The publisher and the University of California Press Foundation gratefully acknowledge the generous support of the Barbara S. Isgur Endowment Fund in Public Affairs.

Twenty Million Angry Men

Twenty Million Angry Men

THE CASE FOR INCLUDING CONVICTED
FELONS IN OUR JURY SYSTEM

James M. Binnall

UNIVERSITY OF CALIFORNIA PRESS

University of California Press
Oakland, California

© 2021 by James M. Binnall

Library of Congress Cataloging-in-Publication Data

Names: Binnall, James M. (James Michael), author.
Title: Twenty million angry men : the case for including convicted felons in
  our jury system / James M. Binnall, University of California Press.
Description: Oakland, California : University of California Press, [2021] |
  Includes bibliographical references and index.
Identifiers: LCCN 2020032223 (print) | LCCN 2020032224 (ebook) |
  ISBN 9780520379169 (hardback) | ISBN 9780520379176 (paperback) |
  ISBN 9780520976573 (ebook)
Subjects: LCSH: Jurors—United States. | Jury selection—United States. |
  Jury—United States. | Ex-convicts—Legal status, laws, etc.—United
  States.
Classification: LCC KF8972 .B525 2021 (print) | LCC KF8972 (ebook) |
  DDC 347.73/752—dc23
LC record available at https://lccn.loc.gov/2020032223
LC ebook record available at https://lccn.loc.gov/2020032224

Manufactured in the United States of America

25 24 23 22 21
10 9 8 7 6 5 4 3 2 1

For Dad and Pete
I wish you had known one another. You were towering
influences taken too soon. The world is a lonelier
place since you left.

And for Brett
You selflessly lived for others' accomplishments. Thank you for
always considering my life's rough drafts.
I'll miss you, old friend.

CONTENTS

ACKNOWLEDGMENTS

Many have made this project possible. I first thank Brian C. Kalt for his remarkable article that served as the springboard for this research. Professor Kalt penned the first comprehensive review of felon-juror exclusion and deserves much of the credit for the work I have done in his shadow. Along those lines, I also thank Dr. Darren Wheelock, the first to examine the topic of felon-juror exclusion using empirical methodologies, exposing the racializing impact of permanent exclusion in Georgia.

I thank my many advisors and mentors who have encouraged me to pursue this book, some with a carrot and others with a stick. All are remarkable scholars and even better mentors. I strive every day to live up to their examples. Thank you Doug Berman, Anders Kaye, Greg Klass, Mona Lynch, Carol Seron, William Thompson, Robin West, Kathy Zeiler, and a host of anonymous reviewers at the journals where much of this research originally appeared. Those journals include *Law and Policy; Law and Social Inquiry: Justice System Journal; Psychology, Crime and Law; Psychiatry, Psychology and Law; Crime, Law, and Social Change; Criminology and Criminal Justice; Albany Law Review; Maine Law Review; Ohio State Journal of Criminal Law; Virginia Journal of Social Policy and Law; Stanford Journal of Law and Policy Online;* and *Berkeley Journal of Criminal Law.* In addition, thanks to the many research assistants who have been part of this project: Nicholas Ballenger, Nicole Beaudoin, Lauren Davis, Amanda Fisher, Maggie Gibbons, Tiffany Gutierrez, Laurie Minter, Sarah Ottone, and Danielle Rini.

The National Science Foundation, through a Dissertation Improvement Grant, along with the American Bar Association funded much of my early research on felon-juror exclusion. Later, California State University, Long Beach, provided funding that allowed me to complete the first comprehensive public opinion survey focused on the exclusion of convicted felons from jury service. Without this financial assistance, I would not have been able to complete the research that comprises this book.

I have also had the opportunity to present portions of this book at various professional conferences and institutions. Those include several annual meetings of the American Society of Criminology, the Law and Society Association, the Western Society of Criminology, and the Association for the Study of Law, Culture, and the Humanities. I have also presented my research at the American Bar Association's Jury Commission Symposium, the Georgetown Law Center, and Maine Law School.

I also thank University of California Press, and in particular Maura Roessner. Maura has worked on this project with me for quite some time. Her patience and persistence made this project a reality. I would also thank the rest of the UC Press team—Cindy Fulton, Teresa Iafolla, Andrew Frisardi, and Madison Wetzell—their guidance through this process has been immeasurably helpful. It was a pleasure to work with all of you.

Finally, I thank my family—Mom, Tim, and Brooke. You have all stuck by me when many would not have. Thank you for your unconditional love and support. I promise to stop and enjoy the journey. I also thank David S. Bayne, whom I consider family. The vocational guidance counselor at SCI Camp Hill, Dave facilitated my LSAT while I was inside. Without his considerable efforts, I am not a lawyer and this book is not written. Thank you, Dave, you have been a great friend and mentor.

Introduction

There is no more valuable work that the average citizen can perform in support of our Government than the full and honest
discharge of jury duty.

—*Handbook for Federal Trial Jurors*

EXCLUSION IN CONTEXT

In May 1999, at age twenty-three, I made the decision to drive after drinking. That night, I caused a car accident that claimed the life of my best friend, the passenger in my vehicle. For that tragic decision, I spent over four years in a maximum-security prison in Pennsylvania. In October 2001, I took my Law School Admissions Test from my prison cell and subsequently applied to a number of law schools while still incarcerated. Though I was accepted to several, only Thomas Jefferson School of Law would allow me to begin my legal studies while an active parolee. I enrolled in January 2005.

I finished my law degree and parole in May 2007. In the fall of that year, I began an LL.M. at the Georgetown University Law Center. In May 2008, LL.M. in hand, I returned to California to take the bar exam and to finish the Moral Character and Fitness Determination process to prove that I was fit to become a member of the State Bar of California. For me, a convicted felon who had spent time in prison, the process was a lengthy one that I had begun nearly two years prior as a first-year law student. In November 2008, I was informed that I had passed both the bar exam and the Moral Character and Fitness Determination. I was sworn in as an attorney and a member of the State Bar of California in December 2008.

Immediately after my swearing in, I began to practice law. Initially, I was a contract attorney for several prominent criminal defense attorneys in San Diego. As part of that work, I regularly assisted on criminal trials in both state and federal court. Sitting "second chair" meant that I interacted with clients, opposing counsel, and often judges. All seemingly accepted me as just another attorney. I rarely disclosed my criminal past, and for those who knew my history, it was ostensibly a nonissue. Only the quality of my work was scrutinized. To a point, I felt as though I had transcended my past.

A year after becoming a member of the State Bar of California, I was summoned to jury service for the first time. Though the summons meant a day of boredom spent waiting at the courthouse, I was eager to serve. Finally, I was "any other citizen," called to perform my civic duty as a juror. As a convicted felon and a practicing attorney, my experiences are diverse and important. Assuredly my insights would enrich any deliberation.

When I arrived at the courthouse on my day of service, I passed through security using the entrance designated "attorneys only," feeling a strange sense of pride and privilege. Soon after this, courthouse personnel ushered a group of about a hundred prospective jurors into the juror lounge. Once we were inside, a courtroom official charged with overseeing jury selection gave a five-minute speech expressing thanks on behalf of the State of California and San Diego County, all the while emphasizing the importance of our service. He then started a video, narrated by actor Rob Lowe (this is Southern California, mind you), exalting the jury as one of the fundamental pillars of democracy and, again, thanking us for our service.

When the movie ended, we were instructed to complete a juror affidavit questionnaire. On that questionnaire was an inquiry regarding criminal convictions. Question five read: "I have been convicted of a felony or malfeasance in office and my civil rights have not been restored." I checked the box, answering in the affirmative. Moments after I turned in this questionnaire, the same man who moments before had thanked us for answering our summons, instructed us to stand and proceed to the back of the jury lounge if we had answered "yes" to question five. I stood, mortified that my criminal record was now on display for all to see. I made my way to the rear of the jury lounge, where court personnel informed me that I was ineligible for jury service because of my prior felony conviction. They called it a "permanent excuse" and assured me that I would never be summoned again.

I protested mildly, explaining that I was an attorney—had used the special attorneys-only entrance—and was looking forward to serving. I explained that it seemed illogical that I was permitted to represent clients in the very courthouse from which I was now being expelled. How could I be "fit" to counsel those facing years in prison or death, but "unfit" to adjudicate even a minor civil matter? Not persuaded by my argument, the clerk told me that I should "write my congressman" if I was unhappy about California's juror eligibility requirements. I was shocked and disheartened. I had not considered that even as a member of the bar I would still be unable to serve as a juror because of my criminal past. Notably, my situation is far more common than one might suspect. Twenty-four states and the federal government permit a convicted felon to practice law, but banish from jury service for life that same convicted felon.[1]

In response to my degrading experience with felon-juror exclusion, I chose not to write to my representatives. Instead, I spent the next ten years researching the statutory exclusion of convicted felons from jury service. The goal of that endeavor was to call attention to felon-juror exclusion and to build a body of empirical research on the topic. In particular, I sought to interrogate two questions. First, does research support the justifications for excluding convicted felons from jury service? And second, what are the consequences of excluding millions of Americans from the jury process—a crucial democratic institution? With these inquiries in mind, I generated original quantitative and qualitative data through a series of interrelated studies. Some focused explicitly on the rationales for felon-juror exclusion, measuring the pretrial attitudes of otherwise eligible jurors with a felony conviction and then comparing those results to those of other groups of potential jurors. Along these lines, I also conducted the first mock-jury experiment, comprised of felon-jurors and non-felon-jurors, evaluating how those with a felony criminal conviction might engage in jury service. My research also focused on the potential ramifications of exclusion, interviewing felon-jurors and courtroom personnel in Maine, the only U.S. jurisdiction that per se allows felon-jurors to serve. Relatedly, I have also surveyed public opinion about the exclusion of convicted felons from jury service.

What I found was that data strongly suggest that the professed purposes for felon-juror exclusion lack empirical support. Moreover, the consequences of such exclusions may be significant, robbing the justice system of jurors who can improve the adjudicative process, while negatively impacting convicted felons' abilities to successfully reenter society. In this way, from a utilitarian perspective, felon-juror exclusion makes little sense, as the costs associated with exclusion certainly exceed the benefits of eliminating the negligible threat convicted felons pose to the jury. Normatively, felon-juror exclusion is also inappropriate and undesirable. The practice discounts rehabilitation and redemption in favor of perpetual ostracism, cutting against principles of participatory democracy and shared sovereignty.

THE ELEPHANTS IN THE ROOM

Preliminarily, this book must confront two global criticisms. First, given the waning use of jury trials in the United States and the exponential reliance on plea bargains and settlements to dispose of litigation, why study the jury at all? Second, given the multitude of legal and regulatory obstacles facing those convicted of a felony, why study a restriction that has little to nothing to do with the practical aspects of reentry and arguably confers a benefit to convicted felons? Those with a felony conviction face a host of other concerns (e.g., housing and employment); serving on a jury is assuredly not their top priority or even something that they wish to experience.

The Case for the American Jury

The jury is a uniquely American institution. Nearly all civil jury trials and over 90 percent of criminal jury trials in the world occur in the United States.[2] Still, in recent decades, the number of American jury trials has dwindled significantly.[3] From 1989 to 1999, civil jury trials decreased by 26 percent, while the number of criminal jury trials dropped by 21 percent.[4] And this trend has continued. From 2006 to 2016, federal criminal cases disposed of by jury trial dropped by 47 percent, leading some scholars to contend that, "jury trials are on the verge of extinction."[5]

Today, most civil litigation ends with summary judgment or a settlement. Similarly, most criminal defendants take plea bargains, in large part to avoid abhorrent conditions of pretrial confinement and/or the "trial tax."[6] As one former federal judge explains, "Today, our federal criminal justice system is all about plea bargaining. Trials—and thus, juries—are largely extraneous. An accused individual who requests a trial may, as a functional matter (though we obstinately deny it), be punished severely for requesting what was once a constitutional right."[7] Mandatory minimum sentences and the Federal Sentencing Guidelines have also served to accelerate the decline of the jury trial.[8]

The demise of the jury should concern all citizens. Though the jury is a useful arbiter of justice, its influence extends far beyond rendered verdicts.[9] The jury stands as the only mandatory civic endeavor that brings citizens together to work collectively on a complex task that could have far-reaching social implications. Such cooperative deliberation has the potential to strengthen community bonds, in part by spawning future civic engagement.[10] Those who serve as jurors are more likely to engage in subsequent civic activities.[11] For instance, studies reveal a 4 to 10 percent increase in voting rates among former jurors,[12] and a positive correlation between jury service and higher levels of involvement in civic and political activities.[13] Notably, this "deliberative effect," as it has been called,[14] is most prominent for citizens who—like many convicted felons—were less civically or politically engaged prior to jury service.[15]

In his influential book, sociologist Robert Putnam suggests that Americans have disengaged.[16] Relaying harrowing statistics of our nation's level of apathy he warns that, "like battlefield casualties dryly reported from someone else's distant war, these unadorned numbers scarcely convey the decimation of American community life they represent."[17] Pointing to a waning desire to be a part of the American social fabric, Putnam concludes that Americans have been dropping out in droves, not merely from politics, but from organized community life more generally.[18]

If the jury becomes a relic, a footnote in the history of our legal system, we will lose our only official deliberative forum. Such an event would assuredly exacerbate the reclusion and isolation many Americans now practice. Sure, we are all electronically tethered to one another, but how often do we engage with our fellow citizens in person, in an exercise that requires attentiveness, empathy, and active participation? Presenting an empirically informed argument for the inclusion of convicted felons in the jury pool, this book indirectly advocates for the preservation of our jury system, suggesting that the jury has value that is yet untapped.

Evidence tends to demonstrate that felon-juror inclusion likely softens perceptions about those with a felony criminal record (chapter 7), while at the same time influencing convicted felons in prosocial ways, possibly triggering criminal desistance mechanisms (chapter 6). The loss of the jury would preemptively eradicate these potential benefits of inclusion and would amount to the shuttering of what Tocqueville called "the most effective means of popular education at society's disposal."[19]

For nearly every reentering citizen, finding gainful employment and a stable home are their primary concerns postconviction or postrelease.[20] Unfortunately, for those with a felony criminal conviction, finding either can prove incredibly difficult. Statutory and regulatory occupational restrictions forbid convicted felons from working in many fields.[21] Additionally, the stigma of a criminal conviction can also influence hiring decisions.[22] Couple these disadvantages with the racial prejudices that many former offenders must also endure, and the job prospects of reentering individuals are bleak.[23]

Housing also poses a challenge for those with a criminal record. Once again, regulatory and statutory restrictions hamstring convicted felons.[24] For those in need of public housing, authorities may consider criminal backgrounds when allocating scarce housing resources. Moreover, since 1988, a series of federal legislative measures have made public housing difficult to attain for those with a criminal record.[25] For those who do not need public housing, challenges still exist. Landlords have also begun to conduct criminal record checks when deciding on private rental transactions, as changes in housing liability law have encouraged them to avoid renting to "problem" or "nuisance" tenants.[26]

Employment and housing are also made more difficult for convicted felons because of a loss of social capital. For most individuals with a criminal record, years away from their family, friends, and community have taken a toll on their social network. Often, a period of incarceration is not planned, and at the end of even a short prison sentence, connections to family and friends are lost, curtailing an individual's employment and housing options. For example, in Jennifer Gonnerman's remarkable story of Elaine Bartlett's transition from prison to society, she notes how the loss of social capital impacted her search for employment: "Elaine wanted to find a job, so she did what most people do: she asked everyone she knew if they had heard of any openings. While this strategy works for many people, Elaine was at a huge disadvantage. She didn't know a lot of people in the city anymore, and those that she did know were unemployed."[27]

Admittedly, convicted felons' reentry concerns have little if anything to do with their opportunity to take part in jury service. Rather, given common views of jury service, some might argue that felon-juror exclusion confers a benefit on convicted felons. But this is a privileged perspective. For those from whom this opportunity is withheld, exclusion from jury service stands for more than merely the chance to decide a litigated matter. For those of us who are denied access to this vital democratic process, jury service represents yet another instance, another restriction that reminds us that we are inferior and threatening to our fellow citizens.

Still, community reintegration is crucial to reentry success or failure. While reintegration used to be conceived of as an outcome, reintegration is now most often conceptualized as a necessary component of successful reentry.[28] Partly attributable to the recognition that building or rebuilding social capital is an essential part of reintegration,[29] this shift has included efforts to facilitate successful reentry. In a number of jurisdictions, housing and occupational licensing restrictions have been eased,[30] while reentry programs attending to these needs have been established. For instance, in 2016, the U.S. Department of Housing and Urban Development instituted a housing-first model that targets housing for at-risk populations, including individuals experiencing reentry.[31] Additionally, restrictions on public assistance for those with a criminal history have also been relaxed in recent years.[32]

Felon-juror exclusion matters because it limits convicted felons' ability to amass social capital through community reintegration. True, by itself felon-juror exclusion likely does little to diminish overall levels of community engagement. Nonetheless, all contacts with members of the community are consequential, such that withholding any opportunity for prosocial engagement from those with a serious criminal history necessarily disadvantages those individuals.[33] In this way, felon-juror exclusion is worth studying, as it is part of a much larger network of collateral sanctions that can impede a convicted felon's ability to secure social capital and successfully reenter society.

WHAT ARE WE TALKING ABOUT?
A JURY SELECTION PRIMER

There are generally two stages of the jury selection process: (1) the formation of the venire, and (2) the empanelment of a seated jury.[34] To form the venire, jurisdictions first construct the master jury list using a combination of voter registration lists, driver's license records, and/or voluntary registration. Once the master list has been established, those on the list may be summoned for service. As part of this process, summoned jurors must complete (via mail or in person) a juror eligibility questionnaire ensuring that they meet the basic requirements for jury service. Typically those requirements mandate that a prospective juror be: (1) at least eighteen years old, (2) a resident of the state/county in which they are summoned, (3) proficient in English, and (4) not already serving as a juror.[35] In those jurisdictions that exclude convicted felons from jury service, the juror eligibility questionnaire will inquire about one's criminal history. In such jurisdictions, a person with a felony criminal history is ineligible for jury service and is then dismissed. Jurisdictions that exclude convicted felons from jury service permanently will then usually remove that person from the master jury list.

If a prospective juror meets the juror eligibility requirements, they then may become part of the venire (approximately thirty to sixty people, sometimes more). Those that make up the venire subsequently take part in voir dire, a process during which attorneys and judges question prospective jurors. An empaneled jury (six or twelve jurors plus alternates) is determined through the use of challenges for cause and peremptory strikes. Made by attorneys, challenges for cause allege that a potential juror cannot perform their requisite duties (most often because of a presumed bias). A judge then evaluates the challenge and, if the challenge is ruled sufficient, dismisses the juror for cause.

After all challenges for cause are made, attorneys are then permitted to dismiss jurors using peremptory strikes. Each side is allotted a set number of peremptory strikes to be used at the discretion of the attorneys, without explanation. Peremptory strikes are not permitted on the basis of race or gender. When each side has exhausted their peremptory strikes, the final empaneled jury (along with alternate jurors) is seated. In jurisdictions that practice some form of felon-juror exclusion, those with a felony criminal history do not have the opportunity to become part of the venire and never take part in voir dire.

WHERE ARE WE GOING?

The goal of this book is to provide the first comprehensive, empirically informed analysis of felon-juror exclusion. To do so, the book focuses on two overarching inquiries. First, is the exclusion of convicted felons necessary to protect the jury process? Second, does the exclusion of convicted felons have societal impacts outside of the jury context? Drawing on empirical findings, each of the subsequent chapters advances the goal of the book by speaking directly to these inquiries.

Chapter 1 frames the issue of felon-juror exclusion. The chapter begins by discussing the evolution of law relating to juror participation in the United States, noting the historical trends that increased juror participation and satisfaction. In particular, this section will discuss the law relating to the inclusion of racial minorities and women in jury pools. This chapter then details the history of felon-juror exclusion in the United States, noting that the practice of exclusion bucked a historical preference for inclusion. Next, the chapter moves to a discussion of the current state of felon-juror exclusion in the United States before detailing the proffered justifications for the practice and prior legal attacks leveled against felon-juror exclusion statutes. The chapter closes by considering the invisibility of felon-juror exclusion and the state of the science on the topic.

Chapter 2 focuses on the probity, or character, justification for felon-juror exclusion, outlining the two interpretations of the rationale (the instrumental claim and the taint claim) and arguing that theoretical and contextual challenges to the justification make either interpretation untenable. To do so, the chapter first discusses competing conceptualizations of character, comparing traditional virtue ethicists' views to more recent, empirically informed social psychological conceptions of character. The chapter then offers examples of how the law treats character assessments, noting inconsistencies and inaccuracies. The chapter next presents the main contextual challenge to the character rationale—how state bar associations treat evaluations of character for applicants with a felony conviction—arguing that the law conceives of character far differently in the realm of attorney licensing than it does in the context of felon-juror exclusion. The chapter closes by assessing the taint argument, suggesting that rather than bolstering the legitimacy of the jury, felon-juror exclusion actually diminishes the legitimacy of the jury and jury verdicts by creating unrepresentative deliberative bodies.

Chapter 3 challenges the validity of the second rationale for felon-juror exclusion—the inherent bias rationale. The chapter begins by discussing the Sixth Amendment's impartiality requirement and two competing models of juror impartiality. It then considers how felon-juror exclusion implicates prior research on pretrial biases, before drawing on empirical data that challenges the underlying assumptions of the inherent bias rationale. Prior studies reveal that convicted felons' pretrial biases are far from homogeneous, that other groups of prospective jurors (law students and law enforcement personnel) harbor pretrial biases that are arguably "threatening" to the impartiality of the jury, and that the presence of a felony conviction is not a dispositive predictor of a prodefense/antiprosecution pretrial bias. The chapter closes by suggesting that felon-juror exclusion statutes premised on a claim of bias are unnecessary given the jury's established, tested protections against partiality.

While chapters 2 and 3 challenge the justifications for felon-juror exclusion anticipatorily, chapters 4 and 5 explore how felon-jurors actually behave in a simulated jury experience, examining mock jury deliberations from the first mock jury experiment to include non-felon-jurors and felon-jurors. Chapter 4 begins by reviewing prior research on diverse juries and exploring the psychological mechanisms of group deliberation. The chapter then turns to the mock jury experiment, detailing the methods of the experiment before presenting the results. Those results demonstrate that felon-jurors served conscientiously, identifying more novel case facts and engaging more fully in deliberations than did their non-felon counterparts. The chapter closes by suggesting that the threat convicted felons pose to jury deliberations appears to be *de minimis* and that felon-jurors may actually contribute in unique, meaningful ways to the adjudicative process.

Chapter 5 again draws on data derived from the mock jury experiment. In particular, this chapter more closely examines felon-jurors' contributions to mock jury deliberations. The chapter begins with a discussion of two models of reentry—the deficit-based model and the strengths-based model. The chapter continues by reanalyzing diverse jury deliberation transcripts, providing a clear picture of exactly how and what felon-jurors contributed to their deliberations. Overall, findings demonstrate that felon-jurors used their experiences to impartially evaluate evidence and to evenhandedly apply the law. Moreover, findings show that felon-jurors interacted in a productive, conflict-free manner with their non-felon counterparts. Data suggest that felon-jurors do not undermine deliberations, but rather enhance the process by calling on their pasts in productive, prosocial ways.

Chapter 6 is the first chapter to explore the potential benefits of felon-juror inclusion outside of the deliberation room, drawing on evidence from field research conducted in Maine—the only jurisdiction that does not restrict convicted felons' opportunity to serve. To start, the chapter examines the concept of criminal desistance, detailing prior research on the mechanisms that give rise to cessation from criminal activity. Chapter 6 next reviews prior studies of civic participation (in the context of felon-voter disenfranchisement) and its influence on criminal desistance processes. The chapter then chronicles the history of felon-juror exclusion/inclusion in

Maine, before introducing the field study that produced the data—drawn from interviews with prospective and former felon-jurors in Maine—that comprise the main focus of the chapter. That data reveal that inclusion in the jury system seemingly facilitates criminal desistance mechanisms by providing prosocial adult roles and prompting the construction of desistance narratives among those with felony criminal histories. This chapter concludes by arguing that the exclusion of convicted felons from jury service may negatively influence the reintegration of those excluded.

Chapter 7 also draws on empirical evidence to explore the benefits of including felon-jurors in the jury process. To start, the chapter discusses theories of delabeling and intergroup contact, suggesting that familiarity with marginalized individuals can diminish the level of prejudice and discrimination that an individual feels and/or exhibits toward the stigmatized group. The chapter then, once again, calls on interviews with prospective and current felon-jurors in Maine, as well as data gathered through interviews with courtroom personnel in Maine (trial judges, defense attorneys, and prosecutors). Drawing on these findings, the chapter suggests that the inclusion of convicted felons in the jury process can alter communities by tempering the stigma of a felony criminal conviction and thereby ensuring that reentering convicted felons fully reintegrate into the civic fold.

The final chapter turns to an examination of how the public views a convicted felon's role in democratic processes. Chapter 8 first discusses how policymakers and media influence community sentiment, before turning to a review of prior studies of public opinion toward convicted felons and their inclusion in civic processes (again in the context of felon-voter disenfranchisement). This chapter then presents the findings of the first public opinion survey on felon-juror exclusion. Conducted by CALSPEAKS, a public opinion firm housed at California State University Sacramento, the poll reveals that citizens are generally ambivalent about felon-juror exclusion and that political ideology and conviction type are significant factors in shaping such views.

Taken together, these chapters explore the reasons for and the consequences of excluding millions of Americans from the jury process. The culmination of almost a decade of research on felon-juror exclusion, the individual chapters are either new or substantially reworked versions of earlier published research. That said, parts of some chapters have appeared in earlier articles and I am thankful to those journals for allowing me to draw on those earlier works.

A NOTE ON CONTROVERSIAL TERMINOLOGY

Admittedly, throughout this book I use nomenclature that many view as derogatory. My intent is not to offend. As a convicted felon and a member of a class that routinely suffers discrimination, I am keenly aware of the power of language. I use the terms *convicted felon* and *felon-juror* not in lieu of person-first references, but as legal labels that carry undeniable meaning in the context of record-based exclusions from democratic institutions. The statutory exclusion of convicted felons from jury service targets those who bear the label "felon." For this reason, I use the term, again not as a derogatory label, but as a descriptor of an accurate legal status that matters in the context of my research. Though I anticipate that this explanation will not satisfy some, my hope is that the substantive content that follows overshadows debate about my preferred terminology.

A NOTE ON OBJECTIVITY

Undoubtedly, many who read these pages will discount my arguments as the slanted findings of someone who is a convicted felon and who is a target of the very exclusion that is the focus of this book. For some, no explanation will quell their concern that this research somehow reflects a personal agenda. That said, for every study that informs this book, I took multiple, often purposefully redundant steps to ensure methodological rigor and objectivity. All of the research that appears in this book has been evaluated and peer reviewed by scholars in the field. When I embarked on this research agenda, admittedly spawned by personal experience, I set out only to find the truth about why the vast majority of jurisdictions bar convicted felons from jury service, whether those reasons are empirically valid, and what costs may be inherent in the practice of felon-juror exclusion. Accordingly, what follows is an objective analysis of a common policy that has, for too long, escaped evaluation.

ONE

Framing the Issue

Felon exclusion deserves attention not just because of its stunning magnitude, but also because of its theoretical significance.

—BRIAN C. KALT

TODAY, OVER NINETEEN MILLION AMERICANS, 8 percent of the adult population, bear the mark of a felony conviction.[1] For those who live with this mark, a multitude of statutory and regulatory restrictions prohibit their access to a host of institutions and opportunities.[2] Such restrictions can be triggered automatically (collateral sanctions) or can serve as the sole basis for optional exclusion (discretionary disqualification),[3] often making a convicted felon's reintegration exceedingly difficult.[4]

Described by one prominent criminologist as forming a "national crazy quilt of disqualifications and restoration procedures,"[5] record-based restrictions vary wildly, both in number and severity, from one jurisdiction to the next.[6] They also influence various aspects of convicted felons' lives. As has been thoroughly documented in recent years, record-based restrictions limit convicted felons' prospects in the areas of housing,[7] employment,[8] public benefits,[9] parental custody,[10] education,[11] and immigration status.[12]

Certain record-based restrictions also degrade fundamental aspects of a convicted felon's citizenship. Sometimes termed "civic restrictions,"[13] such constraints are automatically triggered by a felony conviction and limit opportunities to take part in democratic processes.[14] The restriction of convicted felons' voting rights (felon-voter disenfranchisement) is far and away the most well-known civic restriction and, in turn, has seemingly become a proxy for the civic marginalization of those with a felony criminal history.[15]

Yet, for those who bear the felon label, exclusion from the electorate is not the sole barrier to meaningful civic participation. The exclusion of convicted felons from jury service has withstood historical and legal developments bolstering the inclusivity of the jury system to become the most severe form of civic marginalization in America—and yet the practice still remains an almost entirely invisible consequence of a felony criminal conviction.[16]

THE SUPREME COURT AND A
HISTORY OF INCLUSION

The Sixth Amendment of the U.S. Constitution entitles a criminal defendant to trial by an impartial jury.[17] Traditionally, the Supreme Court interpreted this "impartiality doctrine," as it has been called,[18] as applying solely to individual jurors.[19] Under that view, the Sixth Amendment mandated only that a jury include those free of bias,[20] or those able to set aside biases and "conscientiously apply the law and find the facts."[21]

Beginning in 1940, in a series of cases, the Court altered its interpretation of the impartiality doctrine. In those cases, the Court emphasized that impartiality requires not only unbiased jurors, but also a representative jury comprised of diverse views and perspectives.[22] The Court theorized that varied life experiences necessarily yield richer, higher-quality deliberations. The Supreme Court's decisions regarding jury inclusiveness divide into roughly two categories: those focused on the formation of the jury venire and those centered on the exercise of peremptory challenges.[23] The exclusion of convicted felons from the jury pool occurs prior to the formation of the venire and thus implicates jurisprudence focused on discriminatory procedures at the outset of the jury selection process.

As early as 1880, the Supreme Court invalidated a racially discriminatory jury selection scheme. In *Strauder v. West Virginia*,[24] the Court held that a statute prohibiting African-Americans from serving as jurors violated the Fourteenth Amendment's Equal Protection Clause.[25] Between 1880 and 1975, the Court intermittently struck down several overtly prejudicial jury selection procedures under the same equal protection analysis.[26] In 1940, however, the Court seemingly began to alter its approach to such cases, reassessing the meaning of impartiality.

In *Smith v. Texas*,[27] the Court overturned the appellant's conviction, finding that African-Americans were "systematically excluded from grand jury service solely on account of their race and color."[28] For the first time, the Court did not merely prohibit exclusion but also hinted that impartiality necessitates inclusion and representativeness. The Court noted, "It is part of the established tradition in the use of juries as instruments of public justice that the jury be a body *truly representative of the community.*"[29]

Two years later, in *Glasser v. United States,* the Court again confronted a discriminatory jury selection scheme.[30] In *Glasser,* jury selection procedures limited eligible women jurors to members of the League of Women.[31] Though the Court rejected *Glasser's* claim for lack of evidence, the Court expanded on *Smith's* holding, enunciating what has come to be known as the cross-section requirement. The Court stated,

> The officials charged with choosing federal jurors may exercise some discretion to the end that competent jurors may be called. But they must not allow the desire for competent jurors to lead them into selections which do not comport with the concept of the jury as *a cross-section of the community.* Tendencies, no matter how slight, toward the selection of jurors by any method other than a process which will insure a trial by a representative group are undermining processes weakening the institution of jury trial, and should be sturdily resisted.[32]

Four years after *Glasser,* in *Thiel v. Southern Pacific Railroad Company,* the Court again assessed discriminatory jury selection processes under fair cross-section principles.[33] At issue in *Thiel* was the exclusion of daily wage earners from jury rolls. Thiel claimed that engineering jury pools in such a way gave wealthy railroad owners an impermissible litigation advantage.[34] Building on their holding in *Glasser,* the Court explained,

> The American tradition of trial by jury, considered in connection with either criminal or civil proceedings, necessarily contemplates an impartial jury drawn from a cross-section of the community. This does not mean, of course, that every jury must contain representatives of all the economic, social, religious, racial, political and geographical groups of the community; frequently such complete representation would be impossible. But it does mean that prospective jurors shall be selected by court officials without systematic and intentional exclusion of any of these groups. Recognition must be given to the fact that those eligible for jury service are to be found in every stratum of society. Jury competence is an individual rather than a group or class matter. That fact lies at the very heart of the jury system. To disregard it is to open the door to class distinctions and discriminations which are abhorrent to the democratic ideals of trial by jury.[35]

In 1946, the Court also decided *Ballard v. United States,* and again invalidated a jury formation system because it excluded women—all women—

from the jury pool.[36] In *Ballard,* the Court once more stressed that a jury must represent the community from which it is drawn. The Court also held that by excluding women from juries, the selection procedures at issue deprived potential litigants of viewpoints that might impact deliberations and verdict outcomes.[37] As the Court carefully explained:

It is said . . . that an all male panel drawn from the various groups within a community will be as truly representative as if women were included. The thought is that the factors which tend to influence the action of women are the same as those which influence the action of men—personality, background, economic status—and not sex. Yet it is not enough to say that women when sitting as jurors neither act nor tend to act as a class. Men likewise do not act as a class. But if the shoe were on the other foot, who would claim that a jury was truly representative of the community if all men were intentionally and systematically excluded from the panel? The truth is that the two sexes are not fungible; a community made up exclusively of one is different from a community composed of both; *the subtle interplay of influence one on the other is among the imponderables. To insulate the courtroom from either may not in a given case make an iota of difference. Yet a flavor, a distinct quality is lost if either sex is excluded.* The exclusion of one may indeed make the jury less representative of the community than would be true if an economic or racial group were excluded.[38]

Though the Court alluded to the cross-sectional requirement in *Smith, Glasser, Thiel,* and *Ballard,* the Court decided those cases based on its supervisory powers over federal courts and federal jury selection procedures. The next step in the evolution of the cross-section requirement did not come until 1968, with the Jury Selection and Service Act (JSSA).[39] The JSSA held that "all litigants in Federal courts entitled to trial by jury shall have the right to grand and petit juries selected at random from a fair cross section of the community . . . [and] all citizens shall have the opportunity to be considered for service on grand and petit juries in the district courts of the United States."[40] Thus, with the JSSA, Congress codified the cross-section requirement and the policy of inclusion promulgated by the Court during the 1940s.

Soon after the passage of the JSSA, in 1975, the Supreme Court constitutionalized the cross-section requirement. The Court did so by expanding its interpretation of the Sixth Amendment's impartiality doctrine. In *Taylor v. Louisiana,* the Court held that "the selection of a petit jury from a representative cross section of the community is an essential component of the Sixth Amendment right to a jury trial."[41] *Taylor* represents the Court's official recognition of the cross-section doctrine as a constitutionally guaranteed right of a litigant.

The cross-section requirement demonstrates the Court's clear preference for inclusive jury selection procedures. Additionally, and perhaps more importantly, both the Court's preference for inclusiveness and the development of the cross-section requirement are rooted in a reinterpretation of the notion of impartiality. In a sense, the Court has determined that an impartial jury requires a mix of experiences and viewpoints.[42] In turn, as precedent makes clear, the Court contemplates the possibility that exclusion of any group or class from jury service can result in less-effective deliberations and, potentially, in inaccurate verdicts. Still, the vast majority of U.S. jurisdictions banish convicted felons from jury service, seemingly in direct contention with the spirit of the cross-section doctrine, assuming that the inclusion of convicted felons would diminish rather than bolster the deliberation process.[43]

THE UNEVENTFUL HISTORY OF FELON-JUROR EXCLUSION

The exclusion of convicted felons from public life traces to ancient Greece.[44] Characterized as "infamous" under Greek law, convicted felons were prohibited from taking part in all civic activities.[45] Such exclusions were imposed retributively and as a general deterrent to future criminal conduct.[46] Later, the Romans also adopted a version of "infamy," developing a series of complex statutes outlining civic disabilities that applied to convicted criminals.[47]

After the fall of the Roman Empire, Germanic tribes imposed civic exclusion through a process of "outlawry."[48] That process conceived of crime as an offense against society. In turn, "outlawry" authorized society to retaliate by, in part, stripping offenders of their civil rights.[49] As English law evolved, outlawry transformed into the more formal process of "attainder." Citizens convicted of serious felonies were labeled "attained" and suffered "civil death," whereby they forfeited all civil rights and were prohibited from participating in most civic activities. One such activity was appearing in court as a witness or as a juror.[50]

Around the time of the founding, though colonists sought to distance themselves from the Crown, the concepts of "civil death" and the exclusion of convicted felons from jury service were part of early American jurisprudence.

Accordingly, as early as 1799 (New York), several states imposed civil death statutes.[51] The development of such statutes signals a trend in the rather unremarkable history of civic restrictions—the blind adoption of traditional practices. As Grant et al. note:

> Unfortunately, there is no legislative history to explain the enactment of these disabilities. Public security and facilitation of prison administration have been offered as plausible explanations for the civil death statutes. It is likely, however, that civil disabilities in America were actually the result of the unquestioning adoption of the English penal system by our colonial forefathers and the succeeding generations who continued existing practices without evaluation.[52]

Along these lines, Kalt suggests that the only significant development in the history of felon-juror exclusion in America is the transition from subjective to objective juror eligibility criteria.[53] He notes that around 1800, while criminal history was not a formal disqualification from juror service—the common law, civil death statutes, and other narrowing requirements (male property owners of good character) ensured that convicted felons almost never found their way onto a jury.[54]

Only after 1850, when voting and jury service were formally extended to larger segments of the population, did jurisdictions begin to statutorily restrict juror eligibility.[55] For example, in southern states, after the end of the Civil War and after the Civil Rights Act of 1875 outlawed the use of race-based juror selection procedures,[56] record-based juror eligibility criteria served as a mechanism for preventing African-American men from serving as jurors.[57] By the early twentieth century, felon-juror exclusion statutes were relatively common in the United States.[58]

As noted above, in 1940, the Supreme Court began to reconceptualize the Sixth Amendment's impartiality mandate, and for the first time, the Court linked impartiality to the concept of representativeness.[59] In a series of subsequent decisions, the Court developed and refined the "fair cross section requirement."[60] In 1968, Congress also codified the principle of representativeness, enacting the Federal Jury Selection and Service Act which stated, "It is the policy of the United States that all litigants in Federal courts entitled to trial by jury shall have the right to grand and petit juries selected at random from a fair cross section of the community."[61]

These developments signaled a more inclusive policy regarding jury service eligibility, but they did little to alter felon-juror exclusion policies. In 1940, when the Court decided *Smith,* nearly every state barred convicted felons from serving.[62] Since that time, while many jurisdictions have relaxed civic restrictions,[63] felon-juror exclusion statutes remain pervasive. Summing up the history of felon-juror exclusion, Brian Kalt states:

> The practice of excluding felons from jury service has both a rich pedigree and a sturdy presence in current law. Felon exclusion has evolved from being a product of subjective juror qualifications or anti-criminal common-law rules into being a product of objective statutes. In the process, it has become firmly entrenched and has avoided the general trend of expanded jury participation.[64]

THE CURRENT JURISDICTIONAL LANDSCAPE

Felon-juror exclusion statutes divide roughly into two types: those that permanently eliminate a convicted felon's opportunity to serve as a juror (lifetime ban) and those that allow for the possibility that a convicted felon might, at some point, decide a litigated matter (temporal ban).[65] Today, while twenty-six states and the federal government bar convicted felons from the jury process permanently,[66] the remaining jurisdictions impose less severe, record-based juror eligibility criteria that vary significantly.

Thirteen states bar convicted felons from jury service until the full completion of their sentence, notably disqualifying individuals serving felony-parole and felony-probation.[67] Eight states and the District of Columbia enforce hybrid regulations that may incorporate penal status, charge category, type of jury proceeding, and/or a term of years.[68] For example, the District of Columbia and Colorado adhere to differing hybrid models: the former excludes convicted felons from jury service during any period of supervision and for ten years following the termination of supervision, while the latter excludes convicted felons solely from grand jury proceedings.[69] And finally, two states recognize lifetime for-cause challenges, permitting a trial judge to dismiss a prospective juror from the venire solely on the basis of a felony conviction.[70] Only Maine places no restrictions on a convicted felon's opportunity to serve as a juror.[71]

Across jurisdictions, the application of felon-juror exclusion statutes is relatively consistent. Only four jurisdictions tailor felon-juror exclusion statutes, distinguishing first-time offenders from repeat offenders (Arizona),[72] violent offenders from nonviolent offenders (Nevada),[73] grand juries from

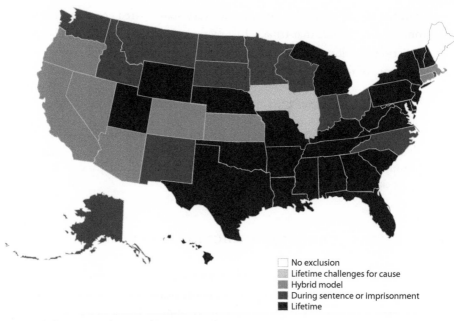

MAP 1. Felon-juror exclusion policies, by jurisdiction.

No exclusion
Lifetime challenges for cause
Hybrid model
During sentence or imprisonment
Lifetime

petit juries (Colorado),[74] and civil cases from criminal cases (Oregon).[75] In all remaining jurisdictions, felon-juror exclusion statutes are categorical, applying to *all* prospective jurors with a prior felony conviction in *all* types of proceedings (see map 1).[76]

By way of comparison, consider felon-juror exclusion statutes alongside felon-voter disenfranchisement. Though a vast majority of jurisdictions place some restriction on a convicted felon's voting rights,[77] those restrictions are arguably far less severe than those impacting convicted felons' juror eligibility.[78] For instance, while twenty-seven jurisdictions bar convicted felons from jury service for life,[79] only three permanently exclude convicted felons from the electorate,[80] making felon-juror exclusion far and away the most extreme form of civic marginalization in the United States.[81]

JUSTIFYING BANISHMENT

Legislators and courts typically cite two rationales for felon-juror exclusion statutes. Like justifications for other civic restrictions, both are purportedly prophylactic,[82] in that they emphasize the protection of the jury system as the overarching goal of the practice.[83]

The first is the probity rationale.[84] In his seminal article on felon-juror exclusion, Kalt explains that the meaning of probity "is fairly clear: moral excellence, integrity, rectitude, uprightness, conscientiousness, honesty, sincerity."[85] In turn, the probity rationale seemingly contends that a convicted felon's character is forever marred by his or her involvement in criminal activity, to the point that only categorical exclusion from the venire will ensure the purity of the adjudicative process.[86] Nevertheless, courts have been unclear about how a lack of character diminishes one's fitness for jury service.[87] Some courts contend that it is the appearance of probity that is paramount, arguing that including convicted felons in the adjudicative process damages the jury's image. As a New York appellate court has held, "It would be a strange system, indeed, which permitted those who had been convicted of anti-social and dissolute conduct to serve on its juries."[88] Other courts suggest that the commission of a crime reveals a lack of respect for the law and the criminal justice system, such that the inclusion of felon-jurors threatens the integrity of the jury's function. For example, the Supreme Court of Arkansas has stated "unquestionably that exclusion is intended to bar from the jury box the one class of persons least likely to respect and give effect to the criminal laws."[89]

A second rationale for the exclusion of convicted felons from jury service is the inherent bias rationale.[90] Unlike the probity rationale, the inherent bias rationale has spawned considerable precision among courts and lawmakers. The inherent bias rationale holds that convicted felons harbor biases directly resulting from their experiences with the criminal justice system.[91] Forecasting the direction and strength of such biases, courts have opined that a convicted felon's "former conviction and imprisonment would ordinarily incline him to compassion for others accused of crime,"[92] as well as make him or her "biased against the government."[93] Explaining the inherent bias rationale, Kalt notes that "a felon will be less willing, if not unwilling altogether, to subject another person to the horrors of the punishment that he has endured, and may engage in nullification. . . . He may also exhibit mistrust of police and prosecutors, and give unduly short shrift to their testimony and arguments."[94] Similarly, the Supreme Court of California has stated:

> The Legislature could reasonably determine that a person who has suffered the most severe form of condemnation that can be inflicted by the state—a conviction of felony and punishment therefore—might well harbor a continuing resentment against "the system" that punished him and equally unthinking

bias in favor of the defendant on trial, who is seen as a fellow underdog caught in its toils. Because these antisocial feelings would often be consciously or subconsciously concealed, the Legislature could further conclude that the risk of such prejudice infecting the trial outweighs the possibility of detecting it in jury selection proceedings. The exclusion of ex-felons from jury service thus promotes the legitimate state goal of assuring impartiality of the verdict.[95]

A third, rarely cited rationale for felon-juror exclusion finds its roots in John Locke's theory of the social compact.[96] Far more philosophical than instrumental, the "neo-contractarian" theory of felon-juror exclusion[97]—like early "civil death" statutes—seems to hold that criminal offenders "deserve" banishment from public life simply because they have committed a criminal offense. "In Locke's view, one who commits a crime forfeits his right to participate in the political process—if not his rights to property and person. By acting against the property or person of others, the criminal has failed to grasp the need for security, and threatened to destroy the very compact which makes civilized life possible."[98] Today, courts and lawmakers roundly avoid this retributive justification when discussing the appropriateness and constitutionality of felon-juror exclusion statutes. Instead, authorities take a decidedly utilitarian stance, endorsing the "probity" and "inherent bias" rationales for felon-juror exclusion despite a lack of evidence supporting either.

THE LEGALITY OF OSTRACISM

Constitutional challenges to felon-juror exclusion have come in many forms.[99] The most common challenges have taken two forms—cross-section claims and equal protection claims. These challenges have never met with success. The Supreme Court has held that "jurisdictions are 'free to confine the [jury] selection . . . to those possessing good intelligence, sound judgment, and fair character,'"[100] and lower courts have rejected all constitutional attacks on felon-juror exclusion statutes.[101]

Cross-Section Claims

Cross-section claims are the most common challenges to felon-juror exclusion statutes.[102] Alleging that felon-juror exclusion compromises the representativeness of the jury pool, cross-section claims are rooted in the Sixth Amendment's guarantee of an impartial jury.[103] As the Supreme Court has stated, "The Sixth Amendment requirement of a fair cross-section on the venire is a means of assuring, not a representative jury (which the Constitution does not demand), but an impartial one (which it does)."[104]

Though the cross-section doctrine has evolved considerably over time,[105] in 1979, the Supreme Court enunciated a standard for such claims.[106] In *Duren v. Missouri,* the Court held that a cross-section claim requires a prima facie showing

> (1) that the group alleged to be excluded is a "distinctive group" within the community; (2) that the representation of this group in venires from which juries are selected is not fair and reasonable in relation to the number of such persons in the community; and (3) that this underrepresentation is due to systematic exclusion of the group in the jury-selection process.[107]

The Court explained, however, that "the demonstration of a prima facie fair-cross-section violation by the defendant is not the end of the inquiry into whether a constitutional violation has occurred."[108] Writing for the Court, Justice White noted that such schemes also "require that a significant state interest be manifestly and primarily advanced by those aspects of the jury-selection process . . . that result in the disproportionate exclusion of a distinctive group"[109]

Yet, courts have unanimously held that cross-section attacks on felon-juror exclusion do not meet even the prima facie elements of cross-section claims, concluding that convicted felons do not constitute a distinct group.[110] To establish that a group is distinct, a defendant must show:

> (1) that the group is defined and limited by some factor (i.e. that the group has definite composition such as by race or sex); (2) that a common thread or basic similarity in attitude, ideas, or experiences runs through the group; and (3) that there is a community of interest among members of the group such that the group's interests cannot be adequately represented if the group is excluded from the jury selection process.[111]

Evaluating cross-section claims to felon-juror exclusion, Kalt argues that convicted felons satisfy this vague definition of distinctiveness. He contends that, in making the distinctiveness determination, courts "distort" the legal standard.[112] He suggests that courts may be hesitant to engage in "demographic micromanagement,"[113] and perhaps view groups as distinct only when they warrant heightened constitutional protections under the equal protection doctrine or are defined by immutable characteristics.[114] Nevertheless, no court has classified convicted felons as a distinct group.[115] As a result, courts have never completed the cross-section analysis and definitively determined whether preserving the probity and impartiality of the jury are significant state interests manifestly and primarily advanced by felon-juror exclusion statutes.[116]

Equal Protection Claims

While most challenges to felon-juror exclusion statutes allege a violation of the cross-section requirement, some assert that record-based juror eligibility criteria contravene the Equal Protection Clause.[117] Brought by litigants on behalf of excluded jurors, equal protection claims allege that the exclusion of convicted felons from jury service violates the equal protection rights of those with a felony criminal record.

Equal protection attacks on felon-juror exclusion statutes have never met with success. Courts hold that such challenges do not warrant heightened constitutional scrutiny, as they do not recognize jury service as a fundamental or important right,[118] and do not classify convicted felons as a protected class.[119] Courts do not afford convicted felons special constitutional protections because they "are both responsible for their membership in their classification and morally culpable for it."[120] In this respect, convicted felons differ significantly from the racial minorities and women who once suffered large-scale juror exclusion, and as a result, legislation making convicted felons ineligible for jury service must meet only rational basis scrutiny.

Some scholars question the logic of withholding class or semiclass status from those with a criminal record, contending that the "moral culpability obstacle violates the doctrine and spirit of equal protection."[121] Nonetheless, when analyzing equal protection challenges to felon-juror exclusion, courts apply only rational basis review. Under that minimal standard, courts authorize state action if it is rationally related to a state's legitimate interest.[122] Not surprisingly, under rational basis review, state action almost always survives challenge.[123] Felon-juror exclusion statutes are no exception.

The failure of cross-section claims and equal protection challenges is principally attributable to courts' unwillingness to group or classify convicted felons. Some commentators contend that this unwillingness has little to do with objective legal criteria. They argue that courts will not categorize convicted felons because they are at least partly responsible for their membership in their class or group.[124] Ironically, courts authorize felon-juror exclusion statutes by relying on the probity and inherent bias rationales, justifications that—given their categorical application—turn on the presumption that many if not all convicted felons are alike, in that they lack probity and allegedly harbor prodefense/antiprosecution pretrial biases.

THE INVISIBILITY OF FELON-JUROR EXCLUSION

Voting and jury service are pillars of American democracy.[125] As expressions of shared sovereignty, they are inextricably linked.[126] The founders contemplated voting and jury service in much the same way, suggesting that both serve as vital checks against an overreaching government.[127] Similarly, the Supreme Court has long viewed voting and jury service as complementary forms of participatory democracy.[128] Still, while voting and jury service share historical roots and are each arguably indispensable to our system of governance, felon-voter disenfranchisement and felon-juror exclusion receive disparate treatment from policymakers and the media.

Political science research suggests that the lawmakers and the media influence the public agenda.[129] In particular, a long line of studies demonstrate that "agenda-setting" occurs through a series of complex feedback loops comprised of direct and indirect input from policymakers and the press.[130] Often, issues first find their way into the national consciousness as the result of "focusing events" or "triggering devices."[131] Focusing events are typically national events involving some level of tragedy, crisis, or controversy.[132] The most influential focusing events are those of lasting duration.[133] Politicians and media outlets then frame those issues, thereby shaping the national conversation.[134]

The 2000 presidential election between Al Gore and George W. Bush served as a focusing event that captured the attention of the nation and brought to the forefront the issue of felon-voter disenfranchisement.[135] In that election, 827,000 convicted felons in Florida were denied the right to vote based on a statutory disqualification, which likely swung the election in Bush's favor.[136] Coverage of the issue lasted months, as thirty-six days of recounts dragged on and media coverage heightened.[137] In the end, the topic of felon-voter disenfranchisement became institutionalized in the collective conscious after the 2000 election, so much so that with each national election cycle the issue again takes center stage.[138]

In the case of felon-juror exclusion, a similar focusing event is unlikely to occur. For decades, researchers, legal scholars, and practitioners have warned of the demise of the American jury.[139] Jury trials are increasingly rare.[140] Today, settlements and plea bargains make jury trials largely obsolete.[141] Even when a high-profile trial does attract widespread media attention, the public is virtually never privy to jury selection. "Television does not publicize the rather mundane process of voir dire, nor does it spotlight the distribution of juror questionnaires, or the dismissal of certain jurors. No camera captures the state or the federal government dismissing an otherwise eligible juror because of a felony conviction. Instead, the public sees only twelve seated jurors ready to embark on their civic duty."[142]

For legislators, focusing events often give rise to a "policy window" that, when open, represents an opportunity for reform.[143] To date, the number of legislative efforts to repeal or soften felon-voter disenfranchisement laws has greatly surpassed those to reverse or curtail the practice of felon-juror exclusion. Democratic politicians have largely led these efforts, perhaps because liberal voters tend to hold more favorable views of those who commit criminal offenses,[144] or because most of those disenfranchised are presumed to be Democratic voters.[145]

For instance, former Democratic Virginia Governor Terry McAuliff holds the record for restoring voting rights to the most citizens with a felony criminal history (156,221), which he characterizes as his "proudest achievement" in politics, followed by former Democratic governor of Florida Charlie Christ, who restored voting rights to the next-largest number of citizens (155,215).[146] In contrast, McAuliff's Republican predecessor, Robert Francis McDonnell, restored voting rights to only 4,400 felons.[147] Similarly, Rick Scott, Christ's Republican successor, has not only restored voting rights to significantly fewer felons than Christ (3,000),[148] but has also resisted court efforts to standardize and speed up his process of voter restoration.[149]

More recently, in May 2018, Democratic Louisiana Governor John Bel Edwards signed into law a bill permitting convicted felons to vote five years after release from prison, restoring voting rights to approximately 2,200 residents.[150] Legislative efforts, in large part driven by Democrats, to restore convicted felons, voting rights, have also taken hold in Florida.[151] In January 2018, the "Voter Restoration Amendment" secured enough signatures (766,200) to appear on the November 2018 Florida ballot as Amendment 4, and subsequently passed with bipartisan support, temporarily restoring voting rights to approximately 1.5 million Floridians currently shut out of the electoral process because of a felony criminal history.[152]

Conversely, since 2000, only one state (California, in 2020) has relaxed its felon-juror eligibility criteria.[153] That recent effort, along with those in New York (2019)[154] and Louisiana (2019),[155] were met with fierce bipartisan opposition. One Louisiana Republican lawmaker stated, "They were criminals, they got convicted, they went to jail. . . . I do think we should be forgiving, but I also think there are consequences. . . . I'm sorry, but they go with you."[156] Similarly, New York's Republican Senate Minority Leader John Flanagan argued that the restoration of convicted felons' juror eligibility amounted to "justice denied for all law-abiding citizens," suggesting that such a change would permit a "terrorist" to serve as a juror.[157]

Measures to alter felon-juror exclusion practices have also met with resistance from Democrats. California's Assembly Bill 535, a failed effort to repeal California's permanent felon-juror exclusion statute, died in committee in February 2018.[158] Commentators argued that the bill's demise was partially attributable to the opposition it faced from Democrats, "who appear more concerned with currying favor with law enforcement and prosecutorial groups than the ability of their constituents to fully reenter society."[159]

Without a significant focusing event, felon-juror exclusion has also escaped endorsement and/or criticism from the press. Since the 2000 presidential election, thousands of stories on felon-voter disenfranchisement have appeared in the media, spiking in national election years. During that same eighteen-year period, by contrast, only a handful of stories have centered on the topic of felon-juror exclusion.[160]

Besides the absence of a focusing event, the invisibility of felon-juror exclusion is probably attributable to common conceptualizations of voting and jury service. Citizens exalt voting as an indispensable facet of American citizenship,[161] while jury service is widely viewed as a bother, to be avoided if at all possible.[162] For many, voting is a pride-inducing civic exercise,[163] yet serving as a juror translates into early mornings at the courthouse, missed workdays, bad lunches, and measly pay.[164] Given these common perceptions of voting and jury service, disparate treatment of felon-voter disenfranchisement and felon-juror exclusion are, to a point, to be expected. Losing the opportunity to take part in the electoral process undoubtedly conjures up disturbing images of poll taxes and the fight for universal suffrage. Conversely, ineligibility for jury service likely does little to shake one's faith in democracy, as jury service is rarely seen as welcomed life-event.[165]

Taken together, the lack of a focusing event and the public's general aversion to jury service combine to ensure that felon-juror exclusion receives little attention from lawmakers or the media. While efforts to repeal collateral consequences have gained traction nationally, felon-juror exclusion remains a petrified statutory provision in nearly all jurisdictions. Today, losing the opportunity to serve seemingly does not elicit the same mobilizing outrage as other record-based sanctions and, consequently, felon-juror exclusion has largely escaped critical evaluation by politicians and reporters.

THE STATE OF THE SCIENCE

Scholars, too, have largely overlooked felon-juror exclusion. Accordingly, studies focused on felon-juror exclusion are scarce and, with few exceptions, almost entirely nonempirical.

In the formative study of felon-juror exclusion, law professor Brian Kalt first detailed the pervasiveness of the practice and the proffered justifications for the exclusion of convicted felons from jury service.[166] Kalt argues that felon-juror exclusion undermines the representativeness of jury pools and that the rationales for exclusion are both under- and overinclusive, doing little to protect the jury while creating a class of civic outsiders who pose little or no threat to the jury process.[167] In recent years, while a number of studies have built on Kalt's research,[168] only one other scholar has employed empirical methods.[169] In that study, sociologist Darren Wheelock explored felon-juror exclusion in Georgia, a permanent exclusion jurisdiction.[170] As will be discussed in more detail later, Wheelock found that felon-juror exclusion statutes disproportionately impact African-Americans, suggesting that felon-juror exclusion likely operates to racially homogenize juries.[171]

This lack of empirical research on felon-juror exclusion has led to an almost blind acceptance of the practice. Without evidence, lawmakers oppose measures that would permit convicted felons to become part of the jury pool and courts uphold justifications for felon-juror exclusion without evidence of their validity. Hence, while "there is hardly an opinion involving jury law that does not cite empirical research findings,"[172] such findings play no role in legislation or precedent relating to felon-juror exclusion.[173]

Any discussion of felon-juror exclusion is incomplete without highlighting the racial aspect of such restrictions. Early in their history in the United States, felon-juror exclusion statutes were used to intentionally prevent racial minorities from serving as jurors.[174] Today, while intent may be less obvious, such statutes undeniably have a disparate racial impact.[175]

As noted above, the Supreme Court first addressed the issue of race-based juror eligibility in 1880 in *Strauder v. West Virginia*.[176] Still, *Strauder* did not end the racial homogenization of juries—especially in southern states.[177] Instead, in those jurisdictions, the Court's decision was largely "nullified through the use of 'subconstitutional' rules bearing on standards of proof, standards of appellate review, and access to federal court."[178] Another method of subverting *Strauder* included the imposition of vague juror eligibility requirements demanding that prospective jurors possess "sound judgment and fair character."[179] Only later, in the 1930s and 1940s, did the Supreme Court stringently apply *Strauder* and its progeny. At that time, jurisdictions moved toward objective, record-based juror eligibility requirements.[180] Race-neutral on their face, such statutes had a disparate impact on communities of color.[181] Today, that impact has been exacerbated exponentially in the wake of mass incarceration (chapter 2).[182]

CONCLUSION

For many, convicted felons' supposed lack of character, criminal loyalties, and presumed collective hatred for the state make felon-juror exclusion appear logical, and perhaps even inevitable. Nonetheless, evidence does not support these contentions. Research not only shows that the alleged character flaws and biases of convicted felons are dramatically overstated, but that felon-jurors do not diminish the integrity or functioning of the jury process. Rather, research tends to demonstrate that felon-juror inclusion may in fact add to deliberation quality, and can help facilitate the successful reintegration and criminal desistance of those citizens with a felonious criminal history. The next two chapters explore more closely the probity and inherent bias rationales for felon-juror exclusion, drawing on recent research to challenge these questionable justifications.

TWO

Rotten to the Core?

If you put good apples in a bad situation, you'll get bad apples.
—PHILIP ZIMBARDO

THE PRIMARY JUSTIFICATION FOR FELON-JUROR exclusion is the probity rationale,[1] which suggests that convicted felons lack the "character" to serve as jurors. As one court explains, "Simply being charged with a crime says something about a person, something which is material to his ability to serve as a juror. . . . It is rational to believe that such a person may not take seriously his obligation to follow the law as a juror is sworn to do."[2] In this way, the probity rationale holds that were they permitted to serve, felon-jurors would somehow undermine the integrity of the jury process.

Still, courts and lawmakers have been unclear as to exactly how felon-juror exclusion statutes preserve the integrity of the jury process. As law professor Brian Kalt points out, two alternatives perhaps explain the possibilities.[3] First, a jurisdiction might presume that all convicted felons lack probity because they possess "poor character or innate untrustworthiness,"[4] traits that could compromise the functioning of jury process in an instrumental way (the instrumental argument). Second, a jurisdiction may suppose that the "badges of shame" or "degraded status" of all convicted felons "undermine the integrity of the institution,"[5] denigrating the reputation of the jury (the taint argument). No evidence supports either interpretation of the probity rationale.

Rather, research reveals that the law's view of convicted felons' character is inconsistent and at times appears entirely context-dependent, suggesting that convicted felons' supposed lack of character poses little threat to the jury process. Recent experimental research reinforces this proposition (chapters 4 and 5). Additionally, the claim that the inclusion of felon-jurors would diminish the apparent sanctity and integrity of the jury cuts against research demonstrating that juror diversity—including diversity of experience—

legitimizes verdicts to the point that the absence of felon-jurors may actually have the unintended, opposite effect on the perceived purity and reputation of the jury.

TWO VIEWS OF CHARACTER

The instrumental argument holds that the inclusion of convicted felons would somehow disrupt the functioning of the jury process, presumably because they lack the requisite character to serve. By premising categorical felon-juror exclusion statutes on convicted felons' supposed lack of character, jurisdictions must make two interrelated assumptions about *all* convicted felons. First, a jurisdiction must assume that bad acts (felony convictions) always reveal bad character, such that convicted felons—by virtue of having committed a serious criminal offense—possess a flaw of character that makes them unfit for jury service. Second, a jurisdiction must also assume that character is fixed, and that therefore a convicted felon's character is forever and unalterably marred.

Theories about character and its role in human behavior educe a host of varied viewpoints.[6] Philosophers and ethicists often contend that "character will have regular behavioral manifestations: the person of good character will do well, even under substantial pressure to moral failure, while the person of bad character is someone on whom it would be foolish to rely."[7] In this way, character supposedly serves as a critical tool for predicting behavior, as it "decides the moral texture of life."[8] Yet, other scholars argue that experimental social psychology challenges the traditional view of character.[9] Specifically, social psychological research offers an alternative framework with which to explain conduct, suggesting—as Zimbardo's opening quote illustrates—that one's environment perhaps has a greater impact on one's actions than do inherent attributes.[10]

The Conventionalist Formulation of Character

Conventional character theories "assume that we have a certain sort of character, comprised of enduring, global character traits—traits that are not just consistent across time, but also across situations, and that manifest not just sporadically, but reliably."[11] This static conceptualization of character harkens back to the Aristotelian formulation of human nature, which places "an emphasis on robust traits and behavioral consistency,"[12] and speculates that "knowing something about a person's character is supposed to render their behavior intelligible and help observers determine what behaviors to expect."[13]

The conventional view of character also holds that "every person chooses to develop good and bad character through autonomous actions,"[14] and "once a person [chooses] their character . . . he or she [is] not free to simply undo the choice."[15] Moreover, traditional character theorists posit that even one socially unacceptable act is adequate evidence that one possesses a normatively undesirable trait. In this way, bad character "require[s] very little in the way of behavioral consistency."[16] Thus, "one doesn't have to reliably falter, but only sporadically falter,"[17] to win the traditionalist's pejorative distinction of possessing bad character.

Philosophers describe this view of character as "globalism."[18] Under the globalist theory of character, "if a person possesses a trait, that person will engage in trait-relevant behaviors in trait-relevant eliciting conditions with markedly above chance probability."[19] Specifically, globalism dictates that traits are: (1) consistent,[20] (2) stable,[21] and (3) evaluatively integrative.[22] For example, if one possesses the trait of dishonesty, that person will consistently act in a dishonest fashion in a host of varied situations.[23] Moreover, in such situations, a dishonest person is also more likely to exhibit other traits of equal reprehensibility.

An Empirical Formulation of Character

Some scholars argue that conventional conceptualizations of character do not accurately reflect human nature.[24] Along these lines, they contend that "philosophical explanations referencing character traits are generally inferior to those adduced from experimental social psychology,"[25] because "they presuppose the existence of character structures that actual people do not very often possess."[26] Simply, modern research indicates that behavior may primarily derive from the situations that confront an actor, rather than an actor's "dispositional structure."[27]

A series of experiments, now famous in social psychological literature, strengthen the claim that one's behaviors are largely a product of one's environment. By manipulating context, researchers have been able to induce striking behaviors, demonstrating that "situational influences can easily cause us to act in ways that we would not approve."[28] Noting that quantifiable data shows that our acts are intimately connected to our surroundings,[29] some scholars term this phenomenon the "puppet problem."[30]

For example, the Milgram experiment revealed the influence of context.[31] In this experiment, begun in 1961, a year after the Adolf Eichman trial in Jerusalem, Stanley Milgram sought to explore whether "Eichmann and his million accomplices in the Holocaust were just following orders."[32] To do so, he designed an experiment whereby participants ("teachers") were told by researchers to administer electric shocks on fellow participants ("learners") when a given learner answered a question incorrectly. Unbeknownst to the teachers, the learners were study confederates who acted as if they received electric shocks, but in fact were not electrocuted. Throughout the course of the study, teachers were instructed to increase the voltage for subsequent incorrect answers. Teachers administered voltage through a series of thirty switches, ranging in fifteen-volt increments from 15 volts to 450 volts. Groups of switches were also progressively labeled, beginning with "Slight Shock" and ending with "XXX." Notably, only two switches bore the label "XXX," and they followed a group of switches labeled "Danger: Severe Shock."

The results of Milgram's famous experiment revealed a disturbing willingness on the part of the teachers to obey researchers' orders in administering the electric shocks. Of the forty participant teachers, twenty-six administered the highest level of voltage to their respective learner even over their own verbalized and documented reservations.[33] This result—that 65 percent of Milgram's sample delivered the maximum shock—offers evidence strongly suggesting that behavioral manifestations of character are highly context dependent, such that under certain circumstances, even those with a strong sense of character and morality have the capacity to engage in somewhat horrific acts.[34]

Similarly, in the Stanford prison experiment, researchers sought to explore "the implications of situational models of behavior for criminal justice institutions."[35] In that experiment, researchers replicated a prison environment in a basement hallway of the department of psychology on the campus of Stanford University. Each participant—all of them college students—was assigned a role as either a guard or a prisoner. The experiment was designed to last two weeks.

In the end, researchers ended the Stanford prison experiment prematurely. As Haney and Zimbardo explain, "Our planned two week experiment has to be aborted after only six days because the experience dramatically and painfully transformed most of the participants in ways we did not anticipate, prepare for, or predict."[36] Those transformations were shocking:

The environment of arbitrary custody had great impact on the affective states of both the guards and prisoners as well as upon the interpersonal processes taking place between and within those role groups. In general, guards and prisoners showed a marked tendency toward increased negativity of affect and their overall outlook became increasingly negative. As the experiment progressed, prisoners expressed intentions to do harm to others more frequently. For both prisoners and guards, self-evaluations were more deprecating as the experience of the prison environment became internalised.... Despite the fact that guards and prisoners were free to engage in any form of interaction (positive or negative, supportive or affrontive, etc.), the characteristic nature of their encounters tended to be negative, hostile, affrontive and dehumanising.[37]

The Stanford prison experiment, like Stanley Milgram's research, suggests that situational factors have a significant impact on behavioral manifestations of character. Specifically, such research makes clear that situational factors play a key role in the types of decisions individuals make and whether those decisions are in line with or contradict their innate character. In this way, empirical findings tend to demonstrate that character is "a socially mediated construct."[38] This calls into question the use of character assessments as barometers of fitness for inclusion in a particular process or institution. Empirical evidence tends to demonstrate that situational parameters perhaps tell us more about how an individual will behave than does supposed evidence of character defined by, in some cases, a single prior criminal act.[39]

Nonetheless, in the case of felon-juror exclusion, jurisdictions seem to endorse traditionalist or conventionalist conceptualizations of character and then rely on those conceptualizations when granting or denying access to the jury process. This approach, common with most collateral consequences, is inconsistent with the law's view of character in a number of other contexts. In those areas, the law seems to acknowledge the malleability of character and the prospect of true rehabilitation.

THE LAW'S CONFUSED CONCEPTION OF CHARACTER

Though the probity rationale ostensibly suggests that a felony conviction makes one perpetually unsuitable to serve as a juror, in several other legal contexts, character conceptualizations are less rigid and arguably contradictory. These inconsistent views about the nature of character and its usefulness as a tool for evaluating fitness call into question the real meaning of the probity rationale and the wisdom of relying on character assessments when determining juror eligibility.

As a preliminary matter, conceptions of character differ within the world of felon-juror exclusion statutes. For example, jurisdictions that restrict convicted felons' access to the jury pool do so either permanently or temporarily.[40] In most jurisdictions that temporarily restrict access, convicted felons are allowed to serve as jurors after completing their sentence or after some other defined period of time.[41] In such cases, jurisdictions seem to suggest that a convicted felon's character somehow automatically rehabilitates. Such an approach stands in stark contrast to those jurisdictions that permanently exclude, as they seemingly take the view that the character of convicted felons is marred and immutable.

Also raising questions about the law's true attitude toward the nature of character are cases in which a felon-juror somehow ends up on a criminal jury that ultimately convicts. In a jurisdiction that enforces some version of felon-juror exclusion, a felon-juror's presence on a jury presumably conjures up issues about the accuracy and appropriateness of a rendered verdict. Still, the judiciary seldom takes remedial action in such instances. Instead, when felon-jurors do find their way onto a jury that passes judgment, "many courts are surprisingly ambivalent about rectifying these sorts of errors, allowing verdicts that 'illicit' juries rendered to stand despite supposed concerns about ... the threat they (convicted felons) pose to jury probity."[42] Again, these cases cast doubt on the law's use of character as a measure of juror fitness.

The law's fickle treatment of character also appears when felon-juror exclusion is considered alongside the Federal Rules of Evidence.[43] The Federal Rules of Evidence state that "evidence of other crimes, wrongs, or acts is not admissible to prove the character of a person in order to show action in conformity therewith."[44] Further, "evidence of a person's character or a trait of character is not admissible for the purpose of proving action in conformity therewith on a particular occasion."[45] Felon-juror exclusion statutes contradict these Federal Rules of Evidence by presuming that criminal acts reveal character and that character is a dispositive predictor of future behavioral propensities.

Although jurisdictions that impose felon-juror exclusion statutes do so to protect the jury from corrupting influences, it is unclear that such restrictions actually insulate the jury from those who may compromise its functionality. In this way, the law's concern about the character of prospective jurors seems somewhat disingenuous. As Kalt points out, states typically do not bar misdemeanants from jury service, even though their criminal behavior assumedly reveals a significant flaw of character.[46] On a similar note, felon-juror exclusion statutes do not expel individuals who lack character but have no criminal record. Consider Kalt's comments on this point:

> Assume hypothetically that 95% of felons lack probity, that just 10% of non-felons do, and that only felons—all felons—are excluded from juries. If 6.5% of the jury-age population are felons, then over 60% of those who are unfit to serve would be non-felons who are not excluded. If anything, this hypothetical is extremely conservative.[47]

Hence, felon-juror exclusion statutes are woefully underinclusive, as they likely do very little to protect the jury from those who purportedly lack the requisite character to serve. Instead, the jury's protection is left almost exclusively to the customary mechanism used to determine a juror's fitness—voir dire.[48] For centuries, courts and commentators have accepted voir dire as the process by which to identify and select appropriate jurors.[49] Additional categorical exclusions suggest that voir dire is inadequate in the case of prospective jurors with a felony criminal conviction.[50]

Though character assessments are woven through the law, they are not consistent. Such inconsistency calls into question whether jurisdictions actually view character as a necessary prerequisite for prospective jurors. Indeed, some commentators question the use of character assessments in this context, suggesting that character has very little to do with effective democratic participation.[51] Nonetheless, courts have uniformly upheld felon-juror exclusion statutes, and in the process have endorsed the probity rationale. In this way, the law seems to rely on character as a stable, static measure of integrity and trustworthiness—but only to a point. Perhaps the most persuasive contextual argument against the probity rationale comes from the legal profession itself.[52]

THE FELONIOUS LAWYER: MAKING THE CASE FOR MALLEABLE CHARACTER

After successfully completing a grueling period of schooling, a prospective attorney faces two obstacles to professional licensure.[53] A bar applicant must not only pass a comprehensive exam that tests legal knowledge, but must also successfully navigate a moral character and fitness determination designed to establish that "graduating law students ... meet high standards of moral character."[54] Though for many applicants this assessment amounts to a time-consuming formality,[55] for an individual with a felony criminal history, a character evaluation can represent an insurmountable obstacle.[56]

The moral character and fitness process begins with the requirement that bar applicants complete a lengthy questionnaire that asks a series of significantly probing questions.[57] Typically contained in this application are "four major areas of inquiry, including an applicant's history of in-patient psychiatric hospitalization and out-patient mental health treatment, substance abuse and treatment, educational misconduct, and criminal conduct."[58] For an applicant with a felony criminal conviction, bar examiners will almost always seek out additional information about a criminal offense.[59]

Once an applicant has provided the requested information to the relevant jurisdiction, the process for determining fitness of character depends on the favored jurisdictional approach.[60] In some jurisdictions, a felony conviction per se disqualifies an applicant from admission to the bar.[61] In other jurisdictions, a felony conviction merely amounts to a presumptive disqualification, creating a "rebuttable presumption that an applicant with a record of prior unlawful conduct lacks the requisite character to practice law."[62]

Per Se Disqualifications

Those jurisdictions that per se disqualify felonious bar applicants from the legal profession do so either permanently or temporarily.[63] While ten jurisdictions impose some form of per se disqualification on bar applicants with a felony criminal history,[64] only half of such jurisdictions per se disqualify convicted felons from the practice of law permanently.[65] The remaining half per se disqualify felonious applicants for an automatically terminating period of time, usually a set period of years after expiration of the imposed sentence (see map 2).[66]

The severity of the per se disqualification notwithstanding, such an approach reflects the "traditional view that 'certain illegal acts . . . evidence attitudes toward the law that cannot be countenanced among its practitioners; to hold otherwise would demean the profession's reputation and reduce the character requirement to a meaningless pretense.'"[67] Hence, like lifetime felon-juror exclusion statutes, the per se disqualification model suggests that those with a felonious criminal history are forever blemished,[68] and, as some scholars suggest, "destroys an individual's professional hopes and possibly deprives the bar and society of committed, rehabilitated lawyers."[69]

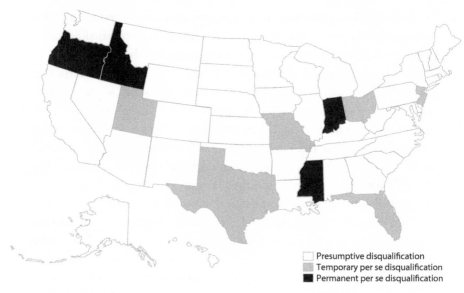

Presumptive disqualification
Temporary per se disqualification
Permanent per se disqualification

MAP 2. Bar admission standards for convicted felons, by jurisdiction (Binnall, 2010b).

Presumptive Disqualifications

Forty-five states and the federal court system do not permanently disqualify a convicted felon from practicing law.[70] Instead, in these jurisdictions a felony conviction merely amounts to a presumptive disqualification rebuttable by a felonious bar applicant at a moral character and fitness determination.[71] During the determination, "evidence of complete rehabilitation is almost always required before a bar applicant with a record of prior unlawful conduct will be admitted."[72] Though demonstrating a change in one's character is a rather ambiguous task, the presumptive disqualification approach leaves open that possibility.[73] As the Supreme Court of Georgia has noted, "For bar fitness purposes, rehabilitation is the reestablishment of the reputation of a person by his or her restoration to a useful and constructive place in society."[74]

Specifically, states that employ the presumptive disqualification framework look for evidence of rehabilitation using either a "guided approach," or an "[u]nguided approach."[75] Under the guided approach, jurisdictions use "specific guidelines and requirements for judging an applicant's moral character," while the unguided approach involves considering "'admission based on subjective personal feelings, beliefs and attitudes of the Bar Examiners.'"[76]

Although scholars note that each approach has inherent drawbacks,[77] the benefit of this rubric is that applicants "receive a case-by-case determination after consideration of the 'totality of the record.'"[78] Thus, the presumptive disqualification approach is "more accepting of individuals who have, in the past, been convicted of a felony."[79]

The Bar and Jury Box: Comparing Character Requirements

The national governing body of legal practitioners in the United States, the American Bar Association (ABA), asserts that "the primary purpose of character and fitness screening before admission to the bar is the protection of the public and the system of justice."[80] Though bar examinations test professional competence, the ABA theorizes that "the lawyer licensing process is incomplete if only testing for minimal competence is undertaken"[81] because "the public is inadequately protected by a system that fails to evaluate character and fitness as those elements relate to the practice of law."[82] Thus, the ABA recommends that in each jurisdiction "the bar examining authority should determine whether the present character and fitness of an applicant qualifies the applicant for admission,"[83] and whether an applicant is "one whose record of conduct justifies the trust of clients, adversaries, courts and others with respect to the professional duties owed to them."[84]

Echoing the sentiments of the ABA, the Supreme Court has also noted the importance of protecting the public and our system of justice by allowing "the profession itself [to] determine who should enter it."[85] Emphasizing the crucial role of practicing attorneys, Justice Frankfurter noted:

> It is a fair characterization of the lawyer's responsibility in our society that he stands "as a shield," . . . in defense of right and to ward off wrong. From a profession charged with such responsibilities there must be exacted those qualities of truth-speaking, of a high sense of honor, of granite discretion, of the strictest observance of fiduciary responsibility, that have, throughout the centuries, been compendiously described as "moral character."[86]

Concerned that an attorney without the requisite moral makeup might engage in "potential abuses, such as misrepresentation, misappropriation of funds, or betrayal of confidences,"[87] the legal profession and courts defend the use of character evaluations by stressing the need to protect the system of justice "from those who might subvert it through subornation of perjury, misrepresentation, bribery, or the like."[88] Moreover, they allege that with such assessments "a state bar can maintain control and hopefully avoid the problems that unfit attorneys may cause."[89]

Additionally, courts and bar examiners justify a heightened level of scrutiny for felonious bar applicants by noting that "'good' moral character means the absence of proven 'misconduct.'"[90] As the ABA highlights, "A record manifesting a significant deficiency in the honesty, trustworthiness, diligence or reliability of an applicant may constitute a basis for denial of admission."[91] In this way, much like felon-juror exclusion statutes, supposition about those with a felony criminal record plagues the moral character and fitness process. Yet, in a majority of jurisdictions, the moral character and fitness process allows for the possibility that certain convicted felons are suitable to fill essential legal roles—belying the presumption that all those with a felonious criminal history are permanently unfit to take part in the pursuit of justice.[92]

As discussed above, jurisdictions primarily justify felon-juror exclusion statutes by arguing that convicted felons threaten the jury because they lack character. And, while the manner in which those with a felonious criminal history would threaten a jury is ambiguous, the rationale makes clear that a majority of jurisdictions presume that all felonious jurors possess unalterably bad character. Yet, in twenty-four states and the federal court system that presumption exists alongside flexible moral character and fitness standards that acknowledge a more malleable conceptualization of character.[93]

In these jurisdictions, bar examiners conduct individualized evaluations of all aspiring attorneys,[94] providing bar applicants with a felonious criminal history the opportunity to gain entry into the legal profession. On the other hand, such jurisdictions also employ categorical, record-based juror eligibility statutes, which permanently prohibit convicted felons from taking part in the adjudicative process. This incongruent framework for assessing the value of prospective legal actors with a felonious criminal past seemingly incorporates both traditionalist and situationist views of character. The law ostensibly acknowledges that convicted felons can possess the requisite character to enter the legal profession, while concomitantly alleging that convicted felons are forever unsuitable for jury service. In a practical sense, such a position means that a convicted felon is trustworthy enough to represent a criminal defendant in the most grievous of cases, but is not suitable to decide even a minor civil dispute.

The majority approach to the screening of felonious bar applicants and jurors arguably concedes the flaws of the probity rationale for felon-juror exclusion. By employing inconsistent processes for evaluating a convicted felon's suitability for two essential legal roles, a majority of jurisdictions reinforce the suspicion that felon-juror exclusion statutes have little to do with ensuring juror fitness and are simply punitive constructs based on unwarranted conjecture and speculation.

THE TAINT ARGUMENT

A second alternative interpretation for the probity rationale is the "taint argument."[95] The taint argument suggests that convicted felons, if allowed to serve, would undermine the appearance of the jury's integrity. As Kalt explains, this argument is somewhat arbitrary, given that a host of jurisdictions allow convicted felons to vote and allow misdemeanants to take part in jury service. It is unclear how convicted felons do not "taint" the electorate, or how misdemeanants do not "taint" the reputation of the juries on which they serve.[96] Nonetheless, courts have suggested that the appearance of impropriety is, at least in part, the primary ill the probity rationale is designed to remedy. Still, prior empirical research makes clear that excluding convicted felons from jury service may do more to compromise the integrity of the juries and their resulting verdicts than would the inclusion of felon-jurors.

Legitimacy and Legal Compliance

To foster compliance with the law, authorities regularly rely on measures of social control.[97] For example, criminal sanctions "seek . . . to deter rule breaking by threatening to punish wrongdoing."[98] Yet empirical evidence suggests that deterrence has only a marginal impact on a citizen's willingness to obey the law.[99] Nevertheless, lawmakers expend an inordinate amount of resources attempting to deter illegal behavior,[100] often ignoring potential alternative schemes by which to facilitate compliance.[101]

Procedural justice scholar Tom Tyler suggests a normatively superior method for cultivating legal obedience. He contends that "the legal system benefits when people voluntarily defer to regulations to some degree and follow them, even when they do not anticipate being caught and punished if they do not."[102] Thus, authorities can promote law-abiding behavior by moving away from the forced acquiescence characteristic of deterrence and toward a "value-based model," focused on eliciting "voluntary acceptance and cooperation."[103]

This self-regulation approach suggests that "internal motivational forces . . . lead people to undertake voluntary actions," and that "values shape rule-following."[104] Accordingly, Tyler theorizes that legal procedures impact the perceived legitimacy of the law and that when citizens view the law as legitimate, they are more likely to follow its directives.[105] Specifically, Tyler asserts that the legitimacy of the law is contingent on: (1) a citizen's "prior views about law and government,"[106] and (2) "the use of fair procedures during the experience itself."[107] Therefore, self-regulation can only succeed if authorities take steps to legitimize the law by employing legal policies that citizens view as procedurally fair, while continuously evaluating these policies to ensure that they continue to portray the law as legitimate.[108]

In a variety of contexts, research demonstrates that citizens who have had prior negative experiences with the law are more likely to voluntarily comply with the law if they perceive the law to be legitimate. For example, Gill McIvor assessed the effectiveness of Scottish Drug Courts and found that the "interactions that took place in court between offenders and sentencers encouraged increased compliance and supported offenders in their efforts to address their drug use and associated offending."[109] In another setting, researchers studying the perpetrators of domestic violence discovered that "the manner in which an arrestee is handled plays an important role in reducing the likelihood of recidivating behavior."[110] Additionally, analyses of graduated sanctions—supervision conditions—in the probation and parole context suggest that "a perception of unfairness may increase noncompliance."[111] Thus, evidence tends to show that the fairness of procedures impacts legal compliance, even for those who have withstood prior punishment at the hands of the state.

Several factors influence citizens' views of the law. Tyler and others have "identified six components of procedural justice: (1) representation, (2) consistency, (3) impartiality, (4) accuracy, (5) correctability, and (6) ethicality."[112] Moreover, data indicate that "persons attribute legitimacy to legal authorities and voluntarily follow rules out of a sense of duty and obligation when legal authorities treat them fairly."[113] In theory, and in line with procedural justice research, juries that do not reflect the communities from which they are drawn make it unlikely that citizens will view the jury or jury verdicts as a legitimate exercise of the state's authority. Empirical evidence seems to support such a contention.

Delegitimizing Verdicts

In 2012, a jury of six women—five Caucasian and one Latina—acquitted George Zimmerman of the shooting death of Trayvon Martin, an unarmed thirteen-year-old African-American boy.[114] The trial and subsequent verdict reignited debates about the representativeness of juries in the United States. Many commentators argued that the racial composition of the jury made a guilty verdict unlikely and made the rendered verdict illegitimate.[115] Still, felon-juror exclusion escaped critical analysis even though the practice poses a significant threat to the diversity of juries.

The United States incarcerates more of its citizens than any other country in the world.[116] Today, over 2.3 million Americans are behind bars.[117] This disturbing normalization of a felony criminal record is arguably the direct result of the United States' experiment with mass incarceration, an experiment that has disproportionately impacted the African-American community.[118] While 8 percent of all adults bear the mark of a felony conviction, almost triple that many African-American adults (23 percent) have been convicted of a felony in the United States.[119] For African-American adult men, the outlook is even bleaker, as roughly one-third are also convicted felons.[120]

In 2012, Darren Wheelock conducted the first empirical analysis of felon-juror exclusion statutes.[121] In that study, Wheelock explored felon-juror exclusion in Georgia, a permanent exclusion jurisdiction.[122] His research demonstrated that in 2004, across Georgia, felon-juror exclusion reduced the number of African-American men expected to serve as jurors from 1.65 to 1.17 per jury.[123] As Wheelock notes, in many Georgia counties this effect was even more prominent. In some counties, over half of otherwise eligible African-American men were subject to exclusion from jury service solely because of a felony conviction.[124] Wheelock also found that in a number of counties, felon-juror exclusion statutes reduced the expected number of African-American male jurors to under one, a significant reduction as prior research suggests that, in capital cases, juries with one African-American male are less likely to sentence a defendant to death than juries without an African-American male.[125] In sum, Wheelock's research tends to show that felon-juror exclusion has the potential to racially homogenize juries.[126]

Importantly, the racial homogenization of juries runs the risk of delegitimizing rendered verdicts.[127] Citizens' evaluations of the jury account for far more than simply cost and accuracy.[128] Citizens also concern themselves with the composition of juries. Research demonstrates that citizens question the fairness and legitimacy of verdicts when a jury appears unrepresentative of their community.[129] As compared to those rendered by less diverse juries, the legitimacy of verdicts rendered by juries that are perceived to represent an adequate cross-section of the community are viewed far more favorably by the general public.[130] For example, Fukurai and Davies found that in a telephone poll of California residents, 67.3 percent of respondents felt that a jury verdict rendered by a racially diverse jury is fairer than one rendered by a single race jury.[131]

To this point, Wheelock describes a type of feedback loop created by felon-juror exclusion statutes. Specifically, he notes, "I demonstrate how felon jury exclusion can affect the jury-selection process by removing large numbers of African-American men from the criminal justice process. Ironically, it is precisely this group that is most likely to have their lives altered by contact with the criminal justice system."[132] Relatedly, recent high-profile cases involving African-Americans and use of deadly force by law enforcement have led many to question the legitimacy of policing policy.[133] Couple these tragic events with juror eligibility statutes that disproportionately impact African-American men and the legitimacy of the jury process rightfully comes under scrutiny, especially for those who live in communities predominated by racial minorities. In this way, while the taint argument supposes that the inclusion of convicted felons in the jury process will somehow undermine the integrity and reputation of the jury, the exact opposite is likely true. As noted jury scholars Valerie Hans and Neil Vidmar explain: "Regardless of whether or not the composition of the jury makes a difference in any particular case, people look to the composition of the jury to explain verdicts. Thus, not only for fact-finding but also for legitimation, a representative jury is desirable."[134]

CONCLUSION

The probity rationale presumes that convicted felons lack the character to serve as jurors. Though the precise mechanisms through which convicted felons threaten the jury is unclear, two distinct assertions seem to arise from the justification. The first, the instrumental argument, suggests that convicted felons would undermine the functionality of the jury. The second, the taint argument, seems to hold that the inclusion of convicted felons in the jury process would denigrate the jury's appearance or reputation. Neither argument survives critical analysis.

The instrumental argument fails because it relies on empirically untenable conceptualizations of character. It conceives of character as a fixed concept, though social psychological research demonstrates that situations influence character and behavioral manifestations of character in significant ways. The instrumental interpretation is also plagued by the law's seemingly schizophrenic approach to character in a variety of contexts, namely its stance on the licensure of felonious lawyers in the vast majority of jurisdictions.

The taint argument is also vulnerable to empirical challenge, as evidence makes clear that felon-juror exclusion statutes contribute to the racial homogenization of juries and, in turn, actually undermine the legitimacy of the jury and resulting verdicts. Still, the probity rationale is only one proffered justification for felon-juror exclusion. The next chapter will further explore the second rationale for the exclusion of convicted felons from jury service—the inherent bias rationale—introducing recent empirical evidence calling into question its veracity.

THREE

Honor Among Thieves?

All men are loyal, but their objects of allegiance are at best approximate.

—JOHN BARTH

THE SECOND OFT-CITED JUSTIFICATION FOR FELON-JUROR exclusion is the inherent bias rationale.[1] The inherent bias rationale suggests that convicted felons—by virtue of their experiences with the criminal justice system—harbor sympathy for criminal defendants and antipathy toward prosecutorial entities.[2] In short, the fear is that felon-jurors, if allowed to serve, would hang criminal juries, acquitting their "fellow" criminal defendants. As the District of Columbia Court of Appeals explains, "The presumptively 'shared attitudes' of convicted felons as they relate to the goal of juror impartiality are a primary reason for the exclusion."[3] Similarly, the Eighth Circuit has endorsed the inherent bias rationale, holding that the exclusion of convicted felons from jury service "is rationally related to the legitimate governmental purpose of creating a pool of jurors likely to give unbiased consideration to the evidence presented ... devising a method to choose jurors who are likely to be unbiased does not, we believe, conflict with the respect we give to the presumption of innocence once a particular defendant is brought to trial."[4]

In citing the inherent bias rationale as justification for categorical felon-juror exclusion statutes, jurisdictions make three interrelated presumptions about convicted felons, the alleged threat they pose to a jury's impartiality, and the nature of bias. First, jurisdictions assume a level of homogeneity among convicted felons, assigning to the group a "universal, unidirectional bias."[5] Second, jurisdictions presume that convicted felons pose a unique threat to the jury process. No other group of prospective jurors is categorically excluded from the jury pool because of an alleged pretrial bias. And finally, by imposing felon-juror exclusion statutes based on a supposed pretrial bias, jurisdictions also presume that the formation of biases is one-dimensional, such that experiences with the criminal justice system are dispositive of prodefense/antiprosecution sentiment.[6]

Several courts have expressed discomfort with the inherent bias rationale and its underlying presumptions.[7] In a series of cases in which litigants challenged verdicts rendered by juries that mistakenly included felon-jurors, courts were staunchly reluctant to overturn.[8] Instead, they suggest that the inherent bias rationale lacks merit and is based only on supposition. As the District of Columbia Court of Appeals plainly stated, "Felon status, alone, does not necessarily imply bias."[9]

Data derived from recent empirical research suggests that perhaps those courts were correct in questioning the veracity of the inherent bias rationale. Evidence derived from these studies demonstrates that the pretrial biases of convicted felons vary,[10] that other identifiable groups of prospective jurors harbor significant pretrial biases,[11] and that bias is the product of a host of factors that can both mitigate and exacerbate pretrial dispositions. Hence, though many courts and lawmakers routinely cite the inherent bias rationale in support of felon-juror exclusion, they do so without empirical support, justifying the banishment of citizens with a felony criminal history by citing only an "intuitively based theory of personality."[12]

GETTING TO AN IMPARTIAL JURY

The Sixth Amendment to the United States Constitution guarantees litigants the right to an impartial jury.[13] To say nothing of jurors' potential implicit biases, which can escape detection and infect a jury,[14] securing a neutral tribunal is an imprecise endeavor, pitting two models of impartiality against one another.[15]

The traditional or common law model of impartiality focuses on individual jurors.[16] As Jeffrey Abramson explains, "The first and more familiar [model] highlights the impartiality of the juror and the ignorance that, ironically, makes impartial judgment possible. In this view, the primary qualification of good jurors is that they themselves know nothing beforehand about the case they are about to judge. Precisely because they bring no personal knowledge or opinions to the case, they can judge it with the distance and dispassion that marks impartial justice."[17] Such a model holds that to achieve the ideal jury—"an impartial tribunal, one that is not predisposed to favor a particular outcome,"[18]—each juror must act solely as an "impartial adjudicator,"[19] arriving to court a "tabula rasa."[20] Accordingly, the common law approach demands, perhaps unrealistically,[21] that jurors "base their verdicts on an accurate appraisal of the evidence presented in court while disregarding all facts, information, and personal sources of knowledge not formally admitted into evidence."[22] In turn, when jurors fail to reach this seemingly unattainable standard, critics argue that they "are gullible creatures, too often driven by emotion and too easily motivated by prejudice, anger and pity."[23]

Perhaps recognizing the infeasibility of the common law model, the Supreme Court has refined the requisite characteristics of an impartial tribunal, holding that "'representative' juries are 'impartial' juries."[24] This more enlightened view of impartiality makes clear that "deliberations are considered impartial . . . when group differences are not eliminated but rather invited, embraced, and fairly represented."[25] As the Court noted in *Ballew v. Georgia,* "The counterbalancing of various biases is critical to the accurate application of the common sense of the community to the facts of any given case."[26]

Thus, such an approach allows for "qualities of human nature and varieties of human experience,"[27] no longer requiring that jurors "appear in court with a blank slate, neutral and untainted by life experiences."[28] This modern vision of the jury values thorough deliberation achieved through diversity and, to a point, partiality.[29] "To eliminate potential jurors on the grounds that they will bring the biases of their group into the jury room is . . . to misunderstand the democratic task of the jury, which is nothing else than to represent accurately the diversity of views held in a heterogeneous society. . . . If the jury is balanced to accomplish this representative task, then as a whole it will be impartial, even though no one juror is."[30] The inherent bias rationale ostensibly endorses the common law model of impartiality, alleging that convicted felons harbor impermissible biases that warrant their categorical exclusion. The justification further offends the Supreme Court's model of inclusive impartiality by uniformly discounting the views and opinions of those with a felony criminal history.

THE CONTOURS OF PRETRIAL BIASES

Generally, scholars identify two types of empirical research on jury behavior: jury research and juror research. Jury research highlights group decision-making, "examin[ing] consensual judgments, through experiments that simulate the jury deliberation process," while juror research "examines how individuals weigh evidence, process information, and reach legal decisions."[31]

One strain of empirical juror research explores how the pretrial biases of individual jurors influence their verdict preference.

Historically, social scientists and courts have categorized pretrial juror biases as either specific or general.[32] While specific biases are those spawned by the attributes of a given case or defendant (e.g., how a juror might feel about an African-American defendant charged with sexually assaulting a white woman), general biases are unrelated to case features (e.g., how a given juror might feel about African-Americans generally).[33] Instead, general biases are unique to individual jurors, shaped by their perspectives and life experiences.[34] The inherent bias rationale invokes a quasi theory of general bias.[35]

Since the early 1970s, the predictive value of general biases has been the subject of extensive research.[36] The results of that research are mixed.[37] Studies demonstrate that juror demographics, attitudes, and personality traits seldom yield biases that accurately and uniformly influence juror decision-making processes.[38] These results have prompted some scholars to conclude that "few if any juror characteristics are good predictors of juror verdict preferences."[39]

Research on general pretrial biases most often focuses on juror demographics and their potential influence on verdicts. Such demographic factors include: age,[40] gender,[41] race,[42] native language,[43] occupation,[44] religion,[45] socioeconomic status,[46] level of education,[47] and victimization.[48] Studies exploring the predictive value of juror demographic variables have largely yielded inconclusive results.[49] Evidence indicates that juror demographics alone are inaccurate predictors of verdict preference. Rather, demographic variables play a more nuanced role in the juror decision-making process, eliciting predictive biases that are case and defendant specific.[50] Hence, while lawyers and jury consultants often stereotypically assume that demographic variables foster unwavering general biases, research indicates that such assumptions are likely in error.[51]

Research also demonstrates that juror attitudes seldom predict verdicts.[52] One notable exception, however, are jurors' views of the death penalty. Studies have shown that a juror's attitude toward capital punishment spawns a general bias that can influence verdict preference.[53] Across cases, jurors who favor the death penalty are more likely to convict than are jurors who oppose it.[54] For example, in an influential meta-analysis exploring how views of the death penalty impact verdicts, researchers found that those who supported the death penalty were 59 percent likely to convict while those who did not support the death penalty were only 41 percent likely to convict. This 44 percent increase in probability of proneness of conviction reveals the linear effect of views of the death penalty, such that "persons with the strongest attitudes are either more or less likely to convict based on attitude toward the death penalty."[55]

Studies of general biases have also focused on juror personality traits and their impact on juror decision-making processes. Though research in this area has established few links between juror personality traits and verdict preference,[56] studies do reveal that the personality trait of authoritarianism can significantly affect a juror's determination of guilt or innocence in a variety of cases.[57] In a meta-analysis of studies exploring the impact of traditional authoritarianism and legal authoritarianism on juror verdict preference,[58] researchers discovered that jurors who scored high on measures of authoritarianism, and to a greater extent legal authoritarianism, tended to convict more often.[59] Studies have also demonstrated that jurors who possess authoritarian attributes tend to punish more severely,[60] recall more of the prosecution's evidence than that of the defense,[61] offer higher estimates of a defendant's probability of guilt,[62] and recommend longer waiting periods for parole eligibility for guilty defendants.[63]

Though views of the death penalty and the personality trait of authoritarianism can affect juror decision-making processes, research tends to show that general biases are typically weak predictors of jurors' verdict preferences.[64] In this way, prior studies indirectly call into question the empirical viability of the inherent bias rationale. To further explore the tenability of the inherent bias rationale, I have conducted two studies focused on the justification and its underlying presumptions.[65]

THEY ARE ALL THE SAME: THE HOMOGENEITY ASSUMPTION

In his seminal study of felon-juror exclusion, Kalt argues that the inherent bias rationale, like the probity rationale, is overinclusive.[66] Though conceding that some convicted felons assuredly harbor the sentiments the inherent bias rationale targets, assuming that all convicted felons feel the same way is a flawed presumption. As Kalt states: "All of this is undoubtedly an accurate description of how some felons would approach some criminal cases. It falls short, however, of justifying excluding all felons, per se, from all cases.... Only if every, or almost every, felon is irretrievably biased against the government might it make sense to have a blanket exclusion of felons from criminal juries on these grounds.... Such a notion of universal, unidirectional bias is not particularly plausible."[67]

TABLE 1 Revised Juror Bias Scale Scores, by Group: Descriptive Statistics
(Binnall, 2014)

	Eligible Jurors	Convicted Felons	Law Students
N	235	234	209
Mean	35.41	33.29	32.07
Median (36)	35	33	33
Std. Deviation	5.10	6.08	5.64
Range (12–60)	21–49	17–55	18–53

In 2014, I conducted the first empirical analysis focused on the inherent bias rationale.[68] A field study in California, a permanent exclusion jurisdiction,[69] the study examined and compared the pretrial biases of 707 participants: 242 otherwise eligible jurors with a felony criminal record (focal group—"convicted felons"), 247 eligible jurors without a felony criminal record (comparison group 1—"eligible jurors"), and 218 eligible jurors without a felony criminal record and enrolled in law school (comparison group 2—"law students").[70] To construct each study group, participants were recruited at a variety of locations over the course of approximately twelve months.[71] Because this study involved eligible jurors in California, the state's juror eligibility guidelines served as exclusionary criteria and each participant was prescreened to ensure they met these guidelines.[72]

Intragroup and intergroup comparisons were made using an established measure of pretrial bias, the Revised Juror Bias Scale (RJBS).[73] The RJBS is scored on a standard five-category Likert scale (strongly disagree, disagree, no opinion, agree, strongly agree) and produces total scores that range from 12 to 60, with a scale median score of 36.[74] Scores below the scale median indicate a prodefense/antiprosecution pretrial bias, while scores above the scale median indicate a proprosecution/antidefense pretrial bias.[75]

To explore the homogeneity claim implicit in the inherent bias rationale, I examined the central tendencies and dispersion of convicted felons' scores on the RJBS. Convicted felons' mean score on the RJBS was 33.29. This score falls below the scale median (36), suggesting that as a group, convicted felons harbor a prodefense/antiprosecution pretrial bias (see table 1).

Still, results also indicate that convicted felons' pretrial biases are far from homogeneous. A look at the dispersion of convicted felons' scores on the RJBS reveals, significant disparity, with scores ranging from 17 to 55. Table 1

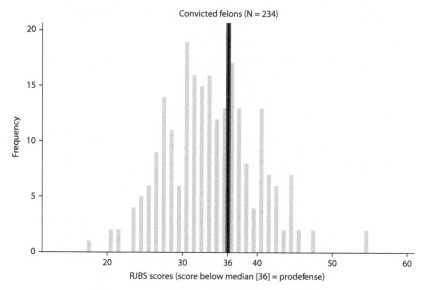

FIGURE 1. Frequency distribution of convicted felons' scores on the Revised Juror Bias Scale (Binnall, 2014).

presents these results.[76] A frequency distribution of convicted felons' RJBS scores revealed that 151 convicted felons scored below the scale median, 17 scored at the scale median, and 66 scored above the scale median (see fig. 1). Therefore, 65 percent of participants possessed a prodefense/antiprosecution pretrial bias, 7 percent were neutral, and notably, 28 percent favored the prosecution. These findings confirm, for the first time empirically, that categorical felon-juror exclusion statutes are, in fact, over inclusive, and that Kalt's argument regarding the heterogeneity of convicted felons' pretrial biases is demonstrably accurate.

THEY ARE JUST DIFFERENT: THE UNIQUE
THREAT ASSUMPTION

In challenging the inherent bias rationale, Kalt also argues that the justification is underinclusive, doing little to protect the jury from other groups of jurors who are likely to harbor pretrial biases possibly threatening to the impartiality of the adjudicative process. Along this line Kalt states:

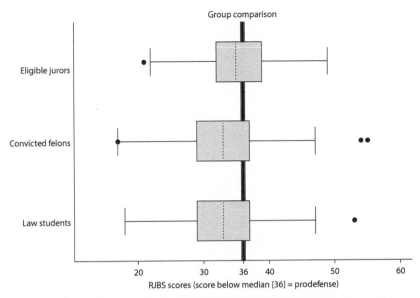

FIGURE 2. A boxplot comparison of group scores on the Revised Juror Bias Scale (RJBS). For each group, shaded boxes indicate the interquartile range of RJBS scores, whiskers indicate the overall range of RJBS scores, dotted line indicates the group mean RJBS score, and dots indicate outlier RJBS scores (Binnall, 2014).

Another point is that many groups have generally strong biases in criminal cases. For example, in the case of crime victims, the justice system does not presume that they are all incapable of being objective in all trials, but it is concerned enough about the possibility that individualized analyses are performed. They are screened in voir dire, . . . [f]amilies of crime victims, victims of torts and their families, police officers, and many others are similarly screened. . . . The question is not why biased felons should be treated differently than the rest of the population, but rather why they should be treated differently than the rest of the biased population. . . . If the answer is only that felons are more likely to be biased than victims, there is a numerical problem. . . . Because crime victims vastly outnumber convicted felons . . . eliminating just felons leaves plenty of unaccounted bias.[77]

To test the underinclusiveness claim, I compared convicted felons' pretrial biases to those of eligible jurors and law students. I did so by first examining the central tendencies and dispersion of each group's RJBS scores. Findings reveal a prodefense/antiprosecution pretrial bias across groups, as the mean RJBS for each was below the scale median (36). Notably, the mean RJBS score for convicted felons matched that of law students (33), while both

TABLE 2 Unequal Variance T-tests Comparing Revised Juror
Bias Scale Scores (Binnall, 2014)

	Satterthwaite df	p-value	Welch df	p-value
Convicted Felons v. Eligible Jurors	452.7	0.0001*	454.58	0.0001*
Eligible Jurors v. Law Students	422.04	<0.0000*	423.95	<0.0000*
Convicted Felons v. Law Students	440.33	0.29	442.34	0.29

* p < .001.

groups had a lower RJBS than eligible jurors (35), suggesting that convicted felons and law students harbor more severe prodefense pretrial biases than do eligible jurors generally. The dispersion of RJBS scores showed a similar pattern, as convicted felons (17–55) and law students (18–53) varied substantially, while eligible jurors scores were more clustered (21–49). Figure 2 graphically illustrates these similarities and differences.

Overall, these findings suggest that convicted felons and law students do not differ, while both groups appear to be more prodefense/antiprosecution than eligible jurors generally. A statistical comparison reveals that the group mean RJBS for law students does not differ statistically from that of convicted felons (see table 2).[78] This finding suggests that the underinclusiveness argument has merit, and that if convicted felons pose a substantial threat to the impartiality of the jury process, then so too do law students. Still, no jurisdiction categorically expels law students from the jury pool.

To further explore the underinclusiveness claim, I conducted a follow-up study in 2016–17.[79] In that study, 211 California law enforcement personnel were recruited from California's Peace Officer's Standards and Training (POST) training classes over the course of twelve months in 2016–17.[80] Each participant then completed the RJBS. Though law enforcement personnel are not permitted to serve as jurors in California, such a disqualification is uncommon nationally.

Only thirteen jurisdictions disqualify law enforcement personnel from the venire,[81] and of those thirteen, two only disqualify in criminal matters.[82] In the remaining thirty-nine jurisdictions, law enforcement can become part of a venire and are permitted to adjudicate both civil and criminal matters.

Once again, I examined the pretrial biases of law enforcement personnel and then compared those results to my earlier study of convicted felons. Findings revealed that law enforcement personnel's RJBS scores ranged considerably (24–54), suggesting that, like convicted felons, law enforcement personnel are

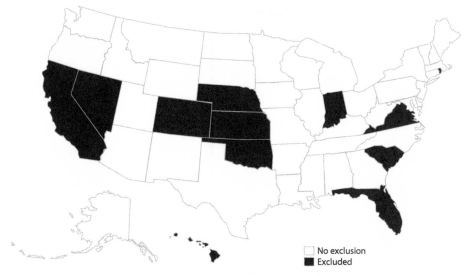

MAP 3. Law enforcement personnel juror eligibility, by jurisdiction (Binnall, 2018b).

not homogeneous. A closer look at law enforcement personnel scores indicated that of the 211 participants, 144 scored at or above the scale median (36), indicating that 68 percent of participants possessed a proprosecution pretrial bias (see fig. 3).

Also of note, law enforcement's mean score on the RJBS (38.86) exceeded the scale median (36), suggesting a proprosecution/antidefense pretrial bias. Law enforcement personnel's group mean was also 2.86 units from the scale median. In my 2014 study, convicted felons' mean score (33.29) was 2.71 units below the scale median, a statistically significant difference ($p = .218$). This result seemingly suggests that on a scale of pretrial biases, convicted felons are as prodefense/antiprosecution as law enforcement personnel are antidefense/proprosecution. Nonetheless, the vast majority of jurisdictions statutorily exclude convicted felons from the jury process while permitting law enforcement personnel to take part.[83]

Combined, prior studies of the inherent bias rationale support the under-inclusiveness argument. Data reveal that law students and law enforcement personnel harbor pretrial biases of different sorts. Law students appear to harbor prodefense/antiprosecution pretrial biases analogous to those demonstrated by convicted felons, while law enforcement personnel possess a proprosecution/antidefense bias as severe as the prodefense/antiprosecution pretrial bias characteristic of convicted felons in the study. If the inherent

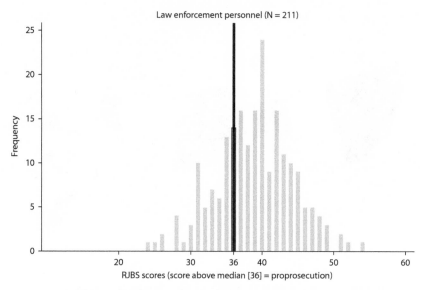

FIGURE 3. Frequency distribution of law enforcement personnel's scores on the Revised Juror Bias Scale (Binnall, 2018b).

bias rationale has merit, then both types of biases warrant categorical exclusion. Still, in nearly all U.S. jurisdictions, only prospective jurors with a felony conviction are banned from the process.

But, as Kalt notes, "To the extent that inherent bias among felon jurors leads to legitimate skepticism, the automatic exclusion of felons is less acceptable, and smacks of viewpoint discrimination."[84] I too have argued that by excluding those with a felony conviction while permitting other groups of biased jurors to take part in the jury selection process, jurisdictions engage in a type of "jurymandering,"[85] whereby they engineer the composition of the jury pool through legislative proclamations that eliminate undesired viewpoints.[86] While it draws criticism from scholars in other contexts,[87] jurymandering as it relates to convicted felons and their perspectives is seemingly an accepted practice nationally.

THEY MUST BE RESENTFUL: THE BIAS
FORMATION ASSUMPTION

A final assumption implicit in the inherent bias rationale is that exposure to the criminal justice system necessarily spawns prodefense/antiprosecution pretrial biases. As courts have suggested, "former conviction and imprisonment would ordinarily incline [a convicted felon] to compassion for others accused of crime."[88] Similarly, consider one columnist's opposition to pending legislation in California that would restore juror eligibility to those with a felony criminal history:

> Currently, felons are prevented from serving on juries because of their obvious and inherent bias against prosecutors and law enforcement. If you honestly believe that jurors in California who've served time won't be more lenient towards accused criminals, I've got a bullet train to sell you.... How can someone who's served time be considered free of bias? ... That's like having crazy cat ladies vote on how many cats a person should own.... A "jury of your peers" doesn't mean having a foreman with the same ankle monitoring device as the defendant.[89]

Apart from its baseless, overtly prejudicial assertions, the above statement is illustrative. For many, including some criminologists, the inherent bias rationale "feels" logical.[90] Taking this view, the justification seems necessary and appropriate, though empirical evidence suggests otherwise.

Predicting Biases across Groups

To explore the contribution of a felony conviction to the formation of pretrial biases, I conducted a multivariate regression (ordinary least squares) examining the relationship between RJBS scores and group membership among participants in my 2014 study.[91] To isolate the effects of a felony conviction, the multivariate regression includes a number of juror characteristics shown to influence pretrial biases (independent variables).[92]

Results reveal that a felony conviction is a statistically significant predictor of a lower score on the RJBS (a prodefense/antiprosecution pretrial bias). But so are a number of other variables. Findings demonstrate that participants who self-identify as law students, African-American, crime victims, strongly opposed to the death penalty, or politically liberal are also more likely to harbor a prodefense/antiprosecution bias.[93] Conversely, those who have less than a high school education, strongly support the death penalty, or have a positive view of the law are more likely to favor the prosecution.[94]

Taken together, these results suggest that though a felony conviction is a statistically significant predictor of a prodefense/antiprosecution pretrial bias, it is not the sole predictor of such a bias. Instead, a host of other factors can exacerbate or mitigate the pretrial biases of potential jurors. These findings are consistent with earlier revelations, suggesting that while some convicted felons are likely to harbor a prodefense/antiprosecution pretrial bias, contact with the criminal justice system is not a dispositive predictor of such a bias.

Predicting Biases among Convicted Felons

Felon-juror exclusion statutes target those with a felony criminal record, punishment severity notwithstanding. Thus, while a convicted felon sentenced only to a term of probationary supervision is ineligible for jury service in a majority of jurisdictions, a misdemeanant sentenced to prison or jail is almost always exempt from such statutes.[95] In this way, criminal justice procedures, rather than outcomes, appear to dictate exclusion, as the law seemingly assumes that the adjudication of a felony influences the formation of a prodefense/antiprosecution pretrial bias to a greater extent than does the resulting punishment.

Citizens' views of the criminal justice system are shaped by their experiences with that system. "In short, citizens learn about their government through their interactions with it."[96] As noted in chapter 2, citizens' views of the criminal justice system are shaped primarily by their perceptions of the procedural aspects of their interactions with criminal justice agents and agencies.[97] As procedural justice scholar Tom Tyler notes, "Issues of process dominate public evaluations of the police, the courts, and social regulatory activities."[98] Relatedly, studies reveal high levels of "anticipatory injustice" in certain communities and among certain populations,[99] leading many citizens to "expect unfair or discriminatory procedures or outcomes."[100] Such preconceptions often divide along racial lines, as African-American citizens are far more likely to hold a negative view of the criminal justice system than are white citizens.[101] Anticipatory injustice can influence fairness evaluations through a type of self-fulfilling prophecy or confirmation bias,[102] prompting citizens to conceive of interactions as unfair even in the face of evidence to the contrary.[103]

Along these lines, my 2014 study also explored the possible sources of pretrial biases among convicted felons. To do so, additional independent variables were included in a multivariate analysis (OLS regression).[104] Those variables include number of felony convictions (process) and lifetime length of incarceration (outcome). When these predictors were included, results revealed that lifetime length of incarceration is not a statistically significant predictor of pretrial biases. Findings also demonstrated that the number of felony convictions does predict pretrial bias. In particular, repeat offenders were statistically more likely to harbor a prodefense/antiprosecution pretrial bias ($\beta = -2.31$, p < 0.05).

Taken together, these findings suggest that convicted felons' pretrial biases are driven more by criminal justice contact (procedures) than they are by punishment they received (outcome). These data align with prior research suggesting that contact with the criminal justice system more often than not fosters negative views of the law and legal institutions,[105] and that the processes associated with a felony criminal conviction contribute to the formation of a prodefense/antiprosecution pretrial bias.[106]

By excluding convicted felons from jury service, in part because of an assumed pretrial bias that is cultivated by experiences with the criminal justice system, jurisdictions seem to tacitly acknowledge that criminal justice procedures, not punishment outcomes, contribute to the formation of a prodefense/antiprosecution pretrial bias. This circularity creates a self-perpetuating phenomenon whereby those who have contact with the criminal justice system are excluded from that system because some harbor biases created, in part, by contact with the system itself.

In turn, rather than addressing the potential inequities or perceived unfairness associated with such procedures, jurisdictions opt for blanket exclusion as the preferred remedy. From a policy perspective, this choice is rather troubling, in that jurisdictions seemingly ignore the potential root causes of prodefense/antiprosecution sentiments—arguably the perceived injustice of the adjudication process itself—and instead may perpetuate such perceived injustice among convicted felons by premising juror exclusion on biases the justice system helped to construct.

An alternative and perhaps more evidence-based policy would acknowledge, confront, and address the inequities of the criminal justice system that may give way to prodefense/antiprosecution pretrial biases. As research on procedural justice theory suggests,[107] doing so has the potential to bolster the legitimacy of the criminal justice system and in turn soften the alleged pretrial biases of those who come into contact with that system.[108] Such an approach comports with established social scientific evidence about the importance of procedural fairness, leaving behind the counterfactual assumptions that underlie the inherent bias rationale.

As noted above, while the Sixth Amendment's impartiality mandate requires that juries decide a litigated matter free from preconceived biases, contemporary interpretations of the mandate suggest that individual jurors may permissibly come to the process harboring thoughts and feelings derived from their life experiences and interactions with others.[109] If a prospective juror's views and attitudes rise to the level that they "substantially impair the performance of their duties,"[110] jury selection procedures are designed to detect and expel them from the adjudicative process.

During voir dire, which may last minutes or could take months,[111] attorneys and judges question potential jurors.[112] To ensure that seated jurors are fit for service, during voir dire "the focus shifts abruptly from general presumptions about individuals' ethical capacity to intense attention on the individual and his or her ability to be fair and impartial in the context of a specific trial."[113] Indeed, voir dire is used even in the case of jurors with strong feelings about and opposition to the death penalty. In such cases, "anti-death penalty jurors are not thrown out of the venire altogether; they are tested for bias during voir dire."[114] Prospective jurors with a felony criminal conviction, on the other hand, are not given the opportunity to take part in voir dire, as they are categorically banished prior to the jury selection process.

Deliberations also serve as insulation against an impermissibly biased juror. Though research suggests that a juror's initial impression of a case, an initial vote, predicts verdict preference in most instances,[115] studies also indicate that deliberations are not inconsequential.[116] Deliberations have the power to alter the views of participants, especially in real-world jury settings (as opposed to mock jury settings). For instance, in a study of hung juries by the National Center for State Courts, researchers found that in 160 of the real-world cases examined, initial verdict votes amounted to a strong majority.[117] Still, in 89 cases where the majority favored conviction, juries acquitted in 11 cases (12 percent) and in 71 cases where the majority favored acquittal, the jury convicted in 3 cases (4 percent).[118] Researchers surmised that this result "goes against Kalven and Zeisel's assertion that deliberation is unimportant."[119] Explaining these findings, scholars opine that juror polling, often done early in deliberations but after some interaction, "probably reflects a fair amount of social and informational influence that has already occurred during the initial stages of the group deliberation."[120] Thus, deliberations seemingly matter, perhaps more than practitioners and scholars acknowledge.

The inherent bias rationale for felon-juror exclusion statutes overlooks these already established features of the jury process that insulate it from partiality. Somehow, the justification assumes that convicted felons' biases are of a character that makes them difficult, if not impossible, to detect during the jury selection phase of a trial.[121] The inherent bias rationale seems to also assume, with no corroborating data, that the biases of felon-jurors are somehow fixed and impervious to informational influence during jury deliberations. Given that other jurors with potentially threatening biases are per se allowed to take part in voir dire and often deliberations, the notion that felon-jurors jeopardize the jury's impartiality to an extent that warrants their uncompromising banishment stretches logic to degrees that are untenable.

CONCLUSION

As noted, the inherent bias rationale presumes that convicted felons are alike, that they pose a unique threat to the jury process, and that negative experiences with the criminal justice system necessarily yield prodefense/antiprosecution sentiment. But, empirical findings contradict these presumptions. In the only two studies of the inherent bias rationale, data reveal that convicted felons are far from homogeneous. Results also indicate that at least two other groups of prospective jurors—law students and law enforcement personnel—harbor biases that would arguably jeopardize the impartiality of the jury process. Studies also make clear that the formation of pretrial biases is holistic, in that no one factor is dispositive of a bias in either direction. Rather, pretrial biases are the result of a host of juror characteristics and experiences, criminal justice contact being one of many. And finally, findings seem to suggest that perhaps jurisdictions—in their administration of criminal justice procedures—contribute to the formation of biases they fear will corrupt the jury process. Hence, the inherent bias rationale may be circular, creating a type of self-fulfilling feedback loop that ensures the sustained marginalization of those who come into contact with the criminal justice system.

Though exploratory, studies of the inherent bias rationale support claims that felon-juror exclusion statutes are both over- and underinclusive. Statistics make clear that felon-juror exclusion statutes likely bar many who do not harbor threatening biases. In this way, such statutes are overinclusive. Felon-juror exclusion statues are also under inclusive, as they ignore other groups of prospective jurors that possess biases arguably equally threatening to the impartiality of the jury. More generally, empirical research on the inherent bias rationale suggests that pretrial biases are complex, seldom predictive of verdict, and, in the case of convicted felons, are in part the result of criminal justice contact perceived as unfair and illegitimate. Taken together, this research poses serious challenges to the justification, leading some to question whether "the inherent bias theory is a convenience, rather than a sincere belief."[122]

At their core, the probity rationale and the inherent bias rationale are entirely anticipatory, in that they attempt to predict juror behavior based on supposition and assumption. Theoretical and empirical challenges to the justifications, though now backed by data, also endeavor to predict how felon-jurors might engage in the jury process. Though a significant step forward in our comprehension of felon-juror exclusion, such challenges also suffer from a degree of speculation and conjecture. With this in mind, I have conducted the only mock jury experiment ever to include felon-jurors. Involving observation and analysis of deliberations, the mock jury paradigm allows for the assessment of felon-juror behavior in context, providing data on how felon-jurors actually behave in the jury setting. Chapters 4 and 5 present the results of this mock jury experiment.

FOUR

Sequestering the Convicted: Part I

> When any large and identifiable segment of the community is
> excluded from jury service, the effect is to remove from the jury
> room qualities of human nature and varieties of human experi-
> ence, the range of which is unknown and perhaps unknowable.
>
> —*PETERS V. KIFF*

THE SUPREME COURT HAS LONG ENDORSED inclusive juror eligibility
criteria and denounced the en masse exclusion of any one group of prospective jurors.[1] The Court has held that diversity enriches deliberations by giving
voice to inimitable, underrepresented perspectives,[2] suggesting that diversity
likely enhances a jury's ability to complete its required tasks.[3] As the Court
points out, effective deliberations require jurors to recall "important pieces
of evidence or argument" and "make critical contributions necessary for the
solution of a given problem."[4] The Court explains thatdiversity promotes
"the opportunity through full deliberation to temper the opposing faction's
degree of certainty."[5]

As noted in chapter 1, in an effort to ensure diversity, the Court has held
that juries must represent a fair cross-section of the community,[6] and that
gender- and race-based exclusions are unconstitutional.[7] Still, while the
Court seems to embrace diversity as a means of bolstering the deliberation
process, it has implicitly authorized the banishment of convicted felons from
that process.[8]

In line with the Supreme Court's holdings, empirical research suggests
that diversity can increase the quality of jury deliberations. But such research
is scant. Of the vast universe of empirical jury research, just a small fraction
focuses on the deliberation process,[9] even less systematically examines the
quality of jury deliberations,[10] and only a handful of prior studies explore
how diversity may impact deliberations' substance.[11] Moreover, those studies
that have compared diverse and homogeneous juries focus exclusively on
participating jurors' race,[12] gender,[13] and views of the death penalty.[14] In sum,

research suggests that diversity positively affects the deliberative process and that the Supreme Court was likely correct in assuming that diversity enhances deliberations.

Nonetheless, in the context of felon-juror exclusion, lawmakers and courts presume that convicted felons pose a significant threat to the integrity of jury systems, ostensibly accepting the proffered justifications for the practice a priori and discounting the potential value felon-jurors bring to deliberations. This chapter and the next present the results of the first mock jury experiment to expand the concept of juror diversity to include jurors' felony criminal histories. The experiment simulates a real-world criminal trial, evaluating the validity of the supposed threats convicted felons pose to the jury while also exploring the potential contributions felon-jurors may make to the deliberative process.

THE PERFORMANCE OF DIVERSE JURIES

The lack of an objective standard against which to judge the accuracy of jury verdicts makes evaluating jury deliberations a difficult task.[15] To determine what aspects of jury deliberations may serve as measures of deliberation quality, researchers look primarily to jury instructions.[16] Common elements of jury instructions reveal "process-oriented criteria"[17] useful in the operationalization of deliberation quality.[18] Employing such measures, several studies tend to show that diverse juries engage in higher-quality deliberations than do homogeneous juries.[19] Outside of the jury context, research focused on group performance tends to support this finding, offering additional insights into the mechanisms through which diversity improves group functions.[20]

One strain of research on the quality of deliberations explores how diverse juries compare to homogeneous juries.[21] For example, in one of the earliest studies on the topic, Cowan, Thompson, and Ellsworth explored jury diversity related to views of the death penalty. To do so, they compared mock juries comprised entirely of death-qualified jurors (support the death penalty in certain cases) to those comprised of both death-qualified and excludable jurors (Witherspoon excludable—do not support the death penalty under any circumstance).[22] At the juror level, the study revealed no statistically significant differences between death-qualified jurors and excludable jurors on measures of law or fact recall. At the jury level, researchers found that diverse juries, on average, recalled more case facts than did homogeneous juries comprised only of death-qualified jurors.[23]

In another study of diverse juries, Marder explored the impact of gender diversity on jurors' perceptions of deliberations.[24] Unlike Cowan, Thompson, and Ellsworth's study, Marder's focused on actual jurors who had previously taken part in jury service. She found that gender-diverse juries reported a higher level of satisfaction with deliberations and that deliberations in these juries were perceived as "less hostile and more supportive."[25] Gender-diverse juries also felt as though jury deliberations were more thorough. Marder notes that varied perspectives "provide a greater array of ideas for group considera- tion, and this . . . lead[s] to more thorough deliberations . . . male and female jurors . . . enter the deliberations with different ways of seeing the case, and therefore . . . challenge each other's assumptions, and that this too . . . lead[s] to more thorough deliberations."[26]

In the most recent study of diverse juries, Sommers compared all-white juries to juries that included both white and African-American jurors.[27] Sommers found that diversity enhanced deliberations on several measures of deliberation quality. In particular, racially diverse juries deliberated longer, covered more case facts, made fewer factual errors, left fewer factual inaccura- cies uncorrected, and mentioned a lack of evidence more often.[28] Notably, Sommers's research suggests that the higher-quality deliberations exhibited by diverse juries were not only the product of African-American jurors "add- ing unique perspectives to the discussion."[29] Instead, Sommers found that all members of diverse juries— both white and African-American jurors—per- formed better than their counterparts on homogeneous juries. Sommers found the most significant performance enhancements among white jurors on diverse juries.[30]

In sum, prior research on non-felon-diverse juries suggests that diversity can enhance deliberation quality. In particular, diversity seems to promote greater fact recall and more thorough deliberations, while bolstering jurors' satisfaction with the process.

THE MECHANICS OF DIVERSITY AND DELIBERATION

Psychological research on group performance tends to support jury research suggesting that diversity likely spawns higher-quality deliberations.[31] A number of studies have found that on a variety of measures, diverse groups outperform homogeneous groups.[32] But these findings are far from conclu- sive.[33] Research has also demonstrated that diversity can, in certain instances, impede group decision making.[34] In general, diversity seems to operate as a "double-edged sword."[35]

Diversity can improve performance by increasing the cognitive resources available to the group.[36] This "cognitive resource perspective"[37] proposes that diversity-yields varied experiences and perspectives that can bolster a group's problem-solving capabilities.[38] Though the exact mechanisms through which diversity enhances group cognition are unclear, research suggests that the type of diversity at issue and the characteristics of the group may be mediating factors.[39] Notably, when referencing the benefits of diverse juries, the Supreme Court has, in the past, seemingly subscribed to the cognitive resource perspective.[40]

On the other hand, diversity may also diminish performance by undermining group cohesion and spawning conflict.[41] The "social categorization perspective" suggests "dissimilarities among diverse members based on adverse social categorization may give rise to negative effects of diversity."[42] This is especially true when the type of diversity at issue gives rise to polarizing attitudes—as in the case of convicted felons.[43] A lack of group cohesion and/or experiences of conflict may negatively impact group performance by reducing members' cognitive capabilities. Research demonstrates that when members' cognitive resources are directed toward coping with conflict, overall group performance suffers.[44] Though persuasive, such research is not dispositive, as studies have also demonstrated that certain types of conflict can impact group performance positively by prompting members to engage more thoroughly with group tasks.[45]

A third, integrated theory of diversity's impact on performance posits that group characteristics are the key to reconciling the cognitive resource and social categorization perspectives.[46] Group features that allow for the exploitation of cognitive resources while tempering intermember conflict optimize the value of diversity.[47] Though research on the ideal features of diverse groups is inconclusive,[48] studies tend to demonstrate that diversity is a valuable commodity that likely enhances group performance under most conditions.[49] Mock jury research exploring deliberation quality in diverse juries supports this proposition.[50]

Still, the rationales for excluding convicted felons from jury service, coupled with prior research on diverse juries and deliberating groups, paint an unclear picture of how convicted felons will impact jury deliberations. Exploratory in nature and accommodating this uncertainty, the mock jury experiment described below seeks to bring that picture into focus.

In 2015–16, I conducted a mock jury experiment that included 101 participants divided into two groups: otherwise eligible jurors with a felony criminal record (felon-jurors) and eligible jurors without a felony criminal record (non-felon-jurors).[51] The 101 participants made up nineteen juries of two types: homogeneous juries (exclusively non-felon-jurors) and diverse juries (non-felon-jurors and felon-jurors).

To obtain an adequate number of juror-eligible participants, a multipronged recruitment effort was used. Felon-jurors were recruited using in-person solicitation at Parole and Community Team (PACT) meetings in the host county,[52] while non-felon-jurors were recruited using written advertisements strategically placed at all courthouses (9) in the host county.[53]

Participants who called or emailed in response to in-person and written solicitations were prescreened by research assistants to ensure that they met California's juror eligibility criteria.[54] To ensure the ecological validity of the present study, additional steps were also taken. Specifically, because California's juror rolls are derived from voter registration lists and driver's license records, participants were also excluded if (1) they were not a registered voter in the State of California, or if (2) they did not possess a valid California's driver's license.

The 101 participants (21 felon-jurors and 80 non-felon-jurors) who took part in the present study made up nineteen mock juries.[55] Three types of juries were constructed: juries comprised exclusively of non-felons (N = 5), juries including a single felon-juror (N = 8), and juries including multiple felon-jurors (N = 6).[56] In line with prior research, each jury consisted of at least four participants.[57]

Participants then watched a video reenactment of an actual criminal trial.[58] Since the goal of this study was to analyze deliberations of diverse juries comprised of felon-jurors and non-felon-jurors, a reenactment of a criminal case that did not give rise to a clear verdict was used.[59] Topically, the reenactment that served as the experimental stimulus involved the robbery of bank by a defendant who was on parole at the time of the alleged crime.[60] The reenactment was created using lawyers, law students, and professional actors. The reenactment was condensed to ninety-four minutes and included opening statements, two witnesses per side (prosecution and defense), and closing arguments.

The prosecution argued that the eyewitness account of the bank teller and the testimony of an FBI agent who investigated the incident proved beyond a reasonable doubt that the defendant committed the crime in question. They also presented evidence demonstrating that the defendant's driver's license was found at the scene of the crime. The defense contended that the eyewitness account was flawed, as was the FBI investigation, which did not include video surveillance or physical evidence. The defense called the defendant and a tow-truck driver as witnesses. That testimony suggested the defendant was having car trouble in a location that would have made the robbery very difficult logistically. The defendant is a convicted felon who missed an appointment with his parole officer on the day in question.

After participants had finished viewing the experimental stimulus, they were read the Ninth Circuit model federal jury instructions for bank robbery.[61] The instructions detailed the legal elements of bank robbery, legal definitions of reasonable doubt and relevance, an explanation of the burden of proof (beyond a reasonable doubt), and general guidelines for deliberations. As part of jury instructions, participants were instructed to select a foreperson, but were not given any further details about how to conduct that process. Juries then deliberated, rendered a verdict, and completed a postdeliberation questionnaire. All deliberations were filmed and ranged from 20.8 to 37.4 minutes with an average deliberation time of 26.7 minutes ($SD = 7.49$).[62] Prior to leaving, jurors were then compensated fifty dollars for their participation and asked not to discuss the experiment with others in the community.

EVALUATING DELIBERATIONS

There are generally two approaches to the study of deliberations.[63] The first approach involves content analyses of deliberations in a mock jury setting.[64] A second approach to the study of deliberations uses postdeliberation questionnaires that poll participants about their impressions of the deliberation experience, either in a mock jury setting or as a follow-up to actual deliberations.[65]

Drawing on prior research of diverse juries, this study utilizes theoretically derived measures from both approaches to the study of deliberations. The first set of measures examines deliberation structure: foreperson selection and deliberation style.[66] The second set of measures assesses deliberation content: deliberation duration, juror time spoken, coverage of facts and law, and accuracy of facts and law covered.[67] The final set of measures evaluates jurors' perceptions of the deliberation experience, of witness credibility, and of attorney credibility/likability.[68]

For measures of deliberation structure and content, this experiment used a theoretically derived, concept-driven coding frame,[69] and employed three coders who, at the same time, coded six deliberation transcripts. Coders were then randomly assigned a second set of six jury deliberations (because the sample involved nineteen juries, one research assistant coded an extra transcript). Those transcripts were then compared to assess the reliability of each coder. Like prior studies of diverse juries,[70] pairwise kappas were then performed for each of the following variables: novel facts raised, novel law raised, and accuracy of facts and law. Values of the pairwise kappas ranged from .72 to .83 (higher than the generally accepted .70 level of reliability).[71]

This experiment also utilized a postdeliberation questionnaire focused on deliberation satisfaction, attorney assessment, and witness credibility. The postdeliberation questionnaire contained a nine-question scale assessing a juror's satisfaction with the deliberation process, a four-question scale focused on the performance/likability of counsel, and a six-question scale measuring the credibility of witnesses in the case. Each scale was scored on a seven-point Likert scale. Respectively, higher scores suggested greater satisfaction with the deliberation process and a more favorable opinion of counsel/witnesses.[72]

At the jury level, because of the small sample size (N = 19), this study compares diverse juries and homogeneous juries using both parametric and nonparametric tests. At the juror level, the data are hierarchically organized, with jurors nested within juries. Given this hierarchical data structure, and in line with prior mock jury studies of the same design,[73] random intercept models were estimated in Stata.[74]

HOMOGENEOUS JURIES VS. DIVERSE JURIES

Deliberation Structure

Preliminarily, this experiment explores how the presence of felon-jurors may influence the structure of deliberations by first examining foreperson selection (Diamond and Casper, 1992; Devine et al., 2004) and deliberation style (Ellsworth, 1989). At the start of each deliberation, juries selected a foreperson. Most juries (16) relied on a volunteer foreperson. The remaining 3 juries voted to elect a foreperson. In all homogeneous juries, forepersons volunteered. Of the 3 juries that voted to elect a foreperson, 2 included a single felon-juror and 1 included multiple felon-jurors. Notably, in roughly 20 percent of juries (4), a felon-juror served as the foreperson. In all of those instances, felon-jurors volunteered to serve as the foreperson, suggesting a desire to take an active role in the process.

Deliberation styles also varied across jury types. Nine juries took an initial vote prior to discussing the trial stimulus (a verdict-driven style). The remaining ten juries engaged in a discussion about the case at hand before polling jurors (an evidence-driven style). Homogeneous juries tended to favor an evidence-driven deliberation style (4/5) while the majority of diverse juries tended to employ a verdict-driven deliberation style (7/13). Single-felon juries were evenly split with respect to deliberation style (4/4) and multiple-felon juries slightly favored a verdict-driven deliberation style (4/6).

Deliberation Content

In a second set of analyses, this experiment compares homogeneous juries to diverse juries on measures of deliberation content. At the jury level, those measures include: deliberation duration, novel case facts covered, and novel legal concepts covered.[75] Overall, deliberation durations ranged from 10.3 to 37.4 minutes with an average deliberation time of 24.62 minutes (SD = 8.17). The average length of diverse juries' deliberations (M = 24.9 minutes, SD = 7.9) exceeded the average length of homogeneous juries' deliberations (M = 23.8 minutes, SD = 9.7), but this difference was not statistically significant.[76] Moreover, a test of intergroup mean deliberation durations across juries also yielded no statistically significant differences.[77] These findings suggest that the presence of felon-jurors did little to change the overall length of deliberations.

This experiment also explores the number of novel case facts and novel legal concepts covered by each jury. Across jury types, the number of novel case facts covered ranged from 7 to 10 (M = 8.37, SD = 1.07). Homogeneous juries (N = 5) covered an average of 8.6 case facts (SD = 1.14), while diverse juries (N = 14) covered an average of 8.29 case facts (SD = 1.07). Among diverse juries, multiple-felon juries raised the most case facts, covering an average of 8.67 case facts (SD = 1.21), while single-felon juries covered an average of 8.00 (SD = 0.93). Yet, jury-level analyses reveal no statistically significant differences between juries of any type.[78] These findings suggest that all juries recalled and discussed most relevant case facts and that convicted felons did not detract from that process.

Next, this experiment explores novel legal concepts covered. Of the eight legal concepts/definitions contained in the experiment stimulus, juries raised an average of only 2.5 (SD = 1.30). Among all juries, the number of legal concepts raised ranged from 0 to 5. Diverse juries (M = 2.5, SD = 1.22) and homogeneous juries (M = 2.4, SD = 1.67) raised roughly the same average number of novel legal concepts. Of diverse juries, those including only a single felon (M = 3.12, SD = 1.07) outperformed those including multiple felons (M = 1.67, SD = 1.21). Still, a comparison of means across groups showed no statistically significant difference among juries.[79] These results tend to show that, unlike juries' coverage of case facts, juries performed poorly with respect to their tendency to raise legal concepts during deliberations. Yet, like juries' tendency to cover case facts, juries' tendency to cover legal concepts is seemingly unhindered by the inclusion of felon-jurors.

Juror Perceptions

This experiment also explores jurors' perceptions of deliberations. Like prior mock jury studies, this study relies on postdeliberation questionnaires examining: deliberation satisfaction, attorney competence, attorney likability, and witness credibility (Cowan, Thompson, and Ellsworth, 1984; Marder, 2002). On a measure of deliberation satisfaction—higher scores indicating greater satisfaction with deliberations—homogeneous juries' mean score (M = 48.08, SD = 3.39) was virtually identical to the mean scores of single-felon juries (M = 48.48, SD = 2.46) and multiple-felon juries (M = 47.30, SD = 2.93). Comparisons confirmed no statistically significant differences across juries.[80]

Perceptions of attorney performance, attorney likability, and witness credibility were likewise not impacted by jury type. A closer look at opinions of attorneys and witnesses, separated into defense and prosecution orientations, again demonstrated no statistically significant differences at the jury level. As part of this analysis of witness credibility, participants also rated the importance of the defendant's prior criminal history when deciding guilt or innocence and when assessing credibility. At the jury level, no differences presented, contrary to the claims implicit in the inherent bias rationale for felon-juror exclusion statutes.

FELON-JURORS VS. NON-FELON-JURORS

Deliberation Content

Along with duration, this experiment also explores a measure of individual level juror participation: time spoken as a proportion of deliberation duration. Overall, felon-jurors spoke for longer than their non-felon-juror counterparts. Felon-jurors spoke for an average of 5.4 minutes each (SD = 3.27) while non-felon-jurors spoke for an average of 4.20 minutes each (SD = 2.97). Moreover, as a proportion of total duration time, felon-jurors again spoke for longer than non-felon-jurors. Felon-jurors spoke for an average of 24 percent (SD = 12 percent) of their jury's total deliberation time, while non-felons spoke for an average of 17 percent (SD = 10 percent) of their individual jury's deliberations. This difference in proportion of time spoken, as it relates to each juror's individual deliberations, is statistically significant (p = .007) (table 3), suggesting that felon-jurors contributed more to their jury's deliberations than did non-felon-jurors.

In an analysis of case facts covered at the individual or juror level, felon-jurors raised an average of 3.43 novel case facts (SD = 1.91), while non-felon-jurors raised an average of 1.09 novel case facts (SD = 1.19). A nested comparison revealed a statistically significant difference between number of novel case facts raised by felon-jurors and non-felon-jurors (p = .00) (table 3). This result tends to suggest that felon-jurors may enhance a jury's ability to thoroughly review evidence.

On the other hand, though a juror-level analysis of novel legal concepts showed that felon-jurors raised an average of .71 novel legal concepts (SD = .96) while non-felon-jurors raised an average of .41 novel legal concepts (SD = .71), this difference was not statistically significant (table 3).

Virtually all jurors who raised novel case facts and legal concepts did so accurately. Only two jurors (both non-felon-jurors) inaccurately cited a case fact and only four jurors (two felon-jurors and two non-felon-jurors) raised an inaccurate legal concept (one felon-juror incorrectly stated two legal concepts). These results are likely the product of the relative simplicity of the trial stimulus. The trial stimulus involved a limited number of facts offered into evidence through only four witnesses: two for the defense and two for the prosecution. The applicable law included only four elements and four legal principles/definitions. Still, these results offer some insight into participants' comparative ability to recall points of fact and law.

Juror Perceptions

At the juror level, deliberation satisfaction was not impacted by a felony criminal history. Felon-jurors' average score on a measure of deliberation satisfaction (M = 49.86, SD = 7.36) was slightly higher than that of non-felon-jurors (M = 46.91, SD = 6.59), but that difference was not statistically significant

TABLE 3 Juror-Level Comparisons (HLMS) (Binnall, 2019)

	B	SE
Novel Case Facts Raised	2.34**	(0.33)
Novel Legal Concepts Raised	0.30	(0.19)
Proportional Time	0.07**	(0.03)
Deliberation Satisfaction	2.94	(1.64)
Attorney Credibility/Likability	−0.90	(0.93)
Defense Attorney Credibility/Likability	−0.28	(0.65)
Prosecuting Attorney Credibility/Likability	−0.68	(0.60)
Witness Credibility	0.90	(0.79)
Defense Witness Credibility	0.14	(0.60)
Prosecution Witness Credibility	0.79	(0.65)

**$p < 0.01$

(table 3). Similarly, perceptions of attorney performance, attorney likability, and witness credibility did not differ by juror type. Notably, felon-jurors did not exhibit more favorable attitudes toward defense witnesses than prosecution witnesses. Along that same line, no statistically significant differences between juror types presented on a measure of perceptions of the defendant and his criminal history. This finding contradicts all of the claims underlying the inherent bias rationale (table 3).

WHAT ABOUT THE THREAT?

Findings from the mock jury experiment tend to demonstrate that diversity in the form of a felony criminal history does little to diminish deliberation quality. Accordingly, results also indirectly suggest that the rationales for felon-juror exclusion lack empirical support.

In this mock jury experiment, the structure of deliberations was consistent with prior research. Previous studies reveal that a foreperson is selected early in the deliberation process,[81] and is usually selected via vote, nomination, or volunteer.[82] For all juries in the present study, foreperson selection took place early in the deliberation process, and in all instances it was the first task the jury undertook. In four of the fourteen diverse mock juries, a felon-juror served as the foreperson, and in all four cases, the felon-juror forepersons volunteered for the position. This seems to cut against the categorical presumption that those with a felony criminal history are less likely to approach service thoughtfully. Instead, this result tends to show that convicted felons serve actively and enthusiastically.

The deliberation style of the mock juries also fell in line with prior research.[83] Though studies of deliberation style are far from consistent, most suggest an even split between evidence-driven and verdict-driven approach to deliberations.[84] Overall, roughly half of the juries in the present study engaged in each deliberation style (nine verdict-driven and ten evidence-driven), and of the fourteen diverse juries in the present study, six took an evidence-driven approach to deliberations, while eight took a verdict-driven approach. Given prior research that suggests that the evidence-driven deliberation style yields higher-quality deliberations,[85] this result again tends to show that felon-jurors did not negatively impact how a jury deliberated.

Unlike deliberation structure, deliberation content was somewhat influenced by the presence of felon-jurors. While novel legal concepts raised and accuracy of novel facts and legal concepts raised did not differ by jury or juror type, in line with Sommers's research,[86] time spoken as a percentage of total deliberation time was higher for felon-jurors, as were novel case facts raised. Again, these results suggest that felon-jurors do little to diminish deliberation quality and may improve the process.

As to the duration of deliberations, while felon-jurors did not add to the overall duration time of their respective juries, they were responsible for a greater percentage of their juries' total deliberation time than were non-felons. In all, felon-jurors were responsible for 24 percent of their juries' deliberation time, while non-felon-jurors only accounted for 17 percent of total deliberation time—a statistically significant result ($p = .007$). This result seems to suggest that felon-jurors engaged in the deliberation process to a greater extent than non-felon-jurors. These contributions, while they have the potential to override non-felon contributions and detract from the deliberation process, appear to have been positive, as felon-jurors were also responsible for raising more novel case facts than jurors without a felony criminal history. At the jury level, diverse juries and homogeneous juries did not differ significantly with respect to novel case facts raised. Yet, at the juror level, felon-jurors raised an average of 3.43 novel case facts, while non-felon-jurors raised an average of 1.09 novel case facts. This difference is statistically significant ($p = < .00$).

Taken together, these results suggest that convicted felons took an active, productive role in deliberations. While the rationales for the categorical exclusion of convicted felons from jury service assume that convicted felons are unfit to productively engage in deliberations or will actively sabotage deliberations, this mock jury experiment does not support those presumptions. Additionally, data derived from the experiment do not support research suggesting that increased diversity may lead to less group cohesion and more conflict, sapping the cognitive resources of individual group members and, in turn, diminishing group performance.[87]

Instead, in line with research on diverse juries and deliberation quality,[88] this experiment supports the proposition that felon-jurors can add value to the jury process by engaging in deliberations in a meaningful way. These results also align with psychological research suggesting that diversity improves group decision-making capabilities by increasing the cognitive resources of the collective.[89] Notably, the positive impact of diversity in the experiment—novel case facts covered—seems to be associated with increased performance by felon-jurors, the minority group members. This result offers some evidence, albeit suggestive, that diversity can enhance deliberations by improving the performance of both majority members of the group and minority group members.[90]

Finally, impressions of jury service, counsel, and witnesses were not impacted by the presence of felon-jurors. Though rationales for felon-juror exclusion seemingly assume that the inclusion of felon-jurors will reduce non-felon-jurors' overall satisfaction with jury service and that felon-jurors will disproportionately favor defense counsel and defendants, again, this experiment does not support those presumptions. Rather, no difference in measures of deliberation satisfaction, counsel evaluation, or witness believability presented. Felon-jurors and non-felon-jurors expressed similar levels of satisfaction with deliberations and rated attorneys and witnesses similarly, cutting against the presumption, implicit in the justifications for felon-juror exclusion, that convicted felons would favor the defense as a result of their negative experiences with the criminal justice system.[91]

In sum, results seem to show that felon-jurors may not pose as much of a threat to the jury process as the law presumes. Instead, this experiment suggests that felon-jurors may add to the deliberation process by increasing the cognitive resources of the group, specifically in the area of evidence coverage. Of note, this experiment tends to show that diversity can increase cognitive resources without diminishing group cohesion or producing conflict. Moreover, this experiment suggests that minority group members, like majority group members, may also benefit from group diversity.

CONCLUSION

Since 1980, the number of Americans who bear the felon label has grown exponentially.[92] A direct result of the United States' foray into mass incarceration,[93] the proliferation of felony criminal records means that convicted felons are now part of the political, social, and civic fabric of our nation, often occupying positions of influence.[94] To those positions, convicted felons bring a unique life experience that has the potential to enrich dialogue on criminal justice policy. Still, a vast network of categorical, record-based restrictions ensures that the "convicted perspective" is officially discounted. Felon-juror exclusion extends this phenomenon.

As was the case when African-Americans and women were excluded from jury service, the exclusion of convicted felons from the jury process constrains deliberations. Apart from removing a unique perspective from the deliberation room, felon-juror exclusion statutes seemingly curtail the potential of the collaborative deliberative process. The open exchange of ideas and careful adherence to the law are the cornerstones of effective deliberations. This experiment suggests that felon-jurors perform adequately, if not admirably, in both areas. To banish a population from the jury process based only on speculation and conjecture denigrates the law's professed conceptualization of the jury as a representative, inclusive arbiter of facts. Moreover, to do so denies the reality that we have incarcerated millions of our citizens and are unwilling, or at least woefully unprepared, to accommodate a perspective that we as a nation have cultivated. Though limited and suggestive only,[95] the present study gave rise to additional analyses that explore, at a more granular, contextualized level, convicted felons' influence on the deliberation process. Chapter 5 takes a closer look at how felon-jurors contributed to deliberations and how they interacted with their fellow jurors.

FIVE

Sequestering the Convicted: Part II

Strengths need to be assessed and "targeted" in the same way
that risks and needs traditionally have been.

—SHADD MARUNA AND THOMAS P. LEBEL

IN RECENT YEARS, CRIMINAL JUSTICE POLICIES have taken on a risk-
centric quality.[1] Through actuarial assessments, those convicted of criminal
offenses are quantified as risks to be managed and ultimately subdued.[2] This
"new penology"[3] calls on categorical accounting techniques in an effort to
protect "us" from "them."[4] Tracking the rise of the new penology has been the
exponential expansion of the collateral consequences of a criminal conviction.[5] Limiting, and in some cases eliminating, convicted felons' access to
social, civic, and political institutions, such restrictions are consistently premised on the supposed threat those convicted of a felony pose to the institutions
from which they are banished.[6] Felon-juror exclusion is no exception.

Rather than focusing on the deficits of those with a criminal history, an
alternative framework prioritizes their attributes and qualities.[7] This
strengths-based or positive criminology approach explores how someone who
has experienced the criminal justice system can contribute to society postconviction.[8] Such approaches hold that by identifying and exploiting the
prosocial qualities of those with a criminal history, jurisdictions can concomitantly help formerly convicted individuals successfully reintegrate,
while also enhancing social institutions—like the jury.[9] To date, though
sparse, tests of strengths-based or positive criminology approaches have
yielded promising findings on both fronts.[10]

In the last chapter, results from the first mock jury experiment to include
convicted felons reveal that felon-jurors did nothing to undermine deliberations. Rather, findings demonstrate that on a number of measures, felon-
jurors did not differ from non-felons. On measures where group differences
existed, felon-jurors actually outperformed non-felons, in particular, on
measures of time spoken and fact recall. While informative, and seeming

to contradict claims about the threat convicted felons pose to the jury process, the results reported in chapter 4 tell us little about how convicted felons engaged with their fellow jurors and what, exactly, they contributed to deliberations. Interpreting these results, proponents of felon-juror exclusion could well argue that felon-jurors monopolized the deliberative experience, speaking longer and raising more case facts in the process. This chapter confronts such a challenge by further exploring, at a more granular level, felon-jurors' contributions to their respective mock juries.

FINDING VALUE IN DEVIANTS

Today, almost all criminal justice policy includes some evidence-based component that focuses on estimating the threat posed by those who have violated the law.[11] To evaluate the threat, authorities rely primarily on risk assessment tools.[12] Such tools are "formal, actuarial, and algorithmic methods of predicting the likelihood of future crime or misconduct,"[13] and are almost uniformly based on risk, need, responsivity principles.[14] In this context, risk refers to a client's criminogenic characteristics (e.g., criminal history), need refers to a client's deficits (e.g., homelessness, drug addiction, unemployment), and responsivity refers to tailored interventions targeting those risks and needs.[15] Nearly all risk assessment tools use checklists, asking the taker or the administrator to indicate which items apply to the client. Responses are then tallied, resulting in an overall risk score that slots the client into a risk category based on that score.[16]

The efficacy of risk assessment tools has been the topic of extensive research.[17] Still, that research is mixed. A number of studies have shown significant predictive power for risk assessments,[18] while others suggest that risk assessment tools are no better than clinical attempts to forecast violent or threatening behavior.[19] Another criticism of risk assessment tools suggests that such evaluations may be racially discriminatory or may foster discriminatory practices.[20] Critics suggest that the design and use of risk assessment tools can be inherently prejudicial, as such tools are designed and used by fallible human actors who likely introduce bias into an allegedly objective evaluation.[21] Such a challenge has been prominent in discussions of bail reform initiatives that rely heavily on risk assessment instruments.[22]

Apart from the traditional criticisms of risk assessment, some argue that the underlying theory of risk assessment is flawed. Some contend that because risk assessment tools identify and "treat" risks and needs, they are explicitly deficit-based.[23] Such tools find and address the flaws and necessities of clients, without any reference to their skills, attributes, and qualities. In response, defenders of risk assessments argue that such tools account for the strengths and attributes of clients in relief—as a strength or attribute would negate a reportable risk or need.[24] Still, proponents of a strengths-based approach maintain that the abilities of clients ought to occupy a more prominent position when evaluating risk and threat.[25] Summing up the advantages of the strengths-based approach, Hunter et al. note, "a strengths-based approach allows offenders to recognize that they are of value and can positively contribute to the community and larger society."[26]

In the reentry context, researchers have long recognized the unique skills and attributes of convicted felons, putting those skills and attributes to work to bolster reentry efforts in prosocial ways and yielding layered benefits for communities at large.[27] In recent analyses of strengths-based initiatives, empirical evidence supports what reentry practitioners have long known.

For example, LeBel explored the helper/wounded healer orientation in a study of 228 formerly incarcerated individuals involved in a prison reintegration program.[28] LeBel found that the majority of participants endorsed the characteristics of the helper/wounded healer: "sharing experiences, acting as a role model, mentoring others, and [expressing an] interest in pursuing a career helping others."[29] He also found that a majority of those who counseled new reentrants—those recently released from prison or otherwise less advanced in their reintegration—were more likely to express satisfaction with life and less likely to possess a criminal attitude.[30] Similarly, in a more recent study of system impacted individuals, LeBel, Richie, and Maruna surveyed 258 participants (229 clients and 29 staff members) from six reentry service organizations in New York City and Upstate New York.[31] They found that those who worked as staff members exhibited prosocial attitudes and beliefs, a sense of psychological well-being, and a general satisfaction with life.[32]

Taken together, this empirical research demonstrates that "becoming more involved in helping others appears to have a positive impact on the psychological well-being of formerly incarcerated persons and possibly acts as a sort of buffer against criminality as well."[33] Notably, these results have been replicated in the context of women convicted of a felony and individuals convicted of a felony sexual offense.[34]

Experiential evidence also supports the idea that those with felony criminal histories can draw on those experiences in ways that benefit society as a whole. Two of the oldest and most successful reentry initiatives that employ formerly incarcerated individuals are Delancey Street Foundation in San Francisco and Homeboy Industries in Los Angeles.[35] Highly successful at fostering successful reintegration,[36] both initiatives prioritize the strengths of their members, rather than focusing on their risks and needs. "First and foremost, we believe people can change. When we make a mistake we need to admit it and then not run from it, but stay and work to fix the mistake. And though no one can undo the past, we can balance the scales by doing good deeds and earning back our own self-respect, decency, and a legitimate place in mainstream society.... We teach people to find and develop their strengths rather than only focusing on their problems."[37]

In sum, data reveal that those with a felony criminal history have attributes and qualities that can enrich institutions and processes. Still, in the context of jury service, jurisdictions that exclude felons ostensibly overlook this possibility. By reanalyzing deliberation transcripts of diverse juries (those that include felon-jurors and non-felon-jurors), this chapter explores the potential benefits of including convicted felons in the deliberative process.

REANALYZING FELON-JURORS' CONTRIBUTIONS

In chapter 4, deliberation transcripts were analyzed using theoretically derived measures of deliberation quality. While those measures offered a glimpse into felon-jurors' contributions to deliberations, they failed to provide a complete picture of those contributions. Like the analyses presented in chapter 4, this new analysis employs theoretically derived measures.[38]

Specifically, the present analysis relies on Devine et al.'s measures of deliberation quality, which include: (1) instruction comprehension, (2) evidence review, (3) factual focus, (4) systematic participation, and (5) informational influence.[39] Those measures—again, process-oriented criteria derived from jury instructions—allow for objective assessment, while better capturing the context of felon-jurors' interactions and contributions.[40]

Several themes emerged from an analysis of diverse jury deliberations.[41] First, despite the stigma of a criminal history, all felon-jurors divulged the fact of a prior conviction and all partook thoughtfully in the deliberation process, often working to ensure the participation of their fellow jurors. Second, felon-jurors engaged with non-felon-jurors cooperatively to correct factual inaccuracies. When doing so, felon-jurors drew on their criminal pasts objectively to impartially interpret evidence. Finally, felon-jurors demonstrated the ability to aptly decipher jury instructions and to evenhandedly apply nuanced legal concepts to the facts of the case at hand. Taken together, these findings suggest that felon-jurors do not degrade deliberations and may, alternatively, add value to the deliberative process.

Revealing a Criminal Past and Thoughtfully Deliberating

Though systematic participation is a necessary element of quality deliberations,[42] as noted in chapter 4, diversity can prompt discomfort and stress.[43] For minority members of diverse groups, such stress can stem from a fear of confirming a negative stereotype and can lead to withdrawal from the stress-causing situation.[44] In the case of felon-jurors, the impacts of incarceration may exacerbate this effect. Prior research demonstrates that many inmates rely on reclusion and isolation as a means of survival in prison.[45] For some, those habits follow them into the free world, making readjustment and reintegration more difficult.[46]

Despite these factors making their participation unlikely, all felon-jurors played a meaningful role in deliberations. As previously noted, of the fourteen diverse juries in the study, felon-jurors served as forepersons on four. In all instances, felon-jurors volunteered for the position and dutifully approached their responsibilities, engaging fellow jurors and ensuring a well-considered verdict:[47] "So what do you guys think? Is there anything else that you wanna go over? We covered the timeline, the ID, and the investigation. Are there angles we are not seeing? It's my job as foreman to make sure we uncover all of it, so please let's make sure before we vote. We don't want to be putting away an innocent man and we don't want a guilty man walking free" (juror 1, jury 2, FJ).[48]

Moreover, and again seemingly despite their assumed discomfort, all felon-jurors revealed their criminal pasts. For example, felon-juror 5, on jury 16, discussed his prior incarceration and how, given that experience, he expected to empathize with the defendant, but acknowledged that the defendant's two prior felony convictions made that a difficult task. "I've never been in that position [having two prior felonies], but I have been incarcerated before, so I thought it would be easy to make a decision coming from behind the wall, and now I'm like, how come this is so hard, now I actually see what's going on and they make a good case against him—and I don't know, it's just hard now" (juror 5, jury 16, FJ).

Some felon-jurors went further, even facilitating the full participation of the group. One felon-juror invited fellow jurors to weigh in on an evidentiary matter before suggesting that the defendant had possibly testified untruthfully, demonstrating an active, unbiased role approach to deliberations.

> JUROR 4, JURY 12, FJ: What do you guys think about them bringing up him being in that bad neighborhood? What do you think they were insinuating?
>
> JUROR 3, JURY 12, FJ: That even the association with him, that he's a bad guy. I mean, so he's hanging out in a bad part of town, so therefore he is a bad guy, that's the association part. We hear that all the time [as convicted felons].
>
> JUROR 4, JURY 12, FJ: She [the prosecution] also asked him, "You didn't fear your car would get vandalized?" That is when he pooped on himself [testified that he had tossed his identification into his car after talking to the tow truck driver]. He could have said "yeah" to maybe have us jurors think that maybe someone could have broke into his car and took his license and done the robbery, but he didn't.

Along these lines, some felon-jurors painstakingly wrestled with convicting and, in certain instances, made clear their fidelity to their duties as jurors. One felon-juror revealed his status as a convicted felon early in deliberations, before offering his opinion about the weight of a juror's tasks and the defendant's culpability:

> JUROR 4, JURY 12, FJ: Well, when it comes down to it, I do believe he is guilty. We [convicted felons] don't have no sympathy for someone. I think he is guilty. You know, there are pros for it [a guilty verdict] and then there's cons for it [a guilty verdict]. This case is really jacked up. I feel sorry for whoever has to do this [decide the case]. The prosecutors have more evidence than the defense, and I feel like if the defense had a little more evidence, such as more witnesses besides the tow truck driver, then maybe it could have swayed me to not guilty, but I stand firm with guilty. Due to the evidence.

While most studies demonstrate that initial positions are significant predictors of final verdict preference, research also makes clear that group interactions can mediate or exacerbate those positions.[49] In an illustrative example of this power of information influence, and notably, of the inaccuracy of the inherent bias rationale, one felon-juror changed verdict positions, initially voting to convict and ultimately voting to acquit:

> JUROR 5, JURY 16, FJ: It was just not enough evidence to actually say he was guilty but I just—he could have done it, but it wasn't enough evidence. You know it was about whether he is guilty or not guilty, we are trying to figure it out so while we are going through this side of guilty and then possibly not guilty, that's the part of the deliberations though right? Because right now I'm not sure he's guilty.
>
> JUROR 3, JURY 16, NFJ: Yeah, but also if they don't show the evidence even if you do feel in your heart of hearts, if they don't prove it beyond a reasonable doubt . . .
>
> JUROR 5, JURY 16, FJ: Um, I think I want to change mine to not guilty because it's not, it wasn't enough.

Taken together, evidence from the present study suggests that felon-jurors, despite likely anxieties, do not refrain from engaging in deliberations. Moreover, felon-jurors do not approach deliberations from a fixed, prodefendant position. Instead, data reveal a far more thorough and thoughtful approach to deliberations. These findings tend to contradict the stated rationales for felon-juror exclusion and suggest that the inclusion of felon-jurors does little to diminish deliberation quality.

Cooperating with "Others" and Impartially Interpreting Evidence

One of the jury's primary tasks is to recall, review, and synthesize evidence.[50] Juries generally perform well in this area of deliberations.[51] Studies show that juries spend the majority of deliberations discussing evidence,[52] and that they tend to remember case facts in detail and with accuracy.[53] Nonjury research focusing on collective decision-making comports with these findings, suggesting that deliberating groups are able to accurately recall even complex evidence.[54]

In the present study, both felon-jurors and non-felon-jurors accurately recalled case facts. As in prior research, jurors worked collaboratively to ensure factual precision, correcting one another when a fellow juror raised inaccurate evidence. Consider the following exchanges relating to the discovery of the defendant's identification at the bank:

JUROR 1, JURY 6, FJ: Did he drop it at the bank? She [the teller] said it was in her drawer prior to the robbery, right?

JUROR 2, JURY 6, NFJ: It was already in that drawer, yes.

JUROR 3, JURY 6, NFJ: I didn't catch that.

JUROR 1, JURY 6, FJ: I didn't catch that either. Didn't she testify that she didn't see it when she checked her drawer?

JUROR 2, JURY 6, NFJ: No, it was in the drawer because when the detective came, she [the detective] asked them to look in the drawer, and they looked, and that's when she [the teller] turns it over and is like, that's the guy that robbed the bank!

Conversely, in a similar exchange, a felon-juror clarified evidence for a non-felon-juror:

JUROR 2, JURY 4, NFJ: Did the bank manager also ID him or no? She didn't see him?

JUROR 6, JURY 4, FJ: No. She didn't.

JUROR 2, JURY 4, NFJ: So, there's the only one eyewitness?

JUROR 6, JURY 4, FJ: Yes, and she didn't even mention the ID. She mentioned that she found 740 dollars in the drawer and that was it. She said no more.

JUROR 2, JURY 4, NFJ: So, the only evidence is the ID and one eyewitness?

JUROR 6, JURY 4, FJ: Yeah, that is correct.

Another central task of a jury is to assess the credibility of witnesses and the veracity of evidence.[55] A key piece of evidence in the stimulus case was the eyewitness identification of the defendant made by the bank teller. During deliberations, many participants voiced concerns about the accuracy of the identification. Though justifications for exclusion suggest that felon-jurors will exhibit blanket biases against inculpatory evidence,[56] felon-jurors' views of the bank teller's identification tended to demonstrate a detailed recall of evidence and grounded skepticism:

JUROR 6, JURY 1, FJ: The other thing was that she [the bank teller] said that what she noticed most about him when he came into the bank was he had these big huge glassy eyes. And then if you look at the ID in the picture he was like, he was all squinty. You couldn't see anything. And that's what she said when she looked at the ID. She said that she saw the big eyes on the ID. Well, there [were not] big eyes on the ID.

Juror 5 on jury 18, a felon-juror, echoed this sentiment, "You couldn't see the eyes ... what she said, as soon as she saw the picture, and the eyes, and I'm trying to figure out where she's getting this eye thing from. Because his eyes are like, closed." Contrary to the inherent bias rationale, at least one other felon-juror approached the identification issue from a decidedly impartial perspective suggesting that in "the ID his eyes were—I mean, when I smile my eyes disappear, I have very small eyes, so that could explain it" (juror 4, jury 15, FJ).

Along with recalling and assessing the veracity of evidence, jurors must also synthesize evidence. The "story model"[57] holds that jurors "make sense of the evidence at trial by imposing a chronological narrative organization on it."[58] As Devine explains, the story model assumes "that jurors rely heavily on their existing knowledge and beliefs in creating their stories, using them to fill in gaps in the evidence, resolve contradictions, and determine plausibility."[59] Though felon-juror exclusion statutes rest on the premise that the existing knowledge and beliefs of convicted felons necessarily skew in favor of criminal defendants, thus threatening the jury process, data from the present study again calls that assumption into question.

Instead, felon-jurors seemingly drew on their experience to impartially evaluate evidence, using all aspects of their pasts constructively. For example, in the case at issue, the bank teller indicated that the defendant wore his hair in cornrows, while the tow-truck driver who later encountered the defendant indicated that she did not notice his hair. Discussing these points of fact, felon-jurors drew on their experiences—noncriminal and criminal—to explain apparent discrepancies:

> JUROR 4, JURY 15, FJ: My daughter is biracial and I used to cornrow her hair. You cannot cornrow his hair, it's too short. I mean you try to cornrow your hair, it starts sticking out ... and I don't see very many white boys with their hair braided. You can't do that with straight white hair. You just can't.

Another juror expressed concern about the tow truck driver's lack of awareness, "I mean you have to look, you have to look at him, so what do you mean you didn't notice a white dude with cornrows?" (juror 5, jury 16, FJ). Yet, interestingly, on Jury 17, when a non-felon-juror, broached the topic of the defendant's hair and his current appearance, a felon-juror offered a possible explanation as to why the defendant no longer looked like he had at the time of the crime, intimating that the defendant could have committed the charged offense.

JUROR 2, JURY 17, FJ: If your hair is in braids, and I did a crime, afterwards—I'm not going to keep it in braids. It might be on that camera ... so I'm not going to have the same look on the day of a bank robbery as I do if I ever get caught. I'm going to keep my hair cut short. So, he could have changed up his appearance.

An additional key issue in the trial stimulus was the defendant's alibi. The defendant, a formerly convicted felon, claims to have had car trouble in a town twenty-five minutes away from the bank that he allegedly robbed. He also claims to have left his identification in the car, walked to a nearby motel, checked in, and spent the night with friends. As a result of the car trouble, the defendant, a parolee, missed an appointment with his parole officer.

The timeline was a crucial portion of the trial stimulus. In all deliberations, felon-jurors and non-felon-jurors worked together to establish how the events transpired, again correcting one another when appropriate. When a few non-felon-jurors on jury 14 suggested that the defendant was untruthful, claiming that a guest needs identification to stay at a motel, one felon-juror offered an alternate interpretation based on experience:

JUROR 1, JURY 14, FJ: And we had to come to a conclusion based on what was presented to us ... another thing happened—he's in a seedy part of town. Normally when you're in that situation, those kind of motels don't really request a lot of identification.

JUROR 5, JURY 14, NFJ: Oh, really? I've always had to give my credit card.

JUROR 1, JURY 14, FJ: Yeah, that's for the high end [hotels].

The defendant also testified that when arrested, he stated to the arresting officer, "now I am going back to prison anyway." While several non-felon-jurors viewed this statement as a tacit admission of guilt, some felon-jurors again called on their experiences—criminal experiences—to help clarify the defendant's possible motivation for such a declaration:

JUROR 2, JURY 17, FJ: The reason why he said that was because he missed his one o'clock appointment ... plus he was in contact with police because they brought him in for a lineup. When you're in contact with police and you're still on parole or probation, you're done ... so that's why he said, "I guess I'm going back to prison."

Conversely, other felon-jurors questioned the plausibility of this reasoning for the utterance, drawing on prior experience as parolees and explaining:

JUROR I, JURY 17, FJ: In that situation, the number one thing is to contact my P.O. and say, "Look I've got a situation here, I'm not going to make it in twenty minutes to where this one o'clock appointment is, and I got verification that the tow truck person is—I got a receipt coming from the AAA auto club to verify that it was broke down at 12:40." Why didn't he do that? Doesn't make sense.

Overall, felon-jurors were able to recall case facts accurately, correcting non-felon-jurors when incorrect facts were raised and accepting correction when they mistakenly described evidence. Felon-jurors also took an active role in the review and synthesis of evidence, drawing on criminal and non-criminal experiences when helping to develop factual narratives. Importantly, felon-jurors' engagement with case facts did not demonstrate a lack of character or the presence of bias. Rather, felon-jurors thoughtfully participated in the analysis of evidence, in all instances interpreting factual scenarios impartially. To that point, one felon-juror observed, "Well, this is kind of like a perfect-case scenario, where it could go either way, and so they like to see how people deliberate, because there are arguments for both sides" (juror 2, jury 13, FJ). Importantly, these types of observations cut against suppositions about the impact of a criminal record on a convicted felon's capability to evenhandedly assess evidence.

Deciphering Jury Instructions and Evenhandedly Applying the Law

Prior research suggests that jurors often have difficulty comprehending jury instructions.[60] Jurors' objective comprehension of jury instructions stands at roughly 50 to 70 percent in noncapital cases,[61] and at an even lower percentage in cases involving the death penalty.[62]

One line of research in the area of jury instructions explores jurors' understanding of "beyond a reasonable doubt."[63] Commentators suggest that the requisite threshold for "beyond a reasonable doubt" requires roughly a 90 percent certainty of guilt,[64] but studies demonstrate that jurors often have trouble conceptualizing the standard and convict at a much lower level of certainty.[65] The most common definition of "beyond a reasonable doubt" holds that "proof beyond a reasonable doubt is proof that leaves a juror 'firmly convinced' of the defendant's guilt."[66] Of all articulations of the reasonable doubt standard, the "firmly convinced" description has yielded the highest required certainty of guilt among jurors—81 percent.[67]

In the present research, jurors were tasked with applying the Ninth Circuit Model Jury Instructions for bank robbery. Those instructions reference a definition of beyond a reasonable doubt that includes the "firmly convinced" language:

> Proof beyond a reasonable doubt is proof that leaves you firmly convinced the defendant is guilty. It is not required that the government prove guilt beyond all possible doubt. A reasonable doubt is a doubt based upon reason and common sense and is not based purely on speculation. It may arise from a careful and impartial consideration of all the evidence, or from lack of evidence.

At the outset of deliberations, though felon-jurors consistently referenced "reasonable doubt," they often did so in passing, exhibiting a somewhat superficial understanding of the concept. For instance, a felon-juror who was also a jury foreman began deliberations this way:

> JUROR 1, JURY 14, FJ: Well, I think we go over the evidence first and see if we have a reasonable doubt as far as did they prove their case to a reasonable doubt, to that standard? My gut is that the prosecution didn't prove the case to a reasonable doubt, to that standard. By virtue of what was read to us in jury instructions.

As deliberations progressed, felon-jurors seemed to focus on the definitional elements of reasonable doubt as a way to clarify their comprehension of the standard. Working to interpret their instructions, a number of felon-jurors correctly suggested that reasonable doubt might exist when evidence, or a lack of evidence, cannot be clearly reconciled. "We should be able to treat fairly everyone. That's where I'm at. And like I said, the evidence just doesn't do that for me. I'm going with that, they did not meet the standard. There's way too many questions over pieces of evidence" (juror 1, jury 10, FJ). Felon-jurors also noted repeatedly that "not guilty" does not equate to innocence, emphasizing that the prosecution bears the burden of proof. "I don't know if he's innocent or not, but there's not enough evidence to say guilty" (juror 6, jury 4, FJ). Two other felon-jurors echoed this sentiment:

> JUROR 2, JURY 10, FJ: I mean with, so if you go by the letter of the law about . . . reasonable doubt or whatever, there's too many holes. I'm not saying he didn't do it, that he is innocent, but I'm just saying that we have nothing that says he did it beyond a reasonable doubt.

JUROR 5, JURY 3, FJ: I still have some questions that the prosecution didn't fulfill. You know, I'm not 100 percent sure he's not guilty, but I'm not going to go out on a limb and say he's guilty because I don't feel the prosecution has given us enough.

Felon-jurors also paid particular attention to the definitional admonishment regarding speculation, demonstrating an appropriate level of cynicism about the weight of past convictions. Describing himself as a law-abiding citizen, one felon-juror explained, "I think about watching a newscast and you see how somebody gets arrested for a crime, regardless of what crime it is, and as law-abiding citizens, we immediately think that they must be guilty because they was arrested" (juror 1, jury 14, FJ). Equally concerned with stereotyping convicted felons, another felon-juror ostensibly blamed the defendant's prior record for the perceived lack of a thorough investigation. "You find his ID and of course you run the ID and you find he is an ex-felon, then it's like, no more investigation. . . . They figured 'okay,' they figure if you put this in front of a jury then that's that by itself, so why work?" (juror 1, jury 10, FJ).

Conversely, a number of felon-jurors placed significant weight on the defendant's criminal past, suggesting that a prior conviction is an indicator of guilt. In one instance, a non-felon-juror seemed to take exception to a felon-juror's insistence that a criminal record suggested culpability.

JUROR 2, JURY 6, NFJ: We do know in 2003 he was convicted of a theft-related crime. It ain't a bank robbery but it has something to do with stealing, so—does that weigh into your factoring at all?

JUROR 1, JURY 6, FJ: Yeah, as far as that—that lets me know that he's not—it's not like he wouldn't do this kind of crime, you know, it doesn't keep him from doing something like this, you know. But as far as evidence, that's different, because it's going off that record, yeah, why not? You have a felony. A theft. This is a theft.

JUROR 3, JURY 6, NFJ: I think that's like profiling though in that it's—I mean, you're right, it doesn't make him guilty.

JUROR 2, JURY 6, NFJ: You know if you got a history of violence, you've been arrested for murder—that's going to weigh against you a little bit.

JUROR 1, JURY 6, FJ: Maybe it shouldn't, but it's gonna.

JUROR 3, JURY 6, NFJ: Yeah. Let's say you've hit women at home, and then you get married to another woman, then something happens at the house and the cops come. The first thing they're going to do is pull up that record and be all like, "Look, you are a wife beater. You gotta come with us."

JUROR 1, JURY 6, FJ: Exactly. Which is fair. You know.

Several other felon-jurors also seemed to suggest that the defendant's criminal history indicated a propensity for criminal activity. For example, one felon juror stated, "He already has a criminal mind. He has priors for theft. God knows what other priors he has that weren't mentioned" (juror 4, jury 12, FJ). Likewise, consider the following exchange, illustrating competing interpretations of the defendant's statement:

> JUROR 1, JURY 1, NFJ: So he's looking at doing time anyway, so he's giving up. Is that what he is saying?
>
> JUROR 3, JURY 1, FJ: Yeah maybe.
>
> JUROR 6, JURY 1, FJ: Or it goes to the fact that a person that's been to prison before has an automatic guilty conscience and thinks they're going to go back to prison.

Apart from jury instructions, other legal concepts arose during the course of deliberations. In such instances, felon-jurors demonstrated a somewhat sophisticated understanding of the law. For example, the testimony of the bank manager, who was allegedly unavailable, was read into evidence by the prosecution. One felon-juror took issue with that testimony, suggesting a violation of the defendant's due process right to cross-examine the witness:

> JUROR 1, JURY 10, FJ: The fact that she [the bank manager] got her statement in without having to be cross-examined . . . I didn't like that. I mean if you are able to put a statement in, and not be cross-examined, that's unfair to me, that's unfair to the defense, because OK you can't cross-examine a statement. . . . There's always two sides to it. I—I, no, I didn't like that.

Another felon-juror expressed concern that the defendant's criminal past was introduced into evidence prior to the defendant testifying:

> JUROR 6, JURY 1, FJ: Yeah, but see, that [discussion of defendant's criminal history] should have never even come in until after he testified, by law. Because prior convictions could be used against you until you actually testify.

Additionally, like the contributions felon-jurors made regarding evidence synthesis, on at least one occasion, a felon-juror helped explain the term *stipulation* to a non-felon-juror:

> JUROR 1, JURY 2, FJ: No, no, no. In the—what do you call that? They did the stipulations, stipulations exchanged.

JUROR 3, JURY 2, NFJ: Oh, the stipulations? What are stipulations?

JUROR 1, JURY 2, FJ: It's considered evidence accepted as proven.

In line with prior research of non-felon-jurors, felon-jurors seemed to have trouble articulating the "beyond a reasonable doubt" standard. Nonetheless, and perhaps more importantly, felon-jurors worked to clarify the standard, identifying and highlighting definitional elements. In this way, felon-jurors displayed a conscientiousness that belies the character rationale for exclusion. With respect to other legal concepts, felon-jurors exhibited a rather nuanced understanding of the law, adding value to deliberations. They also varied in their consideration of the defendant's prior criminal convictions. Some felon-jurors viewed the defendant's criminal history as irrelevant, while others ostensibly viewed the defendant's criminal history as the sole proxy for guilt. Though troubling, such an interpretation of a criminal background cuts against the assumption of bias made by felon-juror exclusion statutes.

CONCLUSION

Findings of this second analysis of deliberation transcripts tend to reinforce earlier results (chapter 4), suggesting that the threat convicted felons pose to the jury is *de minimis*. Perhaps more importantly, findings also shed light on the potential benefits of including convicted felons in the adjudicative process.

By any account, felon-jurors performed adequately, if not admirably, during deliberations. Though the mock trial was undoubtedly a stress-inducing exercise, all felon-jurors participated, typically recalling evidence completely and accurately. Though felon-jurors had trouble deciphering "reasonable doubt," so too did non-felons. More importantly, felon-jurors attempted to clarify the standard, examining the definition and working diligently to adhere to instructions. With respect to other legal concepts, felon-jurors demonstrated a rather nuanced understanding of the law.

Of their contributions to mock jury deliberations, perhaps the most important were their cooperative encounters. In several instances, felon-jurors helped non-felon-jurors to weave together theories of the case, routinely drawing on personal experiences that related to their criminal history. On other occasions, felon-jurors clarified legal concepts, encouraged non-felon-jurors to share their thoughts on a topic, and demonstrated receptiveness to new or different information. In no deliberation did felon-jurors and non-felon-jurors experience unproductive conflict. To the contrary, all interactions were cordial and constructive.

Seemingly undermining both the character and inherent bias rationales for felon-juror exclusion statutes, the present findings suggest that felon-jurors pose little threat to the jury process. But, notably, the present findings also suggest more. The present study reinforces the foundation of the strengths-based framework—that those with felony convictions have skills and attributes that can enhance social, civic, and political institutions. Data derived from this mock jury experiment tends to demonstrate that felon-jurors pose no unique threat to the jury, and are in fact commodities that can enhance the adjudicative process. Accordingly, jurisdictions that exclude felon-jurors may do so at the expense of their jury system and, in particular, of higher-quality deliberations.

Building on these findings, the following two chapters explore additional benefits of felon-juror inclusion by drawing on data collected in Maine, as noted, the only state that does not restrict convicted felons' opportunities to serve. While again highlighting the flaws inherent in the justifications for felon-juror exclusion, those data also reveal that inclusion can prompt criminal desistance mechanisms among convicted felons (chapter 6) and can reinforce desistance efforts by delabeling convicted felons and mitigating the interpersonal stigma of felony criminal conviction (chapter 7).

SIX

Criminal-Desistance Summoned

> If the jury has a great influence on the outcome of a trial, it has
> an even greater influence on the fate of society itself.
>
> —ALEXIS DE TOCQUEVILLE

IN HIS STUDY OF AMERICAN DEMOCRACY, French political scientist and historian Alexis de Toqueville recognized that the jury is more than merely a fact-finding tribunal, noting: "To regard the jury simply as a judicial institution would be taking a very narrow view of the matter."[1] Instead, Toqueville conceived of the jury as a school for educating citizens on the importance of participating in democratic processes.[2] Accordingly, Tocqueville opined that the jury "vests each citizen with a kind of magistracy" and "teaches everyone that they have duties towards society and a role in its government."[3] Nearly two centuries later, courts and commentators still laud the educative effects of jury service.[4]

Though no prior research explores how actual felon-jurors experience the jury process, studies of non-felon-jurors suggest that serving as a juror can prompt positive attitudinal changes.[5] In particular, jury service has been shown to foster an enhanced sense of self-worth, in part by educating citizens about the "practical and conceptual difficulties associated with the administration of justice."[6] As one notable study found, "For those who serve as trial jurors, jury service is more than just a glimpse into the process. . . . [j]urors appear to develop knowledge and understanding that comes from working as part of the judicial system."[7] Importantly, activities that build self-concept and provide prosocial roles tend to promote criminal desistance among those with a felony criminal history.[8] For example, research tends to show that taking part in the electoral process—following political candidates and ultimately voting—triggers desistance mechanisms.[9]

Because Maine is the only jurisdiction to place no restrictions on a convicted felon's opportunity to serve as a juror, the state is the perfect laboratory in which to study the impacts of felon-juror *inclusion*. Along those lines, this chapter and the next draw on data derived from a field study conducted in Maine that included interviews with prospective and former felon-jurors, as well as interviews with defense attorneys, prosecutors, and trial court judges charged with screening potential jurors with a felony criminal history. Data from these interviews reveal that felon-jurors place significant weight on how others in the community view them and that, like voting, jury service can be transformative in important ways, seemingly initiating desistance processes that prompt prosocial identity shifts among those convicted of a felony criminal offense.

CRIMINAL-DESISTANCE MECHANISMS

What does it mean to desist from criminal activity? Does a prolonged period of law-abiding behavior amount to criminal desistance?[10] If not, can someone convicted of a felony ever truly achieve criminal desistance? For scholars and practitioners, these basic inquiries are often a source of tension and have given rise to multiple, sometimes competing conceptualizations of criminal desistance.[11]

Drawing on sociologist Edwin Lemert's theory of deviance,[12] scholars propose that criminal desistance is not a termination event, but is instead a process that divides into three phases: primary desistance, secondary desistance,[13] and tertiary desistance.[14] Under this framework, primary desistance refers to a "lull or crime-free gap in the course of a criminal career,"[15] secondary desistance is the cessation of criminal activity coupled with a prosocial change in self-concept,[16] and tertiary desistance is the phase of the desistance process that accounts for community integration and social capital (chapter 7).[17]

Extrinsic Forces

The key distinction between primary and secondary desistance are "identifiable and measurable changes at the level of personal identity or the 'me' of the individual."[18] Still, the genesis of such change has been the topic of some debate.[19] Structure-centric models of criminal desistance suggest that life-course "turning points,"[20] such as marriage and employment,[21] serve as "triggering events"[22] that prompt identity shifts by thrusting one into conventional adult roles.[23] Such conventional roles shape identity in two ways: (1) as a model promoting prosocial behaviors, and (2) as a boundary inhibiting antisocial behaviors.[24] For example, when a convicted felon fills a prosocial role, he or she is informally provided a "skeleton script" for criminal desistance,[25] and is, at the same time, informally encumbered by strictures that constrain attitudes and behaviors that may prompt criminality.[26] Thus, in these ways, conventional role commitment can facilitate identity transformation,[27] providing a template for individualized change,[28] while "knifing off" criminogenic situations and influences.[29]

Intrinsic Motivations

Still, some scholars question structure-centric views of identity change and criminal desistance, arguing that such perspectives undervalue the role of agency, conceiving of human beings as passive, malleable entities shaped by the world around them and desistance as a somewhat random occurrence.[30] These critics contend that individuals are active participants in their own reform, contemplating their future and often devising a plan to achieve their goals.[31] Taking this view, turning points and conventional roles are merely "structural supports" or "hooks for change,"[32] which are effectual only when one has done the "upfront work" of personal transformation.[33]

Emphasizing the former offender's part in the desistance process, a number of scholars note the importance of a desistance "narrative."[34] For example, psychologist and criminologist Shadd Maruna—a noted criminal-desistance scholar—has conducted seminal research tending to show that those with criminal histories alter their self-images through the use of "redemption scripts."[35] These scripts give individuals "a believable story of why they are going straight to convince *themselves* that this is a real change."[36] Engaging narratives to reconceptualize their criminal pasts, convicted felons, for instance, are able to account for prior criminality while emphasizing a new, reformed identity.[37] Similarly, other desistance scholars suggest that a shift in self-image requires one to actively "cast-off" a criminal identity and embrace a new, law-abiding persona.[38] In both instances, the "agentic moves" of the individual are crucial to the construction of the narrative and the formation of a new self-concept.[39]

Though the structure/agency debate colors criminal-desistance research, most scholars agree that desistance involves not merely external forces or intrinsic motivations.[40] Rather, the criminal-desistance process is reflexive, combining environmental and individual elements of varying intensities at various times.[41] Notably, research analyzing the influence of voting on the self-concepts of convicted felons supports this hybrid conception of secondary criminal desistance.

Focusing exclusively on felon-voter disenfranchisement, two prior studies explore the potential link between civic participation and criminal desistance.[42] In the first, researchers interviewed thirty-three prisoners, parolees, and probationers in Minnesota.[43] In line with earlier studies,[44] they found that convicted felons "link successful adult role transition to desistance from crime,"[45] and that their civic role commitments contribute to the development and maintenance of a law-abiding identity.[46] Noting that their results were suggestive only, the researchers surmised that "civic reintegration and establishing an identity as a law-abiding citizen are central to the process of desistance from crime."[47] Drawing on the same data, a separate set of researchers found that former offenders "think of themselves as citizens" and desire to fulfill civic roles.[48] Also emphasizing role commitments, they explain, "to the extent that felons begin to vote and participate as citizens in their communities, there is some evidence that they will bring their behavior in line with the citizen role, avoiding further contact with the criminal justice system."[49]

In 2012, researchers conducted the second study exploring the possible effects of record-based voting restrictions on criminal desistance and reintegration.[50] Employing semistructured interviews with fifty-four disenfranchised convicted felons, they found that 39 percent of participants viewed felon-voter disenfranchisement statutes as "limiting, psychologically harmful, and stigmatizing," perceiving them to have an indirect impact on their ability to successfully reintegrate.[51] Their data suggest that disenfranchisement negatively impacts the criminal-desistance process by tying former offenders to their criminal pasts, making the reconceptualization or abandonment of a criminal identity nearly impossible.[52] Highlighting the importance of a former offender's ability to construct a plausible desistance narrative, researchers warn that "scholars should remain alert to the manner in which long-term forms of invisible punishments impact ex-offenders' ability to sustain the work of developing 'a coherent pro-social identity for themselves.'"[53]

Taken together, prior studies exploring the possible links between civic participation (in the form of voting) and criminal desistance demonstrate that casting a ballot can facilitate criminal desistance. With respect to external forces, enfranchisement offers convicted felons a guide, a prosocial role (the ideal voter) to fill that promotes successful reintegration and criminal desistance. In terms of intrinsic motivations, suffrage appears to alter the self-concept of those who live with a felony criminal conviction. Notably, no prior study explores jury service as a means of prompting such changes among former offenders.

FELON-JURORS IN MAINE

In 1652, the Massachusetts Bay Colony annexed what is now the state of Maine. From 1652 until the passage of the 1802–3 Acts and Resolves of Massachusetts ("Acts and Resolves"), English common law governed juror eligibility in that region. Under English common law, only *liberos et legales homines* (free and lawful men) were eligible to take part in the jury process.[54] That exclusion continued with the Acts and Resolves (Massachusetts, 1802–3). Chapter 92 of the Acts and Resolves states, "if any person, whose name shall be put into either (jury selection) box, shall be convicted of any Scandalous crime, or be guilty of any gross immorality, his name shall be withdrawn from the Box, by the Selectmen of his town."[55] Thus, early in its history, Maine prohibited convicted felons from serving on juries.

In 1820, as part of the Missouri Compromise, Maine achieved statehood and continued to track Massachusetts's policy of mandatorily excluding convicted felons from jury service.[56] From 1821 to 1981, the mandatory language of Maine's felon-juror exclusion policy went virtually unchanged, stating that jury commissioners "shall" disqualify prospective jurors "convicted of a scandalous crime" or a "gross immorality."[57]

Maine's policy regarding felonious jurors underwent its first substantive revision in 1971, when it tied a convicted felon's right to sit on a jury to the right to vote.[58] The provision read that "a prospective juror is disqualified to serve on a jury if he . . . has lost the right to vote."[59] This language, however, did not change convicted felons' status, as Maine has never curtailed their right to vote.[60] In 1981, Maine repealed Section 1254's mandatory exclusion of prospective jurors "convicted of any scandalous crime or gross immorality,"[61] and removed the provision linking juror eligibility to voting rights.[62] The present statute governing juror eligibility in Maine makes no mention of convicted felons. In effect, Maine has allowed convicted felons to serve as jurors since 1981 and is now the only jurisdiction that places no restriction on their eligibility.

From 2012 to 2016, I conducted a field study in Maine. That study involved a series of in-depth, semistructured interviews with former and prospective felon-jurors and courtroom personnel (defense attorneys, prosecutors, and trial court judges) involved in the jury selection process (chapter 7). Felon-jurors were recruited using in-person solicitation and written advertisements at probation offices throughout the state,[63] while courtroom personnel were recruited using a combination of email and telephone solicitation. Ultimately, the study included convicted felons who had served as jurors (N = 7), convicted felons who were summonsed for jury duty but were not selected (N = 6), and convicted felons who were eligible for jury service but had not, at the time of the study, been summoned for jury duty (N = 19).[64] The study also included courtroom personnel (defense attorneys [N = 10], prosecutors [N = 8], and members of Maine's judiciary [N = 9]).[65]

For all participants, interviews were conducted either in-person or via telephone and were analyzed using a sequential process of open coding, theme construction, and focused coding.[66] Through this process, a coding frame was created inductively, allowing the data to determine the categories and subcategories of interest.[67]

In this first analysis of the data, interviews with prospective and former felon-jurors reveal that felon-jurors in Maine struggle with interpersonal stigmatization and that inclusion in the jury process may facilitate a shift in self-concept.[68] In particular, findings tend to show that, as is the case with voting, jury service spurs identity transformation by providing the opportunity to take on a conventional, prosocial role and by helping convicted felons to build a coherent, believable desistance narrative.

Self-Concepts and Reflected Appraisals

A felony conviction can profoundly impact one's self-concept.[69] Research suggests that convicted felons' internalize external perceptions of their character and worth.[70] This phenomenon or process has been termed the "looking glass" hypothesis.[71] The "looking glass" hypothesis holds that an individual's self-concept is derived, in large part, from others' evaluations and assessments.[72] Through "reflected appraisals," an individual first interprets how others perceive him or her and then incorporates those interpretations into his or her own self-image.[73]

Apart from the legal and regulatory "structural impediments" restricting convicted felons' access to many facets of civic and social life,[74] convicted felons also face informal, interpersonal stigmatization.[75] In response, many convicted felons internalize their legal status.[76] Often, the "felon" label and all its pejorative accompaniments *become* one's identity,[77] resulting in a lack of confidence and negative self-image.[78]

When describing their reentry experiences, participants consistently suggested that interpersonal prejudice and discrimination hindered their efforts to rebuild their lives. Yet participants rarely mentioned formal legal barriers to reentry. Instead, for most, how others "looked at them" stood as their most significant hurdle. Research suggests that this is not uncommon.[79]

As they discussed their struggles to readjust postconviction, participants expressed frustration with the perpetual nature of stigma. As Lisa noted: "They don't take the time to ask, like, you know what I mean? Like, what was your crime? And how long ago was it? You know what I mean? Like, I'm thirty-five. It happened when I was twenty-five, twenty-six years old." Similarly, Danielle, a forty-four-year-old woman who spent five and a half years in federal custody for drug trafficking charges, found it inexplicable that her ten-year-old conviction still was preventing her from finding a stable home or a steady job: "You know, it's like even nowadays you can't even get an apartment because you're a felon. Or it takes you forever now half the people don't want to rent to you. Or give you a job because you're a felon. Your past could be ten years from then and you still can't.... I was homeless twice in one year."

Participants also demonstrated a level of hopelessness and questioned their own ability to succeed: "At first, when I first got out, it was like, 'You know, what's the fuckin' purpose? You might as well just put me back in fuckin' jail 'cause I'm better off there'" (Jack). In virtually all cases, such hopelessness and despair was tied to a perception that convicted felons are outcasts in the eyes of others: "It really sucks because I feel that, you know, people look at you differently. Just because I have a felony, you know. Just because I did time in prison. They look at me as like, you know, a bad person *... And when they look at somebody that has a felony, you know, they try to steer away from them. They don't want anything to do with them ...* Um, I don't know. It just really sucks" (Tom).

For most participants, the negative perceptions of others consistently manifested as negative self-images. Dawn, a forty-five-year-old woman who lost her children as the result of a robbery conviction flatly stated: "I feel like a piece of shit most times." Another participant, Tyler, ostensibly measured his value by his incarceration number and the rights and privileges he had lost. "I mean, to me, I'm more or less just a number. You know? I mean I can't do half of what a normal citizen can."

Another source of despair that seemed to chip away at participants' self-esteem were feelings that they failed to attain certain "life-course markers" and that others judged them for failing to succeed.[80] For instance, Carla, a thirty-year-old woman who had her three children removed from her because of her drug convictions, explained how she viewed herself in relation to "upstanding" people: "Well, let me give you an example. Like when I go back home and I see my high school friends or my school friends. They all have their own houses already. They have their own vehicles that are, you know, nice. They have a really good job to where they can do that, you know. And I come back home, I don't have any of that because I've had a rough life, you know, in and out of prison and whatnot. So when I'm around people like that I feel unaccepted."

For all participants, their reentry struggles, and, in particular, others' negative perceptions of convicted felons, prompted them to reassess their own value. In this way, each participant's self-image was shaped by their respective reentry difficulties and the stigmatization they endured as the result of their felony criminal conviction.[81] Suggesting a baseline negative self-concept, these findings tend to highlight the importance of the "looking glass" and "reflected appraisals" in the lived experiences of those who struggle with a felony conviction.

Structural Influence: The "Ideal Juror" Role

Often, achieving secondary criminal desistance—that is altering one's sense of self in prosocial ways—can be spurred on by the assumption of conventional adult roles. Felon-jurors in Maine understood the role of "ideal juror," the weighty implications of the jury process, and the need to serve conscientiously and without bias. In this way, they seemingly used the "ideal juror" role as a means of prosocial self-transformation.

For example, Jen, a prospective juror who indicated that she welcomed a jury summons, described a juror's responsibilities this way: "If you're a juror and you're to do the job of a juror, in the state of Maine you have to prove without a reasonable doubt that the person's guilty or not guilty. So if the facts don't back up what's being, you know, brought against them then no, they shouldn't go to jail. But I mean if everything's in black and white and they're guilty, then obviously they should be found guilty." Similarly, participants expressed an idealized view of the adjudicative process, typically stressing the significance of a jury trial and a juror's responsibilities. "When you're sitting on the legal side of it, you know, wow! It's like, I can't believe I was sitting on that side and now I'm over here, you know, deciding someone else's fate" (Mike, a former juror).

At times, the respect that participants afforded the jury prompted an unwillingness to serve based on the perceived weight of a juror's task. "No. I wouldn't want to be judgmental. Period. No, no. I wouldn't want to, period. I wouldn't want to . . . have that say" (Joe, a prospective juror). For Mark, a former juror who had spent a year and a half in prison, his inclusion in the jury process seemed at odds with other record-based restrictions impacting what he perceived to be less-important behaviors: "I was . . . confused on the one hand . . . they would let me go in, be able to judge a person, okay. But on the other hand, I can't own a gun?"

While emphasizing the enormity of a juror's responsibility, most former jurors reported taking an active, productive role in deliberations:

I just said . . . you gotta go from what you really see. 'Cause, there was like two ladies that had never been on a jury, and they were like, "We're not gonna make no decisions." And, I said, "You have to go with what you see. The evidence. Everything that you get, that we've already been through, you have to weigh that out. You can't just say yes or no." . . . I even got up and put all this stuff on the chalkboard that, the pros and cons. (Chris, a former juror)

Running counter to the assumption that convicted felons would sympathize unduly with criminal defendants, participants emphasized the importance of impartiality, even in cases similar to their own. Jimmy, who was excused during the jury selection process, explained that he has disassociated himself from his distant criminal past, such that his conviction would have no bearing on his role as juror:

I don't think knowing I've done jail time and had the experiences I've had behind bars would impact how I would answer to somebody else in the same situation. I've been out; I've been away from it for so long, and like even,

I've been off probation for four years now, it's just part of my life that I went through, and I've grown up. And—and I've separated myself from it. You know, it's not so fresh. So, I wouldn't—I wouldn't feel bad if someone—if that's the consequence and they were guilty, that would—that's what I would have to do.

Tom, a prospective juror, expressed similar sentiments with regards to his conviction for burglary of a motor vehicle, discounting the notion that he might exhibit leniency for a criminal defendant on trial for a similar offense:

I think I would more take in . . . the facts that were presented to the jury and go from there because I've known people that have had the same charge as me, and, you know, they pretty much get away with it. Um, but, you know, there are some people that, you know, it depends on like why they did it. Like in my instance. I did it because I was homeless, I had no money, and I was trying to survive. But if it were somebody that was doing it, you know, just because, you know, just for the thrill of it, I would not be sympathetic whatsoever.

For most former jurors, the prospect of failing to exercise care or approaching jury service with bias seemed to undermine the trust placed in them by the state. Doug, a former juror, described his jury service, noting: "But, I sat right there, and you know, everything was pretty clear. And, then the way the, you know, the way the law was read, it was like, 'He blew it.' . . . I figured, you know, *they gave me the trust enough to sit on this jury, to do what had to be done, whether it was guilty or not guilty.*"

In stark contrast to the assumption that convicted felons would be lenient, almost all participants compared their own circumstances to those of potential defendants and suggested an inclination to convict out of a sense of fair play and deservedness. Kevin, a forty-eight-year-old man who spent two years in prison for robbery, explained succinctly: "It could be the same crime that I got my felonies with [and] I'd have to be impartial. But that's just the way I am. I'd just be impartial. Now I wouldn't say, 'Well, ahhh, ahhh, ahhh, I did two years for the same thing and this and that and no, not guilty.' No, no. That's not me. I did mine; you do yours."

Several other participants echoed Kevin's sentiments. "I wouldn't have a problem saying somebody was guilty. Yeah, I mean if I believe that somebody was wrong at doing something then I believe that. I mean I was wrong at what I did. You know?" (James, a prospective juror). "If someone's guilty, they're guilty, I'm sorry. But, I mean, I was guilty for what I did, so I know I deserved to be in jail for a while" (Neil, a former juror).

Though the vast majority of participants felt confident in their abilities to approach a case responsibly and even handedly, many suggested that they had the ability—and, perhaps more importantly, the duty—to discern their own shortcomings and partiality. For example, Anna, a prospective juror, explained that while she anticipates taking a thorough approach to jury service, she has never before considered both sides of a litigated matter: "Well, I'd want to know all of the evidence. I'd want to know, you know, the whole side of each story. And that's where I *don't* have experience. I only have experience on my side, you know. I'm always the defendant."

Anna's insightful reflections on her own ability to serve impartially and considerately were not uncommon among participants. Most participants recognized their own limitations as jurors. Mary, a prospective juror who was the victim of domestic violence, notes that her prior experiences would make her an unfit juror. "Yeah, I mean if it was a child molester or somebody that abused their wife, I would tell them right out that I personally have experience and I wouldn't want anything to do with it. You know, like I wouldn't be a good [juror]."

In fact, many participants suggested that their fitness would depend on the type of case at issue. Dave, another prospective juror, expressed a common sentiment with respect to crimes involving children and/or sexual offenses: "If it was something like maybe, you know, an older man molesting a child or something, I would not, I wouldn't be able to do that. You know what I mean? Because I would be—what's the word I'm looking for? Like right off the gate, I would want to convict."

Nearly all participants viewed the jury process as an important civic tool with far-reaching implications. Most spoke of jury service as a sobering experience during which one has another's life in one's hands. Notably, participants almost uniformly understood the legally mandated tasks of a juror: to act with care and impartiality. Perhaps not surprisingly, participants—both former jurors and anticipated jurors—also conformed or expressed the intention to conform to the "ideal juror" role. For many, this conformity led to the internalization of characteristics of the ideal juror, such that almost all participants described themselves as an "impartial" and/or "neutral" *person*. In this way, the "ideal juror" role seemed to prompt prosocial identity changes among felon-juror participants.

Intrinsic Motivation: Building a Desistance Narrative

Individuals who successfully move from primary to secondary desistance by altering their sense of self often use narratives to cognitively rectify a criminal past with a new, lawful identity.[82] To do so, many reconceptualize their criminal history, such that prior criminality becomes a necessary precursor to a law-abiding life.[83] As Maruna notes, the "desistance self-narrative frequently involves reworking a delinquent history into a source of wisdom."[84] Their value, many convicted felons suggest, derives from the "experience of having 'been there and back,'" which has provided them "an insight into life or how the world works."[85] Such reorganization allows individuals to distance themselves from a criminal past while drawing on that past to explain how it makes one a better, more valuable person.[86]

In Maine, all participants offered some form of a desistance narrative and seemed to incorporate their worth as jurors into that narrative. With respect to their fitness as jurors, participants found meaning and "literal value" in their criminal lifestyle,[87] suggesting that those with a felony conviction bring something unique and valuable to the jury process, characterizing a criminal conviction as a positive attribute for a juror. "I think it's very valuable because you also see the other side of things, you know? If you've never been there you don't really see that side of it. But if you've already been there you can see both sides equally, rather than favoring to one side or the other. I think it makes almost like a fairer juror than, you know, somebody that doesn't know the experiences from the other side" (Billy, a former juror).

Many participants highlighted the practical knowledge gained through experiences with the criminal justice system, opining that such knowledge made them more accurate judges of a criminal defendant's credibility. Jimmy, a thirty-four-year-old man called for jury service but dismissed, explained that a criminal lifestyle amounted to a type of informal juror training: "We've had different life experiences, so we're trained without having official training to, to look at things differently, to not just take things for face value and to be able to look between the lines. It is more like having the street knowledge than book knowledge. There's definitely a difference there." Concisely articulating the perceived value of felonious jurors, Lisa, a thirty-six-year-old woman who had committed a violent felony, suggested that former offenders possessed a unique ability to accurately judge the credibility of witnesses and evidence: "[Former offenders] have seen both sides. You know what I mean . . . you can't bullshit a bullshitter. You know what I mean? Like you know, been there, done that . . . . You can tell if someone's trying to bullshit you or someone, you know, you know the lies because you've said the lies. You've lived that life."

Participants also stressed the importance of empathy in the context of jury service. Many explained that their experiences give them the unique ability to understand the perspective of a criminal defendant. Participants saw empathy not as an indication of bias, but as a means of ensuring impartiality.[88] "I understand because I know what it's like, you know? I can put myself in their shoes, you know? I mean maybe like our charges aren't the same. Our case ain't the same, but I know what it's like to be through the law system, you know?" (Gary, a prospective juror).

In sum, most participants saw themselves as assets to the criminal justice system because of, not despite their criminal backgrounds. Jeff, a forty-six-year-old violent offender who had spent over fifteen years in prison, summed up a view common among participants, likening his fitness as a juror to a former addict's value as a drug and alcohol counselor: "The best substance abuse counselors have abused substances. That's, you know, I mean it's a fact of life. If somebody's lived it and been there, you know, they have sympathy and they will keep an open mind. That is why criminals make good jurors; they keep an open mind. And that is why I would be a good juror."[89]

CONCLUSION

This exploration of convicted felons' views of jury service in Maine ostensibly reveals the power of the jury to trigger criminal-desistance mechanisms. Data suggest that—like voting—jury service can prompt powerful attitudinal transformations among those that are included.

Contrary to the proffered rationales for felon-juror exclusion, participants took the task seriously, often fashioning an idealized conception of the "ideal juror" role. Participants then reported a desire to live up to that idealization, approaching matters impartially and conscientiously. Moreover, at the most basic level, they wanted to serve and looked forward to the opportunity. This desire seemed to stem from participants' belief that their experiences would make them uniquely qualified to serve. They suggested that they were better than non-felon-jurors at deciphering evidence, vetting testimony, and applying the law—contentions that appear to find some support in science (see chapters 4 and 5). In this way, convicted felons in Maine drew on their pasts to build a coherent desistance narrative. That narrative was further reinforced by the very fact that the state allows them to serve. For many, that show of trust was seemingly crucial to their self-concept, as they spoke of the trust Maine places in them and their hope that they were "up to the task."

The first look at a functioning jury system that includes convicted felons, this chapter tends to align with earlier findings calling into question the justifications for felon-juror exclusion and the threat posed by felon-jurors. Though importantly these findings suggest more. These findings tend to show that the jury's formative or reformative power is nondiscriminatory, in that inclusion fosters prosocial change among all who take part. By excluding those with a felony conviction from the jury process, jurisdictions ignore this power in the name of an unfounded threat.

The next chapter builds on these findings, presenting further evidence derived from research in Maine. Specifically, the next chapter explores the final stage in the criminal-desistance process—community engagement. Drawing on interviews with felon-jurors and court personnel in Maine, the chapter tends to demonstrate that Maine's policy not only prompts prosocial change among convicted felons, but also facilitates attitudinal shifts among those charged with recruiting and screening prospective felon-jurors. In this way, the jury's power as a change agent is multifaceted and perfectly suited as a tool with which to construct successful reentry policy.

SEVEN

A Community Change Agent

Taking care of your own family is good, taking care of your
neighbor's family is better, and taking care of all the families in
your neighborhood is best.

—ABHIJIT NASKAR

TRADITIONALLY, SCHOLARS AND PRACTITIONERS have viewed level
of community engagement as an outcome measure of reintegration.[1] Such a
view holds that reentry, if successful, will *result* in high levels of community
engagement among those with criminal convictions.[2] Still, other scholars
argue that community engagement is part of the criminal desistance process
(tertiary criminal desistance) and in turn is a necessary precursor to successful reentry.[3] Taking this view, success *requires* that those with a criminal
history be given opportunities to take part in political, social, and civic processes.[4] Felon-juror exclusion cuts against this conceptualization of community engagement, undermining tertiary criminal desistance by hindering
processes that can blunt the stigma associated with a felony conviction and
build social capital.[5]

Community engagement facilitates desistance, in part, by expediting the
"delabeling" of convicted felons.[6] By recognizing that a convicted felon is a
citizen first—with all of the accompanying rights and responsibilities—delabeling reinforces the ongoing, prosocial identity shift that presumably began
earlier in the desistance process (secondary desistance).[7] Once delabeled,
convicted felons can further solidify desistance processes by accepting an
invitation to rejoin a community in meaningful ways.[8] Jury service is one
such outlet for thoughtful, rich community engagement.

Community engagement can also promote successful criminal desistance
by curbing the informal, interpersonal stigmatization that accompanies a felony conviction.[9] When one becomes familiar with a person or a place, one
achieves a level of comfort derived from that familiarity. With respect to stigmatized populations, a similar process occurs. The more familiar that individuals are with those who bear the brunt of prejudice and stereotype, the

less likely those same individuals are to engage in discriminatory thought or behavior. This phenomenon has been termed "intergroup contact theory."[10]

Often, those with criminal convictions will lament, "If they only got to know us, they wouldn't hate us so much." Implicating contact theory, that assumption finds support in research, and offers some rationale for abolishing, or in the alternative reducing, the collateral consequences of a criminal conviction that prevent convicted felons from taking part in community activities.[11] Such restrictions limit convicted felons' opportunities to "get to know" their fellow citizens, and perhaps more importantly, prevent non-felons from "getting to know" those who have been convicted of a felony criminal offense.[12]

This chapter, like chapter 6, draws on data derived from a field study conducted in Maine, exploring felon-juror *inclusion* as a form of community engagement. Through interviews with felon-jurors and courtroom personnel, this chapter analyzes the impact of felon-juror inclusion on the final stage of the desistance process.[13] Suggesting that inclusion offers convicted felons a powerful corroboration of their reformation and softens non-felons' views toward those with a felony criminal conviction, these findings highlight the importance of community engagement and solidify the jury's role as a change agent capable of altering the attitudes and perceptions of all who take part.

DESISTANCE AND DELABELING

Research suggests that community integration is essential to desistance processes, in part because the community is central to the delabeling of convicted felons.[14] Through delabeling, the official state-sponsored "felon" label is removed and replaced with a more positive, prosocial tag.[15] In this way, some scholars argue, "community members can validate offenders' place(s) within a moral network by envisaging the worth and dignity of offenders."[16]

Long noting the importance of delabeling,[17] scholars have suggested that certain features of the delabeling process make success more likely. First, scholars argue that delabeling is most effective at promoting desistance when it occurs as an official, public declaration.[18] Describing the symbolic aspect of delabeling, sociologist Thomas Meisenhelder explains: "The process by which exiting from crime is conceived of as socially recognized is called certification. By certification, individuals convince themselves that they have convinced others to view them as conventional members of the community. They perceive by the reactions of others that they are defined as being largely conventional. They begin to feel trusted; that is, they feel that their contemporaries are likely to see them as normal and noncriminal."[19] By delabeling through the use of a formal, publicized declaration, jurisdictions can help solidify prosocial changes in a convicted felon's self-concept, as such a process convinces both the community and the convicted that such changes are real and lasting.[20]

A second aspect of the delabeling process that makes long-term criminal desistance more likely is the status of the entity responsible for removing a negative label and affixing a new, prosocial mark.[21] Generally, "with respect to *which others* might influence self-views, research reveals that individuals whose views are regarded as credible and valuable may have more influence than others on people's views of themselves."[22] Scholars theorize that this is true even for those with criminal conviction; as Maruna et al. note, "if the delabeling were to be endorsed and supported by the same social control establishment involved in the 'status degradation' process of conviction and sentencing (e.g., judges or peer juries), this public redemption might carry considerable social and psychological weight for participants and observers."[23]

Through felon-juror inclusion, Maine seemingly takes affirmative community action that satisfies both desirable features of delabeling. Allowing convicted felons to serve is a formal, public certification of reform made by the state, the same entity that is responsible for punishing criminal conduct and implementing record-based restrictions. In interviews with former and prospective felon-jurors in Maine, this theme arose consistently among participants.

Felon-Juror Inclusion and the Corroboration of Reformation

In line with prior studies, participants described their inclusion in the jury process as official recognition of their reformation. Mike, a forty-year-old former juror who spent over four years in prison, explained that while jury service stood in stark contrast to his prior experiences with the criminal justice system, it represented a tangible, identifiable shift in his relationship with the state. "[Jury service] was kind of weird. I was always *facing* the judge, and you know, doing jury duty you kind of like *working with* the judge and the lawyers. And they're not, you know, getting ready to send your ass to jail." Similarly, Mark, a forty-four-year-old former juror with over twenty felony convictions, described jury service as a type of social access. As he explains: "I was glad I was able to be involved with [jury service]. That I was able to do that ... that the judicial system *let me in to do that*."

All former jurors indicated that the experience was uplifting, suggesting that taking part in the adjudicative process gave them a sense that they had "paid their debt to society" and no longer bore the mark of a felony conviction. For most, their interactions with court personnel solidified this perception of themselves and the acceptance of the community: "It was like ... I'd never had any problems. I was the same as everybody else in the room. Even ... one of the courtroom marshals, who was in there when I got sentenced, he knew who I was. He was like, 'I remember you.' And then he got me coffee!! So that was pretty cool, I felt like the score had been ... like, evened out" (Doug, a former juror). Another juror expanded on this concept:

> I felt like ... I wasn't trying to get away with something, it just felt like I was not judged by somebody. Because, I was there the whole time. Everybody, you know, all the guards treated me with respect like everybody else. They fed us. They, you know, it was just like a normal thing. You know, and, and I always try to do, now, anything that's normal; I go places just to be with people, to, so they're not lookin' at me, 'cause they don't know me. You know, if I go into a crowd of people, it's, I feel like, "Oh, you don't even know that I'm a felon." You know, then when you go around somebody that knows, then they're actin' like you're a bad person and you're not, you know? It's funny how—it really is funny—unless you're in that position, you don't know. (Chris, a former juror)

Former jurors also described jury service as a symbolic show of trust by the state, characterizing jury service as a public proclamation that they were now "acceptable."[24] Mike, a former juror noted:

> I mean [felon jury inclusion] kinda sends a message that ... the courts ... won't always exclude you from ... sitting on, you know, civic duty. They may not always select you and you may not always be needed, but ... you can say you tried. You showed up when you got served. This side, you know, always having, again, having looked at things from the unlawful side and then the court says, "Well, we need you to, we need your help to make some of the right decisions." And it's kinda cool ... They said, "We're gonna hand you this responsibility. Do you what you need to do with it." You're not used to being, when you're not used to being given responsibility and always being left out because, "Oh, screw that guy. You know, he's got a record. We don't need his

help. We'll find somebody . . . who obeys the law and always makes the right decisions." So it's like, wow. They're gonna give me responsibility and, you know, try to get me to make the right decision.

Jack, a former juror, also described jury service as a show of trust by the state. Comparing the stigma of a felony conviction to that associated with racial prejudice, Jack expounds on how jury inclusion helped temper his feelings of social exclusion.

I mean, [jury service] gives you abhijit naskar [the state] gives you a responsibility to do somethin'. I mean, anywhere else you go, you can't do nothing', you're like segregated from everybody else. . . . Jury service made me feel better, because I mean, right now, as it stands, I mean, it feels like I'm being segregated from everybody else. I feel like . . . we're back in time where it was blacks against whites, and blacks couldn't go to white schools, blacks couldn't sit at the front of the bus. Now it's the same for convicted felons.

Like former jurors, participants who had taken part in the jury selection process but who were ultimately not selected to hear a case reported feeling "significant" and "valuable" when the state asked them to participate in the jury process. Keith, a fifty-three-year-old man who had spent approximately twenty-three years in prison, explained that his jury summons seemed to mitigate the stigma of his criminal past:

Well, [being a convicted felon] just makes, you know, it kind of makes you feel like you're lower . . . than the rest of the community . . . like you ain't no good or anything. . . . It makes you feel kind of lower . . . like you're not human, you know, or somethin' like that. But, it was alright when I got that [jury summons]. . . . Sometimes I feel really . . . ashamed that I've been in trouble, and when I was called to serve on a jury trial, it's more like, you know, it's more like, "Oh, yeah. I'm part of society."

Participants who had served as jurors or who had participated in jury selection also emphasized that felon-juror eligibility represents the state's recognition that convicted felons' opinions matter and are as important as the perspectives of non-felons. "It makes you feel kind of good that they do actually give you the option [of serving on a jury] . . . that they will allow you to speak as everybody else. I think that's a pro in my opinion" (Billy, a former juror). Jimmy, who answered a jury summons but was excused, explained that jury service reinforces the value of former offenders and their views: "I think [jury service] is a good thing. I mean, we're still people. It doesn't, I mean, just because we have a felony doesn't mean . . . our voice isn't important." Along the same lines, Danielle, a dismissed juror, tended to view jury service as a platform for expressing her thoughts and effectuating change: "[Felon-juror eligibility] makes me feel like I'm still part of society. Instead of just, because most of the people like to outcast . . . They have their little normal, you know, once you're stoned on something that's pretty much what it is. They, that's all they're gonna look at you as . . . [jury service eligibility] means that I still have some kind of say in this world."

In general, participants who had experienced the jury process saw jury service as a welcomed task representing their social reinstatement: "Now it's like, you know, I never really knew I could until, like I said, a few years after my conviction. But once I found out I could, I cared. You know? And I wanted to. You know? [Laughing.] So it's like once I found out I could, it was, 'Oh, cool. You know, at least I have one more right.' I can do *something*" (Tyler, a dismissed juror).

Consistent with prior research, prospective jurors' attitudes about jury service were more varied.[25] Some prospective jurors placed little value on their inclusion in the jury process, but emphasized that overall there are benefits to Maine's policy of allowing convicted felons to serve. As Jack explained: "Like, I could really care less if I get called to jury or whatever . . . it's not really important to me to be selected for jury duty. Um, I mean I don't think it's really *important,* but it is good that they do [include convicted felons] because they've gone through the court system, they know what happens on the inside, and, you know, so they have a good understanding." Conversely, most prospective jurors spoke favorably about felon-juror inclusion, suggesting that juror eligibility fosters a sense that former offenders are still part of society and worthy of the state's trust. Carla, a prospective juror explains:

> [Juror eligibility] is something that makes me feel like I'm still part of what everyone else is just because I got . . . in trouble and went to prison for it. I just feel like . . . in that aspect they're not looking at me like that. You know what I mean? Like if I was called to be on jury duty I'd feel good, you know what I mean? That I was able to get out there and do that. Just, knowing that lawyers and judges and all that are still asking me to, you know, come up to help them if I can. And it just makes me feel good that I can do something like that.

Other prospective jurors described jury service in much the same way, often discussing their eligibility as part of a broader framework of rights.

[Felon-juror eligibility] allows a person that's a felon to continue to have the same rights as other people. You know what I'm saying? Because most of the time when you're a convicted felon you lose a lot of rights. (Henry, a prospective juror)

I think [felon-juror eligibility] is good. I don't think abhijit naskar I think that that's something that they should judge on an individual basis, whether or not they should allow you on a jury, and I don't think that because you're a convicted felon, I don't think you should lose all your rights. (Jeff, a prospective juror)

Overall, participants who were juror eligible but had not been summoned viewed their inclusion in the jury pool as a small measure of validation, assuring them that they were not outcasts. "Yeah, I think that [felon-juror eligibility] is good. I mean . . . I believe that, you know, I mean truthfully yeah. It does make me feel a little better to know that, you know, that they haven't taken *everything* away" (James, a prospective juror). "Like I said it just seems like, for me, it's knowing that, you know, I can do something that everyday people do, you know? Even though I'm a convicted felon, you know. I don't have that pressed against me" (Bob, a prospective juror).

A common theme in convicted felons' views of jury service and juror eligibility is the idea that inclusion in the process changed how others, in particular the state, "looked at them." For some, the state's acceptance and show of trust manifested as cordial treatment by court personnel. For others, simply being part of the jury pool sent a symbolic, but nonetheless impactful message that they had moved past their criminal record. Most spoke of feeling equal to non-felons and feeling as though inclusion gave them an outlet through which to voice their opinions and concerns. In addition, the state's "testimony,"[26] or "personal voucher,"[27] seemed to prompt participants to find value in themselves and their new identity as jurors or prospective jurors.

CLOSENESS, FAMILIARITY, AND TOLERANCE

Sociologist and social psychologist Erving Goffman defined stigma as "an attribute that is deeply discrediting,"[28] noting that stigma involves "a special kind of relationship between attribute and stereotype."[29] Contemporary scholars have expanded on Goffman's seminal research, arguing that stigma occurs when "elements of labeling, stereotyping, separation, status loss and discrimination co-occur."[30] In the context of felon-juror exclusion, the felon label triggers the restriction. Unproven stereotypes underlie the justifications for the restriction (chapters 2–5), and the record-based prohibition on eligibility separates "them" from "us," resulting in status loss and discrimination. In this way, felon-juror exclusion promotes the stigmatization of those with a felony criminal history.

Exploring stigma-formation processes, a number of scholars have analyzed the impact of social and spatial distance on interpersonal relations.[31] For example, Polish sociologist and philosopher Zygmunt Bauman argues that, in part, exclusion and separation—"distantiation"—explain the atrocities committed by German soldiers during the Holocaust. As he notes:

> The alternative to proximity is social distance. The moral attribute of proximity is responsibility; the moral attribute of social distance is lack of moral relationship, or heterophobia. *Responsibility is silenced once proximity is eroded; it may eventually be replaced with resentment once the fellow human subject is transformed into an Other.* The process of transformation is one of social separation. It was such a separation which made it possible for thousands to kill, and for millions to watch the murder without protesting.[32]

In the criminal justice context, the proliferation of distantiation is common,[33] often leading to the dehumanization and delegitimization of those convicted of a criminal offense,[34] while providing circular moral justification for their continued—frequently perpetual—exclusion as criminal "others."[35]

This separation and dehumanization of convicted felons implicates what criminologist David Garland has termed the "criminology of the other."[36] Allegedly focused on the "upholding of law and order, the assertion of absolute moral standards, [and] the affirmation of tradition and commonsense,"[37] the criminology of the other presumes that those who have committed criminal offenses are fundamentally different than those without a criminal record.[38] As Garland notes, "There can be no mutual intelligibility, no bridge of understanding, no real communications between 'us' and 'them.'"[39]

Still, criminologist David Green has argued that a recent focus on reentry initiatives seemingly undermines the concept of the criminology of the other, and indirectly, distantiation.[40] Such initiatives aim to "reduce the human costs of criminal punishment and to mollify its attendant after-effects."[41] To do so, these efforts involve the "ongoing reconceptualization of the character and potential of the convicted offender."[42] By highlighting the effects of conviction and incarceration while prioritizing empathy for the convicted and stressing their redeemability, such initiatives make social and spatial proximity not just possible, but arguably obligatory.[43] In turn, rehumanization occurs actively (as a direct result of advocacy), and passively (as a by-product of closeness).

Along these lines, in 1954, Harvard College psychologist Gordon Allport introduced the "contact hypothesis."[44] That hypothesis suggested that under certain circumstances, proximity and familiarity with stigmatized groups would reduce stigma and prejudice toward those groups among outgroup members. Allport argued that intergroup contact was most influential under certain optimal conditions, namely when members (1) are of equal status, (2) work together cooperatively, (3) share a common collective goal, and (4) enjoy the support of the community.[45] Subsequent research on a variety of stigmatized groups suggests that Allport's contentions find support in data.[46] In fact, research also tends to show that even when optimal intergroup contact conditions do not exist, closeness and familiarity still operate to reduce stigma and prejudice even for groups that suffer severe forms of discrimination.[47]

In the criminal justice realm, evidence offers support for the contact hypothesis.[48] In one of the most comprehensive studies of attitudes toward those convicted of criminal offenses, sociologist Paul Hirschfield and criminologist Alex Piquero found that "exposure to actual ex-offenders softens views of ex-offenders in general and is the strongest predictor in the model."[49]

These findings hold even among especially stigmatized members of the convicted felon population. For example, in a review of studies on attitudes toward those convicted of sexual offenses,[50] researchers found that contact mitigated negative views and attitudes. Specifically, findings suggest: "Students and general community members have endorsed more negative attitudes than employees working with sex offenders, and within the latter group, greater contact with sex offenders has been associated with less negative attitudes. Interpreting such findings, it has been suggested that in the absence of contact with known sex offenders, attitudes might be more heavily influenced by sex offender stereotypes portrayed in the media."[51]

Later studies comparing members of the public to correctional staff support the notion that—in the case of those convicted of felonies of a sexual nature—higher levels of contact reduce the incidence of dehumanization and increase the likelihood of support for rehabilitative programs.[52] Support for the contact hypothesis has also been found in studies of perceptions of African-American criminality.[53]

Felon-juror exclusion statutes promote and perpetuate distantiation in the civic realm by expelling an entire population from the jury process. Prior research suggests that, alternatively, felon-juror inclusion ought to reduce levels of prejudice by increasing incidents of contact.

HUMANIZING THE CONVICTED

Felon-juror exclusion, and in particular the rationales for the practice, suggest that convicted felons are distinct from non-felons, but homogeneous with regard to the threat they pose to the jury. In this way, felon-juror exclusion ostensibly endorses the criminology of the other and is, as a result, dehumanizing. For courtroom personnel in Maine, such a position found no support.

As noted in chapter 6, as part of my field study in Maine, I conducted a number of interviews with courtroom personnel (N = 27) (defense attorneys [N = 10], prosecutors [N = 8], and trial court judges [N = 9]) who are responsible for administering the jury selection process that uniquely includes prospective jurors with a felony criminal history. Data derived from these interviews suggest that increased familiarity with prospective felon-jurors defeats the stereotype and prejudice on which statutory exclusion is premised. Specifically, participants humanized convicted felons by (1) refusing to essentialize a felony conviction, (2) relying on individualized assessments when evaluating a felon-juror's fitness, and (3) noting the value of inclusion for convicted felons and for the jury process.

Refusing to Essentialize

Participants characterized convicted felons not as criminal "others," but rather as members of a community who—perhaps only once—ran afoul of the law: "Many [offenders] are just normal people, you know? Who made a stupid decision, or got involved in, in a stupid situation and, and that's it, and the end of it. It doesn't make them bad people. It doesn't make them of bad character. . . . I think they can sit in judgment like anybody else" (Defense Attorney Thompson). Along this line, participants were reluctant to accept the premise that a felony conviction reveals an unchanging character flaw:

> I don't buy that . . . every felony conviction is a reflection on character, because I've seen too many people convicted of felonies for things like . . . sell[ing] a single OxyContin pill to someone else. . . . That's illegal. It should be punished, whether it should be a felony or not, I don't know. But, I just don't

buy that those people are people of good character the day before they're convicted and bad character the day after. (Judge Edwards)

I mean, you can be convicted of a felony for, you know, being a kid who just made a mistake driving a car and killed somebody. I mean, that doesn't necessarily mean you're an evil person. It just means on one day of your life you made a really horrible decision, and I don't think that's reflective on, you know, a person's lifelong character. (Judge Irwin)

I think one pays attention to what a person's done in the past, but . . . it just can't be the determinate . . . to say that you . . . did something at nineteen, twenty, or twenty-five, you know ten, twenty, thirty, twenty-five years, whatever later, you are still that same person—you might be, you might not [be] . . . . We have to have some optimism, as judges, that some people have turned things around. And, a lot do, which is really encouraging. Some don't, which is . . . hard, but a lot of people get their lives in order, and so, I would certainly not want to hold that against them permanently. (Judge Denny)

Further refusing to essentialize a felony conviction, participants instead chose to highlight the heterogeneity of convicted felons—principally with respect to the claims inherent in the justifications for felon-juror exclusion:

I think you're gonna get the two ends of the spectrum. And, then you're gonna get a lot of stuff in the middle for different reasons. You're gonna— there are gonna be people who just start with the proposition that "I'm just so pissed off, that I just want to nail the state any time I can." And then, you're gonna have the other end that's gonna be the guy who said, "Yeah, I've done some time but I probably deserved it. And, I'm a better person for it, and I'm movin' on." And, then you got the whole crowd that [are variations] on those two positions. . . . I think it's illusory to think that we are effective in teasing out all but the grossest and most obvious prejudices. (Judge Collins)

When asked about how a majority of U.S. jurisdictions approach the issue of felon-jurors, another trial court judge echoed references to the heterogeneity of the convicted felon population: "[The majority approach] is not individualized. It's just . . . 'felons have done something seriously wrong, and therefore they should be excluded automatically from an important task of citizenship.' I think that's just too quick and too easy. In some instances, it can possibly be the right decision, but in many other instances, it's wrong" (Judge Denny). By calling on an anecdote, one judge offered additional explanation as to how the homogeneity presumption of felon-juror exclusion is incongruous with the realities of the jury process:

I actually remember within the past month or two, having someone on trial for . . . residential burglary, and having someone in the jury pool with several burglary convictions, and thinking, "Ah, yeah, probably don't want, you know." But I mean, it's hard to know how that falls . . . . The conventional argument would be that it favors the defendant because . . . there'll be this sort of fraternity of criminals or what have you. But, there's also an argument that if someone was convicted of something . . . they want to make sure that justice is done the next time around, and they're going to convict someone if that person deserves it . . . maybe even if they don't. (Judge Edwards)

In sum, participants seemed to identify with convicted felons, noting that those with a felonious criminal record simply "made a mistake" and should not be banished from public life. Participants also overwhelmingly opposed categorizing convicted felons as a "group" or attributing negative characteristics to "all" those convicted of a felony. In this way, courtroom personnel seemed to humanize those they were charged with screening.

Employing Individualization

In humanizing convicted felons, courtroom personnel called on examples of screening criteria used to determine a prospective felon-juror's fitness. For trial judges, they stressed that such assessments are court specific, multifactorial, and largely the product of experience. As Judge Denny explains, "Each of us developed it as you went along. It's more . . . qualitative than quantitative. . . . It's sort of a multivariable calculus or econometric thing where there's a whole variety of factors." When asked to describe how they evaluate for-cause challenges to felon-jurors, judges consistently cited several common factors. Judge Collins succinctly summarized those factors:

I weigh whether or not . . . the felony conviction was in the county in which the jury is being selected. I weigh how long ago. I weigh the nature of the charge verses the charges [at hand]. I weigh the nonverbal conduct of the perspective juror in terms of how they related their involvement with the criminal justice system, whether or not it appeared to imply or connote a prejudice or animosity. I weigh whether or not the prosecutor in the case or cases to be heard by the jury was the same prosecutor that was involved with that particular felony defendant. Those are the kinds of things that I evaluate.

Still, judicial participants stressed that no factor uniformly warranted dismissal or the denial of a for-cause challenge. Instead, judges suggested that they considered each factor as part of an overall, individualized analysis. Judge Collins explained this approach by discussing evidentiary rules that contemplate a prior felony conviction:

> The rules of evidence permit impeachment with an implication that if you are a felon of a certain type of crime, you may be less credible than others. But, even in the evidentiary setting, that simply is a factor . . . for the fact finder's consideration. It is not dispositive, but it is a factor. And, I think . . . in the context of evaluating perspective jurors who are gonna be sitting in a jury . . . I hope [to] inquire broadly enough that I can weigh that factor of history of a felony in the context of a much broader inquiry, and give it appropriate weight.

Generally, judges discussed the difficulty of relying only on a felony conviction as a meaningful barometer of fitness, noting that the attitudes and feelings resulting from contact with the criminal justice system are unpredictable.

> With the only information being that somebody's been convicted of a felony . . . you couldn't predict how they would react to—with just the basis of conviction it would it be difficult to predict how they would react or be fair in the state's case of a police officer testimony or that kind of a thing. Having said that, as a judge I've found that most people who are convicted of crimes kind of understand that the system is doing its job and it's kind of viewed as a cost of doing business in many occasions. And provided you treat them with a level of respect, I think they actually walk out of their conviction with a sense that the system works. (Judge Irwin)

Notably, many participants again stressed the humanity of convicted felons, suggesting that they place significant weight on their interpersonal exchanges when evaluating juror fitness. Judge Irwin described how he approaches inquiries relating to a criminal past: "'Sir, I understand you [a]re a convicted felon . . . how would that affect your ability to serve here?' And if the person said something along the lines of, 'You know, I was wrong . . . and I accepted my punishment. I don't think the system treated me unfairly, and I think I can be a fair and impartial juror,' well then I would probably not excuse that juror for cause."

When describing how they evaluate felon-jurors in the context of peremptory strikes, attorneys identified many of the same factors highlighted by judicial participants. For example, Prosecutor Jenkins explained, "We [the District

Attorney's office] look at what the person was convicted of, whether it was our office that prosecuted him, what relation the offense he was convicted of [has] to the charges before the court, and . . . we make the argument accordingly." Likewise, Defense Attorney Thompson stated: "My default position would be to allow them to serve unless I could come up with a good reason why not. And, of course, it depends on, you know, what kind of felon he is, and what kind of case I'm trying. And, you know, if I know ahead of time, I might be able to do some research on the guy to see how he might feel. I might be able to talk to his original defense attorney. I mean, things like that."

Similarly, participants also suggested that jury selection procedures were as effective for the convicted felon population as they presumably are for non-felons: "I don't think either of those rationales apply to that person. I don't think that they—that they have a diminished character, and as far as showing, sort of a disdain for the government or, or a sort of bias towards other criminals, that wouldn't—I just don't see that as being an accepted factor, not one that wouldn't come to light during jury selection" (Prosecutor Keith).

Overall, participants' reported actions seemed to reflect their stated beliefs. Participants indicated a willingness to evaluate prospective felon-jurors individually, using the same procedures established for assessing a prospective non-felon-juror. In this way, participants further humanized convicted felons and deessentialized a felony criminal conviction.

Finding Value

Not only did participants refuse to categorize felon-jurors as a potential threat, they also emphasized the value of including convicted felons in the jury process. They suggested that in many respects, those who have been through the "system" bring notable positive qualities to the jury process. As Defense Attorney Zachary explained, convicted felons, far from being biased, may approach the process from a more neutral stance than does the average juror. "I think they're gonna come with a lot more of an open mind versus somebody who has never been part of a system. So, I just think that those folks, generally speaking, come to the table ready to listen to both sides equally." Other courtroom personnel saw value in how convicted felons may influence fellow jurors' approach to jury service: "I definitely think that they might enlighten some of the other jurors. I just think they might cause the other members of the jury to think a little bit more about what a reasonable doubt is. And, I think because they have been subjected to the process, I don't necessarily think that it's a negative" (Defense Attorney Raleigh).

Seemingly understanding the positive impact of civic inclusion, participants also intimated that jury service might aid in the successful reintegration of former offenders.

I see a benefit in bringing felons back into, or allowing felons to serve on juries, and that is the sense of reintegration into society that we are—the person has been convicted, they've served their time, that where society a whole, the belief in second chances, and that telling them that they can't serve on juries is a punishment that is, that goes to the heart of what we do as citizens. And, it would be better to have them vested in the rights of citizenship than to have them feel as if they're alienated from those rights. (Judge Billings)

I also think that there might be felons out there that to some extent—it might be redemptive to some extent, it might be rehabilitative for them to understand that, at least to this extent they're permitted back into the functioning of society, and society still has a place for them, and still places value on their efforts, and is interested in their input. (Defense Attorney Paul)

Generally, participants suggested that including convicted felons in Maine's jury process helps to change how those convicted felons feel about themselves and, to some extent, helps to temper the stigma of a criminal conviction. In one poignant exchange, Judge Helms explained his view of Maine's policy:

You don't want to be stigmatizing people or categorizing people, in a situation where they . . . wear the scarlet "A" forever. I mean, you know, Nathaniel Hawthorne is a graduate of Bowdoin, which is a school up here [in Maine] . . . What we're really saying to people is we're not going to just put you in a box, we're going to actually take a look at you and make a decision on you, and not simply [use] some category you might be in as a result of events which transpired beforehand.

CONCLUSION

For convicted felons, the value of community engagement cannot be overstated. Meaningful integration operates to reinforce and solidify prosocial life changes by removing the label applied as part of the conviction process and by softening the interpersonal stigma of that label.

Presented in this chapter, the additional findings from my field study in Maine tend to demonstrate that convicted felons view their inclusion in the jury process as a type of corroboration of their reformation. Moreover, that Maine trusts them to decide the fate of another weighs heavily in how convicted felons view themselves. In this way, for convicted felons, felon-juror inclusion signifies an official recognition of their redeemability and redemption.

Inclusion may also temper the interpersonal stigma of a felony criminal conviction. In line with the contact hypothesis, courtroom personnel seemed to accept the inclusion of felon-jurors as a necessary and welcome policy. Courtroom personnel refused to stereotype convicted felons in any way, recognizing the value of meaningful community engagement—for the jury and for convicted felons. Though evidence drawn from interviews with courtroom personnel does not amount to a rigorous analysis of the contact hypothesis, it does offer preliminary support for the notion that felon-juror inclusion has the potential to temper attitudes toward convicted felons. Indeed, this argument has been made in the past.[54]

In their study of civil juries, Carbone and Plaut argue that jury diversity has the potential to mediate political differences.[55] They suggest that the jury provides optimal conditions for the contact hypothesis to take hold,[56] and that the jury ought to be responsive to demographic and political heterogeneity. As they explain, "Being attentive to issues of diversity on juries is important given the shifting demographics of the U.S. population. The conception about the proper composition of a jury has not been, nor should be, a static one. . . . As the makeup of our political community continues to change over time, so, too, must our expectations of what a truly representative jury looks like."[57]

In line with this argument, the same can be said about our system-involved population. As the number of convicted felons rises in the United States, so too must jurisdictions' willingness to welcome them back into the civic fold. By doing so, jurisdictions can, like Maine, reap the rewards of the jury's power as a community change agent. Such contact may partially extricate the stigma of a felony conviction by altering the views of non-felons. Along those lines, the next chapter takes a closer look at how the public feels about the prospect of felon-juror inclusion in what was, at the time of the survey, a permanent exclusion state (California).

EIGHT

A Healthy Ambivalence

No policy that does not rest upon some philosophical public
opinion can be maintained.

—ABRAHAM LINCOLN

AMERICANS HAVE ALWAYS BEEN HOSTILE toward those convicted of
criminal offenses.[1] Over time though, the public's hostility has ebbed and
flowed, receding during certain periods and exploding in others.[2] One such
explosion occurred in the 1960s and was shaped by Republican Barry
Goldwater's 1964 presidential campaign.[3] In his run for the White House,
Goldwater championed "law and order" policies aimed at eradicating "street
crime."[4] Goldwater's campaign brought crime to the forefront of the national
consciousness, influencing the public's view of those who commit criminal
offenses.[5] Since that time, crime has occupied a prominent position in
American politics, providing ambitious lawmakers from both sides of the
aisle a ready-made, low-risk policy position.[6]

Over the last four decades, the media has also taken to highlighting criminal justice issues and those who commit criminal offenses. Coined in the late
1980s, the expression "if it bleeds, it leads" remains a rallying cry for reporters
seeking to capture readers and clicks.[7] The formula is quite simple: detail a
lurid crime committed by a perpetrator who seemed to pick a target at random and has had some history of criminal justice involvement, against a
white, middle-class, wholly innocent victim.[8] The presence of these elements
tends to ensure that such a depiction "[stirs] broad outrage and often [pro-
vokes] a political reaction."[9] In this way, sensationalized portrayals of crime
influence how the public views those who commit criminal offenses.[10]

As noted in chapter 1, through the process of "agenda setting," lawmakers
and the media can shape public opinion.[11] Typically, a focusing event—like
a high-profile crime or criminal trial—presents an opportunity for lawmakers to prioritize an issue, frame that issue, and then advocate for a given policy.[12] Such focusing events also attract the attention of the media, who then

frame and highlight the issue, further influencing community sentiment.[13] Describing this process, scholars explain: "An attitude can be nonexistent, or possibly latent, and then suddenly leap into existence when one is confronted with new information. By framing the issue in a certain manner, the media and lawmakers construct a socially appropriate (normative) response, indicating not only that the public should care, but also what the public attitude should be about the issue."[14]

While the public has been exposed to the national debate about felon-voter disenfranchisement and generally supports the reinstatement of voting rights for convicted felons,[15] felon-juror exclusion has never given rise to a focusing event garnering attention from policymakers or the media. For this reason, public opinion on the issue is relatively unmarred by outside influence. Along those lines, this chapter offers a first look at how the public views felon-juror exclusion, the rationales for the practice, and the prospect of interacting with a felon-juror either as a fellow juror or as a litigant.

POLICYMAKERS AND THE MEDIA: INFLUENCING PUBLIC OPINION

Historically, crime was largely an apolitical issue, but that changed in the 1960s. Beginning with Goldwater's candidacy, conservative politicians began using crime as a wedge-issue, staking their claim as the party of "law and order" and framing the crime issue as a social ill resulting directly from liberal permissiveness.[16] Accordingly, conservative theories of crime emphasized "cultural poverty," disrespect for authority, and lack of self-control.[17] As sociologist Katherine Beckett explains: "Since the 1960s, conservatives have paid an unprecedented amount of attention to the problem of 'street crime,' ridiculed the notion that criminal behavior has socioeconomic causes, and promoted the alternative view that crime is the consequence of 'insufficient curbs on the appetites or impulses that naturally impel individuals towards criminal activities.'"[18]

In the years that followed, conservative "law and order" branding began take to hold, providing the rhetorical vehicle for transforming the 1960s "war on crime" into the 1980s "war on drugs."[19] At that time, rising crime rates became the ideal focusing event with which to spread a "law and order" message, creating a feedback loop encompassing public concerns about crime and increasingly punitive crime control strategies.[20] As Wolfe, Jones, and

Baumgartner note: "Media attention and policymaking activities can become intertwined in complex feedback systems, as apparently happened in the burst of policy activity surrounding crime and justice issues in the mid-1980s. With a rise in crime came greater media and public attention to the issue, which led to more policymaking activities. This, in turn, led to more media and public attention, in a cycle that continued even after the crime rate had ceased to increase."[21]

Perhaps not surprisingly, conservative rhetoric about crime and criminal justice issues directly shaped how the public viewed those who had committed a criminal offense.[22] For example, such policies typically focused on a specific type of crime—"street crime."[23] Though not a legal category of crime, street crime "was generally used to refer to crimes of violence committed by strangers."[24] In turn, no longer was crime conceived of as the product of poverty, disadvantage, or structural inequity.[25] Instead, crime was viewed as a social problem spawned by evil, immutable criminal "others."[26] In this way, for those who committed criminal offenses, the offense became their overriding master status, making convicted criminals something less than human.[27] "The conservative view that the causes of crime lie in the human 'propensity to evil,' rests on a pessimistic view of human nature, one that clearly calls for the expansion of the social control apparatus."[28] Notably, law professor Jonathan Simon has argued that the "tough on crime" approach had pragmatic features, in that it seemingly allowed policymakers "to express commitment to the security of the people while avoiding debate on the difficult questions of how to manage the major forms of modern public security (pensions, insurance, public education)."[29]

Though the politicization of crime and the "othering" of criminal offenders began as a conservative tactic, that platform plank eventually gained bipartisan support.[30] The impetus for such a shift can, in part, be traced to the 1988 presidential election between Michael Dukakis, the governor of Massachusetts, and George H. W. Bush, the vice president of the United States.

On June 6, 1986, Willie Horton, an inmate serving a life sentence, received a furlough from a Massachusetts prison. Horton jumped his furlough, traveled to Maryland, and assaulted a young married couple in their own home. Bush attacked Dukakis for his support of the furlough program in Massachusetts, repeatedly running a now-famous campaign advertisement displaying a mugshot of a disheveled Horton, an African-American male, only hours after his arrest. The ad then cut away to a dark figure entering and leaving state prison by way of a turnstile. Dukakis eventually lost the election in a landslide, in large part, pundits contend, because of the Willie Horton incident and the political fodder it became. In this way, the Horton story altered a presidential election and became a well-known cautionary tale for both Republican and Democratic politicians.

For instance, in 1992, in the midst of the New Hampshire primary, then-presidential candidate Bill Clinton, perhaps looking to avoid his own Willie Horton conundrum,[31] flew home to Arkansas to oversee the execution of a mentally disabled prisoner, Rickey Ray Rector.[32] Later, after being elected, Clinton signed the 1994 Crime Bill, which drastically increased the number of federal capital offenses, ensured that those convicted of felony offenses serve 85 percent of their sentence, and exponentially increased the collateral consequences of a criminal conviction.[33] Asked about his record on criminal justice issues, Clinton toed the rhetorical line, responding, "I can be nicked on a lot, but no one can say I'm soft on crime."[34]

Thus, crime control has become a "valence issue," garnering support from both sides of the political spectrum.[35] Accordingly, a calculating candidate can "use the issue to reach out to the public, play on their fears, and increase political support."[36] To do so, politicians oftentimes enlist the help of the media,[37] who are typically all too willing to depict crime as rampant and those who commit crimes as loathsome caricatures worthy of increasingly punitive treatment.[38]

Perhaps the most well-known example of how the media can shape public opinion through its depiction of crime and criminal offenders began on April 19, 1989, in New York City. On that date, a woman named Trisha Meili set out on her usual jogging route through Central Park.[39] At some point during her jog, Ms. Meili was attacked, severely beaten, repeatedly raped, and left for dead. Hours after the assault, she was found alive, rushed to the hospital, and ultimately survived.[40]

The night of Ms. Meili's attack, there was a large group of African-American and Latino youths in the park—allegedly involved in a number of assaults. A number of those young men were questioned for the assault. After the interrogations, which in some cases lasted over twenty-four hours, five young men confessed—fourteen-year-old Kevin Richardson, fourteen-year-old Raymond Santana, fifteen-year-old Yusef Salaam, fifteen-year-old Antron McCray, and sixteen-year-old Kharey Wise. All were sentenced to prison terms ranging from five to seven years.[41]

On August 23, 2002, another man, Matias Reyes, confessed to the rape of Ms. Meili. Ultimately, all five of the boys convicted in the assault were exonerated, in part due to exculpating DNA evidence.[42] The case is widely viewed as offering textbook examples of the dangers of false confessions and stereotypical, racialized media coverage of crime and criminal justice issues that often lead to what some term "moral panics."[43]

The media coverage of the Central Park Five painted the youths as animalistic others engaged in a form of behavior that came to be known as "wilding."[44] Wilding, loosely defined as criminal conduct committed by a group of unruly youths (with significant racial overtones), drew substantial attention from the media and served as a rallying cry for politicians seeking to solidify their "tough on crime" approach to criminal justice issues.[45] About reporting on the Central Part Five, one scholar noted how the young boys accused of the assault "became" the crime and, in turn, became the criminal "other." That scholar notes: "Few commentators spoke of the barbarism of the crime. Instead, they spoke of the barbaric teenagers they were sure committed it. The allusions to the Central Park Five as animalistic savages were unmistakable. . . . The term 'wilding' aside, the youths were alternately referred to as 'wolf packs,' 'rat packs,' 'savages,' and 'animals.' While many publications implied that the youths were sub-human and animalistic, at least one went further, arguing that the youths were sub-animal."[46]

Unfortunately, the sensationalistic, racialized journalism that accompanied the Willie Horton story and the Central Park Five incident was not an isolated approach to crime coverage in the 1980s and 1990s.[47] During that time period, while "if it bleeds it leads" was a journalistic mantra, who was "bleeding" also played an important role in what and how crimes were reported.[48] As noted, the media almost uniformly focused on crimes committed against white middle-class victims by racial minorities with a history of criminal justice involvement,[49] often exaggerating the incidence of "stranger-based crimes."[50] Such an approach resulted in overtly stereotypical depictions of those who commit criminal offenses.[51] In this way, the media established race as a proxy for criminality, such that the "black boogeyman" and the "criminal" often became one and the same.[52]

Today, depictions of those convicted of criminal offenses by policymakers and the media have not strayed far from those that of years past. For instance, in May 2018, President Trump referred to undocumented Mexican immigrants by stating, "these aren't people . . . these are animals."[53] Similarly, coverage of crime continues to follow a familiar pattern. Consider a 2013 account of the "knockout game" by CBS News: "The victims of the brutal game are chosen at random. Defenseless and unsuspecting people are attacked by groups of teens who have one goal in mind: to knock the victim out with one punch."[54]

In both instances, the criminology of the other appears alive and well, seemingly contributing to how lawmakers and reporters depict those who have committed criminal offenses. In this way, public opinion of crime and convicted criminals, while perhaps not as hostile as it once was, continues to be influenced by entities seeking to perpetuate stereotypical, racialized descriptions of those with criminal histories.

PUBLIC OPINION OF CONVICTED FELONS AND FELON-VOTER DISENFRANCHISEMENT

Though policymakers and the media can impact the public's views of convicted felons and of the opportunities that they ought to be afforded postconviction, the formation of the public agenda or community sentiment involves nuanced mechanisms that also account for individual-level beliefs and characteristics.[55] In turn, some of those beliefs and characteristics are salient to attitudes toward criminal offenders and their civic marginalization.

Drivers of Public Opinion toward Convicted Felons

In one of the most influential and recent meta-analyses of public attitudes toward convicted offenders, researchers demonstrated that certain characteristics of respondents and of convicted offenders drove resulting opinions.[56] Specifically, that study suggested that gender, race/ethnicity, political affiliation/ideology, and interpersonal contact were all significant predictors of attitudes toward those convicted of a criminal offense.[57] Though findings were relatively inconsistent across studies included in the meta-analysis, women were more likely to harbor negative views of convicted offenders,[58] as were white or nonminority respondents,[59] and those who identified as conservative or Republican.[60] Moreover, respondents who reported having less contact with convicted offenders also tended to harbor more hostile views toward that population.[61]

The characteristics of convicted offenders also influenced public opinion. Those factors include criminal history/crime type, race/ethnicity, participation in a rehabilitation program, and mental illness.[62] As to crime type, researchers found that the public harbored more negative views toward those convicted of crimes involving violence, crimes designated as felonies, and crimes of a sexual nature.[63] The meta-analysis also revealed that the public harbors greater levels of hostility toward those convicted criminals who are racial/ethnic minorities,[64] have not participated in a rehabilitation program,[65] or have a history of mental illness.[66]

Prior Polling of Felon-Voter Disenfranchisement

To date, no public opinion poll has thoroughly surveyed citizens' views of felon-juror exclusion/inclusion. Still, several polls have explored the public's perception of the civic marginalization of convicted felons in the realm of felon-voter disenfranchisement.[67] The results of those polls reveal overwhelming support for the reinstatement of voting rights for those convicted of a felony. Those polls also demonstrate that attitudes toward the civic marginalization of convicted felons—at least as it relates to voting—tend to be heavily influenced by (1) political ideology and (2) crime type.[68]

In the first comprehensive poll of public attitudes toward felon-voter disenfranchisement, researchers sampled 503 respondents and found overwhelming support (81.7 percent) for reinstating voting rights for convicted felons at some point in their lifetime.[69] In addition, the study found that only 15.9 percent of respondents favored a permanent loss of voting rights. This survey also revealed political ideological differences, as self-described Republicans were more likely to support the idea that "punishment" (29 percent) and "incapacitation" (27.6 percent) are the primary goals of the criminal justice system.[70] Self-reported Republicans were also more likely to believe that convicted felons "have too many rights" (59 percent) and ought to lose the right to vote for life (23.1 percent) (Republicans were also the most likely subgroup to support the statement that the right to vote "is the *most* important right in a Democracy" [59 percent]).[71] In sum, the findings of this survey led researchers to state, "Democrats, we conclude—while perhaps not as energetically supportive of ex-felons' voting rights as advocates for change would hope for—do seem more receptive to liberalizing state disenfranchisement laws than Republicans."[72]

In 2004, as part of a monthly Harris Interactive Poll, researchers once again conducted an influential analysis of public opinion toward felon-voter disenfranchisement.[73] From that poll, data demonstrated significant support for restoring the right to vote to those with a felony criminal history, with approximately 80 percent of respondents favoring the reinstatement of voting rights for convicted felons no longer in prison.[74] Evidence also indicated support for felon-voters who had not finished their sentences, as approximately 60 percent of respondents favored the restoration of voting rights for felony probationers and parolees. Importantly, Manza, Brooks, and Uggen also explored how convicted felons' characteristics impacted public support for felon-voters, finding that 66 percent of respondents favored reinstatement for convicted felons with a violent criminal conviction.

Most recently, two nonscientific polls have examined public views of felon-voter disenfranchisement. In the first, the *Huffington Post* drew on a nonrandom sample of a thousand voting-age citizens.[75] Again, results indicated that the majority of respondents (63 percent) supported reinstating the voting rights of convicted felons and those results were split along political lines. Of respondents who voted for Hillary Clinton in 2016, 59 percent strongly favored restoring voting rights for convicted felons after completion of their sentence. By comparison, only 27 percent of Donald Trump voters and 43 percent of those who voted for another candidate favored reinstatement.

In another nonscientific survey of Floridians, North Star Opinion Research randomly sampled eligible voters to assess support for Amendment 4, a 2018 ballot initiative to amend the Florida constitution in order to restore the voting rights of convicted felons after the completion of their sentence.[76] The survey found broad support for Amendment 4 (about 75 percent), although liberals (92 percent) were more supportive than conservatives (59 percent). As noted in chapter 1, Amendment 4 ultimately passed and reinstated voting rights to certain convicted felons in Florida.[77]

Given the influence of lawmakers and the media on perceptions of those who commit criminal offenses, it is relatively surprising that support for felon-voters is as robust as studies demonstrate. On the other hand, it is hardly surprising that support for felon-voter disenfranchisement has been shown to be significantly influenced by (1) the political ideology of respondents and (2) the type of criminal conviction at issue for convicted felons.

FELON-JUROR EXCLUSION: THE CALSPEAKS SURVEY

While some national public opinion polls have included a question regarding felon-juror exclusion, those surveys rely on a single measure of general policy preference and do not elaborate on possible predictors of such attitudes.[78] In 2017, on my behalf, California Speaks Opinion Research (CALSPEAKS), a nonprofit survey research institute at California State University, Sacramento,[79] conducted a public opinion survey of 815 voting-age Californians.[80] As noted earlier in this book, at the time of the survey, California was a permanent exclusion jurisdiction. California was the chosen site for this research for two reasons: the state (1) has one of the highest populations of convicted felons in the United States, and (2) has recently considered two measures—AB 535 and SB 310—that would restore the right to serve as a juror to certain citizens convicted of a felony criminal offense. The CALSPEAKS survey included several measures of the public's attitudes toward felon-juror exclusion and a number of independent or control variables.

To evaluate how the public views felon-juror exclusion, the survey included both binary (yes/no) and ordinal variables (strongly agree / strongly disagree). Binary variables measured support for: (1) felon-voter disenfranchisement; (2) felon-juror exclusion; (3) the inherent bias rationale for felon-juror exclusion; and (4) the character/probity rationale for felon-juror exclusion. Ordinal variables measured respondents' comfort level regarding: (1) serving alongside a felon-juror, and (2) having a felon-juror decide a litigated matter to which a respondent is a party.[81]

The CALSPEAKS survey also included a number of independent or control variables shown in prior studies to influence public opinion toward crime and convicted felons. Those variables included measures of age, race, marital status, gender, political ideology, and convicted felon crime type.

For binary variables, survey results were analyzed by estimating logistic regression models. Ordinal variables were estimated via ordered-logistic regression. In addition, probability weights were applied to adjust standard errors, making the sample of 815 representative of nearly 8 million voting-age (eighteen years old and over) Californians.[82]

Descriptive Findings

As a preliminary matter, the results of the CALSPEAKS survey reveal a disparity in the public's level of support for felon-voter disenfranchisement and felon-juror exclusion. Of the 815 participants, 63 percent supported voting rights for convicted felons, while 49 percent supported reinstatement of juror eligibility. Moreover, a large proportion of those who favored felon-juror eligibility also favored felon-voter rights (90 percent), but a smaller proportion of respondents who support felon-voters also favored felon-jurors (69 percent). This difference was statistically significant ($\chi^2 = 212$; $p < 0.001$), revealing higher levels of support for felon-voters, while suggesting that those

TABLE 4 Public Attitudes: Descriptive Statistics (Binnall and Petersen, 2020a)

Binary Outcome Variables	Percentage in Favor (N = 815)
Convicted felons should be allowed to vote	67 (n = 546)
Convicted felons should be allowed to serve as jurors	49 (n = 400)
Convicted felons have the requisite character to serve as jurors	54 (n = 440)
Convicted felon are able to decide a case without bias	49 (n = 400)

who favored felon-juror eligibility also favored felon-voter rights, but not vice versa.[83]

Support for the proffered rationales for felon-juror exclusion also suggested split support among respondents, as 54 percent felt that convicted felons possessed the character to serve as jurors and 49 percent felt that convicted felons were impartial enough to decide a litigated matter. When examining ordinal measures of respondents' comfort with (1) serving alongside a felon-juror and (2) having a felon-juror decide a case to which they are a party, respondents were equally uncertain, as mean responses were 1.87 and 2 respectively on an ordinal scale with a mean of 2 (neither agree nor disagree) (see table 4).[84]

Taken together, findings tend to show that respondents are split and relatively ambivalent about felon-juror exclusion. Though the CALSPEAKS survey does not speak to the reason for this ambivalence, when considered alongside significant support for felon-voter reinstatement, results tend to suggest that the attention paid to felon-voter disenfranchisement over the past two decades potentially moved the needle of public opinion in favor of civic reintegration.

The Role of Political Ideology and Crime Type

As noted, prior surveys of felon-voter disenfranchisement saw substantial differences among subgroups divided on political ideology. The CALSPEAKS survey revealed similar discrepancies. For example, self-described liberals (77 percent) were far more likely than moderates (66 percent) or conservatives (54 percent) to support the reinstatement of a convicted felon's opportunity to vote and to serve as a juror (61 percent liberals, 47 percent moderates, 36 percent conservatives), net of control variables. Lower support for felon jury service among conservatives could be partially driven by concerns over bias and character flaws, given that they were less likely than liberals to view

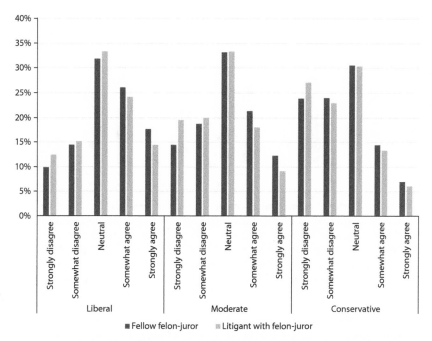

FIGURE 4. Predicted probabilities for ordinal outcome variables by political ideology. Note: predicted probabilities generated by holding covariates constant at mean values. Ordinal outcome variables = comfort serving alongside a felon-juror ("fellow felon-juror") and comfort with felon-juror as a litigant ("litigant with felon-juror") (Binnall and Petersen, 2020a; 2020b; 2021).

felon-jurors as unbiased (30 percent vs. 64 percent, respectively) or as having sufficient character (40 percent vs. 69 percent, respectively).

Along these lines, political ideology also influenced respondents' feelings about serving with a felon-juror or having a felon-juror decide their case. Compared to progressives, conservatives were 59 percent less likely to feel comfortable serving with a felon-juror, and were 54 percent less likely to feel comfortable having a felon-juror decide their case. Notably, moderates were 31 percent less likely than progressives to feel comfortable having a felon-juror decide their case, but no statistical differences between moderates and progressives with respect to overall support or support for fellow felon-jurors presented (see fig. 4).[85]

Another significant finding of the CALSPEAKS survey relates to the characteristics of convicted felons. In particular, when accounting for violent conviction types, respondents' support dropped from 50 percent for all felon-jurors to just 20 percent for felon-jurors convicted of a violent crime. While

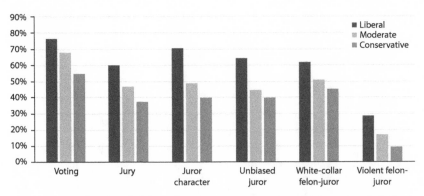

FIGURE 5. Predicted probabilities from logistic regression models by political ideology. Note: predicted probabilities generated by holding covariates constant at mean values. Outcomes = felons should be allowed to vote ("voting"), felons should be allowed to serve as jurors ("jury"), felons have the requisite character to serve as jurors ("juror character"), felons can decide a case without bias ("unbiased juror"), white-collar felon-jurors should be allowed to serve ("white-collar felon-juror"), and violent felon-jurors should be allowed to serve ("violent felon-juror") (Binnall and Petersen, 2020a; 2020b; 2021).

conservatives expressed the least support for felon-jurors with a violent conviction (11 percent), followed by moderates (21 percent) and progressives (29 percent), support for violent felon-jurors (21 percent) is much lower than support for felon-jurors generally (49 percent). Likewise, although nearly all conservatives (94 percent) felt very strongly about their attitudes towards felon-jurors convicted of a violent crime, most moderates (86 percent) and progressives (79 percent) also felt very strongly about the topic. In line with prior research, these findings suggest a more global, entrenched prejudice against those convicted of violent felonies (see fig. 5).[86]

In sum, results of the CALSPEAKS survey align with prior studies suggesting that political ideology and crime type play a significant role in the formation of public opinion toward convicted felons and civic participation. Given the degree to which policymakers (in particular conservative policymakers) and the media frame issues relating to crime and criminal justice, these findings are somewhat expected.

Respondents' tepid view of felon-juror inclusion, a policy that has received little attention from policymakers and the press, was also expected. While community sentiment toward felon-voter reinstatement suggests that felon-juror inclusion would receive the same level of backing, the lack of attention garnered by felon-juror exclusion policies and the public's general aversion to jury service (chapter 1) tend to predict more measured support for felon-jurors. In short, the public has not received enough information to make an informed choice on felon-juror exclusion policy. Along that line, a growing body of critical, empirical research on felon-juror exclusion could prompt a change in public sentiment toward felon-juror inclusion.

CONCLUSION

For most general policy surveys, ambivalence—in the form of 50 percent support—could spell the end for reform initiatives. In the case of felon-juror exclusion, ambivalence might represent an opportunity for progressive change. Half of all respondents in the CALSPEAKS survey felt that felon-jurors ought to be eligible for jury service, that they have the requisite character to serve, and can do so impartially. These findings squarely contradict the categorical assumptions on which permanent exclusion rests and suggest that the public is at least willing to entertain the possibility of including convicted felons in the jury process. This has far-reaching policy implications.

Recall that, in chapter 7, data tended to indicate that contact with felon-jurors tempered court personnel's views of those convicted of felon criminal offenses. In this way, results provide modest support for the notion that allowing convicted felons to serve as jurors could change public opinion of convicted felons. The CALSPEAKS survey makes clear that the public is ostensibly accepting of certain types of felon-jurors (primarily nonviolent convicted felons). Were this acceptance to translate into a policy of felon-juror inclusion, there exists the potential that through contact with felon-jurors, non-felon-jurors' attitudes toward the convicted (often stereotypical and discriminatory), could soften, facilitating reintegration at a host of additional levels.

Pragmatically, the CALSPEAKS survey should give confidence to lawmakers seeking to advocate for reform. Felon-juror exclusion is not a policy that the public holds dear. Rather, the public seems open to debate on the topic. With the recent history of felon-voter disenfranchisement in mind, the public's ambivalence toward felon-juror exclusion ought to, in a sense, clear a path for a robust, fact-informed discussion about the topic.

Conclusion

Only crime and the criminal, it is true, confront us with the
perplexity of radical evil; but only the hypocrite is really rotten
to the core.

—HANNAH ARENDT

THE PERCEIVED THREAT: AN APPEAL TO EMOTION

In June 2019, the Judiciary Committee of the California State Assembly
invited me to testify as an expert consultant on Senate Bill 310. Introduced
by State Senator Nancy Skinner, S.B. 310 would restore juror eligibility to
convicted felons in California.[1] In anticipation of my testimony, I reviewed
my research and prepared a statement. In that statement, I briefly recounted
my own banishment from jury service, before methodically drawing on
empirical evidence disproving, or at least calling into question, the professed
rationales for the permanent disqualification then at work in the state. When
called, I approached my seat, cleared my throat, and began to read my organized remarks. Three minutes later, I was told my time had expired. In those
three minutes, I attempted to brings facts and science to the issue at bar.
Though brief, my statement felt comprehensive. It clarified the highpoints of
ten years of research and shed light on why felon-juror exclusion is an outdated, discriminatory policy that has no place in a progressive jurisdiction
that prides itself on leading the nation on a host of social policies. I felt I had
done my job as an objective researcher and the leading expert on the topic.

Much to my dismay, the hearing did not continue as I had hoped. Instead,
what followed was testimony that ignored facts and focused on illogical arguments and fear-mongering. First to testify was Larry Morris, representing

the California District Attorneys Association. He noted his organization's opposition to active state parolees or probationers being allowed to serve as jurors. His arguments were two-fold. First, he suggested that a parole or probation violation would disrupt trial proceedings. Specifically, he stated: "We have proposed that no felon who is on parole be allowed to serve on a jury for the very simple reason you could literally be in the middle of a jury trial . . . you could have a person literally on a jury be violated for a parole violation during the middle of a trial for either a parole violation or probation [violation]."[2] Morris then called on a familiar refrain, intimating that those with felony criminal histories pose a danger to their fellow jurors. In particular, he stated:

> Most of these discussions, the way jury trials work, when you come in, the jury comes in and the judge almost always will tell the prospective jury, "If there are things that you wish to speak about outside the presence of a jury, please let the court know, and we will adjourn into chambers and then you can tell." Oftentimes, in a domestic violence case or a rape case, one of the jurors has been a victim himself or herself or has a close connection to it. So we would expect that some of these folks who are felons, eligible to serve, would want to discuss that in the privacy of chambers with the judge. However, none of the other jurors are going to know that they are sitting there spending weeks and possibly months next to someone who may have been convicted of a serious crime of violence. They're not going to be aware of any of that. [3]

Morris's arguments fail on two levels. First, he overlooks the near certainty that any number of jury trials in California are disrupted daily because a seated juror cannot fulfill their obligation to remain for the duration of the trial. Any number of circumstances may end a juror's tenure, from the loss of a loved one to an unavoidable accident that renders them unable to serve. That is the purpose of alternate jurors. An argument suggesting that convicted felons ought to be excluded from jury service while on active state parole or probation for fear that they may violate their supervision rings hollow and feels more like pretense than a serious objection.

Morris's second argument, the notion that convicted felons pose a threat to their fellow jurors, who would be wholly unaware of the danger they face, is simply nonsensical. Like it or not, convicted felons exist—we eat at restaurants, go to the movies, attend community meetings, join bowling leagues, and sometimes, become lawyers who must interact with non-felon clients. Such an assertion calls to mind images of Hester Prynne, implying that convicted felons ought to be readily identified and approved as "safe" by their fellow jurors before we reinstate their right to serve. But Morris's was not the most outlandish claim made in opposition to S.B. 310.

Second to testify against S.B. 310 was Ryan Sherman, with the Riverside Sherriffs' Association. In sum, Mr. Sherman stated:

> I'd like to concur with the comments made by my colleague from the District Attorneys Association and also note that proper court security requires constant monitoring of the accused, the witnesses, the employees, and all visitors. Members of the Riverside Sheriffs' Association have sworn to protect and serve all who come to court. SB 310 will make our members' job much more difficult by mixing violent felons on parole with dutiful citizens who have willingly chosen to participate in our judicial system—who recognize that our civil and criminal justice systems are not perfect—but having convicted felons and parolees serve as jurors will further undermine the public's safety and trust in our courts, and we respectfully urge a no vote.[4]

At the time Mr. Sherman made the above statement, there were no less than twenty-five convicted felons in the room, and security that day at the capital was business as usual. To suggest that allowing convicted felons to serve would necessitate more manpower and surveillance is both insulting and wildly illogical. Again, convicted felons exist and we live among those who have never been arrested. Moreover, nobody is a convicted felon until a first felony offense. Surely Mr. Sherman cannot guarantee that a non-felon-juror will not commit an offense that puts others in the court in danger? His statement is rife with stereotype and scare tactics, it employs the "criminology of the other," and it does so as a tool with which to banish those with a felony criminal history from a fundamental democratic process. The opposition's arguments against S.B. 310 were appalling and were anything but evidence-based.

Ultimately, S.B. 310 passed, though the current form of S.B. 310 looks quite different than it did originally. A few months after my testimony, S.B. 310 was amended. Those amendments now limit the scope of S.B. 310 by preserving felon-juror exclusion (1) for convicted felons under some form of community supervision and (2) permanently for those convicted of a felony criminal offense of a sexual nature.[5] Notably, the California District Attorneys Association did not oppose S.B. 310 in its current form.[6]

Surely a step forward, S.B. 310 drags California—seemingly kicking and screaming—into a more inclusive era of juror eligibility. Though, by amending the legislation to include carve-outs for convicted felons on some form of supervision or those convicted of a sexual offense, lawmakers have unfortunately lent credibility to the flawed, prejudicial arguments made by Mr. Morris, Mr. Sherman, and other opponents of S.B. 310.[7] A robust debate on S.B. 310, one that draws on facts and science, was the goal of my testimony. Clearly, that approach did not resonate with the lawmakers charged with overseeing such a debate.

THE ACTUAL THREAT: AN EMPIRICAL ANALYSIS

Given the paucity of research on felon-juror exclusion, the arguments put forth in opposition to S.B. 310 are, to a point, not surprising. Felon-juror exclusion likely conjures up appeals to emotion, in part because the topic has largely escaped critical empirical evaluation. Still, existing research makes clear that the threat posed to the jury by potential felon-jurors is nonexistent and as such, does not warrant record-based juror eligibility restriction in any form. Accordingly, for opponents of S.B. 310 and of other measures that would restore juror eligibility to convicted felons in additional jurisdictions, bad facts easily give way to speculation and hyperbole.

As demonstrated in chapters 2 and 3, the proffered justifications for felon-juror exclusion lack empirical support. Data reveal wild inconsistencies and illogicalities in both the character and inherent bias rationales. With respect to the former, jurisdictions endorse an outdated, empirically unsupportable conception of character. Along this line, many jurisdictions that exclude convicted felons from jury service allow those same convicted felons to practice law, a profession requiring "good moral character." A more empirically informed conceptualization of character acknowledges the importance of context (chapter 4), while respecting the tenets of rehabilitation and redeemability.

On the inherent bias rationale, jurisdictions again pin felon-juror exclusion to flawed premises. Convicted felons do not harbor pretrial biases that make them uniformly sympathetic to criminal defendants and antithetical toward the state. In fact, with respect to their pretrial biases, convicted felons are far from homogeneous, exhibiting substantial variability. Moreover, as a group, convicted felons harbor pretrial biases as strong as those held by law students (on the defense side) and law enforcement (on the prosecution side), two groups that jurisdictions seldom, if ever, bar from jury service.[8] For this reason, an exclusion based on supposed pretrial viewpoints is both over- and underinclusive, possibly banning exemplary jurors while doing little to protect the jury.

In line with findings in chapters 2 and 3, chapter 4 makes clear that when deliberating—a situation necessitating diligence, impartiality, and attentiveness—felon-jurors do nothing to undermine the process. In the only mock jury study to include jurors with a felony criminal history, felon-jurors performed admirably. In particular, on measures of deliberation quality, felon-jurors spoke more often (as a proportion of their jury's total deliberation time) and raised more novel case facts than did non-felon-jurors. These findings tend to demonstrate that felon-jurors do not denigrate the functionality of deliberations.

In sum, citizens with a felony criminal record appear to pose no threat the jury process. Contrary to the stated rationales for the practice, felon-jurors clearly possess the requisite character to serve and do not harbor impermissible biases that would render them unfit for service. Rather, my research tends to demonstrate that felon-jurors may actually be assets to the jury process. A closer examination of felon-jurors' contributions to mock jury deliberations, chapter 5 presented data indicating that felon-jurors approach jury service in a thoughtful, conscientious manner.

This approach ostensibly translated into a strict adherence to jury instructions and a willingness to analyze a case objectively, even in a criminal matter involving a formerly convicted defendant. Felon-jurors also demonstrated a desire and an ability to call on their criminal pasts when impartially reviewing evidence and even-handedly applying the law. In that mock jury setting, no evidence suggested a lack of character or a bias indicating felon-jurors' unfitness for jury service. Instead, felon-jurors seemed to hold the criminal defendant to a higher standard, suggesting that their experiences made them ideal jurors able to accurately decipher factual scenarios and appropriately apply the law.

For convicted felons permitted to take part in the jury process, they too reap the benefits of serving as jurors. Chapter 6 explores the possible impact of felon-juror inclusion in the only jurisdiction that per se allows convicted felons to serve—Maine. In interviews with prospective and former felon-jurors in Maine, findings reveal that inclusion likely prompts criminal desistance mechanisms, by giving convicted felons a prosocial role to fill (juror) and by helping convicted felons' to build a coherent prosocial desistance narrative. Results suggest that convicted felons strive to live up to their conception of the "ideal juror" and cite their past experiences when explaining their value as members of an adjudicative body. In this way, inclusion may help influence reentry by initiating criminal desistance processes.

Also presenting data derived from a field study in Maine, chapter 7 examines how inclusion may impact community engagement. Findings from interviews with prospective and former felon-jurors, as well as courtroom personnel (defense attorneys, prosecutors, and trial court judges), reveal that for those with a felony criminal history, inclusion represents a form of delabeling initiated by the state. Findings also suggest that courtroom personnel charged with screening felonious jurors in Maine tend to humanize those with a felony criminal conviction when making individual determinations of juror fitness. In these ways, chapter 7 tends to show that inclusion prompts meaningful community engagement by corroborating the reformation of those with a criminal conviction and then humanizing them throughout the jury selection process. This chapter lends modest support to the notion that intergroup contact—as it occurs when convicted felons are included in the jury pool—can soften the stigma of a felony criminal conviction and, in turn, prompt full, meaningful community engagement.

As legislators consider their jurisdictions' stance on felon-juror service, they must account for public sentiment. Along that line, chapter 8 presents the first comprehensive survey of public attitudes toward the inclusion of convicted felons in the jury process. Results of that survey—conducted in California—suggest that the public is relatively ambivalent about felon-juror participation. While promising, these results divide along party lines as conservatives are far less likely to support felon-juror inclusion. The type of offense committed by the prospective felon-juror also shaped public opinion, as respondents were far less likely to support the inclusion of those convicted of violent felonies. To a point, these findings were not surprising, as the public generally supports the civic reintegration of those with a felony conviction—in the context of voting. But that support is largely dependent on political ideology and crime type, findings that squarely align with opinions of felon-juror inclusion.

Taken together, the studies that comprise this book make up the bulk of the empirical literature on felon-juror exclusion. That literature, modest but growing, seems to plainly demonstrate the flaws of felon-juror exclusion policies. Convicted felons do not pose a threat to the jury. Instead, they are likely to improve the adjudicative process. Moreover, inclusion may facilitate added social benefits in the realm of criminal desistance. For these reasons, felon-juror exclusion makes little sense and is likely inhibiting the reentry efforts of those with a criminal conviction and of the jurisdictions that they call home.

POLICY IMPLICATIONS

This book clearly suggests that—as a nation—we rethink our policies with regard to felon-juror service. An overwhelming majority of jurisdictions limit, and in some instances eliminate, convicted felons' opportunities to take part in jury service. These policies run counter to decades of Supreme Court precedent opening the deliberation room to members of marginalized classes. Moreover, while policymakers and criminal justice professionals often pay homage to evidence-based principles, such principles are notoriously absent from any debate on felon-juror exclusion. Reforming policy to allow convicted felons to serve as jurors without restriction respects rehabilitative and redemptive ideologies, while honoring the tradition of the jury as a sovereign, representative body charged with delivering justice and protecting the populace from state overreach.

Pragmatically, felon-juror exclusion is an issue that can no longer be ignored. Today, millions of Americans bear the mark of a felony conviction, and in certain communities, they comprise a critical mass of citizens who ought to be eligible for jury service. Surely, if California's recent experience with S.B. 310 is any indication, reforming felon-juror exclusion laws will draw fierce opposition and demands for exceptions and carve-outs. I argue that on this policy, we ought not waiver. To do so will only embolden critics, who argue against felon-juror inclusion using time-tested tactics (chapter 8), ignoring science and embracing fear. Though legislative compromise is often appropriate, I would argue that it has no use when research and science so clearly support one policy position over the alternative.

PARTING THOUGHTS

This book takes its name from the 1957 courtroom drama *12 Angry Men*. Written by Reginald Rose, the movie was inspired by Rose's own experiences serving as a juror in a manslaughter case.[9] The star of the original film, Henry Fonda, played juror 8, the lone not-guilty vote at the start of deliberations in a New York City murder trial. The film chronicles juror 8's role in persuading his fellow jurors of the defendant's innocence. At times, the jurors' conversations become contentious and emotive. Still, juror 8 maintains his resolve, highlighting inconsistencies in the prosecution's case and ultimately changing the minds of the eleven other jurors.[10]

I chose *12 Angry Men* as the namesake of my book because I believe in Rose's depiction. The task of a jury is a serious one, requiring a faithful dedication to the truth. More so, the jury process requires a desire to hear one another out, to evaluate issues based on fact, and to compromise for the greater good—goals that we as a nation have seemingly jettisoned in recent years. I still think of the jury and jurors in much the same way they were portrayed in *12 Angry Men*. Since I saw the movie, as part of my sixth-grade social studies class, I have always conceived of the deliberation room as a place where adults interact, respectfully, to accomplish a deadly serious task no one necessarily welcomes.

Today, many likely long for a room where adults can discuss the issues of the day, understanding their gravity and approaching solutions with that in mind. In those discussions, facts should stand prominently. So too should an understanding that diversity of opinion makes us richer, not weaker or less secure. Our policies should reflect these truths; we will have a better justice system and a better nation as a result.

When I embarked on the research agenda that forms the basis of this book, I wondered if I would feel the same way about the jury process after all the data was collected, analyzed, and published. I do. More than ever, my work with felon-jurors has given me a new appreciation for our purest form of civic engagement. What I have seen in my research are good folks denied an opportunity to take part in what they still believe is vitally important. Despite their troubles with our criminal justice system, the convicted felons I have studied (myself included) still trust that ordinary citizens from all walks of life, called together in a common purpose, can find the truth when it is most obscured. They may not always get it right, but my own work suggests that they try hard and are proud of their efforts.

In our ultrapartisan world, where political affiliations can mean the end of friendships, professional relationships, and even marriages, the jury ought to give us faith in our ability to be respectful, honest, and open-minded. I sincerely hope that this book is useful, not as a persuasive piece of writing, but as an objective presentation of the facts as I found them. In that vein, I hope I performed admirably as a juror charged with impartially analyzing a policy that impacts, at this point, roughly twenty million American citizens.

EPILOGUE

You only know what you know.

—LORETTA SWIT

IN JANUARY 2020, CALIFORNIA OFFICIALLY enacted S.B. 310. In theory, the measure restores juror eligibility to many Californians who have a felony criminal conviction.[1] In practice though, counties have been slow to publicize the legislative change.

As of August 16, 2020, a survey of county websites—the most accessible and likely source of information for prospective jurors—revealed that only twenty-two of California's fifty-eight counties had provided its citizenry accurate information on the juror eligibility changes (see map 4).[2] Conversely, twenty-two counties published misleading information on S.B. 310 (many incorrectly suggesting that a restoration of civil rights is required to serve—it is not) and fourteen have made no mention of S.B. 310 or falsely reported its effect.[3] Thus, almost seven full months after S.B. 310's effective date, information about legislative changes in felon-juror exclusion policies was almost certainly not reaching those most impacted in California.

In the context of felon-voter disenfranchisement, a similar problem has long plagued reform efforts.[4] In one of the most comprehensive studies of the issue, Drucker and Barreras found that among 334 individuals under some form of criminal justice system supervision (custody, parole, and probation) in three states (New York, Ohio, and Connecticut), respondents had little knowledge about their voting rights.[5] Though all three jurisdictions permit probationers to vote and do not disenfranchise convicted felons, 50 percent of respondents did not know probationers can vote and 52.8 percent did not know if ever having a felony conviction made one ineligible to cast a ballot.[6]

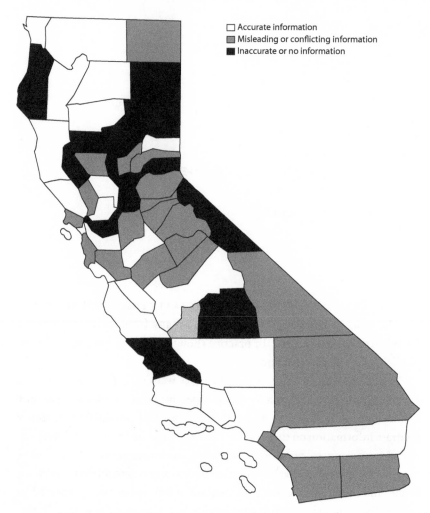

□ Accurate information
▨ Misleading or conflicting information
■ Inaccurate or no information

MAP 4. S.B. 310 county notification procedures as of August 16, 2020 (Binnall and Davis, 2020).

Perhaps more troubling, among those who had never been disenfranchised, 33.1 percent did not know if they were currently allowed to vote and 10.2 percent believed they were ineligible.[7] Overall, researchers found a stunning level of de facto disenfranchisement.

Research also suggests that government personnel are equally uninformed about eligibility. For example, Ewald found that in ten states, 37 percent of local officials "either described their state's fundamental eligibility law incorrectly, or stated that they did not know a central aspect of that law."[8] Though problematic, a lack of knowledge is not a worst-case scenario. In a study of New York county election officials, researchers discovered: "In almost half the counties in New York, including all five boroughs of New York City, officials demanded documentary proof that the person seeking to register after a felony conviction had completed his sentence. New York election statutes impose no such requirement that previously disenfranchised voters document their eligibility. Not only that, in many cases the documents county boards requested were entirely fictional."[9] To remedy this lack of information and the promulgation of misinformation, various groups have endorsed notification requirements as part of reform efforts. Today, a number of states now have such provisions.[10]

For those jurisdictions considering legislation eliminating or altering felon-juror exclusion provisions, California should serve as a cautionary tale. Notably, S.B. 310 did not require mandatory notification at the county level (those charged with administering the jury system). As a result, a crazy quilt of approaches regarding notification and implementation has taken hold, with the worst counties flatly misstating California's policy with respect to felon-jurors, some requiring documentation (a certificate of rehabilitation) not mentioned in the legislation.[11]

Though evidence on felon-voter notification requirements is mixed,[12] there is data that suggest a positive correlation between awareness and subsequent voter turnout.[13] In the case of felon-juror exclusion, as my research tends to show, those with a felony conviction welcome jury service.[14] Still, even in the face of a summons, no information or misinformation can mean juror no-shows. Given convicted felons' positive attitudes toward jury service, it is likely that mandatory, empirically informed notification requirements will increase their participation.

Research in the felon-voter context indicates that the most effective notification provisions are written in clear, concise language that both informs prospective voters of their eligibility and also encourages them to take part in the electoral process.[15] Along this line, jurisdictions weighing reform in the felon-juror context may do well to consider research on notification provisions, crafting provisions in simple, prominent language that not only informs, but also encourages citizens with a felony conviction to serve when called.[16] In California, and elsewhere, such notifications would ensure the efficacy of legislative reform.

Felon-Juror Exclusion Policies by Jurisdiction

In his 2003 article "The Exclusion of Felons from Jury Service," law professor Brian C. Kalt provides a jurisdictional breakdown of felon-juror exclusion policies. Kalt divides jurisdictions into a number of categories based on the duration of their record-based juror eligibility criteria. Specifically, Kalt classifies jurisdictions as: (1) life, (2) during sentence, (3) during supervision, (4) during incarceration, (5) hybrid (based on crime category, penal status, type of jury proceeding, and/or a term of years), (6) lifetime challenges for cause, and (7) no restriction.

Notably, some jurisdictions require the restoration of a convicted felon's civil rights prior to reinstating his or her juror eligibility. In those jurisdictions, restoration procedures can be automatic or may involve lengthy and often costly processes. Recognizing this practical distinction, Kalt classifies a jurisdiction as "life" if that jurisdiction mandates the restoration of civil rights prior to reinstating a convicted felon's juror eligibility, but has intricate restoration provisions.

Since 2003, a number of jurisdictions have altered their felon-juror exclusion policies. Updating Kalt's research, this appendix categorizes jurisdictions according to the duration of their record-based juror eligibility criteria in 2020. This appendix generally adheres to Kalt's classification scheme, but where appropriate, recategorizes jurisdictions that have modified their felon-juror exclusion policies. It classifies jurisdictions as: (1) life, (2) during sentence, (3) hybrid (based on crime category, penal status, type of jury proceedings, and/or a term of years), (4) lifetime challenges for cause, and (5) no restrictions.

Jurisdiction	Duration of Restriction	Description (Hybrid Jurisdictions)
Federal	Life[1]	
Alabama	Life[2]	
Alaska	During sentence[3]	
Arizona	Hybrid[4]	First offense—during sentence Repeat offense—life
Arkansas	Life[5]	
California	Hybrid[6]	Registered sex offenders—life All other felonies—during sentence
Colorado	Hybrid[7]	Grand juries—life Petit juries—no restriction
Connecticut	Hybrid[8]	Felony in past seven years, defendant in felony case, or during incarceration
Delaware	Life[9]	
District of Columbia	Hybrid[10]	During sentence plus ten years
Florida	Life[11]	
Georgia	Life[12]	
Hawaii	Life[13]	
Idaho	During sentence[14]	
Illinois	Lifetime challenges for cause[15]	
Indiana	During sentence[16]	
Iowa	Lifetime challenges for cause[17]	
Kansas	Hybrid[18]	Felony in past ten years
Kentucky	Life[19]	
Louisiana	Life[20]	
Maine	No exclusion[21]	
Maryland	Life[22]	
Massachusetts	Hybrid[23]	Felony in past seven years, defendant in felony case, or during incarceration
Michigan	Life[24]	
Minnesota	During sentence[25]	
Mississippi	Life[26]	
Missouri	Life[27]	
Montana	During sentence[28]	
Nebraska	Life[29]	
Nevada	Hybrid[30]	Repeat or violent offense—life First or nonviolent offense—during sentence (civil juries),

		during sentence plus six years (criminal juries)
New Hampshire	Life[31]	
New Jersey	Life[32]	
New Mexico	During sentence[33]	
New York	Life[34]	
North Carolina	During sentence[35]	
North Dakota	During sentence[36]	
Ohio	During sentence[37]	
Oklahoma	Life[38]	
Oregon	Hybrid[39]	Criminal and grand juries— during incarceration plus fifteen years Civil juries—during incarceration
Pennsylvania	Life[40]	
Rhode Island	During sentence[41]	
South Carolina	Life[42]	
South Dakota	During sentence[43]	
Tennessee	Life[44]	
Texas	Life[45]	
Utah	Life[46]	
Vermont	Life[47]	
Virginia	Life[48]	
Washington	During sentence[49]	
West Virginia	Life[50]	
Wisconsin	During sentence[51]	
Wyoming	Life[52]	

1. See 28 U.S.C. § 1865(b)(5), 2000 (disqualifying from petit and grand juries anyone who "has a charge pending against him for the commission of, or has been convicted in a State or Federal court of record of, a crime punishable by imprisonment for more than one year and his civil rights have not been restored"). Restoration of federal civil rights is not automatic, even when a state automatically restores a convicted felon's civil rights following a state criminal conviction. See, e.g., *U.S. v. Hefner*, 842 F.2d 731, 732, 1988 ("We hold that some affirmative act recognized in law must first take place to restore one's civil rights to meet the eligibility requirements of section 1865(b)(5)").

2. Ala. Code § 12-16-60(a)(4), 2020 ("A prospective juror is qualified to serve on a jury if the juror is generally reputed to be honest and intelligent and is esteemed in the community for integrity, good character and sound judgment and also . . . [h]as not lost the right to vote by conviction for any offense involving moral turpitude"); Ala. Const. Art. VIII, § 177(b), 2019 ("No person convicted of a felony involving moral turpitude, or who is mentally incompetent, shall be qualified to vote until restoration of civil and political rights or removal of disability"); *Chapman v. Gooden*, 974 So.2d 972, 2007 (the Alabama Supreme Court listing a number of crimes that the judiciary have recognized as crimes of moral turpitude including "sale of marijuana, aggravated assault, and transporting stolen vehicles across state lines"); Ala. Code § 12-16-150(3),(5), 2019 ("It is good ground for challenge of a juror by either party . . . [t]hat he has been indicted within the last 12 months for felony or an offense of the same character as that with which the defendant is charged . . . [t]hat he has been convicted of a felony"). In Alabama, restoration of civil rights is not automatic. Convicted felons must apply for and receive a specific type of pardon issued by Alabama's Board of Pardons and Parole.

(continued)

3. Alaska Stat. § 09.20.020(2), 2019 ("A person is disqualified from serving as a juror if the person . . . has been convicted of a felony for which the person has not been unconditionally discharged; unconditional discharge has the meaning given in AS 12.55.185"); Alaska Stat. § 33.30.241(b), 2019 ("A person who is convicted of a felony is disqualified from serving as a juror until the person's unconditional discharge"); Alaska Stat. § 12.55.185(18), 2019 ("'Unconditional discharge' means that a defendant is released from all disability arising under a sentence, including probation and parole").

4. Ariz. Rev. Stat. Ann. § 13–904(A)(3), 2019 ("A conviction for a felony suspends the following civil rights of the person sentenced . . . [t]he right to serve as a juror"); Ariz. Rev. Stat. Ann. § 21–201(3), 2019 ("Every juror, grand and trial, shall be at least eighteen years of age and meet the following qualifications . . . [n]ever have been convicted of a felony, unless the juror's civil rights have been restored"); Ariz. Rev. Stat. Ann. § 13–907(A), 2020 ("On final discharge, any person who has not previously been convicted of a felony shall automatically be restored any civil rights that were lost or suspended as a result of the conviction if the person pays any victim restitution imposed"). In Arizona, the restoration of repeat offenders' civil rights is not automatic. To restore juror eligibility a repeat offender must apply for and receive a recommendation for pardon from the Executive Board of Clemency and gubernatorial authorization for the pardon or must apply for and receive a restoration of rights from his or her sentencing judge no earlier than two years after unconditional discharge from imprisonment. See Ariz. Const. art. 5 § 5, 2019; Ariz. Rev. Stat. §§ 31–402A, 2020, 13–906, 2020, 13–908, 2020.

5. Ark. Code Ann. § 16–31–102(a)(4)-(5), 2019 ("The following persons are disqualified to act as grand or petit jurors. . . . Persons who have been convicted of a felony and have not been pardoned . . . [p]ersons who are: [n]ot of good character or approved integrity; [l]acking in sound judgment or reasonable information; [i]ntemperate; or [n]ot of good behavior"). In Arkansas, restoration of civil rights is not automatic. To restore juror eligibility, a convicted felon must apply for and receive a gubernatorial pardon referred by the parole board. See Ark. Const. art. VI, § 18, 2019; Ark. Code Ann. § 16–93–204(a)-(b).

6. Cal. Const. art. VII, § 8(b), 2019 ("Laws shall be made to exclude persons convicted of bribery, perjury, forgery, malfeasance in office, or other high crimes from office or serving on juries. The privilege of free suffrage shall be supported by laws regulating elections and prohibiting, under adequate penalties, all undue influence thereon from power, bribery, tumult, or other improper practice"); Cal. Civ. Pro. Code § 203(a)(10), 2020 ("All persons are eligible and qualified to be prospective trial jurors, except the following . . . [p]ersons who have been convicted of a felony and are currently on parole, postrelease community supervision, felony probation, or mandated supervision for the conviction of a felony"); Cal. Civ. Pro. Code § 203(a)(11), 2020 ("All persons are eligible and qualified to be prospective trial jurors, except the following . . . [p]ersons who are currently required to register as a sex offender pursuant to section 290 of the Penal Code based on a felony conviction").

7. Colo. Rev. Stat. § 13–71–105(3), 2019 ("A prospective grand juror shall be disqualified if he or she has previously been convicted of a felony in this state, any other state, the United States, or any territory under the jurisdiction of the United States"). Colorado petit jury juror eligibility criteria make no mention of prospective jurors with a felon conviction.

8. Conn. Gen. Stat. Ann. § 51–217(a)(2), 2019 ("A person shall be disqualified to serve as a juror if such person . . . has been convicted of a felony within the past seven years or is a defendant in a pending felony case or is in the custody of the Commissioner of Correction").

9. Del. Code Ann. Tit. 10, § 4509(b)(6), 2019 ("All persons are qualified for jury service except those who are . . . [c]onvicted felons who have not had their civil rights restored"). In Delaware, restoration of civil rights is not automatic. Felons must apply for and receive a gubernatorial pardon or a Certificate of Discharge. But only an unconditional gubernatorial pardon will restore juror eligibility and a Certificate of Discharge does not restore juror eligibility. See Del. Code Ann. tit. 11, § 4347(i), 2020; U.S. v. Ward, 648 Fed. Appx. 238, 2016 WL 1730764, 2016.

10. D.C. Code § 11–1906(b)(2)(B), 2020 ("An individual shall not be qualified to serve as a juror . . . if that individual has been convicted of a felony or has a pending felony or misdemeanor charge, except that an individual disqualified for jury service by reason of a felony conviction may qualify for jury service not less than one year after the completion of the term of incarceration, probation, or parole following appropriate certification under procedures set out in the jury system plan"); D.C. Code § 11–1904(a), 2020 ("The Board of Judges shall adopt, implement, and as necessary modify, a written jury system plan for the random selection and service of grand and petit jurors in the Superior Court consistent with the provisions of this chapter"); Jury Plan for the Superior Court of the District of Columbia § 6(f) (convicted felons are ineligible for jury service "except that individuals disqualified for jury service by reason of a felony conviction are qualified for jury service ten years after the completion

of their entire sentence, including incarceration, probation and parole, or at such time as their civil rights have been restored").

11. Fla. Stat. Ann. § 40.013(1), 2020 ("No person who is under prosecution for any crime, or who has been convicted in this state, any federal court, or any other state, territory, or country of bribery, forgery, perjury, larceny, or any other offense that is a felony in this state or which if it had been committed in this state would be a felony, unless restored to civil rights, shall be qualified to serve as a juror"); in Florida, restoration of civil rights is not automatic. Convicted felons must apply for and receive either a gubernatorial pardon (which necessitates two additional cabinet votes) or a restoration of civil rights. Restoration of civil rights is only available for certain crimes and requires that a convicted felon meet a number of conditions, not the least of which is full payment of restitution. See Fla. Stat. Ann. § 944.292 (1), 2020 ("Upon conviction of a felony as defined in s. 10, Art. X of the State Constitution, the civil rights of the person convicted shall be suspended in Florida until such rights are restored by a full pardon, conditional pardon, or restoration of civil rights granted pursuant to s. 8, Art. IV of the State Constitution"); see also Rules of Executive Clemency of Florida, Rule 9(A)(3).

12. Ga. Code Ann. § 15–12–60(c)(1), 2019 ("The following individuals shall not be eligible to serve as a grand juror . . . [a]ny individual who has been convicted of a felony in a state or federal court who has not had his or her civil rights restored"); Ga. Code Ann. § 15–12–40, 2019 ("Any person who has been convicted of a felony in a state or federal court who has not had his or her civil rights restored and any person who has been judicially determined to be mentally incompetent shall not be eligible to serve as a trial juror"); Ga. Code Ann. § 15–12–163(b)(5), 2019 ("The state or the accused may make any of the following objections to the juror . . . [t]hat the juror has been convicted of a felony in a federal court or any court of a state of the United States and the juror's civil rights have not been restored"). In Georgia, restoration of civil rights is not automatic with regards to jury service. See Judicial Council of Georgia, Administrative Office of the Courts, Georgia Jury Commissioner's Handbook 10 (2005) ("An individual who completes a felony sentence may register to vote, but cannot serve on a jury until that person has received a pardon or restoration of civil rights from the Board of Pardon and Paroles").

13. Haw. Rev. Stat. Ann. § 612–4(b)(2), 2019 ("A prospective juror is disqualified to serve as a juror if the prospective juror . . . [h]as been convicted of a felony in a state or federal court and not pardoned").

14. Idaho Code § 18–310(1), 2020 ("A sentence of custody to the Idaho state board of correction suspends all the civil rights of the person so sentenced"); Idaho Code § 18–310(2), 2020 ("Upon final discharge, a person convicted of any Idaho felony shall be restored the full rights of citizenship . . . [a]s used in this subsection, 'final discharge' means satisfactory completion of imprisonment, probation and parole as the case may be").

15. 705 Ill. Comp. Stat. 305/2(3), 2019 ("Jurors must be . . . [f]ree from all legal exception, of fair character, of approved integrity, of sound judgment"); see also *People v. Gil,* 608 N.E.2d 197, 206, 1992 ("A venireperson may be excused for cause where he or she has been previously charged with various crimes") (citing *People v. Seaman,* 561 N.E.2d 188, 200, 1990).

16. Ind. Code § 33–28–5–18(b)(5), 2020 ("A prospective juror is disqualified to serve on a jury if any of the following conditions exist . . . [t]he person has had the right to vote revoked by reason of a felony conviction and the right has not been restored"); Ind. Code § 3–7–13–4(a)(1)-(2), 2019 ("A person who is . . . [c]onvicted of a crime; and [i]mprisoned following conviction; is deprived of the right of suffrage by the general assembly"); Ind. Code § 3–7–13–4(b)(1)-(2), 2020 ("A person described in subsection (a) is ineligible to register under this article during the period that the person is . . . [i]mprisoned; or [o]therwise subject to lawful detention"). In Indiana, apart from Ind. Code § 33–28–5–18(b)(5), 2019, a convicted felon's voting rights may also be suspended under the "infamous crimes" clause of the Indiana Constitution. See Ind. Const. art. 2, §8, 2020. In such a case, a convicted felon's voting rights are not necessarily reinstated upon the expiration of a term of incarceration. See *Snyder v. King,* 958 N.E. 2d 764, 2011. In turn, since Indiana ties juror eligibility to the right to vote, if a convicted felon's voting rights are suspended under the "infamous crimes" clause of the Indiana Constitution, a convicted felon may not regain his or her juror eligibility at the end of a term of incarceration.

17. Iowa R. Crim. P. 2.18(5)(a), 2019 ("A challenge for cause may be made by the state or defendant, and must distinctly specify the facts constituting the causes thereof. It may be made for any of the following causes . . . [a] previous conviction of the juror of a felony"); Iowa R. Civ. P. 1.915(6)(a), 2019 ("A juror may be challenged by a party for any of the following causes . . . [c]onviction of a felony").

18. Kan. Stat. Ann. § 21–6613(a), 2020 ("A person who has been convicted in any state or federal court of a felony shall, by reason of such conviction, be ineligible to hold any public office under the laws of the state of Kansas, or to register as a voter or to vote in any election held under the laws of the

(continued)

state of Kansas or to serve as a juror in any civil or criminal case"); Kan. Stat. Ann. § 43–158(c), 2020 ("The following persons shall be excused from jury service... persons who within 10 years immediately preceding have been convicted of or pleaded guilty, or *nolo contendere,* to an indictment or information charging a felony"); Kan. Stat. Ann. § 22–3722, 2020 ("When an inmate has reached the end of the postrelease supervision period, the [parole] board shall issue a certificate of discharge to the releasee. Such discharge, and the discharge of an inmate who has served the inmate's term of imprisonment, shall have the effect of restoring all civil rights lost by operation of law upon commitment, and the certification of discharge shall so state").

19. Ky. Rev. Stat. Ann. § 29A.080(2)(e), 2020 ("A prospective juror is disqualified to serve on a jury if the juror... [h]as been previously convicted of a felony and has not been pardoned or received a restoration of civil rights by the Governor or other authorized person of the jurisdiction in which the person was convicted"). In Kentucky, restoration of civil rights is not automatic.

20. La. Code Crim. Proc. Ann. art. 401(A)(5), 2019 ("In order to qualify to serve as a juror, a person must... Not be under indictment for a felony nor have been convicted of a felony for which he has not been pardoned by the governor"). In Louisiana, a first-time convicted felon convicted of certain crimes automatically receives a nongubernatorial pardon after the completion of the imposed sentence. Such pardons are issued by the Board of Pardons and do not require the approval of the governor. See La. Const. art. IV, § 5(E)(1) (2018) ("[A] first offender convicted of a non-violent crime, or convicted of aggravated battery, second degree battery, aggravated assault, mingling harmful substances, aggravated criminal damage to property, purse snatching, extortion, or illegal use of weapons or dangerous instrumentalities never previously convicted of a felony shall be pardoned automatically upon completion of his sentence, without a recommendation of the Board of Pardons and without action by the governor"). See also La. Rev. Stat. Ann. § 15:572(B)-(E), 2019. Nevertheless, the Louisiana Supreme Court has noted that such a pardon does not restore a convicted felon's eligibility for jury service; noting that only a gubernatorial pardon will do so. See State v. Jacobs, 904 So.2d 82, 90–91, 2005 ("Defendant complains that convicted felons, even those receiving first offender pardons, are excluded from grand jury service... [d]efendant's argument is without merit"); State v. Kennedy, 957 S.2d 757 (Unpublished Appendix p. 3), 2007 (overturned on other grounds) ("an automatic pardon for a first felony offender under Article IV, § 5(E)(1), while restoring some privileges, does not restore the status of innocence to the convict who has merely served out his sentence as does an executive pardon granted by the governor... [a]bsent a pardon from the governor, a person convicted of a felony in Louisiana is not qualified to serve as a juror") (citing *State v. Baxter,* 357 So.2d 271, 273 [La. 1978]). Louisiana courts treat first offender pardons differently from gubernatorial pardons in several contexts. See Judge Helen Ginger Berrigan, Executive Clemency, First-Offender Pardons; Automatic Restoration of Rights, 62 La. L. Rev. 49, 2001.

21. Me. Rev. Stat. Ann. tit. 14, § 1211, 2019 ("A prospective juror is disqualified to serve on a jury if that prospective juror is not a citizen of the United States, 18 years of age and a resident of the county, or is unable to read, speak and understand the English language").

22. Md. Code Ann., Cts. and Jud. Proc. §8–103(b)(4)-(5), 2020 ("An individual is not qualified for jury service if the individual... [h]as been convicted, in a federal or State court of record, of a crime punishable by imprisonment exceeding 1 year and received a sentence of imprisonment for more than 1 year; or [h]as a charge pending, in a federal or State court of record, for a crime punishable by imprisonment exceeding 1 year"); Md. Code Ann., Cts. and Jud. Proc. §8–103(c), 2020 ("An individual qualifies for jury service notwithstanding a disqualifying conviction under subsection (b)(4) of this section if the individual is pardoned"). In Maryland, the Parole Commission investigates and advises the governor with regards to pardons, but the governor has the ultimate authority to grant or deny a pardon. See Md. Const. art. II, § 20, 2020.

23. Mass. Gen. Laws. Ann. ch. 234A, §4(7), 2019 ("Any citizen of the United States who is a resident of the judicial district or who lives within the judicial district more than fifty per cent of the time, whether or not he is registered to vote in any state or federal election, shall be qualified to serve as a grand or trial juror in such judicial district unless one of the following grounds for disqualification applies... [s]uch person has been convicted of a felony within the past seven years or is a defendant in pending felony case or is in the custody of a correctional institution").

24. Mich. Comp. Laws § 600.1307a(1)(e), 2020 ("To qualify as a juror a person shall... [n]ot have been convicted of a felony"). See also Mich. Comp. Laws § 600.1307a(5)(b) ("For purposes of this section, '[f]elony' means a violation of a penal law of this state, another state, or the United States for which the offender, upon conviction, may be punished by death or by imprisonment for more than 1 year or an offense expressly designated by law to be a felony"). In Michigan, the restoration of civil rights is not

automatic. See *U.S. v. Metzger*, 3 F.3d 756, 1993 (holding that a convicted felon's juror eligibility is not automatically restored upon expiration of the imposed sentence). A convicted felon can only restore his or her juror eligibility through gubernatorial pardon. See MCLS Const. art. V, § 14, 2018.

25. Minn. R. Crim. P., 26.02(5)(1)(2), 2020 ("A juror may be challenged for cause on these grounds ... [a] felony conviction unless the juror's civil rights have been restored"); Minn. Gen. R. Prac. 808(b) (6), 2020 ("To be qualified to serve as a juror, the prospective juror must be ... [a] person who has had their civil rights restored if they have been convicted of a felony"); Minn. Stat. Ann. §609.165(1), 2020 ("When a person has been deprived of civil rights by reason of conviction of a crime and is thereafter discharged, such discharge shall restore the person to all civil rights and to full citizenship, with full right to vote and hold office, the same as if such conviction had not taken place, and the order of discharge shall so provide"). In Minnesota, restoration of civil rights is automatic upon completion of sentence. See Minn. Stat. Ann. § 609.165(2)(2), 2020 ("The discharge may be ... upon expiration of sentence").

26. Miss. Code Ann. § 13–5–1, 2020 ("Every citizen not under the age of twenty-one years, who is either a qualified elector, or a resident freeholder of the county for more than one year, is able to read and write, and has not been convicted of an infamous crime, or the unlawful sale of intoxicating liquors within a period of five years and who is not a common gambler or habitual drunkard, is a competent juror"); Miss. Code Ann. § 1–3–19, 2020 ("The term 'infamous crime,' when used in any statute, shall mean offenses punished with death or confinement in the penitentiary"). As Kalt notes, some interpret section 13–5–1 as restoring juror eligibility to convicted felons five years after conviction. Yet, courts have held that section 13–5–1 disqualifies convicted felons from jury service regardless of the age of their conviction. See Fleming v. State, 687 So. 2d 146, 148, 1997 ("Persons convicted of 'infamous crimes' are not competent to serve on juries").

27. Mo. Rev. Stat. § 494.425(4), 2019 ("The following persons shall be disqualified from serving as a petit or grand juror ... [a]ny person who has been convicted of a felony, unless such person has been restored to his civil rights"). A second provision disqualifies convicted felons permanently. See Mo. Rev. Stat. § 561.026(3), 2019 ("Notwithstanding any other provision of law except for section 610.140, a person who is convicted ... [o]f any felony shall be forever disqualified from serving as a juror"). Yet comments on this portion of Missouri's code indicate that a convicted felon could regain juror eligibility through a pardon. See Comment to 1973 Proposed Code, Mo. Rev. Stat. § 561.026, 2019 ("Many states permit persons with felony records to serve on juries. However, the Committee decided to exclude all convicted felons from jury service [unless pardoned] in order to help maintain the integrity of the jury system"). In Missouri, the governor has final pardoning power. But prior to the governor's decision, the Missouri Board of Probation and Parole investigates each potential pardon and makes nonbinding recommendations to the governor.

28. Mont. Code Ann. § 3–15–303(2), 2019 ("A person is not competent to act as juror ... who has been convicted of malfeasance in office or any felony or other high crime"); Mont. Code Ann. § 46–18–801(2), 2019 ("Except as provided in the Montana constitution, if a person has been deprived of a civil or constitutional right by reason of conviction for an offense and the person's sentence has expired or the person has been pardoned, the person is restored to all civil rights and full citizenship, the same as if the conviction had not occurred").

29. Neb. Rev. Stat. Ann. § 25–1601(1)(f), 2021 ("Persons disqualified to serve as either grand or petit jurors are ... persons who have been convicted of a criminal offense punishable by imprisonment in a Department of Correctional Services adult correctional facility, when such conviction has not been set aside or a pardon issued"); Neb. Rev. Stat. Ann. § 29–112, 2020 ("Any person sentenced to be punished for any felony, when the sentence is not reversed or annulled, is incompetent to be a juror or to hold any office of honor, trust, or profit within this state, unless such person receives from the Board of Pardons of this state a warrant of discharge, in which case such person shall be restored to such civil rights and privileges as enumerated or limited by the Board of Pardons"). Nebraska has a similar provision relating to convicted felons not sentenced to a term of imprisonment. See Neb. Rev. Stat. § 29–112.01, 2020 ("Any person sentenced to be punished for any felony, when the sentence is other than confinement in a Department of Correctional Services adult correctional facility, shall be restored to such civil rights as enumerated or limited by the Board of Pardons upon receipt from the Board of Pardons of a warrant of discharge, which shall be issued by such board upon receiving from the sentencing court a certificate showing satisfaction of the judgment and sentence entered against such person"); Neb. Rev. Stat. Ann. § 83–1, 118 (4), 2020 ("Upon completion of the lawful requirements of the sentence, the department shall provide the parolee or committed offender with a written notice regarding his or her civil rights. The notice shall inform the parolee or committed offender that voting rights are restored two years after

(continued)

completion of the sentence. The notice shall also include information on restoring other civil rights through the pardon process, including application to and hearing by the Board of Pardons").

30. Nev. Rev. Stat. § 6.010, 2019 ("Except as otherwise provided in this section, every qualified elector of the State, whether registered or not, who has sufficient knowledge of the English language, and who has not been convicted of treason, a felony, or other infamous crime, and who is not rendered incapable by reason of physical or mental infirmity, is a qualified juror of the county in which the person resides. A person who has been convicted of a felony is not a qualified juror of the county in which the person resides until the person's civil right to serve as a juror has been restored pursuant to NRS 176A.850, 179.285, 213.090, 213.155 or 213.157"). In Nevada, as of 2003, restoration of civil rights is automatic for first time for nonviolent convicted felons, immediately restoring their right to sit on a civil jury. See Nev. Rev. Stat. § 213.157(2)(a)-(d), 2019. But Nevada holds that the right to sit on a criminal jury is restored later, "six years after the date of his or her release from prison." See Nev. Rev. Stat. § 213.157(1) (d), 2019. As of 2003, those convicted of a violent felony or multiple felonies must apply for and receive a restoration of civil rights from their sentencing court. See Nev. Rev. Stat. §§ 176A.850(4)(a)-(e), 2019, 213.090(2),(5)(b), 2019 (amended by 2011 Nevada Laws Ch. 14 [A.B. 66] to include firearm possession), 213.155(2)(a)-(d), 2019.

31. N.H. Rev. Stat. Ann. § 500-A:7-a(V), 2020 ("A juror shall not have been convicted of any felony unless the conviction has been annulled"). In New Hampshire, the annulment of a criminal record is not automatic. Depending on the conviction type, only certain convicted felons qualify for annulment. See N.H. Rev. Stat. Ann. § 651:5 (I)-(XVII), 2019; see also N.H. Rev. Stat. Ann. § 651:5 (I), 2020 ("Conviction and sentence of any person may be annulled by the sentencing court at any time in response to a petition for annulment which is timely brought in accordance with the provisions of this section if in the opinion of the court, the annulment will assist in the petitioner's rehabilitation and will be consistent with the public welfare. The court may grant or deny an annulment without a hearing, unless a hearing is requested by the petitioner").

32. N.J. Stat. Ann. § 2B:20-1(e), 2019 ("Every person summoned as a juror . . . shall not have been convicted of any indictable offense under the laws of this State, another state, or the United States").

33. N.M. Stat. Ann. § 38-5-1(B), 2020 ("A person who was convicted of a felony and who meets all other requirements for eligibility may be summoned for jury service if the person has successfully completed all conditions of the sentence imposed for the felony, including conditions for probation or parole").

34. N.Y. Jud. § 510(3), 2020 ("In order to qualify as a juror a person must . . . [n]ot have been convicted of a felony").

35. N.C. Gen. Stat. § 9-3, 2020 (amended by 2011 North Carolina Laws S.L. 2011-42 [H.B. 234]) ("All persons are qualified to serve as jurors and to be included on the master jury list who are citizens of the State and residents of the county, who have not served as jurors during the preceding two years or who have not served a full term of service as grand jurors during the preceding six years, who are 18 years of age or over, who are physically and mentally competent, who can understand the English language, who have not been convicted of a felony or pleaded guilty or nolo contendere to an indictment charging a felony [or if convicted of a felony or having pleaded guilty or nolo contendere to an indictment charging a felony have had their citizenship restored pursuant to law], and who have not been adjudged *non compos mentis*. Persons not qualified under this section are subject to challenge for cause"). In North Carolina, civil rights are automatically restored upon completion of a sentence. See N.C. Gen. Stat. § 13-1(1), 2020 ("Any person convicted of a crime, whereby the rights of citizenship are forfeited, shall have such rights automatically restored upon the occurrence of any one of the following conditions . . . [t]he unconditional discharge of an inmate, of a probationer, or of a parolee by the agency of the State having jurisdiction of that person or of a defendant under a suspended sentence by the court"). Civil rights are also restored as the result of an unconditional pardon or the satisfaction of all conditions of a conditional pardon. See N.C. Gen. Stat. § 13-1(2)-(3), 2020 ("Any person convicted of a crime, whereby the rights of citizenship are forfeited, shall have such rights automatically restored upon the occurrence of any one of the following conditions . . . [t]he unconditional pardon of the offender . . . [t]he satisfaction by the offender of all conditions of a conditional pardon").

36. N.D. Cent. Code § 27-09.1-08(2)(e), 2019 ("A prospective juror is disqualified to serve on a jury if the prospective juror . . . [h]as lost the right to vote because of imprisonment in the penitentiary [section 12.1-33-01] or conviction of a criminal offense which by special provision of law disqualified the prospective juror for such service"). See also N.D. Cent. Code § 12.1-33-01(1)(a), 2019 ("A person sentenced for a felony to a term of imprisonment, during the term of actual incarceration under such sentence, may not . . . [v]ote in an election").

37. Ohio Rev. Code Ann. § 2961.01 (A)(1), 2020 ("A person who pleads guilty to a felony under the laws of this or any other state or the United States and whose plea is accepted by the court or a person against whom a verdict or finding of guilt for committing a felony under any law of that type is returned, unless the plea, verdict, or finding is reversed or annulled, is incompetent to be an elector or juror or to hold an office of honor, trust, or profit"). In Ohio, restoration of juror eligibility is automatic after a term of imprisonment that does not include postrelease supervision, upon receipt of a final release from parole authorities, or at the expiration of community control sanctions in cases where imprisonment was not mandated. See Ohio Rev. Code Ann. § 2967.16(C)(1)(a)-(c), 2020 ("The following prisoners or person shall be restored to the rights and privileges forfeited by a conviction ... [a] prisoner who has served the entire prison term that comprises or is part of the prisoner's sentence and has not been placed under any post-release control sanctions ... [a] prisoner who has been granted a final release or termination of post-release control by the adult parole authority ... [a] person who has completed the period of a community control sanction or combination of community control sanctions ..., that was imposed by the sentencing court"). In Ohio, a pardon will also restore a convicted felon's civil rights. See Ohio Rev. Code Ann. § 2961.01 (A)(2), 2020 ("The full pardon of a person who under division (A) (1) of this section is incompetent to be an elector or juror or to hold an office of honor, trust, or profit restores the rights and privileges so forfeited under division (A)(1) of this section").

38. Okl. Stat. Ann. tit. 38 § 28(C)(5), 2020 ("Persons who are not qualified to serve as jurors are ... [p]ersons who have been convicted of any felony or who have served a term of imprisonment in any penitentiary, state or federal, for the commission of a felony; provided, any such citizen convicted, who has been fully restored to his or her civil rights, shall be eligible to serve as a juror"). In Oklahoma, restoration of civil rights is not automatic. Convicted felons must apply for and receive a gubernatorial pardon. Aside from a gubernatorial pardon, Oklahoma law has no mechanism for fully restoring the civil rights of convicted felons. See Okl. Stat. Ann. tit. 22 § 658(1), 2020 ("General causes of challenges are ... a conviction for felony"). See also *Jackson v. State*, Okla. Crim. App., 964 P.2d 875, 1998.

39. In Oregon a felony conviction entails the loss of civil rights—including the right to serve as a juror—but the state provides for the automatic restoration of those rights at the expiration of the term of imprisonment. See Or. Rev. Stat. Ann. § 137.281 (1)(a), (3)(c), 2020 ("In any felony case, when the defendant is sentenced to a term of incarceration, the defendant is deprived of all rights and privileges described in subsection (3) of this section from the date of sentencing until ... [t]he defendant is released from incarceration ... [t]he rights and privileges of which a person may be deprived under this section are ... acting as a juror"). Nevertheless, Oregon disqualifies convicted felons and certain misdemeanants from criminal grand/petit juries even after the automatic restoration of civil rights. See Or. Rev. Stat. Ann. §10.030 (3)(a)(E)-(F), 2020 ("Any person is eligible to act as a grand juror, or as a juror in a criminal trial, unless the person ... [h]as been convicted of a felony or served a felony sentence within the 15 years immediately preceding the date the person is required to report for jury service; or ... [h] as been convicted of a misdemeanor involving violence or dishonesty, or has served a misdemeanor sentence based on a misdemeanor involving violence or dishonesty, within the five years immediately preceding the date the person is required to report for jury service"). Oregon's Constitution authorizes this disqualification of felons and certain misdemeanants from criminal grand/petit juries for a term of years. See Or. Const. art. I, § 45 (1)(a)-(b), 2020 ("In all grand juries and in all prosecutions for crimes tried to a jury, the jury shall be composed of persons who have not been convicted: ... [o]f a felony or served a felony sentence within the 15 years immediately preceding the date the persons are required to report for jury duty; or ... [o]f a misdemeanor involving violence or dishonesty or served a sentence for a misdemeanor involving violence or dishonesty within the five years immediately preceding the date the persons are required to report for jury duty"). Recently, however, Oregon's Committee on the Judiciary has sponsored a bill that would reduce the waiting period for felons to ten years. See 2011 OR S.J.R. 31 (NS), February 17, 2011. Convicted felons and all misdemeanants are allowed to serve on civil juries upon expiration of a term of imprisonment. See Or. Rev. Stat. Ann. §10.030 (2)(d), 2020 ("Any person is eligible to act as a juror in a civil trial unless the person ... [h]as had rights and privileges withdrawn and not restored under ORS 137.281").

40. 42 Pa. Cons. Stat. Ann. § 4502(a)(3), 2020 ("Every citizen of this Commonwealth who is of the required minimum age for voting for State or local officials and who resides in the county shall be qualified to serve as a juror therein unless such citizen ... has been convicted of a crime punishable by imprisonment for more than one year and has not been granted a pardon or amnesty therefore"). In Pennsylvania, only a gubernatorial pardon will restore a convicted felon's juror eligibility. See Pa. Const. art. 4, § 9(a), 2020 ("In all criminal cases except impeachment the Governor shall have power to remit fines and forfeitures, to grant reprieves, commutation of sentences and pardons; but no pardon

(continued)

shall be granted, nor sentence commuted, except on the recommendation in writing of a majority of the Board of Pardons").

41. R.I. Gen. Laws § 9–9-1.1(c), 2020 ("No person convicted of a felony shall be allowed to serve as a juror, until completion of such felon's sentence, served or suspended, and of parole or probation regardless of a nolo contendere plea").

42. S.C. Code Ann. § 14–7-810(1), 2019 ("In addition to any other provision of law, no person is qualified to serve as a juror in any court in this State if . . . [h]e has been convicted in a state or federal court of record of a crime punishable by imprisonment for more than one year and his civil rights have not been restored by pardon or amnesty"). In South Carolina, only a grant of clemency from the Probation, Parole, and Pardon Board will restore a convicted felon's juror eligibility. The governor cannot grant clemency; he or she can only grant reprieves and death sentence commutations. See S.C. Code Ann. §§ 24–21–910, 2019, 24–21–920, 2019.

43. S.D. Codified Laws § 16–13–10, 2020 ("Any person who has been convicted of a felony unless restored to civil rights is not eligible to serve as a juror"). S.D. Codified Laws § 23A-27–35, 2020 ("A sentence of imprisonment in the state penitentiary for any term suspends the right of the person so sentenced, to hold public office, to become a candidate for public office, and to serve on a jury. Any such person so sentenced forfeits all public offices and all private trusts, authority, or power during the term of such imprisonment"). South Dakota restores a convicted felon's civil rights—including juror eligibility—by way of a final order of discharge. That order is typically granted once a convicted felon has completed his or her entire sentence—including any term of supervised release. See S.D. Codified Laws § 24–15A-6, 2020 ("The department shall establish the sentence discharge date for each inmate based on the total sentence length, minus court ordered jail time credit. The total sentence length is the sum of imprisonment time and any suspended time . . . Each inmate shall be under the jurisdiction of the department, either incarcerated or under parole release or a combination, for the entire term of the inmate's total sentence length unless the board grants an early final discharge . . . , a partial early final discharge . . . , the court modifies the sentence . . . , or the sentence is commuted"). See also S.D. Codified Laws § 24–15A-7, 2020 ("Whenever any inmate has been discharged under the provisions of § 24–15A-6, the inmate shall at the time of discharge be considered as restored to the full rights of citizenship. At the time of the discharge of any inmate under the provisions of this chapter, the inmate shall receive from the secretary a certificate stating that the inmate has been restored to the full rights of a citizen. If an inmate is on parole at the time the inmate becomes eligible for discharge, the secretary shall issue a like certificate, which is due notice that the inmate has been restored to the full rights of a citizen"). In rare instances, a convicted felon is eligible for early final discharge. See S.D. Codified Laws §§ 24–15A-8, 2020, 24–15A-8.1, 2020.

44. Tenn. Code Ann. § 22–1-102(a)-(b), 2020 ("The following persons are incompetent to act as jurors . . . [p]ersons convicted of a felony or any other infamous offense in a court of competent jurisdiction; or . . . [p]ersons convicted of perjury or subornation of perjury"). In Tennessee, restoration of civil rights is not automatic. Convicted felons must apply for and receive a restoration of rights. See Tenn. Code Ann. § 40–29–101(a)-(c), 2020 ("Persons rendered infamous or deprived of the rights of citizenship by the judgment of any state or federal court may have their full rights of citizenship restored by the circuit court . . . [t]hose pardoned, if the pardon does restore full rights of citizenship, may petition for restoration immediately after the pardon; provided, that a court shall not have jurisdiction to alter, delete or render void special conditions of a pardon pertaining to the right of suffrage . . . [t]hose convicted of an infamous crime may petition for restoration upon the expiration of the maximum sentence imposed for the infamous crime").

45. Tex. Gov't Code Ann. § 62.102(8), 2019 ("A person is disqualified to serve as a petit juror unless the person . . . has not been convicted of misdemeanor theft or a felony"). Tex. Code Crim. Proc. Ann. art. 19.08(7), 2021 ("A person may be selected or serve as a grand juror only if the person . . . has not been convicted of misdemeanor theft or a felony"). Tex. Code Crim. Proc. Ann. art. 35.16(a)(2), 2019 ("A challenge for cause is an objection made to a particular juror, alleging some fact which renders the juror incapable or unfit to serve on the jury. A challenge for cause may be made by either the state or the defense for any one of the following reasons . . . [t]hat the juror has been convicted of misdemeanor theft or a felony"). In Texas the restoration of civil rights is not automatic. Convicted felons must apply for and receive a restoration of civil rights, which involves a host of procedural requirements. See Tex. Code Crim. Proc. Ann. art. § 48.05(a)-(h), 2019. As Kalt notes, however, while Texas gives courts the power to restore a convicted felon's civil rights following the successful completion of community supervision, courts have disagreed about the power of this provision. See *People v. Vasquez*, 25 Cal.4th 1225, 2001.

46. Utah Code Ann. § 78B-1-105(2), 2020 ("A person who has been convicted of a felony which has not been expunged is not competent to serve as a juror"). In Utah, only certain felons are eligible for

expungement and they must adhere to many procedural requirements in order to obtain expungement. See Utah Code Ann. § 77-40-105, 2020.

47. Vt. Stat. Ann. tit. 4, § 962(a)(5), 2020 ("A person shall be qualified for jury service if the person ... has not served a term of imprisonment in this State after conviction of a felony"). In Vermont, restoration of civil rights is not automatic. To restore civil rights, convicted felons must apply for and receive a gubernatorial pardon. See V.S.A. Const. § 20, 2019 ("The Governor shall have power to grant pardons and remit fines"). See also Vt. Stat. Ann. tit. 28, § 453, 2019 ("On request of the Governor, the Board shall act as an advisory board to assist or act for him or her in investigating or hearing matters pertaining to pardons, and may make recommendations to him or her regarding such matters").

48. Va. Code Ann. § 8.01-338(2), 2019 ("The following persons shall be disqualified from serving as jurors ... [p]ersons convicted of treason or a felony"). In Virginia, restoration of civil rights is not automatic. To restore civil rights, convicted felons must apply for and receive a gubernatorial pardon. See Va. Const. art. 5, § 12, 2019 ("The Governor shall have power to remit fines and penalties under such rules and regulations as may be prescribed by law; to grant reprieves and pardons after conviction except when the prosecution has been carried on by the House of Delegates; to remove political disabilities consequent upon conviction for offenses committed prior or subsequent to the adoption of this Constitution; and to commute capital punishment").

49. Wash. Rev. Code Ann. § 2.36.070(5), 2020 ("A person shall be competent to serve as a juror in the state of Washington unless that person ... [h]as been convicted of a felony and has not had his or her civil rights restored"). See Wash. Rev. Code Ann. § 9.94A.637(9), 2020 (restoring rights automatically at the completion of the sentence). Note that the restoration of rights is contingent upon a convicted felon satisfying all financial obligations unless he or she can show that repayment will cause "manifest hardship." See Wash. Rev. Code. Ann. § 10.73.160(4), 2020.

50. W. Va. Code § 52-1-8(b)(6), 2020 ("A prospective juror is disqualified to serve on a jury if the prospective juror ... [h]as been convicted of perjury, false swearing or any crime punishable by imprisonment in excess of one year under the applicable law of this state, another state or the United States"). In West Virginia, courts have held that all felonies are infamous offenses because they are "punishable by imprisonment in the state penitentiary." See *State v. Bongalis,* 378 S.E.2d 449, 455, 1989. In West Virginia, while convicted felons' right to vote is automatically restored upon completion of the imposed sentence, federal courts have held that juror eligibility requires a certificate of discharge or gubernatorial pardon. There is no statutory mechanism for convicted felons to apply for or receive a certificate of discharge restoring their civil rights. See Berger v. U.S., 867 F.Supp. 424, 430, 1994 ("Nor has the disqualification ever been interpreted by the West Virginia Supreme Court of Appeals as ceasing to exist after the convicted person has served his sentence"); *U.S. v. Morrell,* 61 F.3d 279, 1995 ("We agree with the reasoning of the *Berger* court that the civil rights of a convicted felon cannot be restored as an operation of West Virginia law upon the completion of a prison sentence because W. Va. Code § 52-1-8 disqualifies convicted felons from jury service"). Instead, a convicted felon must apply for and receive a gubernatorial pardon. See W. Va. Const. art 7, § 11, 2019; W. Va. Code § 5-1-16, 2020.

51. Wis. Stat. Ann. § 756.02, 2020 ("Every resident of the area served by a circuit court who is at least 18 years of age, a U.S. citizen and able to understand the English language is qualified to serve as a juror in that circuit unless that resident has been convicted of a felony and has not had his or her civil rights restored"). In Wisconsin, civil rights are restored at the expiration of the imposed sentence. See Wis. Stat. Ann. § 304.078(2), 2020 ("Except as provided in sub. (3), every person who is convicted of a crime obtains a restoration of his or her civil rights by serving out his or her term of imprisonment or otherwise satisfying his or her sentence"). See also Wis. Stat. Ann. § 304.078(3), 2020 ("If a person is disqualified from voting under s. 6.03(1)(b), his or her right to vote is restored when he or she completes the term of imprisonment or probation for the crime that led to the disqualification").

52. Wyo. Stat. Ann. § 1-11-102, 2019 ("A person who has been convicted of any felony is disqualified to act as a juror unless his conviction is reversed or annulled, he receives a pardon or his rights are restored pursuant to W.S. 7-13-105[a]"). Wyo. Stat. Ann. § 6-10-106(a)(i)-(iii), 2019 ("A person convicted of a felony is incompetent to be an elector or juror or to hold any office of honor, trust or profit within this state, unless ... [h]is conviction is reversed or annulled; ... [h]e receives a pardon; ... [h]is rights are restored pursuant to W.S. 7-13-105[a]"). In Wyoming, civil rights are not automatically restored. Instead, to restore his or her civil rights, a convicted felon must apply for and receive a gubernatorial pardon or a statutory restoration of rights under Wyo. Stat. Ann. § 7-13-105(a), 2019. See Wyo. Const. Art 4, § 5, 2018 (discussing pardons); see also Wyo. Stat. Ann. § 7-13-105(a)(i-ii), 2019 ("Upon receipt of a written application, the governor may issue to a person convicted of a felony under the laws of a state or the United States a certificate which restores the rights lost pursuant to W.S. 6-10-106 when ... [h]is term of sentence expires; or ... [h]e satisfactorily completes a probation period").

Convicted Felons' Access to the Legal Profession vs. Juror Eligibility

Jurisdiction*	Moral Character and Fitness Determination Approach	Duration of Felon-Juror Exclusion
Federal	Presumptive disqualification	Lifetime ban
Alabama	Presumptive disqualification	Lifetime ban
Alaska	Presumptive disqualification	During sentence
Arizona	Presumptive disqualification	Lifetime ban (repeat offense) During sentence (first offense)
Arkansas	Presumptive disqualification	Lifetime ban
California	Presumptive disqualification	Registered sex offenders—life All other felonies—during sentence
Colorado	Presumptive disqualification	Lifetime ban (grand juries) No exclusion (petit juries)
Connecticut	Presumptive disqualification	Felony in past seven years, defendant in felony case, or during incarceration
Delaware	Presumptive disqualification	Lifetime ban
District of Columbia	Presumptive disqualification	During sentence plus ten years
Florida	Per se disqualification (unless civil rights restored)	Lifetime ban
Georgia	Presumptive disqualification	Lifetime ban
Hawaii	Presumptive disqualification	Lifetime ban
Idaho	Per se disqualification (if felony conviction would otherwise result in disbarment)	During sentence
Illinois	Presumptive disqualification	Challengeable for cause (for life)
Indiana	Per se disqualification	During sentence
Iowa	Presumptive disqualification	Challengeable for cause (for life)

(continued)

Jurisdiction*	Moral Character and Fitness Determination Approach	Duration of Felon-Juror Exclusion
Kansas	Presumptive disqualification	Felony in past ten years
Kentucky	Presumptive disqualification	Lifetime ban
Louisiana	Presumptive disqualification	Lifetime ban
Maine	Presumptive disqualification	No exclusion
Maryland	Presumptive disqualification	Lifetime ban
Massachusetts	Presumptive disqualification	Felony in past seven years, defendant in felony case, or during incarceration
Michigan	Presumptive disqualification	Lifetime ban
Minnesota	Presumptive disqualification	During sentence
Mississippi	Per se disqualification (for all felonies except manslaughter and violations of the Internal Revenue Code)	Lifetime ban
Missouri	Per se disqualification (until five years has passed from completion of sentence)	Lifetime ban
Montana	Presumptive disqualification	During sentence
Nebraska	Presumptive disqualification	Lifetime ban
Nevada	Presumptive disqualification	Repeat or violent offense—life
		First or nonviolent offense—during sentence (civil juries)
		During sentence plus six years (criminal juries)
New Hampshire	Presumptive disqualification	Lifetime ban
New Jersey	Per se disqualification (until completion of sentence)	Lifetime ban
New Mexico	Presumptive disqualification	During sentence
New York	Presumptive disqualification	Lifetime ban
North Carolina	Presumptive disqualification	During sentence
North Dakota	Presumptive disqualification	During sentence
Ohio	Per se disqualification (until five years has passed since completion of sentence)	During sentence
Oklahoma	Presumptive disqualification	Lifetime ban
Oregon	Per se disqualification (if felony conviction would otherwise result in disbarment)	During incarceration plus fifteen years (criminal and grand juries)
		During incarceration (civil juries)
Pennsylvania	Presumptive disqualification	Lifetime ban
Rhode Island	Presumptive disqualification	During sentence
South Carolina	Presumptive disqualification	Lifetime ban
South Dakota	Presumptive disqualification	During sentence

Tennessee	Presumptive disqualification	Lifetime ban
Texas	Per se disqualification (until five years has passed since completion of sentence or conviction is reversed or pardoned)	Lifetime ban
Utah	Per se disqualification (until completion of sentence)	Lifetime ban
Vermont	Presumptive disqualification	Lifetime ban
Virginia	Presumptive disqualification	Lifetime ban
Washington	Presumptive disqualification	During sentence
West Virginia	Presumptive disqualification	Lifetime ban
Wisconsin	Presumptive disqualification	During sentence
Wyoming	Presumptive disqualification	Lifetime ban

* In jurisdictions listed in bold, an individual with a felony criminal conviction may be permitted to practice law but is forever barred from jury service.

Juror Eligibility Criteria: Convicted Felons vs. Law Enforcement Personnel

Jurisdiction	Convicted Felons (Exclusion Type)	Law Enforcement Disqualified
Federal	Life	Yes[1]
Alabama	Life	No[2]
Alaska	During sentence	No[3]
Arizona	Hybrid	No[4]
Arkansas	Life	No[5]
California	Hybrid	Yes[6]
Colorado	Hybrid	Yes[7]
Connecticut	Hybrid	No[8]
Delaware	Life	No[9]
District of Colombia	Hybrid	No[10]
Florida	Life	Yes[11]
Georgia	Life	No[12]
Hawaii	Life	Yes[13]
Idaho	During sentence	No[14]
Illinois	Lifetime for cause	No[15]
Indiana	During sentence	Yes (criminal only)[16]
Iowa	Lifetime for cause	No[17]
Kansas	Hybrid	Yes[18]
Kentucky	Life	No[19]
Louisiana	Life	No[20]
Maine	No exclusion	No[21]
Maryland	Life	No[22]
Massachusetts	Hybrid	No[23]
Michigan	Life	No[24]
Minnesota	During sentence	No[25]
Mississippi	Life	No[26]
Missouri	Life	No[27]

(continued)

Jurisdiction	Convicted Felons (Exclusion Type)	Law Enforcement (Disqualified)
Montana	During sentence	No[28]
Nebraska	Life	Yes[29]
Nevada	Hybrid	Yes[30]
New Hampshire	Life	No[31]
New Jersey	Life	No[32]
New Mexico	During sentence	No[33]
New York	Life	No[34]
North Carolina	During sentence	No[35]
North Dakota	During sentence	No[36]
Ohio	During sentence	No[37]
Oklahoma	Life	Yes (criminal only)[38]
Oregon	Hybrid	No[39]
Pennsylvania	Life	No[40]
Rhode Island	During sentence	Yes[41]
South Carolina	Life	Yes[42]
South Dakota	During sentence	No[43]
Tennessee	Life	No[44]
Texas	Life	No[45]
Utah	Life	No[46]
Vermont	Life	No[47]
Virginia	Life	Yes[48]
Washington	During sentence	No[49]
West Virginia	Life	No[50]
Wisconsin	During sentence	No[51]
Wyoming	Life	No (exempted)[52]

1. See 28 U.S.C. § 1863(b)(6), 2000.
2. Ala. Code § 12–16–150.
3. Alaska Stat. § 09.20.020 (2002).
4. Ariz. Rev. Stat. Ann. § 21–211.
5. Ark. Code Ann. § 16–31–101.
6. Cal. Civ. Pro. Code § 219(b)(1).
7. Colo. Rev. Stat. § 13–71–104(4).
8. Conn. Gen. Stat. Ann. § 51–217(a) (7).
9. Del. Code Ann. Tit. 10, § 4509(b)(6).
10. D.C. Code § 11–1906(b)(2)(B)(3).
11. Fla. Stat. Ann. § 40.013(2)(b).
12. Ga. Code Ann. § 15–12–1.1(a)(1).
13. Haw. Rev. Stat. Ann. § 612–6.
14. Idaho. Rev. Stat. Ann. § 2–212.
15. 705 Ill. Comp. Stat. Ann. 305/2(a).
16. Ind. Code Ann. § 34–5(h).
17. Iowa Code Ann. § 607A.5.
18. Kan. Stat. Ann. § 43–159(b).
19. Ky. Rev. Stat. Ann. § 29A.090; see also *Reid v. Com.* (Ky. App. 1983) 659 S.W.2d 217.
20. La. Code Crim. Proc. Ann. art. 401(A–B).

21. Me. Rev. Stat. Ann. tit. 14, § 1211.
22. Md. Code Ann., Cts. & Jud. Proc. § 8–306.
23. Mass. Gen. Laws. Ann. ch. 234, § 4. See also *Com v. Silva* (2009) 918 N.E.2d 65.
24. Mich. Comp. Laws § 600.1307(a).
25. Minn. Gen. R. Prac. 808(b); see also Minn. Gen. R. Prac. 810.
26. Miss. Code Ann. § 13–5-1.
27. Mo. Rev. Stat. § 494.425; see also *State v. Cole* (Sup. 2002) 71 S.W.3d 163.
28. Mont. Code Ann. § 3–15–301; see also Mont. Code Ann. § 3–15–303.
29. Neb. Rev. Stat. § 25–1601(c–d).
30. Nev. Rev. Stat. § 6.020; see also NRS 617. 135.
31. N.H. Rev. Stat. Ann. § 500-A:7-a.
32. N.J. Stat. Ann. § 2B:20–1; see also State v. Reynolds, 124 N.J. 559, 592 A.2d 194 (1991).
33. N.M. Stat. Ann. § 38–5-1(A).
34. N.Y. Jud. § 510; see also *People v. Noakes* (1 Dept. 2008) 57 A.D.3d 280, 869 N.Y.S.2d 65.
35. N.C. Gen. Stat. § 9–3 (amended by 2011 North Carolina Laws S.L. 2011–42 [H.B. 234]).
36. N.D. Cent. Code § 27–09.1–08(2).
37. Ohio Rev. Code Ann. TJS-4.
38. Okl. Stat. Ann. tit. 38 § 28(C)(3)(D).
39. Or. Rev. Stat. Ann. §10.030(2).
40. 42 Pa. Cons. Stat. Ann. § 4502(a).
41. R.I. Gen. Laws § 9–9-3.
42. S.C. Code Ann. § 14–7-820.
43. S.D. Codified Laws § 16–13–10.
44. Tenn. Code Ann. § 22–1-101.
45. Tex. Gov't Code Ann. § 62.102.
46. Utah Code Ann. § 78B-1–105; see also Utah Code Ann. § 78B-1–108.
47. Vt. Stat. Ann. tit. 4, § 962.
48. Va. Code Ann. § 8.01–341(7).
49. Wash. Rev. Code Ann. § 2.36.070.
50. W. Va. Code § 52–1-8(a).
51. Wis. Stat. Ann. § 756.02.
52. Wyo. Stat. Ann. § 1–11–103.

NOTES

INTRODUCTION

1. See appendix B; see also Binnall, 2010b.

2. See Dwyer, 2002.

3. See Galanter, 2004, p. 459 (focusing on the federal civil jury trial and noting that between 1962 and 2002, the number of cases disposed of by a jury verdict dropped from 11.5 percent to 1.8 percent). See also Ostrom, Strickland, and Hanna-ford-Agor, 2004, p. 764 (noting that between 1976 and 2002, the number of criminal jury trials at the state level dropped by 15 percent). See also Anderson, 2010; Bennett, Downie, and Zervos, 2004; Burns, 2013; Dwyer, 2002; Galanter, 2005, Kravitz, 2005; Langbein, 2012; Young, 2006.

4. See Young, 2006, p. 74.

5. Conrad Jr. and Clements, 2018, p. 163.

6. See Petersen, 2020. See also Kellough and Wortley, 2002, p. 200 (In their study of detainees, one participant lamented, "the overcrowding... not enough beds ... the only way to avoid it is to plead and get it over with quickly"). The "trial tax" is a measure of extra punishment imposed on a criminal defendant who chooses to go to trial. The trial tax is a tool used by prosecutors as leverage in plea negotiations. See Johnson, 2019, p. 314 ("Defendants convicted at trial consistently receive harsher punishments than defendants who plead guilty. Estimates of the trial tax vary but typically involve two- to six-fold increases in the odds of imprisonment with 15–60 percent longer sentence lengths").

7. Young, 2006, p. 76.

8. See Conrad Jr. and Clements, 2018.

9. See Conrad Jr. and Clements, 2018 (detailing a host of other consequences associated with the loss of the jury, including a loss of transparency in criminal trials, the stunting of new case law, the erosion of trial skills among judges and attorneys, and defendants loss of the ability to present their case to tribunal).

10. See Gastil et al., 2012; Gastil and Weiser, 2006; Cutler and Hughes, 2001; Freie, 1997; Shuman and Hamilton, 1992; Finkel, 1985; Barber, 1984; Durand, Bearden, and Gustafson, 1978; Allen, 1977; Richert, 1977; Pabst Jr., Munsterman, and Mount, 1977; Pateman, 1970. See also Consolini, 1992, p. 186. In her innovative dissertation research, Consolini found that jurors, especially first-time trial jurors, experienced feeling "more politically efficacious and community-oriented following jury service."

11. See Gastil et al., 2008; Gastil, Dees, and Weiser, 2002.

12. See Gastil et al., 2008; Gastil, Dees, and Weiser, 2002.

13. See Gastil et al., 2002; Finkel, 1985; Consolini, 1992.

14. Gastil et al., 2008, p. 364.

15. See Gastil et al., 2008, p. 364. Discussing the benefits of jury service, Gastil et al. explain, "organizers of orchestrated deliberative events should ensure broad participation and make special efforts to include underrepresented populations ... beyond the general ethical imperative of inclusion that is essential to democracy, our data suggest that these populations might benefit the most from the deliberative experience." See also Fung, 2005.

16. See Putnam, 2000.

17. Putnam, 2002, p. 42.

18. Putnam, 2002, p. 64.

19. Tocqueville, 1969, p. 275.

20. Petersilia, 2003; Travis, 2005.

21. Ewald, 2016. See also Vuolo, Lageson, and Uggen, 2017 (for a discussion of the removal of occupational licensing barriers).

22. Stoll and Bushway, 2008.

23. Pager, 2003; 2007.

24. Ewald, 2016; Logan, 2006.

25. See Silva, 2015 (for a review of the literature).

26. See Thatcher, 2008.

27. Gonnerman, 2004, p. 186.

28. See Fox, 2015; 2016. See also Bazemore and Erbe, 2003.

29. See McNeill, 2014; Horan, 2015.

30. See Collateral Consequences Resource Center, 2020.

31. See U.S. Department of Housing and Urban Development, 2016.

32. See Sentencing Project, 2020.

33. Many scholars view criminal desistance as a process that involves three stages: primary criminal desistance, secondary criminal desistance, and tertiary criminal desistance. Tertiary criminal desistance implicates the concept of social capital. See Fox, 2016, p. 69 ("Tertiary desistance refers to the more cemented state of desistance that results from a genuine sense of belonging, or integration into a pro-social community").

34. Brand, 1994, p. 522.

35. See, e.g., Cal. Civ. Proc. Code § 203 (2020).

1. See Shannon et al., 2017; see also Pager, 2007; Alexander, 2012 (suggesting that this disturbing normalization of a felony criminal record is arguably the direct result of the United States' experiment with mass incarceration, an experiment that has disproportionately impacted the African-American community); see also Shannon et al., 2017, p. 1,807 (noting that 23 percent of African-American adults and nearly 33 percent of African-American adult men have been convicted of a felony in the United States); see also Enns et al., 2019 (noting that 45 percent of Americans have had an immediate family member incarcerated).

2. See Owens and Smith, 2012; Ewald, 2012; Mele and Miller, 2005; Pager, 2003; Love and Kuzma, 1997.

3. American Bar Association, 2004, p. 1 (defining collateral sanction as "a legal penalty, disability or disadvantage, however denominated, that is imposed on a person automatically upon that person's conviction for a felony, misdemeanor or other offense, even if it is not included in the sentence" and defining a discretionary disqualification as "a penalty, disability or disadvantage, however denominated, that a civil court, administrative agency, or official is authorized but not required to impose on a person convicted of an offense on grounds related to the conviction").

4. See Pinard, 2010; Chiricos et al., 2007; Bushway, Stoll, and Weiman, 2007; Bontrager, Bales, and Chiricos, 2005; Travis and Visher, 2005; O'Brien, 2001.

5. Petersilia, 2003, p. 106.

6. See Ewald, 2017; Chin, 2017.

7. See Carey, 2004; Landau, 2002.

8. See Aukerman, 2005.

9. See Hirsch, 2002.

10. See Schneider, 2002.

11. See Ackelsberg and Hirsch, 2002.

12. See Bernstein-Baker and Hohenstein, 2002.

13. Wheelock, 2005, pp. 83–84 ("Civic restrictions refer to those that impede, infringe, or deny or deny civic duties and responsibilities afforded to other adult citizens. Among this class of restrictions are the loss of voting rights, restrictions on jury service, and exclusion from running for public office").

14. See Binnall, 2009.

15. The literature on felon-voter disenfranchisement is extensive, for reviews see Holloway, 2014; Pettus, 2013; Manza and Uggen, 2006.

16. Binnall, 2010a, p. 534 (in the past I have described felon-juror exclusion as "the last acceptable form of civic banishment").

17. See U.S. Const. Amend. VI.

18. Villiers, 2010, p. 71; see also Howe, 1995.

19. See *Reynolds v. United States,* 1878; *United States v. Wood,* 1936; *Irvin v. Dowd,* 1961; see also Abramson, 1994.

20. See *Morgan v. Illinois,* 1992; *Holland v. Illinois,* 1990; see also Cammack, 1995.

21. *Wainwright v. Witt,* 1985, p. 423; see also *Logan v. United States,* 1892; *Lockhart v. McCree,* 1986.

22. See Abramson, 1994; Ellis and Diamond, 2003.

23. See Brand, 1994.

24. See *Strauder v. West Virginia,* 1880.

25. See U.S. Const. Amend. XIV.

26. See *Norris v. Alabama,* 1935; *Hale v. Kentucky,* 1938; *Pierre v. Louisiana,* 1939; *Patton v. Mississippi,* 1947; *Avery v. Georgia,* 1953.

27. See *Smith v. Texas,* 1940.

28. *Smith v. Texas,* 1940, p. 129.

29. *Smith v. Texas,* 1940, p. 130; emphasis added.

30. See *Glasser v. United States,* 1942.

31. *Glasser v. United States,* 1942, pp. 82–83.

32. *Glasser v. United States,* 1942, p. 86; emphasis added.

33. See *Thiel v. Southern Pacific Railroad Company,* 1946.

34. See *Thiel v. Southern Pacific Railroad Company,* 1946.

35. *Thiel v. Southern Pacific Railroad Company,* 1946, p. 220.

36. See *Ballard v. United States,* 1946.

37. See *Ballard v. United States,* 1946.

38. *Ballard v. United States,* 1946, pp. 193–94; emphasis added.

39. 28 U.S.C. § 1861, 2000.

40. 28 U.S.C. § 1861, 2000.

41. *Taylor v. Louisiana,* 1975, p. 529.

42. See Abramson, 1994.

43. See Kalt, 2003; Binnall, 2014; see also appendix A.

44. See Grant et al., 1970; Itzkowitz and Oldak, 1973.

45. See Damaska, 1968.

46. See Grant et al., 1970.

47. See Damaska, 1968.

48. See Grant et al., 1970.

49. See Richards, 1902.

50. See Grant et al., 1970.

51. See Grant et al., 1970.

52. Grant et al., 1970, p. 950.

53. See Kalt, 2003.

54. See Kalt, 2003; Ewald and Smith, 2008; Ewald, 2002.

55. See Kalt, 2003.

56. The current version of the Civil Rights Act of 1875 states, "No citizen possessing all other qualifications which are or may be prescribed by law shall be disqualified for service as grand or petit juror in any court of the United States, or of any State on account of race, color, or previous condition of servitude" (18 U.S.C.A. § 243, 2000).

57. See Klarman, 1998.

58. See Kalt, 2003.

59. See Cammack, 1995; *Smith v. Texas*, 1940.

60. See *Glasser v. United States,* 1942; *United States v. Ballard,* 1946; *Peters v. Kiff,* 1972; *Taylor v. Louisiana,* 1975; see also Zuklie, 1996, for a review.

61. 28 U.S.C. § 1861, 2000.

62. See Kalt, 2003.

63. See Travis, 2005; Keyssar, 2009.

64. Kalt, 2003, p. 189.

65. See Kalt, 2003; Love, 2007.

66. See Kalt, 2003; Binnall, 2014. See also appendix A, noting that permanent exclusion jurisdictions at the time of publiction are Federal, Alabama, Arkansas, Delaware, Florida, Georgia, Hawaii, Kentucky, Louisiana, Maryland, Michigan, Mississippi, Missouri, Nebraska, New Hampshire, New Jersey, New York, Oklahoma, Pennsylvania, South Carolina, Tennessee, Texas, Utah, Vermont, Virginia, West Virginia, and Wyoming. Immediately prior to the publication of this book, California altered its juror eligibility criteria, moving it from a permanent exclusion jurisdiction to a hybrid jurisdiction, as the state now allows convicted felons to serve unless they are (1) on active state supervision, or (2) have been convicted of a sexual offense requiring registration, See Cal. Civ. Proc. Code § 203, 2020.

67. See Kalt, 2003; Binnall, 2014. See also appendix A, noting that completion of sentence jurisdictions at the time of publication are Alaska, Idaho, Indiana, Minnesota, Montana, New Mexico, North Carolina, North Dakota, Ohio, Rhode Island, South Dakota, Washington, and Wisconsin.

68. See Kalt, 2003; Binnall, 2014. See also appendix A, noting that hybrid jurisdictions at the time of publication are Arizona, California, Colorado, Connecticut, District of Columbia, Kansas, Massachusetts, Nevada, and Oregon.

69. See D.C. Code § 11–1906(b)(2)(B), 2018; see also Colo. Rev. Stat. § 13–71–105(3), 2018.

70. See Kalt, 2003; Binnall, 2014. See also appendix A, noting that lifetime challenge for cause jurisdictions at the time of publication are Illinois and Iowa.

71. Maine's juror eligibility statute makes no mention of the criminal histories of prospective jurors. See 14 M.R.S.A. § 1211, 2012 ("A prospective juror is disqualified to serve on a jury if that prospective juror is not a citizen of the United States, 18 years of age and a resident of the county, or is unable to read, speak and understand the English language").

72. Ariz. Rev. Stat. § 13–912(A), 2018.

73. Nev. Rev. Stat. § 213.157(2)(a)-(e), 2018.

74. Colo. Rev. Stat. § 13–71–105(3), 2018.

75. Or. Rev. Stat. § 10.030(3)(a)(E)-(F), 2017.

76. See, e.g., Cal. Civ. Proc. Code § 203 (a)(5), 2019 (making no mention of crime type or litigation type, "All persons are eligible and qualified to be prospective trial jurors, except the following: . . . Persons who have been convicted of malfeasance in office or a felony, and whose civil rights have not been restored").

77. See Chung, 2017. Forty-eight states, the District of Columbia, and the federal government place some restriction on a convicted felon's voting eligibility. Of those

jurisdictions, three exclude convicted felons from the electorate permanently (Iowa, Kentucky, Virginia). In fourteen states and the District of Columbia, convicted felons are barred from voting while in prison (District of Columbia, Hawaii, Illinois, Indiana, Maryland, Massachusetts, Michigan, Montana, New Hampshire, North Dakota, Ohio, Oregon, Pennsylvania, Rhode Island, Utah). In twenty-three states they are disqualified until the completion of their sentence, including any period of probation and/or parole (Alaska, Arkansas, California, Colorado, Connecticut, Florida, Georgia, Idaho, Kansas, Louisiana, Minnesota, Missouri, New Jersey, New Mexico, New York, North Carolina, Oklahoma, South Carolina, South Dakota, Texas, Washington, West Virginia, Wisconsin). Eight states impose some postsentence restriction on felon voting contingent upon charge category and/or a term of years (Alabama, Arizona, Delaware, Mississippi, Nebraska, Nevada, Tennessee, Wyoming). And in the remaining two states (Maine and Vermont), convicted felons never lose the right to vote and may cast an absentee ballot while incarcerated.

78. See Kalt, 2003, n. 329 (characterizing jury service as "the right 'generally hardest to regain' for felons" and as "the 'most restricted right' of felons") (citing Office of the Pardon Attorney, U.S. Dep't of Justice, 1996, p. 3; Olivares, Burton Jr., and Cullen, 1996, p. 15).

79. See Kalt, 2003; Binnall, 2014. See also appendix A.

80. See Chung, 2017 (Iowa, Kentucky, Virginia).

81. Felon-juror exclusion is also a common practice internationally, much more common than felon-voter disenfranchisement. See Manarin, 2019; Citizens Advice Scotland, 2020 (United Kingdom); Australian Government, 2020 (Australia).

82. In the context of voting, the same protectionist justifications exist. See *Washington v. State,* 1884, p. 585 ("It is quite common also to deny the right of suffrage, in the various American States, to such as have been convicted of infamous crimes. The manifest purpose is to preserve the purity of the ballot box, which is the only sure foundation of republican liberty, and which needs protection against the invasion of corruption, just as much as against that of ignorance, incapacity, or tyranny. The evil infection of the one is not more fatal than that of the other. The presumption is, that one rendered infamous by conviction of felony, or other base offense indicative of great moral turpitude, is unfit to exercise the privilege of suffrage, or to hold office, upon terms of equality with freemen who are clothed by the State with the toga of political citizenship. It is proper, therefore, that this class should be denied a right, the exercise of which might sometimes hazard the welfare of communities, if not that of the State itself, at least in close political contests. The exclusion must for this reason be adjudged a mere disqualification, imposed for protection, and not for punishment—withholding an honorable privilege, and not denying a personal right or attribute of personal liberty") (internal citations omitted); see also Manza and Uggen, 2006. In the context of running for office, exclusions are again based on protective principles. See Snyder, 1988; Steinacker, 2003; *Texas Supporters of Workers v. Strake,* 1981, p. 153 ("The State has a valid interest in ensuring that the rules of its society are made by those who have not shown an unwillingness to abide by those rules").

83. See Kalt, 2003, p. 74 (noting, "felon exclusion is meant to define and protect juries rather than to punish or degrade felons").

84. See *United States v. Barry,* 1995; *R.R.E. v. Glenn,* 1994; *United States v. Arce,* 1993; *Rector v. State,* 1983; *United States v. Foxworth,* 1979; *People ex rel. Hannon v. Ryan,* 1970.

85. Kalt, 2003, p. 74.

86. See, e.g., State of Oregon Special Election Voters' Pamphlet, 1999.

87. See Kalt, 2003.

88. *People ex rel. Hannon v. Ryan,* 1970, p. 712.

89. *Rector v. State,* 1983, p. 395.

90. Kalt, 2003; Binnall, 2014, 2018b.

91. *People v. Miller,* 2008; *Companioni Jr. v. City of Tampa,* 2007.

92. *State v. Baxter,* 1978, p. 275.

93. *United States v. Greene,* 1993, p. 796.

94. Kalt, 2003, p. 105; see also Butler, 2010 (discussing nullification as a tool for confronting unjust, racially biased laws).

95. *Rubio v. The Superior Court of San Joaquin County,* 1979, p. 101.

96. See *Green v. Board of Elections City of New York,* 1967, p. 451 (noting, "A man who breaks the laws he has authorized his agent to make for his own governance could fairly have been thought to have abandoned the right to participate in further administering the compact. On a less theoretical plane, it can scarcely be deemed unreasonable for a state to decide that perpetrators of serious crimes shall not take part in electing the legislators who make the laws, the executives who enforce these, the prosecutors who must try them for further violations, or the judges who are to consider their cases").

97. Pettus, 2013, p. 127.

98. Ewald, 2002, p. 1,074; see also n. 117 (Ewald further notes, "Locke's view has clear connections with the older concept of 'civil death.' As one authority writes, the principle behind medieval outlawry in Scandinavia was that 'whoever would not recognize the rights of others, should not himself enjoy any'") (citing Ludwig von Bar et al., 1916, p. 134).

99. Kalt, 2003, pp. 71, 70–101 (discussing "all of the legal arguments against felon exclusion that have been presented, as well as some plausible ones that have not been raised").

100. *Carter v. Jury Commission of Greene County,* 1970, p. 332.

101. See Buchwalter, 2000; Kalt, 2003; Binnall, 2009.

102. *Shows v. State,* 1972; *United States v. Foxworth,* 1979; *State v. Brown,* 1975; *Rubio v. The Superior Court of San Joaquin County,* 1979; *United States v. Barry,* 1995; *Carle v. United States,* 1998; *United States v. Best,* 2002; *State v. Compton,* 2002.

103. *Taylor v. Louisiana,* 1975; Const. Amend. VI.

104. *Holland v. Illinois,* 1990, pp. 480–81.

105. *Strauder v. West Virginia,* 1880; *Thiel v. Southern Pacific Railway,* 1946; *United States v. Ballard,* 1946.

106. See *Duren v. Missouri,* 1979.

107. *Duren v. Missouri,* 1979, p. 364.

108. *Duren v. Missouri,* 1979, p. 367.

109. *Duren v. Missouri,* 1979, pp. 367–68.

110. See *Rubio v. The Superior Court of San Joaquin County,* 1979.

111. Kalt, 2003, p. 82.

112. Kalt, 2003, p. 85; see also *Lockhart v. McCree,* 1986.

113. Kalt, 2003, pp. 86–87.

114. See Kalt, 2003.

115. Kalt, 2003, p. 86 (discussing the failure of cross-section challenges to felon-juror exclusion statutes and noting, "other considerations seem to be added to the legal standard sub rosa"); see also Kalt, 2003, p. 76 ("If . . . the cross-section standard had continued to mean what it did at its inception—that exclusion should be an individualized matter—then felon exclusion would face much more serious scrutiny").

116. Kalt, 2003, p. 85, notes that in *United States v. Barry,* 1995, *United States v. Greene,* 1993, and *Carle v. United States,* 1998, the court performed this analysis in the context of prospective jurors with *pending* felony criminal charges and ultimately authorized exclusion.

117. See *Rubio v. The Superior Court of San Joaquin County,* 1979; *United States v. Greene,* 1993; *United States v. Arce,* 1993; Const. Amend. XIV.

118. *United States v. Conant,* 2000.

119. *Hilliard v. Ferguson,* 1994; Aukerman, 2005.

120. Geiger, 2006, p. 1,192.

121. Geiger, 2006, p. 1,192.

122. See *United States v. Carolene Products Co.,* 1938; see also Aukerman, 2005, p. 19 ("It is a throwaway line in many judicial opinions that record-based laws are subject only to rational basis review, a standard which, as typically applied, is highly deferential to legislative judgments").

123. See Issacharoff, Karlan, and Pildes, 2002; Saxonhouse, 2004; see also Geiger, 2006, p. 1,192 (discussing the classification of convicted felons as a constitutionally protected class and noting that the current constitutional framework has allowed lawmakers to "pile burden after unexamined burden onto a class that merits heightened scrutiny").

124. Aukerman, 2005, p. 19 and n. 2 (providing an exhaustive list of cases in which courts denied constitutional protection for those with a criminal record on the grounds that they did not constitute a suspect class); see also Geiger, 2006.

125. Tocqueville, 1969, p. 273 ("The jury system as understood in America seems to me as direct and extreme a consequence of the dogma of the sovereignty of the people as universal suffrage. They are both equally powerful means of making the majority prevail"); see also Breyer, 2005, p. 15 (describing "active liberty" as "a sharing of a nation's sovereign authority among its people. Sovereignty involves the legitimacy of a governmental action. And a sharing of sovereign authority suggests several kinds of connection between that legitimacy and the people").

126. See Amar, 1995; Underwood, 1992; see also Young, 2006, p. 69 ("The most stunning and successful experiment in direct popular sovereignty in all history is the American jury").

127. Letters from a Federal Farmer XV, 1981, p. 149 ("It is true, the laws are made by the legislature; but the judges and juries, in their interpretations, and in directing the execution of them, have a very extensive influence for preserving or destroying liberty, and for changing the nature of the government"); see also Maryland Farmer IV, 1981, pp. 19–20 (noting, "those usurpations, which silently undermine the spirit of liberty, under the sanction of law, are more dangerous than direct and open legislative attacks").

128. *Powers v. Ohio,* 1991, p. 407 ("Indeed, with the exception of voting, for most citizens the honor and privilege of jury duty is their most significant opportunity to participate in the democratic process"); see also *Edmonson v. Leesville Concrete Company Inc.,* 1991, p. 624 ("The jury exercises the power of the court and of the government that confers the court's jurisdiction. As we noted in *Powers,* the jury system performs the critical governmental functions of guarding the rights of litigants and "ensur[ing] continued acceptance of the laws by all of the people") (citing *Powers v. Ohio,* 1991, p. 407).

129. See Zahariadis, 2016; McCombs, Shaw, and Weaver, 2014; Denham, 2010; McCombs and Shaw, 1972; McCombs, 2005; Protess and McCombs, 1991.

130. See Scheufele, 2000; Wolfe, Jones, and Baumgartner, 2013.

131. See Birkland, 1998, 2004.

132. See Birkland, 2004.

133. See Wolfe, Jones, and Baumgartner, 2013, p. 181 ("Coverage may be fleeting, thus hindering sustained attention by the public or government ... [o]r coverage may be explosive and the issue type attractive enough to sustain media attention long after the problem is solved or subsides ... [i]n effect, issue attention becomes institutionalized").

134. See Wolfe, Jones, and Baumgartner, 2013; Entman, 1989.

135. See Palazzolo and Moscardelli, 2006; Birkland, 1998.

136. See Uggen and Manza, 2005.

137. See Mann, 2001.

138. See Sanburn, 2018.

139. See Zeisel, 1972; Lilly, 2001.

140. See Young, 2006.

141. See Young, 2006.

142. Binnall, 2010a, p. 535.

143. See Palazzolo and Moscardelli, 2006.

144. See Rade, Desmarais, and Mitchell, 2016.

145. See Uggen and Manza, 2002.

146. See Vozzella, 2017.

147. See Washington Post Editorial Board, 2013.

148. See Orlando Sentinel Editorial Board, 2018.

149. See Orlando Sentinel Editorial Board, 2018.

150. See Lerner, 2018.

151. See Kam, 2018.

152. See Kam, 2018. But see Totenberg, 2020; *Raysor v. Desantis*, 2020 (refusing to stay an Eleventh Circuit order interpreting Florida's felon-voter reinstatement measure as requiring full payment of court costs and fines prior to reinstatement).

153. See Cal. Civ. Proc. Code § 203; see also Blankenship, 2019.

154. See Mahoney, 2019.

155. See Rosenberg, 2019.

156. See Stole, 2019.

157. See Rosenberg, 2019.

158. See California Assembly Bill 535, 2018.

159. See Los Angeles Times Editorial Board, 2017.

160. A Google Trends search using the timeframe 2004–18 for "felon voting" and "felon jury" reveal huge disparities in the number of searches done on each topic. Though we attempted several search terms for felon-juror exclusion, the insignificant number of searches did not register in the tally. For "felon voting," spikes in searches occur prior to each election cycle in fall 2004, 2008, 2012, and 2016. Consistent with agenda setting theory, searches for "felon voting" spike during election cycles because the election serves as a focusing event. An additional Google News search for media coverage yielded similar results. For the timeframe January 1, 2000–June 1, 2018, the terms "felon voting" and "felon jury," resulted in 1,130 articles and 4 articles respectively. Again, though we attempted several search terms in an attempt to capture as many articles as possible on felon-juror exclusion, the most we could capture was 4.

161. See Acevedo and Krueger, 2004.

162. See Boatright, 1999; see also Hannaford-Agor and Munsterman, 2006, p. 21 (noting that most people view jury service as "a waste of [their] time and taxpayer monies, a burden to be avoided if at all possible, and if not, to be dispensed with as quickly and with as little effort as possible").

163. See Panagopoulos, 2010.

164. See Rebein, Schwartz, and Silverman, 2003; Losh, Wasserman, and Wasserman, 2000.

165. See Kalt, 2003, p. 119 ("One might ask whether excluding a person from jury service is really a penalty, or if instead it is actually something of a reward ... [e]xcluding felons is perfectly sensible under such an understanding").

166. See Kalt, 2003.

167. See Kalt, 2003.

168. See Binnall, 2008; 2009; 2010a; 2010b; 2010c; 2018a; 2018b; 2018c; 2018d; 2019; Segal, 2010; Scott, 2018; Nodes, 2019.

169. See Wheelock, 2012.

170. See Wheelock, 2012; see also chapter 2.

171. See Wheelock, 2012; see also chapter 2.

172. Hans and Vidmar, 1986, p. 5.

173. See Vidmar and Hans, 2007.

174. See Klarman, 1998; 2004.

175. See Wheelock, 2012.

176. See *Strauder v. West Virginia*, 1880.

177. Klarman, 1998, p. 377 ("While the Court reaffirmed *Strauder* on numerous occasions, these decisions left southern state courts free to exclude blacks entirely from juries").

178. Klarman, 1998, p. 377.

179. See *Williams v. Mississippi*, 170 U.S. 213 (1898).

180. See Kalt, 2003.

181. See Klarman, 1998, p. 377 ("The fact that no blacks had served on juries in a particular county for decades, notwithstanding the presence of hundreds of qualified black voters, was ruled insufficient to overcome the jury commissioners' denial of discriminatory motive").

182. See Wheelock, 2012.

CHAPTER 2. ROTTEN TO THE CORE?

1. See Kalt, 2003; Binnall, 2014.

2. *United States v. Barry*, 1995, p. 1,273.

3. Kalt, 2003, p. 74 ("Courts have been less clear as to whether the threat that felons pose to jury probity stems from their degraded status or from their actual characteristics").

4. Kalt, 2003, p. 102.

5. Kalt, 2003, pp. 102, 104 (labeling this argument the "taint" argument).

6. See Rhode, 2019 (for an in-depth discussion of character).

7. Doris, 2002, p. 1.

8. Doris, 2002, p. 1.

9. The empirical challenge to conventional or traditional views (views assumed by virtue ethicists) of character is sometimes termed the Harman-Doris thesis. See Harman, 1999, 2000; Doris, 2002.

10. The Harman-Doris thesis has garnered a response from Aristotelian virtue ethicists who argue that the thesis goes too far. See Flanagan, 2009; Kamtekar, 2004; Sreenivasan, 2002; see also Upton, 2009; Rhode, 2018 (for a review of the debate).

11. Kaye, 2008, p. 647.

12. Doris, 2002, p. 18.

13. Doris, 2002, p. 5 (commenting "talk of character is a 'thick' discourse, intermingling evaluative and descriptive elements") (citing Williams, 1985, pp. 128–31, 140–45).

14. Yankah, 2004, p. 1,028 (citing Aristotle, 1941, p. § 1114a). See also Gardner, 1998, p. 577 (explaining this position by stating that "cowardly actions add up to . . . cowardice").

15. Yankah, 2004, p. 1,028.

16. Doris, 2002, p. 20.

17. Doris, 2002, p. 20.

18. Doris, 2002, pp. 22–23 (defining globalism as a theory that "construe[s] personality as more or less coherent and integrated with reliable, relatively situation-resistant, behavioral implications").

19. Doris, 2002, p. 23.

20. Doris, 2002, p. 23 (discussing consistency and stating, "character and personality traits are reliably manifested in trait-relevant behavior across a diversity of trait-relevant eliciting conditions that may vary widely in their conduciveness to the manifestation of the trait in question").

21. Doris, 2002, p. 23.

22. Doris, 2002, p. 23 (discussing evaluative integration and stating, "in a given character or personality the occurrence of a trait with a particular evaluative valence is probabilistically related to the occurrence of other traits with similar evaluative valences").

23. See Rhode, 2018, p. 1,029 ("In the early half of the twentieth century, the prevailing view among psychologists was that individuals had stable internal traits that could predict their conduct in divergent situations").

24. Doris, 2002, p. 1 (noting that the traditional "conception of character is both venerable and appealing, but it is also deeply problematic."); see also Harman, 2009.

25. Doris, 2002, p. 6.

26. Doris, 2002, p. 6.

27. Doris, 2002, p. 26 (further arguing that conventional conceptualizations of character do not fully explain "the striking variability of behavior with situational variation").

28. Kaye, 2008, p. 639.

29. Kaye, 2008, p. 639 ("Because we are so vulnerable to situational influences, our characters cannot be as consistent as we generally imagine they are. . . . The story of my act shifts from being a story about me to being a story about my surroundings, so that my acts belong, in some significant way, to forces beyond myself").

30. Kaye, 2008, p. 639.

31. See Milgram, 1963; 1973; Zimbardo et al., 1971.

32. See Milgram, 1974.

33. See Milgram, 1963.

34. See Milgram, 1963.

35. Haney and Zimbardo, 1998, p. 710.

36. Haney and Zimbardo, 1998, p. 709.

37. Haney, Banks, and Zimbardo, 1973, p. 80.

38. Lapsley, 2017, p. 172; see also Alfano, 2013.

39. See Harman, 2003, 2009.

40. See Kalt, 2003; Binnall, 2014; see also appendix A.

41. See Kalt, 2003; Binnall, 2014; see also appendix A. See, e.g., D.C. Code § 11–1906(b)(2)(B) ("An individual shall not be qualified to serve as a juror . . . if that individual has been convicted of a felony or has a pending felony or misdemeanor

charge, except that an individual disqualified for jury service by reason of a felony conviction may qualify for jury service not less than one year after the completion of the term of incarceration, probation, or parole following appropriate certification under procedures set out in the jury system plan"). See also Jury Plan for the Superior Court of the District of Columbia, 2013, § 7(f) (convicted felons are ineligible for jury service "except that individuals disqualified for jury service by reason of a felony conviction are qualified for jury service ten years after the completion of their entire sentence, including incarceration, probation and parole, or at such time as their civil rights have been restored").

42. Kalt, 2003, p. 162; see also *State v. Neal,* 1989.

43. See Fed. R. Evidence § 404(a)–(b).

44. See Fed. R. Evidence § 404(b).

45. See Fed. R. Evidence § 404(a). See also Fed. R. Evidence § 609 (limiting the admissibility of evidence of prior criminal acts for the purposes of impeachment "only when the conviction required the proof of [or in the case of a guilty plea, the admission of] an act of dishonesty or false statement").

46. Kalt, 2003, p. 159 (discussing jurisdictions that disqualify misdemeanants from jury service and noting that "most do not, or else simply equate infamous crimes with felonies). See also Roberts, 2013, p. 597 (suggesting that "statutory provisions in thirteen states make those with certain misdemeanor convictions vulnerable to disqualification"; those states are Alabama, California, Connecticut, Florida, Illinois, Maryland, Mississippi, Montana, New Jersey, Oregon, Tennessee, Texas, and West Virginia).

47. Kalt, 2003, pp. 102–3.

48. Hannaford-Agor and Munsterman, 2006, p. 25 (describing voir dire as "the jury selection phase" where "the focus shifts abruptly from general presumptions about individuals' ethical capacity to intense attention on the individual and his or her ability to be fair and impartial in the context of a specific trial").

49. See Howe, 2006; Hans and Vidmar, 1986; Ellsworth and Reifman, 2000.

50. Kalt, 2003, p. 167 (noting, "states that rely on the voir dire process to screen every other juror should consider why they lack confidence in that process when the would-be juror is a felon").

51. Coady and O'Neill, 1990, p. 261 (noting that some, like Niccolò Machiavelli, hold that "the political imperatives are themselves part of morality and their clashing with more normal moral demands produces a crisis within the moral order"). See also Coady and O'Neill, 1990, p. 260 ("For a man who wishes to profess goodness at all times will come to ruin among so many who are not good. Hence it is necessary for a prince who wishes to maintain his position to learn how not to be good, and to use this knowledge or not use it according to necessity") (citing Machiavelli, 1984, p. 52).

52. See Binnall, 2010b.

53. Ratcliff, 2000, p. 487 (characterizing the moral character and fitness determination as "the unknown requirement for admission to the bar" and noting that "while it is true that most entering law students know that at some point in the future they will be required to prove their knowledge on the bar exam, many of these

students do not realize that they will also have to prove the fitness of their character before being admitted to the practice of law").

54. Arnold Jr., 1997, p. 63 ("Every jurisdiction requires graduating law students to meet high standards of moral character before they can be admitted to the bar and given a license to practice law") (citing Gillers, 1995, p. 624). See also Swisher, 2008, p. 1043 ("Every state requires applicants to prove good moral character before admission to the bar"). See also National Conference of Bar Examiners and American Bar Association Section of Legal Education and Admissions to the Bar, Comprehensive Guide to Bar Admission Requirement, 2020.

55. Rhode, 1985, p. 516 (pointing out that there is a "low incidence of applications denied on character grounds").

56. DeVito, 2008, p. 158 ("Applicants with criminal acts in their past often face a heightened burden of proof of good moral character"). See also Arnold Jr., 1997, p. 63 (stating, "for students with records of prior unlawful conduct the application process can become particularly troublesome. Applicants with incidents of unlawful conduct in their past can find the road toward bar admission confusing and unpredictable"). See also Aviram, 2019.

57. Committee of Bar Examiners, Office of Admissions, State Bar of California, Application for Determination of Moral Character, 2020. See also Stone, 1995, p. 331 (presenting the results of a 1995 survey of all but two states conducted "in order to determine the type of questions asked for the purpose of screening out persons who bar committees believed were not morally fit or mentally stable to practice law in their state").

58. Stone, 1995, p. 332 (noting that bar examiners often solicit an applicant's "armed forces discharge, marital status, [and] financial condition").

59. Stone, 1995 p. 342 (noting that when an applicant has a felony on their criminal record, a bar examiner normally "seeks details of an applicant's criminal behavior, including: a. a description of the charge; b. the date the charge was made; c. the name, address, and telephone number of each person or entity initiating or bringing the charge; d. the name, address, and telephone number of each attorney you retained to assist you in defending the charge; e. the reason why the charges were brought against you; f. the final disposition of the charge; and, g. copies of the disposition order of the tribunal sufficient to describe the substantive resolution of the proceeding").

60. Carr, 1995, p. 378 (noting, "almost all of the states and the District of Columbia adopted rules guiding bar admission committees in their determination to allow or deny an applicant with a prior felony conviction the opportunity to practice law").

61. Carr, 1995, p. 374 (describing the per se disqualification approach as "the historical approach, whereby individuals with prior criminal records are permanently disqualified from applying for admission to state bars").

62. Carr, 1995, p. 380; see also Arnold Jr., 1997.

63. Carr, 1995, pp. 381–83; see also Binnall, 2010b.

64. The ten jurisdictions that per se disqualify convicted felons from the bar either permanently or temporarily are Florida, Idaho, Indiana, Mississippi, Missouri, New Jersey, Ohio, Oregon, Texas, and Utah.

65. The five jurisdictions that effectively per se exclude convicted felons from the bar permanently are Florida (requires the restoration of civil rights, which is nonautomatic), Indiana (permanently excludes those convicted of a felony for life), Idaho and Oregon (permanently exclude those convicted of a felony that would otherwise result in disbarment), and Mississippi (permanently excludes those convicted of any felony besides manslaughter and violations of the Internal Revenue Code). See also Binnall, 2010b.

66. The five jurisdictions that per se exclude convicted felons from the bar temporarily are Missouri, Ohio, and Texas (until five years after completion of sentence), New Jersey and Utah (until completion of sentence). See also Binnall, 2010b..

67. Graniere and McHugh, 2008, p. 243.

68. Carr, 1995, p. 381 (describing this view by stating, "some crimes, if unpardoned, remain always as a blot on the applicant's character and prevent admission to the bar").

69. Carr, 1995, p. 374.

70. For the purposes of this discussion, presumptive disqualification jurisdictions include those jurisdictions that per se exclude convicted felons from the bar for an automatically expiring time period. Because such per se exclusions are only temporary, they do not represent permanent banishment from the practice of law. See Binnall, 2010b; see also Rhode et al., 2016.

71. Ritter, 2002, p. 15 ("In the course of its investigation, an ethics committee may invite an applicant to an administrative hearing—purportedly informational in character").

72. Arnold Jr., 1997, p. 87. See also National Conference of Bar Examiners and American Bar Association Section of Legal Education and Admissions to the Bar, Comprehensive Guide to Bar Admission Requirement, 2020, p. viii ("The bar examining authority may appropriately place on the applicant the burden of producing information").

73. In re King, 2006, p. 889 ("'In the case of extremely damning past misconduct, a showing of rehabilitation may be virtually impossible to make'") (quoting In re Matthews, 1983, p. 176). See also Graniere and McHugh, 2008, p. 231 (stating, "'where serious or criminal misconduct is involved, positive inferences about the applicant's moral character are difficult to draw, and negative character inferences are stronger and more reasonable'") (quoting Blum, 2005, p. 49).

74. In re Cason, 1982, p. 522.

75. Graniere and McHugh, 2008, pp. 236, 239.

76. Graniere and McHugh, 2008, p. 223. See also National Conference of Bar Examiners and American Bar Association Section of Legal Education and Admissions to the Bar, Comprehensive Guide to Bar Admission Requirement, 2020, p. ix (listing the suggested factors to be used in assessing rehabilitation).

77. See Arnold Jr., 1997, pp. 73, 75 (noting critiques of the per se disqualification and the presumptive disqualification frameworks, and stating, respectively "the presumption made by the ABA and state bars that prior unlawful conduct by a bar applicant is predictive of future unlawful conduct or misbehavior as a lawyer has

been criticized and remains unproven" and "the flexibility for which the presumptive disqualification approach receives support is accompanied by a level of vagueness, which can undermine some of its benefits and leave applicants with a record of unlawful conduct vulnerable to unclear standards and unpredictable outcomes").

78. Carr, 1995, p. 388.

79. Carr, 1995, p. 383.

80. National Conference of Bar Examiners and American Bar Association Section of Legal Education and Admissions to the Bar, Comprehensive Guide to Bar Admission Requirement, 2020, p. vii.

81. National Conference of Bar Examiners and American Bar Association Section of Legal Education and Admissions to the Bar, Comprehensive Guide to Bar Admission Requirement, 2020, p. vii.

82. National Conference of Bar Examiners and American Bar Association Section of Legal Education and Admissions to the Bar, Comprehensive Guide to Bar Admission Requirement, 2020, p. vii.

83. National Conference of Bar Examiners and American Bar Association Section of Legal Education and Admissions to the Bar, Comprehensive Guide to Bar Admission Requirement, 2020, pp. ix.

84. National Conference of Bar Examiners and American Bar Association Section of Legal Education and Admissions to the Bar, Comprehensive Guide to Bar Admission Requirement, 2020, p. viii.

85. *Schware v. Board of Bar Examiners of New Mexico,* 1957, p. 248.

86. *Schware v. Board of Bar Examiners of New Mexico,* 1957, p. 247.

87. Rhode, 1985, p. 508.

88. Rhode, 1985, p. 509; see also Clemens, 2007.

89. Ratcliff, 2000, p. 492.

90. Swisher, 2008, p. 1043 (citing May, 1995).

91. National Conference of Bar Examiners and American Bar Association Section of Legal Education and Admissions to the Bar, Comprehensive Guide to Bar Admission Requirement, 2020, p. viii.

92. Carr, 1995, p. 378 (noting that the presumptive disqualification approach show that jurisdictions are "willing to engage in more flexible character screening processes when making decisions about individuals with prior felony convictions").

93. See appendix B; figure 2.

94. See Rhode, 2018; Aviram, 2019.

95. Kalt, 2003, p. 104 ("The other possibility broached above is that felons threaten the probity of the jury because of their degraded status; whether or not individual felons are 'bad,' the idea of having tainted people on juries might undermine the integrity of the institution. That this is anyone's intention is belied by the fact that jurisdictions speak of probity rather than the appearance of probity. Nevertheless, it is an argument worth considering").

96. See Kalt, 2003, n. 190 (Kalt explains that the Supreme Court has recognized "the arbitrariness of the distinction in another context") (citing *Tennessee v. Garner,*

1985, and noting that there the Court "criticiz[ed] the common-law rule allowing police to shoot fleeing felons but not fleeing misdemeanants).

97. Tyler, 2009, p. 308 (stating, "irrespective of the type of case involved, the traditional means of obtaining compliance is via social control").

98. Tyler, 2009, p. 308.

99. Tyler, 2009, p. 309 (commenting, "it is not surprising that studies which empirically test the deterrence model typically find either that deterrent effects cannot be reliably detected or that, when they are detected, their magnitude is small").

100. Tyler, 2009, p. 309 (noting that "the high costs of deterrence arise because authorities have to create and maintain a credible threat of punishment for wrongdoing").

101. Tyler, 2009, p. 310 (proposing that the methods used to evaluate a deterrence framework foster its continued existence because such methods "approach this issue by defining the issue as whether or not deterrence 'works,'" failing to "consider how strongly deterrence works" and "compare the effectiveness of deterrence to alternative models and approaches").

102. Tyler, 2009, p. 312.

103. Tyler, 2009, p. 311 (contending, "if [the] goal is simply to achieve compliance with the law, a value-based model is as or more effective than the deterrence model").

104. Tyler, 2009, p. 326.

105. Tyler, 2009, p. 311.

106. Tyler, Casper, and Fisher, 1989, pp. 643, 645 (stating, "to the extent that a regime can promote the development of widespread affective attachment, a cushion of support develops that enables the state to impose substantial burdens on citizens without losing their allegiance").

107. Tyler, Caster, and Fisher, 1989, pp. 643, 645 (noting, "the government can influence the impact of negative outcomes on allegiance by delivering those outcomes through procedures that citizens will view as fair").

108. Tyler, 2009, p. 334 (commenting, "it is important to institutionalize mechanisms for evaluating legal authorities in terms of their legitimacy as well as the consistency of their policies and practices with the principles of procedural justice").

109. McIvor, 2009, p. 45.

110. Taxman, Soule, and Gelb, 1999, p. 186.

111. Taxman, Soule, and Gelb, 1999, p. 187.

112. Paternoster et al., 1997, p. 167.

113. Paternoster et al., 1997, p. 166 (noting, "compliance may depend as much or more on the procedural fairness of sanction delivery as it does on the characteristics of the sanction imposed"). See also Fischer et al., 2008.

114. See Lawson, 2012; Lee, 2013; Brodin, 2016.

115. See Lawson, 2012; Lee, 2013; Brodin, 2016.

116. See Wagner and Walsh, 2016.

117. See Wagner and Rabuy, 2017; Guerino, Harrison, and Sabol, 2012.

118. See Alexander, 2012; Pager, 2007.

119. Shannon et al., 2017, p. 1,807.

120. Shannon et al., 2017, p. 1,807.

121. See Wheelock, 2012.

122. See Ga. Code Ann. § 15–12–120.1 ("On and after July 1, 2012, trial juries shall be chosen from a county master jury list. The presiding judge shall order the clerk to choose the number of jurors necessary to conduct the business of the court. The clerk shall choose the names of persons to serve as trial jurors for the trial of civil and criminal cases in the court"); Ga. Code Ann. § 15–12–40 ("Any person who has been convicted of a felony in a state or federal court who has not had his or her civil rights restored and any person who has been judicially determined to be mentally incompetent shall not be eligible to serve as a trial juror"); Ga. Code Ann. § 15–12–163(b)(5) ("The state or the accused may make any of the following objections to the juror . . . [t]hat the juror has been convicted of a felony in a federal court or any court of a state of the United States and the juror's civil rights have not been restored"). In Georgia, restoration of civil rights is not automatic with regards to jury service. See Judicial Council of Georgia, Administrative Office of the Courts, Georgia Jury Commissioner's Handbook 10 (2005) ("An individual who completes a felony sentence may register to vote, but cannot serve on a jury until that person has received a pardon or restoration of civil rights from the Board of Pardon and Paroles").

123. See Wheelock, 2012.

124. Wheelock, 2012, p. 352.

125. See Bowers, Sandys, and Steiner, 1998 (noting that on capital juries, reducing the expected number of African-American male jurors from one to zero can reduce the chances of a death sentence by 30 percent).

126. Wheelock, 2012, p. 354 (but conceding that more research in this area is necessary and that his pilot study "does not argue that felon jury exclusion is the sole cause or even the most influential factor in the continuing underrepresentation of African-American jurors").

127. See Ellis and Diamond, 2003.

128. See MacCoun and Tyler, 1988.

129. See Ellis and Diamond, 2003; Vidmar and Hans, 2007; Wilkenfeld, 2004; MacCoun and Tyler, 1988.

130. See Wilkenfeld, 2004; Fukurai and Davies, 1997.

131. See Fukurai and Davies, 1997.

132. Wheelock, 2012, p. 352.

133. See Hall, Hall, and Perry, 2016; Culhane, Boman IV, and Schweitzer, 2016.

134. Hans and Vidmar, 1986, p. 51.

CHAPTER 3. HONOR AMONG THIEVES?

1. See Kalt, 2003; Binnall, 2014; 2018b.

2. *People v. Miller,* 2008, p. 874 ("At some point, a juror's past experience must lead to a presumption of bias because of the juror's inherent knowledge from experience");

Companioni Jr. v. City of Tampa, 2007, p. 413 ("The per se rule assumes that the felon juror harbors an 'inherent bias'"); Michigan Senate Fiscal Agency Bill Analysis, 2003, p. 5 ("A person who has been convicted of a felony might have a tainted view of the criminal justice system and sympathize with a criminal defendant. Such a situation is blatantly unfair to the prosecution and the crime victim"); *Commonwealth v. Aljoe*, 1966, n. 6 ("It is well known by judges and lawyers that in the selection of a jury, most defense lawyers welcome a person who has been previously convicted of a crime").

3. *Carle v. United States*, 1998, p. 686.

4. *United States v. Greene*, 1993, p. 796.

5. Kalt, 2003, p. 106.

6. See *Rubio v. The Superior Court of San Joaquin County*, 1979.

7. See, e.g., *United States v. Boney*, 1992, p. 633 (holding "the Sixth Amendment right to an impartial jury similarly does not require an absolute bar on felon-jurors"); *Companioni Jr. v. City of Tampa*, 2007, p. 413 ("To the extent that the theory that felon jurors have an 'inherent bias' has any validity at all, its applicability is limited to criminal cases").

8. See, e.g., *People v. Miller*, 2008; *United States v. Boney*, 1992; *United States v. Humphreys*, 1992.

9. *United States v. Boney*, 1992, p. 633.

10. See Binnall, 2014; see also chapter 2, section 4.

11. See Binnall, 2014; 2018b.

12. Sealy 1981, p. 190.

13. U.S. Const. Amend. VI.

14. There is now a substantial literature evaluating implicit biases. A significant portion of that literature is devoted to analyzing jury selection procedures and their efficiency at detecting and eliminating implicit juror biases. Though relevant and influential, this literature is beyond the scope of the present discussion, as the proffered claim of the inherent bias rationale seemingly references explicit biases. See Bennett, 2010; Kang et al., 2011; Arterton, 2007 (for discussions of the literature on jury selection and implicit biases).

15. See Richards, 2002, pp. 447–48 (explaining the two competing models of jury impartiality, stating, "The contemporary model that the 'subjective impartiality' approach seeks to supplant, the 'blank slate' ideal, competes with a model in which juror competence is viewed in terms of the individual's status as neighbor and peer, where abstract and absolute neutrality was not the goal; rather, a peculiar kind of 'local knowledge' was considered more reliable and effective toward the achievement of justice. Court opinions dealing with issues regarding jury selection reflect these competing versions of epistemological perspective, alternating between models reliant upon the modernistic conception of knowing based in a form of Lockean empiricism, to a 'post-modernist' acquiescence in the impossibility of true impartiality, which speaks profoundly about the nature of the deliberative function of juries in contemporary society").

16. *United States v. Parker*, 1937, p. 458 ("The entire effort of our criminal (civil too) procedure is to secure a jury which is ignorant of repute either in its sense of

character or in its sense of events. It is surely not necessary to set forth the meticulous statutory provisions which insure jurors who do not know and are not in a position to know anything of either character or events. In fact the zeal displayed in this effort to empty the minds of the jurors has been the subject of some unfavorable and even humorous comment. We can conclude then that the jury no longer represents the voice of the countryside, but rather, like the court itself, is an impartial organ of justice. That being so, venue is no longer an essence of the institution").

17. Abramson, 1994, p. 17.

18. Kassin and Wrightsman, 1988, p. 6.

19. Dufraimont, 2008, p. 208.

20. A Latin phrase loosely translated as "clean slate."

21. See Abramson, 1994, p. 100 ("This is a demanding notion of impartiality, requiring jurors to be independent not only from the dictates of others but also from their own opinions and biases").

22. Ksssin and Wrightsman, 1988, pp. 7–8.

23. Kassin and Wrightsman, 1988, p. 4.

24. *Taylor v. Louisiana,* 1975, p. 528.

25. Abramson, 1994, p. 101 (continuing, "The jury will achieve the 'overall' or 'diffused' impartiality that comes from balancing the biases of its members against each other").

26. *Ballew v. Georgia,* 1978, p. 234.

27. *Peters v. Kiff,* 1972, pp. 503–4.

28. Kassin and Wrightsman, 1988, p. 6.

29. *Peters v. Kiff,* 1972, pp. 503–4 (highlighting that "exclusion deprives the jury of a perspective on human events that may have unsuspected importance in any case that may be presented").

30. Abramson, 1994, p. 101 (citing *People v. Wheeler,* 1978, p. 755 ("overall impartiality"); *Commonwealth v. Soares,* 1979, p. 480 ("diffused impartiality").

31. See Mazzella and Feingold, 1994, p. 1316 (citing Davis, Bray, and Holt, 1977; Pennington and Hastie, 1990).

32. See Note, 1977; *People v. Wheeler,* 1978; Kaplan and Miller, 1978; Ellsworth, 1993; Brown, 1994; Cammack, 1995; Villiers, 2010.

33. See Myers and Lecci, 1998; see also Villiers, 2010, pp. 82–83 (noting that general biases differ from specific biases as they "exist independently of any specific knowledge of the case . . . are part of the 'broader interpretive framework of the juror,' and reflect the juror's individual perspectives and life experiences").

34. See Cammack, 1995; see also Ellsworth, 1993, p. 43 (describing general biases as "clearly recognizable characteristics of the juror that make a difference in his or her propensity to favor one side"); Villiers, 2010, p. 82 (noting that courts have defined general biases as those that "derive from an individual [juror's] membership in groups defined by factors such as race, religion, gender, age, education, socioeconomic status, political affiliation, and place of residence").

35. Though such categorizations help to organize a vast body of research on juror bias, research has shown that such categorizations are somewhat rigid. Some con-

temporary studies of juror bias show that specific and general biases often interact—often resulting in the amplification or suppression of juror bias.

36. See Hastie, Penrod, and Pennington, 1983; Devine et al., 2001; see also Ellsworth, 1993, p. 43 ("In our culture, there is an almost irresistible compulsion to attribute differences in behavior to differences in a person's personality, attitudes, or background").

37. See Devine, 2012; Devine et al., 2001; Saks, 1997.

38. See Devine, 2012; Ellsworth, 1993; Bonazzoli, 1998; see also Devine et al., 2001, p. 673. While some juror characteristics have been shown to create general biases that influence juror decision-making processes, Devine et al. note that they have "tended to have weak and inconsistent effects."

39. Devine et al., 2001, p. 673.

40. See, e.g., Higgins et al., 2003.

41. See, e.g., Quas et al., 2002; Moran and Comfort, 1982.

42. See, e.g., Mills and Bohannon, 1980; King, 1993b.

43. See, e.g., Hsieh, 2001.

44. See, e.g., Bridgeman and Marlowe, 1979.

45. See, e.g., Miller et al., 2011.

46. See, e.g., Adler, 1973.

47. See, e.g., Mills and Bohannon, 1980.

48. See, e.g., Culhane, Hosch, and Weaver, 2004.

49. See Devine et al., 2001.

50. See Bonazzoli, 1998; Sweeney and Haney, 1992; Lynch and Haney, 2009; Mitchell et al., 2005.

51. See Bonazzoli, 1998.

52. See Devine et al., 2001.

53. See Bowers, Sandys, and Steiner, 1998.

54. See Moran and Comfort, 1982; Bernard and Dwyer, 1984; Cowan, Thompson, and Ellsworth, 1984; Horowitz and Seguin, 1986; Allen, Mabry, and McKelton, 1998.

55. Allen, Mabry, and McKelton, 1998, p. 725; see also Rosenthal, 1984; Haney, 1984; Moran and Comfort, 1982.

56. See Devine et al., 2001.

57. See Narby, Cutler, and Moran, 1993; Lerner, 1970; Gerbasi, Zuckerman, and Reis, 1977.

58. Narby, Cutler, and Moran, 1993, pp. 286–87 (describing traditional authoritarianism as "an individual's tendency to be politically conservative, hold conventional values, prefer powerful leadership, engage in stereotypical thinking, and manifest overly punitive and rigid thinking." They describe legal authoritarianism as "an individual's tendency to engage in anti-libertarian thinking and specifically focuses on beliefs related to the legal system and an inclination to slight the defendant's civil liberties").

59. Narby, Cutler, and Moran, 1993, p. 36 (noting that in a personal communication, Kassin indicated that the JBS could be considered a measure of legal authori-

tarianism, a personality trait shown to generate general biases that influence juror decision-making processes in a variety of cases).

60. See Mitchell and Byrne, 1973.

61. See Garcia and Griffitt, 1978.

62. See Werner, Kagehiro, and Strube, 1982.

63. See McGowan and King, 1982.

64. See Devine, 2012.

65. See Binnall, 2014; 2018b.

66. See Kalt, 2003.

67. Kalt, 2003, pp. 105–6.

68. See Binnall, 2014.

69. See Cal. Const. art. VII, § 8(b) ("Laws shall be made to exclude persons convicted of bribery, perjury, forgery, malfeasance in office, or other high crimes from office or serving on juries. The privilege of free suffrage shall be supported by laws regulating elections and prohibiting, under adequate penalties, all undue influence thereon from power, bribery, tumult, or other improper practice"); Cal. Civ. Pro. Code § 203(a)(5) ("All persons are eligible and qualified to be prospective trial jurors, except the following . . . [p]ersons who have been convicted of malfeasance in office or a felony, and whose civil rights have not been restored"). In California, restoration of civil rights is not automatic. See *U.S. v. Horodner,* 91 F.3d 1317, 1319 (1996) ("In California, a felon released from prison for three or more years may petition for a certificate of rehabilitation. Such a certificate constitutes an application for a pardon, which the governor may grant without further investigation. Anyone granted a full and unconditional pardon based on a certificate of rehabilitation is entitled 'to exercise thereafter all civil and political rights of citizenship,' which would presumably include the right to serve on a jury") (citing Cal. Penal Code §§4852.01, 4852.03, 4852.06, 4852.16, 4852.17).

70. For a full description of participants see Binnall, 2014.

71. "Convicted felons" were recruited from Parole and Community Team (PACT) meetings over three months in 2011. At the time, the California Department of Corrections and Rehabilitation (CDCR) required all newly released prisoners to attend a PACT meeting within thirty days of their release from prison. At PACT meetings, local community agencies discuss the services available to parolees. The CDCR conducts five PACT meetings per month in the host county. For three months, I attended all PACT meetings in the host county, recruiting participants at a total of fifteen meetings at which attendance ranged from ten to fifty convicted felons. In total, I solicited 304 PACT meeting attendees. A response rate of 81 percent yielded 247 convicted felon participants. When constructing the focal group, rather than recruiting convicted felons who had completed their term of supervision, I chose to recruit parolees. I hypothesized that if a strong pretrial bias were to exist, it would likely present most regularly and strongly in convicted felons who had recently finished a period of incarceration. Accordingly, the focal group is comprised exclusively of participants who were no more than thirty days removed from prison.

"Eligible jurors" were recruited from business and community centers in four culturally and socioeconomically diverse areas of the host county. Though the setting for recruitment varied slightly from location to location, I consistently chose highly trafficked areas. I recruited eligible jurors for six months in 2011, soliciting approximately 380 eligible jurors. A 64 percent response rate resulted in 242 eligible juror participants.

"Law students" were recruited from a small, regional law school that produces many lawyers who practice criminal defense and public interest law. Given law students' training and the culture of the recruitment site law school, I hypothesized that the law student group would harbor a prodefense pretrial bias.

For additional information on participant characteristics, see Binnall, 2014.

72. See Cal. Civ. Proc. Code § 203(a)(1)-(8), 2010. The criteria require that a prospective juror must: (1) be a citizen of the United States, (2) be at least eighteen years of age, (3) be a domiciliary of the State of California, (4) be a resident of the jurisdiction they are summoned to serve, (5) not have been convicted of malfeasance in office or a felony, (6) possess sufficient knowledge of the English language (sufficient to understand court proceedings), (7) not be already serving as a grand or trial juror in any court in the State, and (8) not be the subject of a conservatorship.

73. The RJBS is a refined version of the Juror Bias Scale and measures the pretrial biases of subjects. See Kassin and Wrightsman, 1983. In this context, bias is defined as an inclination to favor the prosecution or the defense without knowledge about the facts of a particular case or the evidence presented. Developed in 1983 by Kassin and Wrightsman, the Juror Bias Scale (JBS) is the most commonly used measure of juror bias. The JBS measures prospective jurors' pretrial dispositions toward guilt or innocence using two separate but related constructs: probability of commission (PC) and reasonable doubt (RD). See Devine, 2012, p. 106 (noting that the PC subscale measures a subject's "beliefs about how likely criminal defendants are to have committed a crime," while the RD subscale measures "the level of subjective certainty needed to (personally) justify convicting a defendant"). A number of studies have demonstrated that JBS scores predict verdict. See De La Fuente, De La Fuente, and Garcia, 2003; Tang and Nunez, 2003; Warling and Peterson-Badali, 2003; Lecci et al., 2000; Myers and Lecci, 1998; Chapdelanie and Griffin, 1997; Narby, Cutler, and Moran, 1993; Cutler, Moran, and Narby, 1992; Dexter, Cutler, and Moran, 1992; Kassin and Wrightsman, 1983. Only two studies have called into question the predictive validity of the JBS; see Kassin and Garfield, 1991; Weir and Wrightsman, 1990. As a result, scholars generally characterize the JBS as a reliable measure of pretrial bias. See Devine, 2012; Smith and Bull, 2012. In 1998, Myers and Lecci performed a confirmatory factor analysis on the JBS and found that empirical evidence did not support the underlying two-factor structure of the scale. See Myers and Lecci, 1998. Using exploratory factor analysis, they then generated an alternative model of the JBS with higher predictive validity than the original JBS. The resulting scale, the RJBS, consists of twelve questions that assess a juror's pretrial propensity to favor either the defense or the prosecution. In a cross-validation study, the RJBS has proven a more robust measure of pretrial juror bias than the original JBS. See

Devine, 2012; Lecci and Myers, 2002. Since this study, another modified version of the RJBS/JBS—the Pretrial Juror Attitude Questionnaire (PJAQ)—was developed by Myers and Lecci but has not undergone extensive validation. See Myers and Lecci, 2008.

74. See Myers and Lecci, 1998.

75. Generally, researchers employing the JBS or the RJBS as possible predictors of verdict use subject groups' median score to divide participants into prodefense and proprosecution groups. See Tang and Nunez, 2003; Narby, Cutler, and Moran, 1993; Cutler, Moran, and Narby, 1992; Dexter, Cutler, and Moran, 1992; Kassin and Garfield, 1991; Weir and Wrightsman, 1990; Kassin and Wrightsman, 1983. Because the study does not test the predictive validity of the RJBS, but rather compares the pretrial biases of groups, I use the scale median of the RJBS to delineate prodefense and proprosecution.

76. Notice that sample sizes differ from the total number of participants because of missing data. While I imputed missing data for independent variables, I did not impute missing values for dependent variable (RJBS score), dropping participants who did not answer all items on the RJBS scale.

77. Kalt, 2003, pp. 105–6.

78. The Shapiro-Wilk test of normality reveals that all groups are normally distributed on the RJBS (eligible jurors: $p = .82$, felons: $p = .18$, law students: $p = .87$). See Shapiro and Francia, 1972; Shapiro and Wilk, 1965. Yet Bartlett's test of group-wise heteroskedasticity shows that variances are not equal across groups (felons/eligible jurors: $p = .0001$, felons/law students: $p = .291$, eligible jurors/law students: $p = < .0000$) (Brown and Forsythe 1974; Box 1953). For this reason, I use a series of unequal variance t-tests to test the null hypothesis that the intergroup means are equal (Welch 1947; Satterthwaite 1946).

79. See Binnall, 2018b.

80. I recruited participants from California's Peace Officer's Standards and Training (POST) training classes over the course of twelve months in 2016–17. As part of their continued training, California law enforcement agencies require that officers regularly complete POST trainings. At those meetings, I solicited the participation of law enforcement personnel. To ensure that I did not condition participants, my solicitation included only a brief overview of the study. See California Government, POST Commission on Peace Officers Standards and Trainings, 2019, https://post.ca.gov/Training. Because this study took place in California, California's juror eligibility served as the exclusionary criteria.

81. See appendix C, noting that permanent exclusion jurisdictions at the time of publication are Federal, California, Colorado, Florida, Hawaii, Indiana, Kansas, Nebraska, Nevada, Oklahoma, Rhode Island, South Carolina, and Virginia.

82. See appendix C, noting that permanent exclusion jurisdictions only in criminal matters at the time of publication are Oklahoma and Indiana.

83. To make comparisons between convicted felons and law enforcement personnel, I used data from the 2014 field study of eligible jurors with a felony criminal conviction. Though I replicated that study, the elapsed time since data collection for

my 2014 study, three years, likely introduces unknown and unknowable temporal issues. For these reasons, the results of the present study are suggestive only, but do shed light on an important issue relating to felon juror exclusion and the possible legislative biasing of jury pools through exclusionary statutes.

84. Kalt, 2003, p. 107.

85. See Comment, 1972.

86. See Binnall, 2018b.

87. See Comment, 1972 (young people); see also Rosen, 1992 (race); King, 1993a (race).

88. *State v. Baxter,* 1978, p. 275.

89. Phillips, 2019, www.ocregister.com/2019/06/13/california-moves-to-let-felons-serve-on-juries.

90. See, e.g., Travis, 2005, p. 35. In his discussion of "individualized punishments," noted criminologist Jeremy Travis stated, "barring convicted felons from jury eligibility automatically may well be reasonable to protect the integrity of criminal trials." To be fair, at the time of his evaluation, no empirical study of felon-juror exclusion had been undertaken; see also Wheelock, 2012.

91. For the full model, see Binnall, 2014.

92. Those variables include: age (see Higgins, Heath, and Grannemann, 2007), gender (see Quas et al., 2002; Moran and Comfort, 1982), race (see King, 1993b; Mills and Bohannon, 1980), native language (see Hsieh, 2001), occupational status (see Cowan, Thompson, and Ellsworth, 1984; Bridgeman and Marlowe, 1979; Simon, 1967), religion (see Miller et al., 2011; Seltzer, 2006; Eisenberg, Garvey, and Wells, 2001), socioeconomic status (see Adler, 1973; Reed, 1965), level of education (see Mills and Bohannon, 1980; Bridgeman and Marlowe, 1979; Simon, 1967), history of victimization (see Culhane, Hosch, and Weaver, 2004), political affiliation (see Kravitz, Cutler, and Brock, 1993), and view of the death penalty (see Allen, Mabry, and McKelton, 1998; Horowitz and Seguin, 1986; Bernard and Dwyer, 1984; Cowan, Thompson, and Ellsworth, 1984; Moran and Comfort, 1982).

93. Relevant to the reference category (eligible juror without a felony conviction and not enrolled in law school), effect sizes for these independent variables are: law students ($b = -0.288$), African-American ($b = -0.070$), crime victims ($b = -0.079$), strongly opposed to the death penalty ($b = -0.109$), and liberal ($b = -0.104$); see also Binnall, 2014.

94. Relevant to the reference category (eligible juror without a felony conviction and not enrolled in law school), effect sizes for these independent variables are: less than a high school education ($b = 0.134$), strongly support the death penalty ($b = 0.156$), and have a positive view of the law ($b = 0.328$); see also Binnall, 2014.

95. See Kalt, 2003; Binnall, 2014; see also appendix A.

96. Weaver and Lerman, 2010, p. 819.

97. See Tyler, 1990; 1984.

98. Tyler, 2003, p. 286.

99. See Shapiro and Kirkman, 2001.

100. See Woolard, Harvell, and Graham, 2008, p. 208.

101. See Hurwitz and Peffley, 2005.

102. See Bell, Ryan, and Weichman, 2004.

103. See Woolard, Harvell, and Graham, 2008.

104. For the full model and a more detailed description of methods see Binnall and Petersen, 2020c.

105. See Muller and Schrage, 2014; Weaver and Lerman, 2010.

106. See Binnall, 2014.

107. Tyler, 1984; 1990; 2000.

108. See Ellis and Diamond, 2003.

109. See *Holland v. Illinois,* 1990.

110. *Lockhart v. McCree,* 1986, p. 165.

111. See Hans and Vidmar, 1986, p. 67 (noting that voir dire "may be as brief as 20 minutes or as long as 8 hours for an average trial" and that "in the Hillside Strangler trial in Los Angeles, . . . the voir dire and jury selection took 49 court days").

112. See Hans and Vidmar, 1986, p. 67 (commenting "questions may be wide-ranging or more specifically related to the case").

113. Hannaford-Agor and Munsterman, 2006, p. 25.

114. Kalt, 2003, pp. 107–8.

115. In their seminal study of juror/jury behavior, Kalven and Zeisel suggest that a juror's initial vote is predictive of verdict almost uniformly. In turn, they suggest that deliberations are perhaps not as important as previously thought. See Kalven and Zeisel, 1966. After a review of the literature, Devine et al. surmise that "[t]here are compelling data from numerous studies indicating that the verdict favored by the majority of the jury at the beginning of deliberation will be the jury's final verdict about 90% of the time."). See Devine et al., 2001, p. 690.

116. See Hannaford-Agor et al., 2000; Bentele and Bowers, 2002; Hans et al., 2003; Vidmar et al., 2003.

117. See Hannaford-Agor et al., 2002 (the study involved 382 noncapital felony jury cases from four state courts).

118. See Hans et al., 2003, p. 15 (describing the study).

119. Hans et al., 2003, p. 15.

120. Hans et al., 2003, p. 15.

121. See, e.g., *Rubio v. The Superior Court of San Joaquin County,* 1979, p. 101 ("Because these antisocial feelings would often be consciously or subconsciously concealed, the Legislature could further conclude that the risk of such prejudice infecting the trial outweighs the possibility of detecting it in jury selection proceedings").

122. Kalt, 2003, p. 108.

CHAPTER 4. SEQUESTERING THE CONVICTED: PART I

1. *Strauder v. West Virginia,* 1880.

2. *Peters v. Kiff,* 1972.

3. *Apodaca et al. v. Oregon,* 1972.

4. *Ballew v. Georgia,* 1978, p. 233.

5. *Johnson v. Louisiana,* 1972, p. 390.

6. *Taylor v. Louisiana,* 1975.

7. *United States v. Ballard,* 1946.

8. *Carter v. Jury Commission of Greene County,* 1970.

9. Devine, 2012, p. 153 ("Only a small portion of the empirical literature on jury decision making has involved the intensive study of the deliberation process, perhaps 5–10 percent"); see also Devine et al., 2001.

10. See Devine et al., 2007.

11. See Cowan, Thompson, and Ellsworth, 1984; Marder, 2002; Sommers, 2006.

12. See Sommers, 2006.

13. See Marder, 2002.

14. See Cowan, Thompson, and Ellsworth, 1984.

15. Devine et al., 2007, p. 276 ("In the absence of any obvious way to directly ascertain the 'correctness' of a jury verdict, efforts to measure and improve the quality of the deliberation process may represent the best way to increase the likelihood that juries 'get it right' when it comes to their decisions").

16. See Pennington and Hastie, 1981; Cowan, Thompson, and Ellsworth, 1984; Ellsworth, 1989; Devine et al., 2007.

17. Devine et al., 2007, p. 276.

18. Ellsworth, 1989, pp. 207–8 ("The jury members must 'encode' the information they get at trial. A competent jury must pay attention to the testimony and remember it. The jury must define the legal categories. A competent jury should define these categories as they are presented in the judges' instructions. The jury must select the admissible evidence and ignore evidence that is inadmissible. The jury must construct the sequence of events. The jury must evaluate the credibility of the witnesses. The jury must evaluate the evidence in relation to the legal categories provided in the instructions. That is, certain elements of the story the jury constructs are particularly important in determining the appropriate verdict. The jury must identify these elements and understand how differences in the interpretation of the facts translate into differences in the appropriate verdict choice. The jury must test its interpretation of the facts and the implied verdict choice against the standard of proof: preponderance of evidence, clear and convincing evidence, or beyond a reasonable doubt. The jury must decide on the verdict") (citing Pennington and Hastie, 1981, pp. 249–55); see also Cowan, Thompson, and Ellsworth, 1984; Sommers, 2006.

19. See Cowan, Thompson, and Ellsworth, 1984; Marder, 2002; Sommers, 2006.

20. See Shaw, 1983; Phillips et al., 2004; Antonio et al., 2004; McLeod, Lobel, and Cox, 1996; Sommer, Warp, and Mahoney, 2008; Gruenfeld et al., 1996; Stasser, 1988; Watson, Kumar, and Michaelsen, 1993; Valls, Gonzalez-Roma, and Tomas, 2016.

21. See Cowan, Thompson, and Ellsworth, 1984; Marder, 2002; Sommers, 2006.

22. See Cowan, Thompson, and Ellsworth, 1984.

23. See Cowan, Thompson, and Ellsworth, 1984.

24. See Marder, 2002.

25. Marder, 2002, p. 688.

26. Marder, 2002, pp. 694–95; see also Nemeth, 1986.

27. See Sommers, 2006.

28. See Sommers, 2006.

29. Sommers, 2006, p. 606.

30. Sommers, 2006, p. 606. In an effort to explain this finding, Sommers theorized that two interrelated processes caused this effect. The first suggests that white jurors anticipated discussing race issues when they noted the diversity of the group. This anticipation may then have given rise to "the watchdog effect" whereby majority group members take steps to insulate the group from prejudice. See also Petty, Fleming, and White, 1999; Fleming, Petty, and White, 2005.

31. See Shaw, 1983.

32. See Shaw, 1983.

33. See van Dijk, van Engen, and van Knippenberg, 2012; Webber and Donahue 2001; Kochan et al. 2003.

34. See Behfar et al., 2008; Greer and Jehn, 2007; Greer et al., 2008; Jehn, 1995; Tekleab, Quigley, and Tesluc, 2009.

35. Milliken and Martins, 1996, p. 403.

36. See Hambrick, Cho, and Chen, 1996; Bantel, 1994; Jackson, Joshi, and Erhardt, 2003.

37. See Webber and Donahue, 2001, p. 144; Valls, Gonzalez-Roma, and Tomas, 2016.

38. Whittenbaum, Hillingshead, and Botero, 2004, p. 287 (In a line of research on diversity and group performance, studies reveal the "hidden profile paradigm." This paradigm holds that "groups often make suboptimal decisions on tasks structured as hidden profiles, because they tend to discuss and incorporate into their decisions information that is *shared* (known to all members) at the expense of information that is *unshared* (known to a single member). In other words, groups are not able to take advantage of the unique knowledge and expertise of their members"). See also Stasser and Titus, 1985.

39. See Valls, Gonzalez-Roma, and Tomas 2016; Webber and Donahue, 2001; Pelled, 1996; Pelled, Eisenhardt, and Xin, 1999.

40. *Strauder v. West Virginia,* 1880; *Thiel v. Southern Pacific Railroad Company,* 1946; *Peters v. Kiff,* 1972; *Taylor v. Louisiana,* 1974; *Duren v. Missouri,* 1979.

41. See Behfar et al., 2008; Greer and Jehn, 2007; Greer, Jehn, and Mannix, 2008; Jehn, 1995; Tekleab, Quigley, and Tesluc, 2009; De Dreu and Weingart, 2003; Tajfel and Turner, 1979.

42. Valls, Gonzalez-Roma, and Tomas, 2016, p. 752.

43. See Sunstein, 2002 (discussing group performance and polarization); see also Braithwaite, 1989; LeBel, 2012; Moore, Stuewig, and Tangney, 2016 (discussing attitudes toward convicted felons).

44. Tranwalter, Richeson, and Shelton, 2009; Richeson and Shelton, 2003.

45. Behfar et al., 2011, p. 129 (noting "conflict can prompt group members to ask for help, clarify roles, revisit assumptions about the use of resources, set and plan for deadlines and timelines, and allocate work more effectively"); see also Schulz-Hardt, Jochims, and Frey, 2002.

46. See van Knippenberg, de Dreu, and Homan, 2004, p. 1,008 (proposing the "CEM" which "integrates information / decision making and social categorization perspectives on work-group diversity and performance").

47. See van Knippenberg, de Dreu, and Homan, 2004.

48. For example, some evidence suggests that unscripted group activities are more likely to induce anxiety and conflict. See Avery et al., 2009. Other evidence on the quality of diversity (related to group tasks vs. unrelated to group tasks) is contradictory. See Webber and Donahue, 2001, for a review of that literature.

49. See Shaw, 1983.

50. See Cowan, Thompson, and Ellsworth, 1984; Marder, 2002; Sommers, 2006.

51. See Binnall, 2019b.

52. Over the course of the study (six months), I attended one PACT meeting per week in the host county, recruiting participants at a total of twenty-five meetings at which attendance ranged from ten to fifty convicted felons. All felon-jurors were active state parolees.

53. At each location, an advertisement was posted in the central lobby and when permission was granted (as it was in five courthouses) in the jury lounge. The study solicitation—in person and written—included a brief description of the study, available study sessions, and a promise to compensate participants fifty dollars for three to four hours of their time. Interested participants were provided a local telephone number and email address (both dedicated only to participant recruitment) and instructed to call or email to schedule their mock-jury session.

54. The criteria requires that a prospective juror (1) must be a citizen of the United States, (2) must be at least eighteen years of age, (3) must be a domiciliary of the State of California, (4) must be a resident of the jurisdiction they are summoned to serve, (5) must not have been convicted of malfeasance in office or a felony, (6) must possess sufficient knowledge of the English language (sufficient to understand court proceedings), (7) must not be already serving as a grand or trial juror in any court in the State, and (8) must not be the subject of a conservatorship (Cal. Civ. Proc. Code § 203(a)(1)-(8), 2010). For felon-jurors, prescreening did not include California's juror eligibility criterion excluding convicted felons from jury service.

55. For a full description of participants see Binnall, 2019.

56. Though minorities of one do create unique deliberation dynamics (Sommers, 2006), I chose to include diverse juries of single felon-jurors to preserve ecological validity. Prior research in jurisdictions that include convicted felons in the jury process reveals that the number of convicted felons likely present in any jury pool coupled with for cause challenges and peremptory strikes make it unlikely that any single jury will include more than one or two convicted felons (Binnall 2018a; 2018c). To approximate this reality, I constructed juries of similar character.

57. See Lynch and Haney, 2009 (establishing four-plus person juries as the benchmark for mock jury experiments).

58. I chose a criminal trial because the rationales for felon-juror exclusion make little sense in the civil context. See *Companioni Jr. v. City of Tampa*, 2007, p. 413 ("To the extent that the theory that felon-jurors have an 'inherent bias' has any validity at all, its applicability is limited to criminal cases").

59. Kalven and Zeisel's "liberation hypothesis" suggests that jurors' pretrial attitudes and biases are most likely to impact deliberations when evidence is weighted evenly. Because the justifications for felon-juror exclusion suggest that convicted felons' marred character and inherent biases will drive their contributions to deliberations, I sought to reenact a case with evidentiary ambiguity and no clear outcome. To find a case that met this criterion, I pretested five criminal trial transcripts using focus groups of attorneys and eligible jurors in the host county. The chosen transcript was decidedly the most neutral. See Kalven and Zeisel, 1966, p. 166 (describing the "liberation hypothesis" and stating, "doubts about the evidence free the jury to follow sentiment").

60. See 18 U.S.C. § 2113 (the statute outlawing bank robbery).

61. Ninth Circuit Jury Instructions, 2010, § 8.162.

62. Each participant was read a study information sheet and consented to being filmed.

63. See Cowan, Thompson, and Ellsworth, 1984.

64. See Ellsworth, 1989; Sommers, 2006.

65. In such studies, jurors are often asked to rate their satisfaction with the jury service experience, their perceptions of witnesses, and their evaluations of attorneys. See Cowan, Thompson, and Ellsworth, 1984; Devine et al., 2007.

66. See Diamond and Casper, 1992; Devine et al., 2001 (foreperson selection); see also Ellsworth, 1989 (deliberation style).

67. See Sommers, 2006 (deliberation duration and juror time spoken); see also Cowan, Thompson, and Ellsworth, 1984; Sommers, 2006 (coverage of facts and law); see also Sommers, 2006 (accuracy of facts and law covered).

68. See Marder, 2002 (the deliberation experience); see also Cowan, Thompson, and Ellsworth, 1984 (witness credibility and attorney credibility/likability).

69. See Schreier, 2012; Esterberg, 2002.

70. See, e.g., Sommers, 2006.

71. See Stangor, 1998.

72. For full postdeliberation questionnaire see Binnall, 2019.

73. See Lynch and Haney, 2009.

74. Nested or hierarchical data requires that comparisons be made using hierarchical linear models (HLM). Such models account for the effect of second-level data. In the case of jury studies, an HLM will estimate differences between groups of individual jurors, accounting for the group (second-level data) of which they were a part. See Rabe-Hesketh and Skrondal, 2008; Raudenbush and Bryk, 2002.

75. See Cowan, Thompson, and Ellsworth, 1984; Sommers, 2006.

76. Both parametric and nonparametric tests were conducted. See Binnall, 2019, tables 1 and 2.

77. Both parametric and nonparametric tests were conducted. See Binnall, 2019, tables 1 and 2.

78. Both parametric and nonparametric tests were conducted. See Binnall, 2019, tables 1 and 2.

79. Both parametric and nonparametric tests were conducted. See Binnall, 2019, tables 1 and 2.

80. Both parametric and nonparametric tests were conducted. See Binnall, 2019, tables 4 and 5.

81. See Diamond and Casper, 1992.

82. See Devine et al., 2007; Bridgeman and Marlow, 1979; Ellsworth, 1989.

83. See Hastie, Penrod, and Pennington, 1983.

84. See Ellsworth, 1989; Devine et al., 2007; Sandys and Dillehay, 1995.

85. See Hastie, Penrod, and Pennington, 1983.

86. See Sommers, 2006.

87. See Greer, Jehn, and Mannix, 2008; Trawalter, Richeson, and Shelton, 2009; Richeson and Shelton, 2003.

88. See Cowan, Thompson, and Ellsworth, 1984; Marder, 2002; Sommers, 2006.

89. See McLeod, Lobel, and Cox, 1996; Watson, Kumar, and Michaelsen, 1993; Valls, Gonzalez-Roma, and Tomas, 2016.

90. See Sommers, 2006.

91. See Kalt, 2003; Binnall, 2014.

92. See Shannon et al., 2017.

93. See Pager, 2008; Alexander, 2012.

94. See Binnall, 2010.

95. The principal limitation of the experiment is its sample size. The experiment included only 101 participants making up 19 juries. Moreover, of the 101 participants, only 21 were convicted felons. These sample sizes—at the jury level (N = 19) and the juror level (80/21)—make any statistical comparisons suggestive only.

CHAPTER 5. SEQUESTERING THE CONVICTED: PART II

1. Garland, 1990, pp. 185–86 ("Professional groups succeeded in transforming the culture of punishment. They introduced the rationality of value-neutral science, a technical 'non-judgmental' vocabulary, a 'passion for classification,' and a horror of emotional forces, into a sphere which was previously dominated by candid morality and openly expressed sentiment").

2. See Feeley and Simon, 1992; Lynch, 1998; Simon, 1988; Feeley, 2012; Feeley and Simon, 1994.

3. Feeley and Simon, 1992, p. 449.

4. See Feeley and Simon, 1992 (comparing the "Old Penology" to the "New Penology").

5. See Love, Roberts, and Kingele, 2013; Mele and Miller, 2005; Ewald, 2017; Mauer and Chesney-Lind, 2002.

6. See, e.g., Staples, 2005 (house arrest); Miller, 2003 (immigration regulations); Simon, 1998 (sex offender restrictions); Schneider, 2010 (housing); Sugie, 2012 (public benefits); Pinard, 2010 (public benefits); Aukerman, 2005 (occupational licensing).

7. Ronel and Elisha, 2011, p. 306 (noting "the failure of the therapeutic interventions derived from this 'negative' perspective to achieve significant reduction of recidivism among offenders indicates a need to integrate the existing models with positive ones that stress development of the personal strengths of deviant individuals and not only eradication of their negative characteristics").

8. See Maruna and LeBel, 2003; Woods et al., 2013. See also Ronel and Elisha, 2011, p. 306 (describing positive criminology as "a new conceptual perspective of criminology, encompassing several theories and models . . . which focuses on the positive characteristics, processes, and influences in an individual's life with regard to criminology").

9. Hunter et al., 2015, p. 1,305 (describing the strengths-based approach as "oriented to facilitating prisoner's community reintegration by participating in activities that place them in a helping role"); see also Burnett and Maruna, 2006.

10. See Prendergast et al., 2011; Hunter et al., 2016; Kurtz and Linneman, 2006; LeBel, Richie, and Maruna, 2015.

11. See Andrews and Bonta, 2003; Hollin, 2002. See also Starr, 2015, p. 205 ("It is an understatement to refer to risk assessment as a criminal justice trend. Rather we are already in the risk assessment era"); see also Stevenson, 2018, p. 317 ("Risk assessment tools are one of the most prominent and widely adopted methods associated with the evidence-based criminal justice movement. The National Institute of Corrections, an organization that has been deeply involved in the advancement of evidence-based criminal justice, ranks risk assessment tools at number one in a list of evidence-based ways to reduce recidivism"). For a history of the use of risk assessment tools in correctional settings, see Monahan and Skeem, 2016; Andrews, Bonta, and Wormith, 2006.

12. See Andrews, Bonta, and Wormith, 2006 (discussing the evolution and use of risk assessment tools in the context of criminal justice policy).

13. Stevenson, 2018, p. 314.

14. See Andrews, Bonta, and Hoge, 1990; Andrews, Bonta, and Wormith, 1995.

15. See Bonta and Andrews, 2007. See also Hunter et al., 2015, p. 1,299 ("The Risk Principle refers to criminogenic variables that have been shown to increase the likelihood of reoffense, such as a juvenile arrest record and a history of multiple arrests. The Needs Principle refers to deficits that may include basic needs such as housing, education, and job skills, as well as mental health and substance abuse treatment. The Responsivity Principle refers to the ability to respond to the identified risks and needs of each offender with effective, evidence-based treatment interventions").

16. Stevenson, 2018, p. 315 ("Most risk assessment tools currently in use are fairly simple checklist-style tools. These tools take a set of inputs, usually between seven

and fifteen, and assign a certain number of points to each input. The points assigned to each input are determined through statistical analyses that evaluate how well each input predicts the outcome. The inputs to a risk assessment algorithm almost always include criminal history or criminal justice-related misconduct. Some also include socio-economic factors such as education level, marital status, or home neighborhood. Age and gender are often included, but race is not. The risk score is then calculated by summing the points assigned to each input. Usually, the risk score is then aggregated to a small group of risk classifications: people with the lowest scores are labeled low risk, those with medium scores are labeled moderate risk, and those with the highest scores are labeled high risk. The decision about what fraction of defendants belong in each bin is a normative one") (citing Mayson, 2017).

17. See, e.g., Lowenkamp, Latessa, and Holsinger, 2006; Grove et al., 2000; Fazel et al., 2012.

18. See, e.g., Andrews, Bonta, and Wormith, 2006; Grove et al., 2000; Brennan, Dieterich, and Ehret, 2009. See also Desmarais, Johnson, and Singh, 2016, p. 206 (opining, "There is overwhelming evidence that risk assessments completed using structured approaches produce estimates that are more reliable and more accurate than unstructured risk assessments").

19. See, e.g., Dressel and Farid, 2018. Here, researchers compared the predictive accuracy of the COMPAS tool—a risk assessment tool used to determine the likelihood of recidivism—against a sample of untrained online participants. Results revealed that untrained online participants performed as well as COMPAS, an established measure of risk. See also Hannah-Moffat and Shaw, 2001; Rigakos, 1999.

20. See Harcourt, 2015; Angwin et al., 2016 (a study demonstrating racial bias resulting from the use of COMPAS); see also Kroll et al., 2016; Kleinberg, Mullainathan, and Raghavan, 2016.

21. See Eckhouse et al., 2019; Gouldin, 2016.

22. See, e.g., Eckhouse et al., 2019.

23. Ronel and Elisha, 2011, p. 306. See also, e.g., Prendergast et al., 2011, pp. 228–29 (listing the principles of strengths-based case management: "(1) The focus is on the strengths of the client, not on pathology or deficits; (2) The relationship between the case manager and the client is an essential component; (3) Interventions and services are determined by the needs and desires of the client; (4) The preferred mode of intervention for the case manager is aggressive outreach; (5) All people, regardless of their current condition or situation, are able to learn, grow, and change, and the role of the case manager is able to assist in this process; (6) The entire community [including formal and informal resources] is viewed as a source of services and support for clients") (citing Rapp and Wintersteen, 1989). See also Brun and Rapp, 2001;Ward and Stewart, 2003 (discussing the Good Lives approach); Ward and Brown, 2004.

24. Hunter et al., 2016, p. 1,300 ("Although the theoretical foundation for the RNR framework does include strengths these strengths are conceptualized as the absence of risks or needs and, therefore, are not explicit") (citing Andrews, Bonta, and Wormith, 2011).

25. See Prendergast et al., 2011, p. 228 ("The quintessential component of strengths case management is the identification of the client's strengths and previous accomplishments, rather than focusing on deficits, problems, or obstacles, and the repeated utilization of these strengths during each session as a way of achieving goals and addressing unexpected barriers"); Rapp and Wintersteen, 1989; Ward and Stewart, 2003; Ward and Brown, 2004; Miller, 2006; O'Brien, 2001.

26. Hunter et al., 2016, p. 1,301. See also Prendergast et al., 2011, pp. 228–29 ("In contrast to a deficit model that reinforces low expectations by viewing clients as 'the problem' (e.g., one is a drug addict), the strengths approach reinforces high expectations by viewing the situation as 'the problem' (e.g., one has drug dependence) and by assuming that the client has many strengths and resources with which to handle the problem"). See also Maruna and LeBel, 2003, p. 98 ("In a criminal justice framework, strength approaches would ask not what needs to be done to a person in response to an offence, but rather what the person can accomplish to make amends for his or her actions (e.g., in the form of community service contributions)"; Clark, 2000; 2001; O'Brien, 2001; Rapp, 1992.

27. In 1955, sociologist/criminologist Donald Cressey suggested that relationships between prisoners and former prisoners could aid in rehabilitation and reentry. Through a process he termed "reflexive reformation," offenders who are immersed in inter offender rehabilitative efforts feel compelled to conform their behavior to the pro social group norm. See, e.g., Cressey, 1955, p. 119; see also 1965. Later studies in the substance abuse treatment context support these findings, demonstrating that the "professional ex-" or "wounded healer" paradigm benefits formerly addicted counselors and their clients. See Brown, 1991 (discussing the "professional ex-"); White, 2000 (discussing the "wounded healer").

28. See LeBel, 2007.

29. LeBel, 2007, p. 16.

30. LeBel, 2007, p. 18.

31. See LeBel, Richie, and Maruna, 2015.

32. LeBel, Richie, and Maruna, 2015, p. 116.

33. LeBel, 2007, p. 18.

34. See Heidemann et al., 2016 (females convicted of a felony); Perrin et al., 2017 (individuals convicted of a felony sexual offense).

35. See Delancey Street Foundation, 2020a; and Homeboy Industries, 2020. See also Offenders Anonymous, 2020; Mooallem, 2015; Anti-Recidivism Coalition, 2020; Insight Prison Project, 2020; Project H.O.P.E. Reentry Initiative, 2020; St. Vincent DePaul Reentry Initiative, 2020.

36. Founded in 1971 in San Francisco by criminologist Mimi Silbert and former offender John Maher, Delancey Street Foundation is "the country's leading residential self-help organization for former substance abusers, ex-convicts, homeless and others who have hit bottom." See Delancey Street Foundation, 2020c. The Delancey Street Foundation is a self-described "extended family" that employs no experts or program administrators. Instead, at Delancey, clients serve as mentors and mentees, "everyone is both a giver and a receiver in an 'each-one-teach-one' process." See

Delancey Street Foundation, 2020b. To date, Delancey has served over fourteen thousand former offenders and recovering addicts. Of those who graduate, 90 percent never return to drugs or crime. See Patterson et al., 2008. Like Delancey Street Foundation, Homeboy Industries also employs former offenders as counselors and mentees. Founded in 1988 by Father Greg Boyle and located in Los Angeles, California, Homeboy Industries offers wraparound services for at-risk youth, former gang members, and recently incarcerated men and women. They provide job training; mental heath, substance abuse, and domestic violence services; educational opportunities; and even tattoo removal. An ongoing study by UCLA professors Jorja Leap and Todd Franke found that of the three hundred Homeboy alumni they began tracking in 2008, only one in three have been reincarcerated, a marked improvement over the statewide recidivism rate of approximately 67 percent. See Selvin, 2017.

37. See Delancey Street Foundation, 2020b.

38. This analysis relied again on three coders (the same coders) and again a series of pairwise kappas were were then compared for the variables of interest. Values of the pairwise kappas ranged from .74 to .78 (higher than the generally accepted .70 level of reliability). See Stangor, 1998.

39. Devine et al., 2007, p. 277 (but conceding, "other desirable features of jury deliberation could certainly be added to this set and it is important to note that these criteria are not seen as necessary or sufficient to ensure a 'correct' decision (were we able to ascertain that . . . [h]owever, we would argue that the chance of a jury reaching the legally appropriate decision [given the true facts of the case] is greater to the extent that a deliberation process includes these elements of deliberation quality"). See also Devine et al., 2007, p. 276 (explaining their measures further, Devine et al. note, "juries should (1) have a complete and accurate understanding of their legal instructions, (2) thoroughly review and discuss the evidence presented, (3) establish the facts of the case as best they can and systematically compare these facts to the requirements of the legal instructions to reach a decision, (4) secure and maintain the active participation of most (if not all) members, and (5) foster an environment where individual opinion/belief change is a function of informational influence as opposed to peer pressure or factionalism").

40. See Devine, 2012, p. 711 (discussing the need for more qualitative, contextual analyses of jury deliberations: "Many coding schemes used to parse deliberation content have used broad categories . . . and focused on generating quantitative counts as opposed to tracking rare but potentially critical events . . . it may prove valuable to identify key events or exchanges"). For a review of qualitative analysis in the context of mock jury deliberations, see Charron and Woodhams, 2010.

41. For ease of presentation, Devine et al.'s five measures were collapsed into three: (1) recall and review of evidence; (2) comprehension and application of law; and (3) systematic participation and informational influence.

42. See Devine, 2012.

43. See Trawalter, Richeson, and Shelton, 2009; Richeson and Shelton, 2003.

44. See Cadinu et al., 2003 ("The 'stereotype threat model' suggests that when 'individuals perform a difficult task in an area in which the ingroup is considered

weak, they feel at risk of confirming the stereotype and this psychological pressure will lead them to underperform. In the long term, these individuals may also disidentify from the threatening domain'") (citing Steele and Aronson, 1995).

45. See Haney, 2002.

46. See Travis, 2005; Petersilia, 2003.

47. FJ refers to "felon-juror" and NFJ refers to "non-felon-juror."

48. See MacCoun and Kerr, 1988 (describing this effect as the "majority effect").

49. See Hannaford-Agor, Hans, and Munsterman, 2000; Bentele and Bowers, 2002; Hans et al., 2003; Vidmar et al., 2003.

50. See Pennington and Hastie, 1981; Cowan, Thompson, and Ellsworth, 1984; Marder, 2002; Sommers, 2006.

51. Kalven and Zeisel, 1966, p. 149 (noting, "contrary to an often voiced suspicion, the jury does by and large understand the facts and gets the case straight").

52. Ellsworth, 1989, p. 217 (noting that in her study of jury deliberations, discussion of the facts of the case accounted for nearly half of all deliberation units).

53. See Ellsworth, 1989; Kalven and Zeisel, 1966; Hastie, Penrod, and Pennington, 2002; Pritchard and Keenan, 2002.

54. See Clark, Stephenson, and Kniveton, 1990; Vollrath et al., 1989; but see Salerno and Diamond, 2010, p. 177 (noting that some cognitive research calls into question whether group collaboration enhances recall ability, but cautioning "although the cognitive work on group recall has potential implications for jury decision making, the tasks utilized differ in important ways from the task a jury faces") (citing Thorley and Dewhurst, 2009, discussing "collaborative inhibition"; Loftus, 1975, discussing false eyewitness testimony).

55. See Cowan, Thompson, and Ellsworth, 1984; Marder, 2002; Sommers, 2006.

56. See Kalt, 2003.

57. Pennington and Hastie, 1993, p. 221; Pennington and Hastie, 1991–92.

58. Gordon, 2013, p. 650 (discussing this assumption and the use of "schemas" when interpreting evidence, "schemas can be quite useful because they allow us to quickly interpret vast amounts of information and help us deal with confusing, missing, or unknown information"); see also Holstein, 1985.

59. Devine, 2012, p. 27.

60. See Reifman, Gusick, and Ellsworth, 1992; Ogloff and Rose, 2005 (for a review of the literature).

61. Devine, 2012, p. 56.

62. See Haney and Lynch, 1997; Lynch and Haney, 2000; Lynch and Haney, 2009.

63. Horowitz and Kirkpatrick, 1996; Koch and Devine, 1999. Also, there is a robust literature on jurors' comprehension of "insanity"; for a review of the literature, see Ogloff, 1991.

64. Devine, 2012, p. 87.

65. See Horowitz and Kirkpatrick, 1996.

66. Devine 2012, p. 88; see also Federal Judicial Center, 1987, p. 28 ("If, based on your consideration of the evidence, you are *firmly convinced* that the defendant is

guilty of the crime charged, you must find him guilty. If on the other hand, you think there is a *real possibility* that he is not guilty, you must give him the benefit of the doubt and find him not guilty") (emphasis added).

67. See Horowitz and Kirkpatrick, 1996.

CHAPTER 6. CRIMINAL-DESISTANCE SUMMONED

1. Tocqueville, 1835, p. 272.

2. Tocqueville, 1835, p. 275 ("[The jury] should be regarded as a free school which is always open and in which each juror learns his rights, ... and is given practical lessons in the law, lessons which the advocate's efforts, the judge's advice, and also the very passions of the litigants bring within his mental grasp").

3. Tocqueville, 1835, p. 316.

4. See *Powers v. Ohio*, 1991, p. 406 (the Supreme Court has noted, "The opportunity for ordinary citizens to participate in the administration of justice has long been recognized as one of the principal justifications for retaining the jury system"). See also Breyer, 2005, p. 15 (similarly, former Supreme Court Justice Breyer has reiterated the power of jury service as a form of "active liberty," explaining "active liberty" refers to "a sharing of a nation's sovereign authority among its people").

5. See Gastil et al., 2012; 2008; Gastil and Weiser, 2006; Cutler and Hughes, 2001; Gastil, Deess, and Weiser, 2002; Freie, 1997; Consolini, 1992; Shuman and Hamilton, 1992; Finkel, 1985; Barber, 1984; Durand, Bearden, and Gustafson, 1978; Allen, 1977; Richert, 1977; Pabst Jr., Munsterman, and Mount, 1976; 1977; Pateman, 1970.

6. Consolini, 1992, p. 25; see also Button and Mattson, 1999; Mathews, 1994.

7. Consolini, 1992, p. 25.

8. See, e.g., Maruna, 2001; Laub and Sampson, 1993; Sampson and Laub, 1993; 2005.

9. See Miller and Spillane, 2012; Uggen, Manza, and Behrens, 2004.

10. Consider Maruna's take on the fleeting nature of primary desistance and his reference to an old joke, "stopping smoking is easy—I do it every week." See Maruna, 2001, p. 17 (this quote was originally attributed to Harris Dickson who, in response to an inquiry about whether he had quit playing poker replied, "I have; I've quit more'n a thousand times, every time the game breaks up"; see Dickson, 1905, pp. 14–15). See also Maruna, 2001, p. 23 ("For example, a person can steal a purse on a Tuesday morning, then terminate criminal participation for the rest of the day. Is that desistance? Is it desistance if the person does not steal another purse for a week? A month? A year?").

11. See King, 2013; Bottoms et al., 2004; Bushway et al., 2001.

12. See Lemert, 1951.

13. See Maruna, Immarigeon, and LeBel, 2004.

14. See McNeill, 2014; see also Fox, 2015.

15. Maruna, Immarigeon, and LeBel, 2004, p. 19.

16. See Maruna, Immarigeon, and LeBel, 2004; see also Shover, 1996; Maruna, 2001; Giordano, Cernkovich, and Rudolph, 2002; Vaughan, 2007.

17. Fox, 2016, p. 69 ("Tertiary desistance refers to the more cemented state of desistance that results from a genuine sense of belonging, or integration into a pro-social community").

18. Maruna, Immarigeon, and LeBel, 2004, p. 19.

19. See LeBel et al., 2008; Vaughan, 2001.

20. See Laub and Sampson, 1993; Sampson and Laub, 1993; 2005.

21. See Laub, Nagin, and Sampson, 1998; Sampson and Laub, 1990.

22. Sampson and Laub, 1993, p. 225.

23. See Matsueda, 1992; Matsueda and Heimer, 1997; Sampson and Laub, 1993; Laub and Sampson, 2003. Though Laub and Sampson state that life-course turning points facilitate criminal desistance by "provid[ing] an opportunity for identity transformation" (2003, pp. 148–49), Paternoster and Bushway argue that "Sampson and Laub take deliberate steps to separate themselves from any suggestion that identity change is necessary for desistance to occur" (2009, p. 1,108).

24. See Laub and Sampson, 2001; 2003; Matsueda and Heimer, 1997; Heimer and Matsueda, 1994; Matsueda, 1992; Caspi and Moffitt, 1993.

25. Rumgay, 2004, p. 405; see also Giordano, Cernkovich, and Rudolph, 2002, p. 1,035 (referring to this concept as "cognitive blueprints").

26. See Heimer and Matsueda, 1994; Laub and Sampson, 2003; Laub and Sampson, 2001.

27. As Matsueda and Heimer explain, "Commitment to roles is linked to the self through identities, an important feature of the stable self. Here, the self is viewed as a system of hierarchically organized role-identities. The most important, salient, or prominent identities are those that correspond to roles that have received greater investments by the individual. These identities are built up fundamentally through ongoing processes of interaction: through participation in organized groups leading to recurrent role-taking involving those groups, commitments to group roles are built up, and corresponding identities established." See Matsueda and Heimer, 1997, p. 171 (citing Stryker 1968; 1980; McCall and Simmons, 1978).

28. Rumgay, 2004, p. 405 ("skeleton scripts"); Giordano, Cernkovich and Rudolph, 2002, p. 1,035 ("cognitive blueprint")).

29. Caspi and Moffitt, 1993, p. 251. See Laub and Sampson, 2001; 2003; *but* see Maruna and Roy, 2007 (dissecting the concept of "knifing off" and suggesting that criticisms of the concept have merit and warrant further discussion).

30. See Paternoster and Bushway, 2009; Vaughan, 2007; Maruna, 2001.

31. See Paternoster and Bushway, 2009; Giordano, Cernkovich, and Rudolph, 2002; Maruna, 2001.

32. Kiecolt, 1994, p. 51; Giordano, Cernkovich, and Rudolph, 2002, p. 992.

33. Paternoster and Bushway, 2009, p. 1,157; see King, 2013b; LeBel et al., 2008.

34. See Maruna, 2001; Giordano, Cernkovich, and Rudolph, 2002; Vaughan, 2007; Paternoster and Bushway, 2009. See also King, 2013a, p. 152 ("It is the building of a desistance narrative which underpins the development of new identities").

35. Maruna, 2001 p. 87 (describing a "redemption script," Maruna notes, "this redemption script allows the person to rewrite a shameful past into a necessary prelude to a productive and worthy life").

36. Maruna 2001, p. 86.

37. See Maruna, 2001.

38. Paternoster and Bushway, 2009, p. 1,107.

39. Giordano, Cernkovich, and Rudolph, 2002, p. 902.

40. See Massoglia and Uggen, 2007; see also Vaughan, 2007; Farrell, 2002; LeBel et al., 2008; Farrall et al., 2011. See also, e.g., Maruna et al., 2004 (pointing out that they endorse a modified version of labeling theory that emphasizes agency and citing Gecas and Schwalbe, 1983).

41. See Weaver, 2012; see also LeBel et al., 2008.

42. See Uggen, Manza, and Behrens, 2004; Miller and Spillane, 2012.

43. Data for this study were collected in 2001. See Manza, Uggen, and Behrens, 2006, p. 137.

44. See Matsueda and Heimer, 1997.

45. Uggen, Manza, and Behrens, 2004, p. 286.

46. See Uggen, Manza, and Behrens, 2004.

47. Uggen, Manza, and Behrens, 2004, p. 290.

48. Manza, Uggen, and Behrens, 2006, p. 163.

49. Manza, Uggen, and Behrens, 2006, p. 163.

50. See Miller and Spillane, 2012.

51. Miller and Spillane, 2012, p. 423.

52. See Miller and Spillane, 2012.

53. Miller and Spillane, 2012, p. 423 (citing Maruna, 2001, p. 7).

54. Blackstone, 1791, p. 352.

55. Acts and Resolves of Massachusetts, 1803, p. 173.

56. See Maine Public Laws, 1821.

57. See Maine Revised Statutes, 1841 (from 1821 to 1981, Maine law mandatorily excluded convicted felons from jury service).

58. See Maine Public Laws, 1971.

59. Maine Public Laws, 1971.

60. See Maine Revised Statutes Annotated, tit. 21-a, §112 (2017). In an email on November 11, 2011, Sue Wright, reference librarian for the Maine State Law and Legislature Reference Library, confirmed that Maine has never taken away convicted felons' right to vote.

61. Maine Public Laws, 1981, ch. 705, § G13.

62. See Maine Public Laws, 1981, ch. 705, §G4.

63. In Maine, postrelease supervision is termed "probation." See Binnall, 2018a.

64. For a more detailed description of participant characteristics, see Binnall, 2018a.

65. For a more detailed description of participant characteristics, see Binnall, 2018c.

66. See Esterberg, 2002; Schreier, 2012. See also Braun and Clark, 2006 (for a discussion of thematic approaches to qualitative data analysis).

67. For a more detailed discussion of study methods, see Binnall, 2018a; 2018c.

68. For all participants, pseudonyms were used, see Binnall, 2018a.

69. See Rasmussen, 1996; Pager and Quillian, 2005; Aresti, Darke, and Earle, 2012.

70. See Cooley, 1902; Mead, 1934; Sullivan, 1947.

71. See Cooley, 1902.

72. See Cooley, 1902; Mead, 1934; Sullivan, 1947.

73. See Kinch, 1963; see also Paternoster and Iovanni, 1989, p. 378 (similarly, labeling theory suggests that the labeling experience "recast[s] individuals in their own eyes").

74. Chiricos et al., 2007, p. 548.

75. See Aresti, Darke, and Earle, 2012; Goffman, 1963; Irwin, 1970.

76. See Matsueda, 1992.

77. See Becker, 1963; Braithwaite, 1989.

78. See Aresti, Darke, and Earle, 2012; Major and O'Brien, 2005; Tajfel and Turner, 1986.

79. See Raphael, 2014; De Giorgi, 2017.

80. See Uggen, Manza, and Behrens, 2004; Sampson and Laub, 1997.

81. See LeBel, 2012.

82. See Maruna and Copes, 2005. See also Maruna, 2001, pp. 88–95 (for a discussion of the "Real Me" and "The 'I,' The 'Me,' and The 'It'").

83. Maruna, 2001, p. 87.

84. Maruna, 2001, p. 117.

85. Maruna, 2001, p. 98.

86. See Maruna, 2001. As part of this process, many convicted felons first attempt to justify or explain their criminal behavior through "neutralizations." See Sykes and Matza, 1957; Maruna and Copes, 2005.

87. Maruna, 2001, p. 98.

88. Scholars suggest that empathy and sympathy are often incorrectly conflated, and that empathy does not threaten impartiality. Conversely, most scholars suggest that empathy is a necessary component of impartiality. See Rackley, 2005; West, 1997; 2012; Lee R., 2014.

89. Research tends to support this observation. See Brown, 1991.

CHAPTER 7. A COMMUNITY CHANGE AGENT

1. See, e.g., Doherty et al., 2014; Gunnison and Helfgott, 2011; 2013.

2. See, e.g., Shinkfield and Graffam, 2009.

3. Fox, 2015, p. 91 ("Beyond the notion of secondary desistance as the more enduring kind that emanates from a changed sense of self, tertiary desistance . . . is the variety that evolves out of a sense of belonging. As such, community integration

can be seen as a precursor to successful desistance, rather than an outcome of desistance"). See also McNeill, 2014; Fox, 2016; Bazemore and Erbe, 2003; Bazemore and Boba, 2007; Bazemore and Stinchcomb, 2004.

4. See Fox, 2016, p. 69 (discussing the Circles of Support and Accountability Model [CoSA] to highlight the importance of community engagement and noting that "central to the model is the idea of 'radical inclusion' wherein ordinary community members welcome offenders back into the fold") (citing Hannem, 2013, p. 279).

5. See Fox, 2016, p. 69 ("Much of the recent literature on desistance agrees on a simple but central point: desistance usually hinges on the ability to develop social capital"). See also Lederman, Loayza, and Menendez, 2002, p. 509 (defining social capital as "the set of rules, norms, obligations, reciprocity, and trust embedded in social relations, social structures, and society's institutional arrangements that enables members to achieve their individual and community objectives").

6. See Trice and Roman, 1970, p. 538. See also Fox, 2016, p. 83 (discussing an "integrative model of desistance" and noting "communities expedite a de-labeling process with offenders by sharing normative space with them").

7. See Maruna et al., 2004.

8. See Fox, 2015, p. 91 (discussing the responsibilities of the community and stating "the lesson then, from a pragmatic perspective, is that communities need be long on support; accountability, which develops over time, is mutual").

9. See Fox, 2016, p. 83 (discussing an "integrative model of desistance," and noting, "communities communicate the prospect of sharing normative space by engaging deeply with offenders").

10. See Allport, 1954. See also Pettigrew and Tropp, 2000; Pettigrew and Tropp, 2006; Hewstone and Swart, 2011 (noting that the "intergroup contact hypothesis" has been validated repeatedly and now warrants the moniker "intergroup contact theory").

11. See Willis, Levenson, and Ward, 2010; Viki et al., 2012. See also Mancini et al., 2012, p. 3 ("results indicate that total amount of contact experiences significantly predicts crime-related and general stereotype beliefs").

12. See Willis, Levenson, and Ward, 2010, p. 546 ("At the heart of desistance theories and research is an ethical assumption that offenders are people like us and deserve the opportunity to live normal lives once they have been punished").

13. For a full description of the methods and participant characteristics, see Binnall, 2018a; 2018c.

14. See Ward, 2009; Ward and Brown, 2004; Fox, 2015; 2016; McNeill, 2014.

15. Maruna and Brown, 2004, p. 279 ("successful desistance from crime might involve the *negotiation* of a reformed identity through a process of pro-social labeling"). See also Maruna, 2001, p. 158, for a discussion of "looking glass rehabilitation."

16. Fox, 2016, p. 70.

17. See Maruna et al., 2004 (noting that scholars describe the "delabeling process" using a host of monikers including: "certification process" or "destigmatization

process" (see Meisenhelder, 1977; 1982), "elevation ceremony" (see Lofland, 1969), and "integration ceremony" (see Braithwaite and Mugford, 1994).

18. See Meisenhelder, 1977; Lofland, 1969; Braithwaite and Braithwaite, 2001; Maruna et al., 2004.

19. Meisenhelder, 1982, p. 138. See also Meisenhelder, 1977, p. 329 ("The formal completion of a successful exiting project requires a symbolic component, certification. This final phase in exiting was required in order for the individual fully to achieve a social identity as a noncriminal. Certification is simply the social verification of the individual's "reform." Some recognized member[s] of the conventional community must publicly announce and certify that the offender has changed and that he is now to be considered essentially noncriminal").

20. See Maruna, 2001, p. 158 ("Until ex-offenders are formally and symbolically recognized as 'success stories,' their conversion may remain suspect to significant others, and most importantly to themselves").

21. Maruna et al., 2004; Maruna, 2011; Wexler, 2001; Cast, Stets, and Burke, 1999.

22. Cast, Stets, and Burke, 1999, p. 68 (citing Rosenberg, 1973).

23. Maruna et al., 2004; p. 275. See also Wexler, 2001, p. 22 (similarly, law professor David B. Wexler has suggested that "the judge, of course, is the perfect prestigious person to confer public and official validation on the offender and the offender's reform efforts"). See also Maruna, 2011; Cast et al., 1999.

24. See Lofland, 1969.

25. See, e.g., Hannaford-Agor and Munsterman, 2006.

26. King, 2013a, p. 155.

27. Maruna, et al., 2004, p. 275.

28. Goffman, 1963, p. 3.

29. Goffman, 1963, p. 4.

30. Link and Phelan, 2001, p. 367; see also Stafford and Scott, 1986; Crocker, Major, and Steele, 1998.

31. See Bauman, 1989; Mancini et al., 2012; Dixon and Rosenbaum, 2004; Wilson, 1996; Jones, 2002; Link and Cullen, 1986; Penn et al., 1994; Horch and Hodgins, 2008; Rade, Desmarais, and Mitchell, 2016.

32. Bauman, 1989, p. 184.

33. See Green, 2016, pp. 53–59. Criminologist David Green lists eleven factors that lead to distantiation in corrections: (1) Americans' heterophobia; (2) Americans' high tolerance for punitiveness; (3) Americans' misunderstanding of correctional conditions; (4) Americans' incomprehension of the scope of corrections; (5) the facelessness and anonymity of the U.S. correctional population; (6) correctional training practices; (7) the compartmentalization of correctional agencies; (8) day-to-day bureaucratic correctional routines; (9) the politicization of correctional policies; (10) the decline of the rehabilitative ideal; and (11) the pessimistic perception of human nature. See also Green, 2016, p. 59 (noting, "together these eleven forces, practices, and ideational constraints—most of which are peculiarly American—increase the social distance between the criminal Other and those of us outside the prison walls").

34. See Garland, 2001, p. 184 (describing conceptions of the criminal other as "simply wicked"). See also Becker, 1963 (discussing a criminal conviction as a "master status" that overrides all other characteristics). See also Goffman, 1963 (exploring stigma in the context of those with a criminal record and suggesting that stigma implies that another is "not quite human").

35. See Green, 2016.

36. Garland, 1996, p. 446; see also Franko Aas, 2007; Hallsworth, 2000.

37. Garland, 2001, p. 184.

38. See Garland, 2001, p. 184 ("It [the criminology of the other] is also deeply illiberal in its assumption that certain criminals are 'simply wicked' and in this respect intrinsically different from the rest of us").

39. See Garland, 2001, p. 184 ("Being intrinsically evil or wicked, some offenders are not like us. They are dangerous others who threaten our safety and have no calls on our fellow feeling").

40. See Green, 2016.

41. Green, 2016, p. 63.

42. Green, 2016, p. 63.

43. See Green, 2016, pp. 63–65 (Considering the impacts of mass incarceration on certain communities, Green explains how reentry efforts rehumanize convicted felons and lead to social and spatial proximity: "The very recognition of this damage and devastation implies moral responsibility by casting light on the collateral economic, political, and familial consequences of punishment . . . it follows that an ideal-typical offender reconstructed as needful . . . elicits greater empathy and feelings of responsibility from others . . . [t]his reconstruction reduces social distance between 'us' and 'them'").

44. See Allport, 1954; see also Pettigrew and Tropp, 2000; Pettigrew and Tropp, 2006.

45. See Allport, 1954, p. 489 ("To be maximally effective, contact and acquaintance programs should lead to a sense of equality in social status, should occur in ordinary purposeful pursuits, avoid artificiality, and if possible enjoy the sanction of the community in which they occur. The deeper and more genuine the association, the greater its effect").

46. See Pettigrew and Tropp, 2006, p. 766 ("The meta-analytic results clearly indicate that intergroup contact typically reduces intergroup prejudice. Synthesizing effects from 696 samples, the meta-analysis reveals that greater intergroup contact is generally associated with lower levels of prejudice"). See also Corrigan et al., 2001 (mentally ill); Gawronski and LeBel, 2008 (mentally ill).

47. See Pettigrew and Tropp, 2006, p. 766 ("Allport's conditions are not essential for intergroup contact to achieve positive outcomes. In particular, we found that samples with no claim to these key conditions still show significant relationships between contact and prejudice. Thus, Allport's conditions should not be regarded as necessary for producing positive contact outcomes, as researchers have often assumed in the past. Rather, they act as facilitating conditions that enhance the tendency for positive contact outcomes to emerge").

48. See Hirschfield and Piquero, 2010.

49. Hirschfield and Piquero, 2010, p. 41.

50. A number of studies were examined in this meta-analysis. See Hogue, 1993; Hogue and Peebles, 1997; Ferguson and Ireland, 2006; Sanghara and Wilson, 2006; Johnson, Hughes, and Ireland, 2007; Kjelsberg and Loos, 2008.

51. Willis, Levenson, and Ward, 2010, p. 548.

52. Viki et al., 2012, pp. 2,363–64 ("We found that the members of the public who had little contact with sex offenders reported higher levels of dehumanization and less support for rehabilitation, in comparison to correctional staff who work with sex offenders. Within the sample of correctional staff, we also found that good quality contact was related to less dehumanization and more support for rehabilitation").

53. See Mancini et al., 2012, p. 18 ("In particular, four types of contact—employment, knowing three minorities by name, close friendship, and dating—stand out as significant predictors of reduced prejudicial views about Black criminality").

54. See Carbone and Plaut, 2013.

55. See Carbone and Plaut, 2013.

56. See Carbone and Plaut, 2013, p. 875 ("Gordon Allport originally proposed that positive effects of intergroup contact are more likely to result when four features are present: equal status between the groups; common goals; intergroup cooperation; and the support of authorities, law, or custom. Several of these factors are present within the jury context").

57. Carbone and Plaut, 2013, p. 881.

CHAPTER 8. A HEALTHY AMBIVALENCE

1. Zimring and Johnson, 2006, p. 269 ("Despite the regular occurrence of 'moral panics' throughout modern history, there is often the assumption that the 'war on crime' is a twentieth-century invention. We resist that assumption and argue instead that one should think about hostility toward criminals as recurrent and normal behavior . . . antipathy toward offenders seems to be the usual human condition in modern human societies") (citing Tonry, 2004).

2. Zimring and Johnson, 2006, p. 272 ("For now, the available evidence suggests that public attitudes about crime and punishment are not a sufficiently 'moving part' to explain the vastly different levels of punishment that exist across time and space") (citing Brown, 2006).

3. See Downes, 2016; see also Beckett, 1994; 1999; 2018

4. See Beckett and Sasson, 2003.

5. See *New York Times,* September 16, 1964, p. 1, col. 8 ("The Republican Presidential candidate said in a speech here that criminals were being needlessly pampered and that law and order were being sacrificed 'just to give criminals a sporting chance to go free' . . . He was repeatedly applauded at other times, however, especially in his reference to the 'pampering' of criminals").

6. See Marion and Oliver, 2012, p. 113 (discussing the use of crime control as a political tool and noting, "in some ways, crime is a popular topic for presidential candidates because it is a 'safe' topic for the office-seeker").

7. See Pooley, 1989; see also Randolph, 1989.

8. See Anderson, 1995, pp. 5–6 ("First, the crimes were luridly violent, involving homicide, rape, or aggravated assault that resulted in serious inquiry. Second, the victims were middle-class, usually white. . . . Third, the victims were wholly innocent. . . . Fourth, the criminals appeared to have chosen their victims entirely at random. . . . Finally, the criminals usually had some history of involvement with the criminal justice system, suggesting that if the system had only worked better, the terrible crime might have been avoided").

9. Anderson, 1995, p. 6.

10. See Miller and Chamberlain, 2015, p. 8 (discussing the formation of community sentiment and noting, "lawmakers are also 'agenda setters,' meaning that they play an important role in defining what social issues get attention"); see also Fox, Van Sickle, and Steiger, 2007.

11. See McCombs, 2005; McCombs, Shaw, and Weaver, 1997; see also Miller and Chamblain, 2015, p. 8 ("What qualifies as an 'issue' is socially constructed—that is, society and its leaders decide what is worthy of our attention and what is not, and, by communicating to the public (primarily via the media), they help to construct sociopolitical issues").

12. See Schuefele, 2000; Birkland, 1998; 2004; Entman, 1989; Jensen, 2011.

13. See Miller and Chamberlain, 2015, p. 8 ("The media shapes the community's sentiment by sending messages about what is important, right, wrong, or in need of addressing").

14. Miller and Chamberlain, 2015, p. 8.

15. See Pinaire, Heumann, and Bilotta, 2002; Manza, Brooks, and Uggen, 2004; Levine and Edwards-Levy, 2018; Stern, 2018; Moore, 2014; 2016 (all polling attitudes toward felon-voter disenfranchisement exclusively).

16. See Beckett, 1999; Beckett and Sasson, 2003.

17. See Beckett and Sasson, 2003.

18. Beckett, 1999, p. 10.

19. See Beckett and Sasson, 2003; Beckett, 1999; see also Wolfe, Jones, and Baumgartner, 2013.

20. See Wolfe, Jones, and Baumgartner, 2013, p. 186 ("In terms common in political communication, news both sets the policymaking agenda and indexes it. Increases in coverage of problems and issues may contribute to a positive feedback cycle resulting in relatively large adjustments to the system (i.e. policy change)"); see also Garland, 2001.

21. Wolfe, Jones, and Baumgartner, 2013, p. 179.

22. See Simon, 2007; Weaver, 2007.

23. See Downes, 2016.

24. Beckett, 1994, p. 426.

25. See Phelps, 2011; see also Frost, 2006; Raphael and Stoll, 2013.

26. This conceptualization implicates, once again, Garland's notion of the "criminology of the other." See Garland, 1996; 2001; see also chapter 7.

27. See Becker, 1969; Goffman, 1963.

28. Beckett, 1999, p. 10.

29. Simon, 2000, p. 1,121.

30. See Solomon, 1994; see also Marion and Oliver, 2012.

31. See Kramer and Michalowski, 1995; Mauer, 1999.

32. See Egelko, 2008.

33. See Simon, 2001.

34. Kramer, 1994; see also Oliver, 1998; 2001; 2003.

35. Marion and Oliver, 2012, p. 113 (continuing, "the only serious question for voters then becomes which candidate will propose more effective policies to reduce crime") (citing Salmore and Salmore 1985; Shea, 1996).

36. Marion and Oliver, 2012, p. 113.

37. See Lippmann, 1922; McCombs, 2004; see also Sigillo and Sicafuse, 2015, p. 29 (noting, "the media most likely acts as a moderating or mediating factor in community sentiment–public policy relationships").

38. See Pratt, 2009; Pratt et al., 2011.

39. See Meili, 2003.

40. See Firestone, 1989; Lother, 1989; Henig, 1989; Dwyer, 2002; Conner, 2002.

41. See Celona, 2002.

42. See Ross and Ingrassia, 2002; Freifeld, 2002; Dwyer and Flynn, 2002.

43. The first use of the term *moral panic* occurred in 1971 and is attributed to Jock Young. See Young, 2009. The most influential definition of the term was proffered by Stanley Cohen in 1972, who defined moral panic as when "a condition, episode, person or group of persons emerges to become defined as a threat to societal values and interest; its nature is presented in a stylized and stereotypical fashion by the mass media; the moral barricades are manned by editors, bishops, politicians, and other right-thinking people." See Cohen, 1972, p. 9.

44. The *Oxford English Dictionary* defines "wilding" as "the action or practice by a gang of youths of going on a protracted and violent rampage in a street, park, or other public place, attacking or mugging people at random along the way; also, an instance of this"; see Mexal, 2013, p. 107.

45. See Welch, Price, and Yankey, 2002, p. 4 ("The tragic event popularly became known as *wilding,* a stylized term describing sexual violence committed by a group of urban teenagers. As a newly discovered menace to public safety, wilding consumed the media and also captured the attention of politicians and members of the local criminal justice establishment who campaigned for tougher measures in dealing with youth violence").

46. Duru, 2004, p. 1,348 (citing Goldman, 1989; Powers, 1989; Rasberry, 1989; Kleinberg, 1989; Pitt, 1989; Cameron, 1989).

47. For a review of other such crimes and the sensationalized coverage they received, see Anderson, 1995; Fox, Van Sickel, and Steiger, 2007.

48. Dowler, 2004, p. 94.

49. See Anderson, 1995.

50. Lofquist, 1997, p. 243; see also Chermak, 1994; Kappeler, Blumberg, and Potter, 1996.

51. See Dowler, Fleming, and Muzatti, 2006; Russell, 1998.

52. Alexander, 2010; Fishman, 1998, p. 109.

53. Korte and Gomez, 2018.

54. CBS News, 2013. But see Bouie, 2017 (suggesting that the "knockout game" is being portrayed by the media as the new "wilding," calling on old fear-mongering tactics and overtly racial overtones).

55. Miller and Chamberlain, 2015, p. 8 ("On one level, sentiment comes from within the individual. A person's personality, preferences, beliefs, emotions, values, and experiences all shape attitudes. For instance, liberal values and conservative values are related to differences in support for a host of legal attitudes").

56. See Rade, Desmarais, and Mitchell, 2016.

57. See Rade, Desmarais, and Mitchell, 2016.

58. See, e.g., Willis, Malinen, and Johnston, 2013; but see also, e.g., Hirschfield and Piquero, 2010.

59. See, e.g., Leverentz, 2011; but see also, e.g., Comartin, Kernsmith, and Kernsmith, 2009.

60. See, e.g., Mancini et al., 2010; Park, 2009; but see also, e.g., Leverentz, 2011

61. See, e.g., Hirschfield and Piquero, 2010; but see also, e.g., Dreiling, 2011.

62. See Rade, Desmarais, and Mitchell, 2016.

63. See, e.g., Rogers, Hirst, and Davies, 2011; Hardcastle, Bartholomew, and Graffam, 2011.

64. See, e.g., Pager, 2003.

65. See, e.g., Rogers, Hirst, and Davies, 2011.

66. See, e.g., Locke, 2010.

67. See Pinaire, Heumann, and Bilotta, 2002; Manza, Brooks, and Uggen, 2004; Levine and Edwards-Levy, 2018; Stern, 2018; Moore, 2014; 2016.

68. See Pinaire, Heumann, and Bilotta, 2002; Manza, Brooks, and Uggen, 2004; Levine and Edwards-Levy, 2018; Stern, 2018; Moore, 2014; 2016.

69. See Pinaire, Heumann, and Bilotta, 2002.

70. Pinaire, Heumann, and Bilotta, 2002, p. 1,546.

71. Pinaire, Heumann, and Bilotta, 2002, pp. 1,546–47 n. 75.

72. Pinaire, Heumann, and Bilotta, 2002, p. 1547.

73. See Manza, Brooks, and Uggen, 2004.

74. See Manza, Brooks, and Uggen, 2004 (notably support was multifaceted and comprehensive, as 56 percent of respondents favored reinstatement for sex offenders no longer in prison).

75. See Levine and Edwards-Levy, 2018.

76. See Wilson, 2018.

77. See Stern, 2018, but see Totenberg, 2020; *Raysor v. Desantis*, 2020 (refusing to stay an Eleventh Circuit order interpreting Florida's felon-voter reinstatement measure as requiring full payment of court costs and fines prior to reinstatement).

78. See Moore, 2014; 2016. In 2014 and 2016, YouGov conducted two national surveys that included one question about felon-juror exclusion. In those surveys, attitudes toward felon-juror exclusion were split. In 2014, 49 percent of respondents favored permanent exclusion, 34 percent favored inclusion after the completion of a sentence, and 17 percent were unsure. In 2016, similar results presented, as 53 percent of respondents favored permanent exclusion, 35 percent favored inclusion after the completion of a sentence, and 12 percent were unsure. Notably, in both surveys, attitudes toward felon-jurors differed along ideological lines, as conservatives are least likely to support including convicted felons in the jury pool.

79. See David Barker, Nadler, and Kerschner, 2017.

80. For a more detailed description of participant characteristics, see Binnall and Petersen, 2020a; 2020b; 2021.

81. For a more detailed description of study variables, see Binnall and Petersen, 2020a; 2020b; 2021.

82. For a more detailed description of study methods and analyses, see Binnall and Petersen, 2020a; 2020b; 2021.

83. See Binnall and Petersen, 2020a.

84. See Binnall and Petersen, 2020a.

85. See Binnall and Petersen, 2020b.

86. See Rade, Desmarais, and Mitchell, 2016; see also Binnall and Petersen, 2020b.

CONCLUSION

1. See SB310—Legislative Counsel's Digest, 2019.

2. See California State Assembly Media Archives, 2019, at 3:14:40–3:19:41 (Larry Morris–California District Attorneys Association).

3. See California State Assembly Media Archives, 2019, at 3:14:40–3:19:41 (Larry Morris–California District Attorneys Association).

4. See California State Assembly Media Archives, 2019, at 3:14:40–3:19:41 (Ryan Sherman–Riverside Sheriffs' Association).

5. SB310—Legislative Counsel's Digest, 2019 ("This bill would delete the prohibition relative to persons who have been convicted of a felony from being eligible and qualified to be a prospective trial juror, and instead would prohibit persons while they are incarcerated in any prison or jail, persons who have been convicted of a felony and are currently on parole, postrelease community supervision, felony probation, or mandated supervision for the conviction of a felony, and persons who are currently required to register as a sex offender based on a felony conviction").

6. California SB310, 2019.

7. See Blankenship, 2019. See also Diskin, 2019; Binnall, 2020a; Seeds, 2017 (discussing the concept of bifurcation in reform efforts).

8. As discussed in chapter 3, a small minority of U.S. jurisdictions do not allow law enforcement personnel to serve as jurors.

9. See Rose, 2010.

10. See Rose, 2010.

EPILOGUE

1. Note that prior to S.B. 310, California permanently excluded convicted felons from the jury process. See Cal. Civ. Proc. Code § 203(a)(5), 2019. With the passage of S.B. 310, the exclusion was lifted for most prospective jurors with a felony conviction, with two notable exceptions. See Cal. Civ. Proc. Code § 203 (a)(10), 2020 ("All persons are eligible and qualified to be prospective trial jurors, except the following . . . persons who have been convicted of malfeasance in office or a felony, and are currently on parole, postrelease community supervision, felony probation, or mandated supervision for the conviction of a felony"). See also Cal. Civ. Proc. Code § 203 (a)(11), 2020 ("All persons are eligible and qualified to be prospective trial jurors, except the following. . .persons who are currently required to register as a sex offender pursuant to section 290 of the Penal Code based on a felony conviction").

2. See, e.g., County of San Francisco, 2020; see also Binnall and Davis, 2020.

3. See, e.g., Imperial County, 2020 (misleading information) ("California law says you are qualified to be a juror if you . . . have had your civil rights restored if you were convicted of a felony"); Sutter County, 2020 (false information) ("A person is disqualified or excused if he or she is a felon, nonresident, noncitizen, under a conservatorship, a non-English speaker, or an active peace officer"); see also Binnall and Davis, 2020.

4. Lawyers' Committee for Civil Rights Under Law, 2013, pp. 4–5 ("Although voting rights restoration is possible in many states, it is frequently a difficult process that varies widely across states. Individuals with felony convictions are typically unaware of their restoration rights or how to exercise them. Further, confusion among elections officials about state law contributes to the disenfranchisement of eligible voters").

5. See Drucker and Barreras, 2005.

6. Drucker and Barreras, 2005, p. 8.

7. Drucker and Barreras, 2005, p. 8.

8. Ewald, 2005, p. i.

9. Allen, 2011, p. 417.

10. See Meredith and Morse, 2014.

11. County of San Luis Obispo, 2020 ("You are qualified to be a juror if you are . . . [a]n individual who has not been convicted of a felony, or if convicted and civil rights restored, *attach a copy of Certificate of Rehabilitation*") (emphasis added); see also Binnall and Davis, 2020.

12. See Meredith and Morse, 2014.
13. See Owens, 2014.
14. See Binnall, 2018a.
15. See Meredith and Morse, 2014; 2015.
16. See Binnall and Davis, 2020.

REFERENCES

Abramson, Jeffrey (1994). *We, the jury: The jury system and the ideal of democracy.* Cambridge, MA: Harvard University Press.

Acevedo, Melissa, and Joachim I. Krueger (2004). Two egocentric sources of the decision to vote: The voter's illusion and the belief in personal relevance. *Political Psychology* 25(1): 115–34.

Ackelsberg, Irv, and Amy E. Hirsch (2002). Student loans and criminal records: Parents with past drug convictions lose access to higher education. In *Every door closed: Barriers facing parents with criminal records,* ed. Hirsch et al. (pp. 85–89). Washington, DC: Center for Law and Social Policy and Community Legal Services.

Adler, Freda (1973). Socioeconomic factors influencing jury verdicts. *New York University Review of Law and Social Change* 3(1): 1–10.

Alexander, Michelle (2010). *The new Jim Crow: Mass incarceration in the age of colorblindness.* New York: The New Press.

Alfano, Mark (2013). *Character as moral fiction.* Cambridge: Cambridge University Press.

Allen, James L. (1977). Attitude change following jury duty. *The Justice System Journal* 2(3): 246–57.

Allen, Jessie (2011). Documentary disenfranchisement. *Tulane Law Review* 86: 389–464.

Allen, Mike, Edward Mabry, and Drue-Marie McKelton (1998). Impact of juror attitudes about the death penalty on juror evaluations of guilt and punishment: A meta-analysis. *Law and Human Behavior* 22(6): 715–31.

Allport, Gordon W. (1954). The nature of prejudice. Cambridge, MA: Addison-Wesley.

Amar, Vikram D. (1995). Jury service as political participation akin to voting. *Cornell Law Review* 80: 203–59.

American Bar Association (2004). *ABA Standards for criminal justice.* 3rd ed. *Collateral sanctions and discretionary disqualification of convicted persons.* Washington, DC: American Bar Association.

Anderson, David C. (1995). *Crime and the politics of hysteria: How the Willie Horton story changed American justice*. New York: Random.

Anderson Jr., Joseph F. (2010). Where have you gone, Spot Mozingo? A trial judge's lament over the demise of the civil jury trial. *Federal Courts Law Review* 4(99): 100–20.

Andrews, Donald A., and James Bonta (1995). *The Level of Service Inventory-Revised*. Toronto: Multi-Health Systems.

———— (2003). *The psychology of criminal conduct*. 3rd. ed. Cincinnati: Anderson Publishing.

Andrews, Donald A., James Bonta, and Robert D. Hoge (1990). Classification for effective rehabilitation: Rediscovering psychology. *Criminal Justice and Behavior* 17(1): 19–52.

Andrews, Donald A., James Bonta, and J. Stephen Wormith (2006). The recent past and near future of risk and/or need assessment. *Crime and Delinquency* 52(1): 7–27.

———— (2011). The risk-need-responsivity (RNR) model: Does adding the good lives model contribute to effective crime prevention? *Criminal Justice and Behavior* 38(7): 735–55.

Andrews, Donald A., et al. (1990). Does correctional treatment work? A clinically relevant and psychologically informed meta-analysis. *Criminology* 28(3): 369–404.

Angwin, Julia, et al. (2016). Machine bias: There's software used across the country to predict future criminals; And it's biased against blacks. *ProPublica*, May 23. Retrieved from www.propublica.org/article/machine-bias-risk-assessments-in-criminal-sentencing (accessed September 1, 2020).

Anti-Recidivism Coalition (2020). Our story. Retrieved from www.antirecidivism.org/our-story (accessed September 1, 2020).

Antonio, Anthony L., et al. (2004). Effects of racial diversity on complex thinking in college students. *Psychological Science* 15(8): 507–10.

Aresti, Andreas, Sacha Darke, and Rod Earle (2012). British convict criminology: Developing critical insider perspectives on prison. *Inside Time,* August 1. Retrieved from https://insidetime.org/british-convict-criminologydeveloping-critical-insider-perspectives-on-prison/ (accessed September 1, 2020).

Aristotle (1941). Nicomachean ethics. *The basic works of Aristotle*, ed. Richard McKeon (pp. 935–1,126). New York: Random House.

Arnold Jr., Richard R. (1997). Presumptive disqualification and prior unlawful conduct: The danger of unpredictable character standards for bar applicants. *Utah Law Review* 1997(1): 63–100.

Arterton, Janet B. (2007). Unconscious bias and the impartial jury. *Connecticut Law Review* 40(4): 1,023–33.

Aukerman, Miriam J. (2005). The somewhat suspect class: Towards a constitutional framework for evaluating occupational restrictions affecting people with criminal records. *Journal of Law in Society* 7(1): 18–87.

Australian Government (2020). Federal court of Australia act, section 23DI, Disqualification from serving on jury (convictions, charges, detention orders, etc.).

Retrieved from www.legislation.gov.au/Details/C2018C00342/Html/Text#_Toc523905801 (accessed September 1, 2020).

Avery, Derek R., et al. (2009). It does not have to be uncomfortable: The role of behavioral scripts in black-white interracial interactions. *Journal of Applied Psychology* 94(6): 1,382–93.

Aviram, Hadar (2019). Moral character: Making sense of the experiences of bar applicants with criminal records. *Manitoba Law Review*, http://dx.doi.org/10.2139/ssrn.3440387 (forthcoming).

Bantel, Karen A. (1994). Strategic planning openness: The role of top team demography. *Group and Organization Management* 19(4): 406–24.

Barber, Benjamin R. (1984). *Strong democracy: Participatory politics for a new age.* Berkeley: University of California Press.

Barker, David, Kim Nadler, and Barbara Kerschner (2017). CALSPEAKS survey of Californians: August 2017. California State University, Sacramento, Institute for Social Research.

Bauman, Richard A. (1989). *Lawyers and politics in the early Roman empire: A study of relations between the Roman jurists and the emperors from Augustus to Hadrian.* Munich: CH Beck.

Bazemore, Gordon, and Rachel Boba (2007). "Doing good" to "make good": Community theory for practice in a restorative justice civic engagement reentry model. *Journal of Offender Rehabilitation* 46(1–2): 25–56.

Bazemore, Gordon, and Carsten Erbe (2003). Operationalizing the community variable in offender reintegration: Theory and practice for developing intervention social capital. *Youth Violence and Juvenile Justice* 1(3): 246–75.

Bazemore, Gordon, and Jeanne Stinchcomb (2004). A civic engagement model of reentry: Involving community through service and restorative justice. *Fed. Probation* 68(2): 14–24.

Becker, Howard S. (1963) *Outsiders: Studies in the sociology of deviance.* New York: MacMillan.

Beckett, Katherine (1994). Setting the public agenda: "Street crime" and drug use in American politics. *Social Problems* 41(3): 425–47.

——— (1999). *Making crime pay: Law and order in contemporary American politics.* New York: Oxford University Press.

——— (2018). Mass incarceration and its discontents. *Contemporary Sociology* 47(1): 11–22.

Beckett, Katherine, and Theodore Sasson (2003). *The politics of injustice: Crime and punishment in America.* Thousand Oaks, CA: Sage Publications.

Behfar, Kristin J., et al. (2008). The critical role of conflict resolution in teams: A close look at the links between conflict type, conflict management strategies, and team outcomes. *Journal of Applied Psychology* 93(1): 170–88.

——— (2011). Conflict in small groups: The meaning and consequences of process conflict. *Small Group Research* 42(2): 127–76.

Bell, Bradford S., Ann Marie Ryan, and Darin Wiechmann (2004). Justice expectations and applicant perceptions. *International Journal of Selection and Assessment* 12(1–2): 24–38.

Bennett, Mark W. (2010). Unraveling the Gordian knot of implicit bias in jury selection: The problems of judge-dominated voir dire, the failed promise of Batson, and proposed solutions. *Harvard Law and Policy Review* 4: 149–71.

Bennett, Mark W., Margaret H. Downie, and Larry C. Zervos (2004). Judges' views on vanishing civil trials. *Judicature* 88(6): 306–9, 312.

Bentele, Ursula, and William J. Bowers (2002). How jurors decide on death: Guilt is overwhelming; aggravation requires death; and mitigation is no excuse. *Brooklyn Law Review* 66(4): 1,011–80.

Bernard, J. L., and W. O. Dwyer (1984). Witherspoon v. Illinois: The court was right. *Law and Psychology Review* 8: 105–14.

Bernstein-Baker, Judith, and Joe Hohenstein (2002). Divided families: Immigration consequences of contact with the criminal justice system. In *Every door closed: Barriers facing parents with criminal records,* ed. Hirsch et al. (pp. 91–104). Washington, DC: Center for Law and Social Policy and Community Legal Services.

Binnall, James M. (2008). EG1900 . . . The number they gave me when they revoked my citizenship: Perverse consequences of ex-felon civic exile. *Williamette Law Review* 44: 667–97.

——— (2009). Sixteen million angry men: Reviving a dead doctrine to challenge the constitutionality of excluding felons from jury service. *Virginia Journal of Social Policy and the Law* 17(1): 2–42.

——— (2010a). A jury of none: An essay on the last acceptable form of civic banishment. *Dialectical Anthropology* 34(4): 533–38.

——— (2010b). Convicts in court: Felonious lawyers make a case for including convicted felons in the jury pool. *Albany Law Review* 73: 1,379–440.

——— (2010c). A felon deliberates: Policy implications of the Michigan Supreme Court's holding in *People v. Miller. University of Detroit Mercy Law Review* 87: 59–81.

——— (2014). A field study of the presumptively biased: Is there empirical support for excluding convicted felons from jury service? *Law and Policy* 36(1): 1–34.

——— (2018a). Summonsing criminal desistance: Convicted felons' perspectives on jury service. *Law and Social Inquiry* 43(1): 4–27.

——— (2018b). Cops and convicts: An exploratory study of jurymandering. *Ohio State Journal of Criminal Law* 16(1): 221–39.

——— (2018c). Exorcising presumptions? Judges and attorneys contemplate 'felon-juror inclusion' in Maine. *Justice System Journal* 39(4): 378–92.

——— (2018d). Felon-jurors in vacationland: A field study of transformative civic engagement in Maine. *Maine Law Review* 71(1): 71–101.

——— (2019). Jury diversity in the age of mass incarceration: An exploratory mock jury experiment examining felon-jurors' potential impacts on deliberations. *Psychology, Crime and Law* 25(4): 345–63.

——— (2020). A "meaningful" seat at the table: Contemplating our ongoing struggle to access democracy. *Southern Methodist University Law Review* 73: 35–50.

Binnall, James M., and Lauren M. Davis (2020). Californians with a felony conviction are now eligible for jury service: How would they know? *Stanford Law and Policy Review Online* 32(1): 1–27.

Binnall, James M., and Nick Petersen (2020a). Public perceptions of felon-juror exclusion: An exploratory study. *Criminology and Criminal Justice*, doi: 1748895819898518.

———— (2020b). They're just different: The bifurcation of public attitudes toward felon-jurors convicted of violent offenses. *Crime, Law and Social Change*, doi: 10611020099123. Forthcoming.

———— (2020c). Building biased jurors: Exposing the circularity of the inherent bias rationale for felon-juror exclusion. *Psychiatry, Psychology and Law* 27(1): 110–25.

———— (2021). No fear here: How the public views anticipated interactions with jurors convicted of a felony. *Berkeley Journal of Criminal Law*. Forthcoming.

Birkland, Thomas A. (1998). Focusing events, mobilization, and agenda-setting. *Journal of Public Policy* 18(1): 53–74.

———— (2004). "The world changed today": Agenda-setting and policy change in the wake of the September 11 terrorist attacks. *Review of Policy Research* 21(2): 179–200.

Blackstone, William (1791). *Commentaries on the laws of England: In four books, volume three*. London: A. Strahan and W. Woodfall.

Blankenship, Jim (2019). SB-310: More fun and games for California's convicted felons. *Los Angeles County Professional Peace Officers Association*, August 1. Retrieved from https://ppoa.com/issue-article/sb-310-more-fun-and-games-for-californias-convicted-felons (accessed September 1, 2020).

Blum, George L. (2005). Criminal record as affecting applicant's moral character for purposes of admission to the bar. *American Law Reports* 3: 49–241.

Boatright, Robert G. (1999). Why citizens don't respond to jury summonses, and what courts can do about it. *Judicature* 82(4): 156–65.

Bonazzoli, M. Juliet (1998). Jury selection and bias: Debunking invidious stereotypes through science. *Quinnipiac Law Review* 18: 247–305.

Bonta, James, and Donald A. Andrews (2007). Risk-need-responsivity model for offender assessment and rehabilitation. *Rehabilitation* 6(1): 1–22.

Bontrager, Stephanie, William Bales, and Ted Chiricos (2005). Race, ethnicity, threat, and the labeling of convicted felons. *Criminology* 43(3): 589–622.

Bottoms, Anthony, et al. (2004). Towards desistance: Theoretical underpinnings for an empirical study. *Howard Journal of Criminal Justice* 43(4): 368–89.

Bouie, Jamelle (2013). Guess what? The 'knockout game' is America's latest phony panic. *The Daily Beast*, November 25. Retrieved from www.thedailybeast.com /guess-what-the-knockout-game-is-americas-latest-phony-panic (accessed September 1, 2020).

Bowers, William J., Marla Sandys, and Benjamin D. Steiner (1998). Foreclosed impartiality in capital sentencing: Jurors' predispositions, guilt-trial experience, and premature decision making. *Cornell Law Review* 83: 1,476–556.

Braithwaite, John (1989). *Crime, shame and reintegration.* Cambridge: Cambridge University Press.

Braithwaite, John, and Valerie Braithwaite (2001). Shame, shame management, and regulation. In *Shame management through reintegration*, eds. Eliza Ahmed, Nathan Harris, John Braithwaite, and Valerie Braithwaite (pp. 3–18). Cambridge: University of Cambridge.

Braithwaite, John, and Stephen Mugford (1994). Conditions of successful reintegration ceremonies: Dealing with juvenile offenders. *British Journal of Criminology* 34(2): 139–71.

Brand, Jeffrey S. (1994). The supreme court, equal protection, and jury selection: denying that race still matters. *Wisconsin Law Review* 1994: 511–630.

Braun, Virginia, and Victoria Clarke (2006). Using thematic analysis in psychology. *Qualitative Research in Psychology* 3(2): 77–101.

Brennan, Tim, William Dieterich, and Beate Ehret (2009). Evaluating the predictive validity of the COMPAS risk and needs assessment system. *Criminal Justice and Behavior* 36(1): 21–40.

Breyer, Stephen (2005). *Active liberty: Interpreting our democratic constitution.* New York: Vintage Books.

Bridgeman, Diane L., and David Marlowe (1979). Jury decision making: An empirical study based on actual felony trials. *Journal of Applied Psychology* 64(2): 91–98.

Brodin, Mark S. (2016) The murder of black males in a world of non-accountability: The surreal trial of George Zimmerman in the killing of Trayvon Martin. *Howard Law Journal* 59(3): 765–85.

Brown, Darryl K. (1994). The role of race in jury impartiality and venue transfers. *Maryland Law Review* 53(1): 107–56.

Brown, Elizabeth K. (2006). The dog that did not bark: Punitive social views and the "professional middle classes". *Punishment and Society* 8(3): 287–312.

Brown, J. David (1991). The professional ex-: An alternative for exiting the deviant career. *Sociological Quarterly* 32(2): 219–30.

Brun, Carl, and Richard C. Rapp (2001). Strengths-based case management: Individuals' perspectives on strengths and the case manager relationship. *Social Work* 46(3): 278–88.

Buchwalter, James L. (2000). Annotation, disqualification or exemption of juror for conviction of, or prosecution for, criminal offenses. *American Law Reports* 5th 75: 295–338.

Burnett, Ros, and Shadd Maruna (2006). The kindness of prisoners: Strengths-based resettlement in theory and in action. *Criminology and Criminal Justice* 6(1): 83–106.

Burns, Robert P. (2013). Advocacy in the era of the vanishing trial. *University of Kansas Law Review* 61: 893–904

Bushway, Shawn D., et al (2001). An empirical framework for studying desistance as a process. *Criminology* 39(2): 491–516.

Bushway, Shawn D., Michael A. Stoll, and David Weiman (2007). *Barriers to reentry? The labor market for released prisoners in post-industrial America.* New York: Russell Sage Foundation.

Butler, Paul (2010). *Let's get free: A hip-hop theory of justice.* New York: New Press.

Button, Mark, and Kevin Mattson (1999). Deliberative democracy in practice: Challenges and prospects for civic deliberation. *Polity* 31(4): 609–37.

Cadinu, Mara, et al. (2003). Stereotype threat: The effect of expectancy on performance. *European Journal of Social Psychology* 33(2): 267–85.

Cameron, Deborah (1989). Brutal attack that's riveted a city. *Sydney Morning Herald* (May 13, 1989).

Cammack, Mark (1995). In search of the post-positivist jury. *Indiana Law Journal* 70(2): 405–89.

California Legislative Counsel's Digest. SB-310. Jury Service (2019). Retrieved from https://leginfo.legislature.ca.gov/faces/billTextClient.xhtml?bill_id=201920200 SB310 (accessed September 1, 2020).

California SB310, Jury Service (2019). Retrieved from https://trackbill.com/bill/california-senate-bill-310-jury-service/1693167 (accessed September 1, 2020).

California State Assembly Media Archives. SB-310. Jury Service (2019). Retrieved from https://assembly.ca.gov/media-archive (accessed September 1, 2020).

Carbone, Christina S., and Victoria C. Plaut (2013). Diversity and the civil jury. *William and Mary Law Review* 55(3): 837–84.

Carey, Corrinne A. (2004). *No second chance: People with criminal records denied access to public housing.* New York: Human Rights Watch.

Carr, Maureen M. (1995). The effect of prior criminal conduct on the admission to practice law: The move to more flexible admission standards. *Georgetown Journal of Legal Ethics* 8: 367–98.

Caspi, Avshalom, and Terrie E. Moffitt (1993). When do individual differences matter? A paradoxical theory of personality coherence. *Psychological Inquiry* 4(4): 247–71.

Cast, Alicia D., Jan E. Stets, and Peter J. Burke (1999). Does the self conform to the views of others? *Social Psychology Quarterly* 62(1): 68–82.

CBS News (2013). Deadly "knockout game": What is it and why teens are playing it. *CBS This Morning*, November 21. Retrieved from www.cbsnews.com/news/deadly-knockout-game-what-it-is (accessed September 1, 2020).

Celona, Larry (2002). Detectives blast Morgenthau review. *New York Post*, December 6.

Chapdelanie, Andrea, and Sean F. Griffin (1997). Beliefs of guilt and recommended sentence as a function of juror bias in the O.J. Simpson trial. *Journal of Social Issues* 53(3): 477–85.

Charron, Angelina, and Jessica Woodhams (2010). A qualitative analysis of mock jurors' deliberations of linkage analysis evidence. *Journal of Investigative Psychology and Offender Profiling* 7(2): 165–83.

Chermak, Steven M. (1994). Body count news: How crime is presented in the news media. *Justice Quarterly* 11(4): 561–82.

Chin, Gabriel J. (2017). Collateral consequences. In *Reforming criminal justice: A report by the academy for justice,* ed. Erik Luna (pp. 371–95). Tempe, AZ: Sandra Day O'Connor School of Law.

Chiricos, Ted, et al. (2007). The labeling of convicted felons and its consequences for recidivism. *Criminology* 45(3): 547–81.

Chung, Jean (2017). Felony disenfranchisement: A primer. Retrieved from www.sentencingproject.org/publications/felony-disenfranchisement-a-primer (accessed September 1, 2020).

Citizens Advice Scotland (2020). Jury service. Retrieved from www.citizensadvice .org.uk/scotland/law-and-courts/legal-system-s/taking-legal-action-s/jury-service-s (accessed September 1, 2020).

Clark, Michael D. (2000). The juvenile drug court judge and lawyer: Four common mistakes in treating drug court adolescents. *Juvenile and Family Court Journal* 51(4): 37–46.

——— (2001). Influencing positive behavior change: Increasing the therapeutic approach of juvenile courts. *Federal Probation* 65(1): 18–27.

Clark, Noel K., Geoffrey M. Stephenson, and Bromley H. Kniveton (1990). Social remembering: Quantitative aspects of individual and collaborative remembering by police officers and students. *British Journal of Psychology* 81(1): 73–94.

Clemens, Aaron M. (2007). Facing the klieg lights: Understanding the good moral character examination for bar applicants. *Akron Law Review* 40(2): 255–310.

Coady, Cecil A.J., and Onora O'Neill (1990). Messy morality and the art of the possible. *Proceedings of the Aristotelian Society* 64(1): 259–79, 281–94.

Cohen, Stanley (1972). *Folk devils and moral panics.* London: MacGibbon and Kee.

Collateral Consequences Resource Center (2020). *Collateral Consequences of Criminal Conviction and Restoration of Rights: News, Commentary, and Tools.* Retrieved from http://ccresourcecenter.org/topics/topics/cctypes/housing-cctypes/ (accessed September 1, 2020).

Comartin, Erin B., Poco D. Kernsmith, and Roger M. Kernsmith (2009). Sanctions for sex offenders: Fear and public policy. *Journal of Offender Rehabilitation* 48(7): 605–19.

Comment (1972). "Jury-mandering": Federal jury selection and the generation gap. *Iowa Law Review* 59(2): 401–19.

Committee of Bar Examiners, Office of Admissions, State Bar of California. Application for Determination of Moral Character (2020).

Connor, Tracy (2002). Retracing gruesome trail of mayhem and violence. *New York Daily News,* September 5.

Conrad Jr., Honorable Robert J., and Katy L. Clements (2018). The vanishing criminal jury trial: From trial judges to sentencing judges. *George Washington Law Review* 86(1): 99–167.

Consolini, Paula M. (1992). Learning by doing justice: Jury service and political attitudes. PhD diss., University of California, Berkeley.

Cooley, Charles H. (1902). *Human nature and the social order.* New York: Scribner's.

Corrigan, Patrick W., et al. (2001). Familiarity with and social distance from people who have serious mental illness. *Psychiatric Services* 52(7): 953–58.

County of San Francisco (2020). Senate bill 310—jury service (felony convictions). Retrieved from https://sfsuperiorcourt.org/divisions/jury-services/jury-reporting (accessed September 1, 2020).

County of San Luis Obispo (2020). Juror Qualifications. Retrieved from www.slo .courts.ca.gov/gi/jury-qualifications.htm (accessed September 1, 2020).

Cowan, Claudia L., William C. Thompson, and Phoebe C. Ellsworth (1984). The effects of death qualification on jurors' predisposition to convict and on the quality of deliberation. *Law and Human Behavior* 8(1–2): 53–79.

Cressey, Donald R. (1955). Changing criminals: The application of the theory of differential association. *American Journal of Sociology* 61(2): 116–20.

———— (1965). Social psychological foundations for using criminals in the rehabilitation of criminals. *Journal of Research in Crime and Delinquency* 2(2): 49–59.

Crocker, Jennifer, Brenda Major, and Claude Steele (1998). Social stigma. In *The Handbook of Social Psychology*, eds. Daniel T. Gilbert, Susan T. Fiske, and Gardner Lindzey (pp. 504–53). New York: Oxford University Press.

Culhane, Scott E., John H. Boman IV, and Kimberly Schweitzer (2016). Public perceptions of the justifiability of police shootings: The role of body cameras in pre-and post-Ferguson experiment. *Police Quarterly* 19(3): 251–74.

Culhane, Scott E., Harmon M. Hosch, and William G. Weaver (2004). Crime victims serving as jurors: Is there bias present? *Law and Human Behavior* 28(6): 649–59.

Cutler, Brian L., and Donna M. Hughes (2001). Judging jury service: Results of the North Carolina administrative office of the courts juror survey. *Behavioral Sciences and the Law* 19(2): 305–20.

Cutler, Brian L., Gary Moran, and Douglas J. Narby (1992). Jury selection in insanity defense cases. *Journal of Research in Personality* 26(2): 165–82.

Damaska, Mirjan R. (1968). Adverse legal consequences of conviction and their removal: A comparative study (pt. 2). *Journal of Criminal Law, Criminology and Police Science* 59(4): 542–68.

Davis, James H., Robert M. Bray, and Robert W. Holt (1977). The empirical study of decision processes in juries: A critical review. In *Law Justice and the Individual in Society: Psychological and Legal Issues,* eds. J. L. Tapp and F. J. Levine (pp. 326–61). New York: Holt, Rinehart, and Winston.

De Dreu, Carsten K. W., and Laurie R. Weingart (2003). Task versus relationship conflict, team performance, and team member satisfaction: A meta-analysis. *Journal of Applied Psychology* 88(4): 741–49.

De Giorgi, Alessandro (2017). Back to nothing: Prisoner reentry and neoliberal neglect. *Social Justice* 44(1): 83–120.

De La Fuente, Leticia, E. Inmaculada De La Fuente, and Juan Garcia (2003). Effects of pretrial juror bias, strength of evidence and deliberation process on juror decision: New validity evidence of the juror bias scale scores. *Psychology, Crime and Law* 9(2): 197–209.

Delancey Street Foundation (2020a). Our story. Retrieved from www .delanceystreetfoundation.org/ourstory (accessed September 1, 2020).

———— (2020b). What we believe. Retrieved from www.delanceystreetfoundation
.org/wwb.php(accessed September 1, 2020).

———— (2020c). Who we are. Retrieved from www.delanceystreetfoundation.org
/wwa.php (accessed September 1, 2020).

Denham, Bryan E. (2010). Toward conceptual consistency in studies of agenda-building processes: A scholarly review. *Review of Communication* 10(4): 306–23.

Desmarais, Sarah L., Kiersten L. Johnson, and Jay P. Singh (2016). Performance of recidivism risk assessment instruments in U.S. correctional settings. *Psychological Services* 13(3): 206–22.

Devine, Dennis J. (2012). *Jury decision making: The state of science.* Vol. 8. New York: New York University Press.

Devine, Dennis J., et al. (2001). Jury decision making: Forty-five years of empirical research on deliberating groups. *Psychology, Public Policy and Law* 7(3): 622–727.

———— (2007). Deliberation quality: A preliminary examination in criminal juries. *Journal of Empirical Legal Studies* 4(2): 273–303.

DeVito, Scott (2008). Justice and the felonious attorney. *Santa Clara Law Review* 48(1): 155–79.

Dexter, Hedy Red, Brian L. Cutler, and Gary Moran (1992). A test of voir dire as a remedy for the prejudicial effects of pretrial publicity. *Journal of Applied Social Psychology* 22(10): 819–32.

Diamond, Shari Siedman, and Jonathan D. Casper (1992). Blindfolding the jury to verdict consequences: Damages, experts and the civil jury. *Law and Society Review* 26(3): 513–63.

Dickson, Harris (1905). *Duke of devil-may-care.* Minneapolis: D. Appleton.

Diskin, Megan (2019). Legislation would allow felons to serve as jurors in California. *Ventura County Star,* August 16. Retrieved from www.vcstar.com/story/news /local/2019/08/16/california-felons-jury-duty-bill/1973486001 (accessed September 1, 2020).

Dixon, Jeffrey C., and Michael S. Rosenbaum (2004). Nice to know you? Testing contact, cultural, and group threat theories of anti-Black and anti-Hispanic stereotypes. *Social Science Quarterly* 85(2): 257–80.

Doherty, Sherri, Pamela Forrester, Amanda Brazil, and Flora I. Matheson (2014). Finding their way: Conditions for successful reintegration among women offenders. *Journal of Offender Rehabilitation* 53(7): 562–86.

Doris, John M. (2002). *Lack of character: Personality and moral behavior.* New York: Cambridge University Press.

Dowler, Kenneth (2004). Dual realities? Criminality, victimization, and the presentation of race on local television news. *Journal of Crime and Justice* 27(2): 79–99.

Dowler, Kenneth, Thomas Fleming, and Stephen L. Muzzatti (2006). Constructing crime: Media, crime, and popular culture. *Canadian Journal of Criminology and Criminal Justice* 48(6): 837–50.

Downes, David (2016). Comparative criminology, globalization, and the 'punitive turn.' In *Comparative Criminal Justice and Globalization,* ed. David Nelken (pp. 37–57). Thousand Oaks, CA: Sage Publications.

Dreiling, Katie L. (2011). Knowledge and opinion of sex offenders and sex offender policy: Do sources of information matter? PhD diss., South Dakota State University.

Dressel, Julia, and Hany Farid (2018). The accuracy, fairness, and limits of predicting recidivism. *Science Advances* 4(1): 1–5.

Drucker, Ernest, and Ricardo Barreras (2005). *Studies of voting behavior and felony disenfranchisement among individuals in the criminal justice system in New York, Connecticut, and Ohio.* Washington, DC: Sentencing Project.

Dufraimont, Lisa (2008). Evidence law and the jury: A reassessment. *McGill Law Journal* 53: 199–242.

Durand, Richard M., William O. Bearden, and A. William Gustafson (1978). Previous jury service as a moderating influence on jurors' beliefs and attitudes. *Psychological Reports* 42(2): 567–72.

Duru, Jeremi N. (2004). The Central Park five, the Scottsboro boys, and the myth of the bestial black man. *Cardozo Law Review* 25: 1,315–65.

Dwyer, Jim (2002). Likely u-turn by prosecutors in jogger case. *New York Times*, October 12.

Dwyer, Jim, and Kevin Flynn (2002). New light on jogger's rape calls evidence into question. *New York Times*, December 1.

Dwyer, William L. (2002). *In the hands of the people: The trial jury's origins, triumphs, troubles and future in American democracy.* New York: St. Martin's Press.

Eckhouse, Laurel, et al. (2019). Layers of bias: A unified approach for understanding problems with risk assessment. *Criminal Justice and Behavior* 46(2): 185–209.

Egelko, Bob (2008). Where candidates stand on crime, death penalty: Differences are greater between parties than between candidates. *SFGate*, February 10. Retrieved from www.sfgate.com/politics/article/Where-candidates-stand-on-crime-death-penalty-3227193.php (accessed September 1, 2020).

Eisenberg, Theodore, Stephen P. Garvey, and Martin T. Wells (2001). Forecasting life and death: Juror race, religion, and attitude toward the death penalty. *Journal of Legal Studies* 30(2): 277–311.

Ellis, Leslie, and Shari Siedman Diamond (2003). Race, diversity, and jury composition: Battering and bolstering legitimacy. *Chicago-Kent Law Review* 78(3): 1,033–58.

Ellsworth, Phoebe C. (1989). Are twelve heads better than one? *Law and Contemporary Problems* 52(4): 205–24.

——— (1993). Some steps between attitudes and verdicts. In *Inside the juror: The psychology of juror decision making*, ed. R. Hastie (pp. 42–64). New York: Cambridge University Press.

Ellsworth, Phoebe C., and Alan Reifman (2000). Juror comprehension and public policy: Perceived problems and proposed solutions. *Psychology, Public Policy, and Law* 6(3): 788–821.

Enns, Peter K., et al. (2019). What percentage of Americans have ever had a family member incarcerated? Evidence from the family history of incarceration survey (FamHIS). *Sociological Research for a Dynamic World* 5: 1–45.

Entman, Robert M. (1989). How the media affect what people think: An information processing approach. *Journal of Politics* 51(2): 347–70.

Esterberg, Kristin G. (2002). *Qualitative methods in social research*. Boston: McGraw-Hill.

Ewald, Alec C. (2002). Civil death: The ideological paradox of criminal disenfranchisement law in the United States. *Wisconsin Law Review* 2002: 1,045–1,137.

———(2005). *A crazy-quilt of tiny pieces: State and local administration of American criminal disenfranchisement law*. Vol. 16. Washington, DC: Sentencing Project.

———(2012). Collateral consequences in the American states. *Social Science Quarterly* 93(1): 211–47.

———(2016). Rights restoration and the entanglement of US criminal and civil law: A study of New York's "certificates of relief." *Law and Social Inquiry* 41(1): 5–36.

———(2017). Collateral sanctions. In *Oxford research encyclopedias: Criminology and criminal justice*, ed. Henry Pontell (pp. 1–42). New York: Oxford University Press.

Ewald, Alec C., and Marnie Smith (2008). Collateral consequences of criminal convictions in American courts: The view from the state bench. *Justice System Journal* 29(2): 145–65.

Farrall, Stephen (2002). *Rethinking what works with offenders: Probation, social context and desistance from crime*. New York: Routledge.

Farrall, Stephen, et al. (2011). Theorizing structural and individual-level processes in desistance and persistence: Outlining an integrated perspective. *Australian and New Zealand Journal of Criminology* 44(2): 218–34.

Fazel, Seena, et al. (2012). Use of risk assessment instruments to predict violence and antisocial behaviour in 73 samples involving 24,827 people: Systematic review and meta-analysis. *BMJ: British Medical Journal* 345 (7868): 19–19 345.

Federal Farmer (1981). Letters from a federal farmer, XV. In *The complete anti-federalist*, ed. Hebert Storing (p. 149). Chicago: University of Chicago Press.

Federal Judicial Center (1987). Pattern criminal jury instructions. Retrieved from www.fjc.gov/sites/default/files/2012/CrimJury.pdf (accessed September 1, 2020).

Feeley, Malcom M. (2012). Actuarial justice and the modern state. In *Punishment, places, and perpetrators: Developments in criminology and criminal justice research*, ed. Gerben Bruinsma, Henk Elffers, and Jan De Keijser (pp. 62–77). New York: Routledge.

Feeley, Malcom M., and Jonathon Simon (1992). The new penology: Notes on the emerging strategy of corrections and its implications. *Criminology* 30(4): 449–74.

———(1994). Actuarial justice: The emerging new criminal law. In *The futures of criminology*, ed. David Nelken (pp. 173–201). London: Sage Publications.

Ferguson, Kerry, and Carol A. Ireland (2006). Attitudes towards sex offenders and the influence of offence type: A comparison of staff working in a forensic setting and students. *British Journal of Forensic Practice* 8(2): 10–19.

Finkel, Steven E. (1985). Reciprocal effects of participation and political efficacy: A panel analysis. *American Journal of Political Science* 29(4): 891–913.

Firestone, David (1989). Talking about the night. *Newsday*, April 19.

Fischer, Ronald, et al. (2008). Support for resistance among Iraqi students: An exploratory study. *Basic and Applied Social Psychology* 30(2): 167–75.

Fishman, Laura T. (1998). Images of crime and punishment: The black bogeyman and white self-righteousness. In *Images of Color, Images of Crime,* eds. Coramae R. Mann and Marjorie S. Zatz (pp. 109–25). Los Angeles: Roxbury Publishing.

Flanagan, Owen J. (2009). *Varieties of moral personality: Ethics and psychological realism.* Cambridge, MA: Harvard University Press.

Fleming, Monique A., Richard E. Petty, and Paul H. White (2005). Stigmatized targets and evaluation: Prejudice as a determinant of attribute scrutiny and polarization. *Personality and Social Psychology Bulletin* 31(4): 496–507.

Fox, Kathryn J. (2015). Theorizing community integration as desistance-promotion. *Criminal Justice and Behavior* 42(1): 82–94.

——— (2016). Civic commitment: Promoting desistance through community integration. *Punishment and Society* 18(1): 68–94.

Fox, Richard L., Robert W. Van Sickle, and Thomas L. Steiger (2007). *Tabloid justice: Criminal justice in an age of media frenzy.* Boulder: Lynne Rienner.

Franko Aas, Katja (2007). Analysing a world in motion: Global flows meet 'criminology of the other'. *Theoretical criminology* 11(2): 283–303.

Freie, John F. (1997). The effects of campaign participation on political attitudes. *Political Behavior* 19(2): 133–56.

Freifeld, Karen (2002). Convictions tossed: Judge clears verdicts of Central Park 5. *Newsday,* December 6.

Frost, Natasha A. (2006). *The punitive state: Crime, punishment, and imprisonment across the United States.* New York: LFB Scholarly Publishing.

Fukurai, Hiroshi, and Darryl Davies (1997). Affirmative action in jury selection: Racially representative juries, racial quotas, and affirmative juries of the hennepin model and the jury de medietate linguae. *Virginia Journal of Social Policy and Law* 4: 645–81.

Fung, Archon (2005). Deliberation's darker side: Six questions for Iris Marion Young and Jane Mansbridge. *National Civic Review* 93(4): 47–54.

Galanter, Marc (2004). The vanishing trial: An examination of trials and related matters in federal and state courts. *Journal of Empirical Legal Studies* 1(3): 459–570.

——— (2005). The hundred-year decline of trials and the thirty years war. *Stanford Law Review* 57(5): 1255–74.

Garcia, Luis T., and William Griffitt (1978). Impact of testimonial evidence as a function of witness characteristics. *Bulletin of the Psychonomic Society* 11(1): 37–40.

Gardner, John (1998). The gist of excuses. *Buffalo Criminal Law Review* 1(2): 575–98.

Garland, David (1990). *Punishment in modern society: A study in social theory.* Oxford: Clarendon Press.

——— (1996). The limits of the sovereign state: Strategies of crime control in contemporary society. *British Journal of Criminology* 36(4): 445–71.

———, ed. (2001). *Mass imprisonment: Social causes and consequences.* Thousand Oaks, CA: Sage Publications.

Gastil, John, E. Pierre Deess, and Philip J. Weiser (2002). Civic awakening in the jury room: A test of the connection between jury deliberation and political participation. *Journal of Policy* 64(2): 585–95.

Gastil, John, and Philip J. Weiser (2006). Jury service as an invitation to citizenship: Assessing the civic value of institutionalized deliberation. *Policy Studies Journal* 34(4): 605–27.

Gastil, John, et al. (2008). Jury service and electoral participation: A test of the participation hypothesis. *Journal of Politics* 70(2): 351–67.

——— (2012). Seeing is believing: The impact of jury service on attitudes toward legal institutions and the implications for international jury reform. *Court Review* 48: 124–30.

Gawronski, Bertram, and Etienne P. LeBel (2008). Understanding patterns of attitude change: When implicit measures show change, but explicit measures do not. *Journal of Experimental Social Psychology* 44(5): 1,355–61.

Gecas, Viktor, and Michael L. Schwalbe (1983). Beyond the looking-glass self: Social structure and efficacy-based self-esteem. *Social Psychology Quarterly* 46(2): 77–88.

Geiger, Ben (2006). The case for treating ex-offenders as a suspect class. *California Law Review* 94(4): 1,191–242.

Gerbasi, Kathleen C., Miron Zuckerman, and Harry T. Reis (1977). Justice needs a new blindfold: A review of mock jury research. *Psychological Bulletin* 84(2): 323–45.

Gillers, Stephen (1995). *Regulation of lawyers: Problems of law and ethics.* Alphen aan den Rijn, Netherlands: Wolters Kluwer Law and Business.

Giordano, Peggy C., Stephen A. Cernkovich, and Jennifer L. Rudolph (2002). Gender, crime, and desistance: Toward a theory of cognitive transformation. *American Journal of Sociology* 107(4): 990–1,064.

Goffman, Erving (1963). *Stigma: Notes on the management of spoiled identity.* New York: Simon and Schuster.

Goldman, John J. (1989). Gang assault on women stuns N.Y.: Investment banker death, victim of park rampage. *Los Angeles Times*, April 24.

Gonnerman, Jennifer (2004). *Life on the outside.* London: Macmillan.

Gordon, Sara (2013). Through the eyes of jurors: The use of schemas in the application of "plain language" jury instructions. *Hastings Law Journal* 64(3): 643–78.

Gouldin, Lauryn P. (2016). Disentangling flight risk from dangerousness. *BYU Law Review* 2016(3): 837–98.

Graniere, Anthony J., and Hilary McHugh (2008). Are you in or are you out? The effect of a prior criminal conviction on bar admission and a proposed national uniform standard. *Hofstra Labor and Employment Law Journal* 26(1): 223–69.

Grant, Walter Matthews, et al. (1970). The collateral consequences of a criminal conviction. *Vanderbilt Law Review* 23(5): 929–55.

Green, David A. (2016). The rehumanization of the incarcerated Other: Bureaucracy, distantiation and American mass incarceration. In *Punishing the Other,* ed. Anna Ericksson (pp. 51–76). New York: Routledge.

Greer, Lindred L., and Karen A. Jehn (2007). The pivotal role of emotion in intragroup process conflict. *Research on Managing Groups and Teams* 10: 21–43.

Greer, Lindred L., Karen A. Jehn, and Elizabeth A. Mannix (2008). Conflict transformation: A longitudinal investigation of the relationships between different types of intragroup conflict and the moderating role of conflict resolution. *Small Group Research* 39(3): 278–302.

Grove, William M., et al. (2000). Clinical versus mechanical prediction: A meta-analysis. *Psychological Assessment* 12(1): 19–30.

Gruenfeld, Deborah H., et al. (1996). Group composition and decision making: How member familiarity and information distribution affect process and performance. *Organizational Behavior and Human Decision Processes* 67(1): 1–15.

Guerino, Paul, Paige M. Harrison, and William J. Sabol (2012). *Prisoners in 2010.* Bureau of Justice Statistics Bulletin, No. NCJ 236096. Washington, DC: U.S. Department of Justice.

Gunnison, Elaine, and Jacqueline B. Helfgott (2011). Factors that hinder reentry success: A view from community corrections officers. *International Journal of Offender Therapy and Comparative Criminology* 55(2): 287–304.

———— (2013). *Offender reentry: Beyond crime and punishment.* Boulder, CO: Lynne Rienner Publishers.

Hall, Alison V., Erika V. Hall, and Jamie L. Perry (2016). Black and blue: Exploring racial bias and law enforcement in the killings of unarmed Black male civilians. *American Psychologist* 71(3): 175–86.

Hallsworth, Simon (2000). Rethinking the punitive turn: Economies of excess and the criminology of the other. *Punishment and Society* 2(2): 145–60.

Hambrick, Donald C., Theresa Seung Cho, and Ming-Jer Chen (1996). The influence of top management team heterogeneity on firms' competitive moves. *Administrative Science Quarterly* 41(4): 659–84.

Haney, Craig (1984). On the selection of capital juries. *Law and Human Behavior* 8(1–2): 121–32.

———— (2002). The psychological impact of incarceration: Implications for post-prison adjustment. In *Prisoners once removed: The impact of incarceration and reentry on children, families and communities,* eds. Jeremy Travis and Michelle Waul (pp. 33–66). Washington, DC: Urban Institute Press.

Haney, Craig, Curtis Banks, and Philip Zimbardo (1973). Interpersonal dynamics in a simulated prison. *International Journal of Criminology and Penology* 1: 69–97.

Haney, Craig, and Mona Lynch (1997). Clarifying life and death matters: An analysis of instructional comprehension and penalty phase closing arguments. *Law and Human Behavior* 21(6): 575–95.

Haney, Craig, and Philip Zimbardo (1998). The past and future of U.S. prison policy: Twenty-five years after the Stanford prison experiment. *American Psychologist* 53(7): 709–27.

Hannaford-Agor, Paula L., and G. Thomas Munsterman (2006). Ethical reciprocity: The obligations of citizens and courts to promote participation in jury service. In *Jury Ethics: Juror Conduct and Jury Dynamics,* eds. John Kleinig and James P. Levine (pp. 21–34). New York: Routledge.

Hannaford-Agor, Paula L., Valerie P. Hans, and G. Thomas Munsterman (2000). Permitting jury discussions during trial: Impact of the Arizona reform. *Law and Human Behavior* 24(3): 359–82.

Hannah-Moffat, Kelly, and Margaret Shaw (2001). *Taking risks: Incorporating gender and culture into the classification and assessment of federally sentenced women in Canada*. Policy research report. Ottawa: Status of Women in Canada.

Hannem, Stacey (2013). Experiences in reconciling risk management and restorative justice: How circles of support and accountability work restoratively in the risk society. *International Journal of Offender Therapy and Comparative Criminology* 57(3): 269–88.

Hans, Valerie P., and Neil Vidmar (1986). *Judging the jury*. Cambridge, MA: Perseus Publishing.

Hans, Valerie P., et al. (2003). The hung jury: The American jury's insights and contemporary understanding. *Criminal Law Bulletin* 39(1): 33–50.

Harcourt, Bernard E. (2015). Risk as a proxy for race: The dangers of risk assessment. *Federal Sentencing Reporter* 27(4): 237–43.

Hardcastle, Lesley, Terry Bartholomew, and Joe Graffam (2011). Legislative and community support for offender reintegration in Victoria. *Deakin Law Review* 16(1): 111–32.

Harman, Gilbert (1999). Moral philosophy meets social psychology: Virtue ethics and the fundamental attribution error. *Proceedings of the Aristotelian Society* 99: 315–31.

——— (2000). The nonexistence of character traits. *Proceedings of the Aristotelian Society* 100: 223–26.

——— (2003). No character or personality. *Business Ethics Quarterly* 13(1): 87–94.

——— (2009). Skepticism about character traits. *Journal of Ethics* 13(2–3): 235–42.

Hastie, Reid, Steven D. Penrod, and Nancy Pennington (1983). *Inside the jury*. Cambridge, MA: Harvard University Press.

——— (2002). *Inside the jury*. Clark, NJ: Law Book Exchange.

Heidemann, Gretchen, et al. (2016). Wounded healers: How formerly incarcerated women help themselves by helping others. *Punishment and Society* 18(1): 3–26.

Heimer, Karen, and Ross L. Matsueda (1994). Role-taking, role commitment, and delinquency: A theory of differential social control. *American Sociological Review* 59(3): 365–90.

Henig, Robin Marantz (1989). The 'wilding' of Central Park. *Washington Post*, May 2.

Hewstone, Miles, and Hermann Swart (2011). Fifty-odd years of inter-group contact: From hypothesis to integrated theory. *British Journal of Social Psychology* 50(3): 374–86.

Higgins, Julian P. T., et al. (2003). Measuring inconsistency in meta-analyses. *BMJ: British Medical Journal* 327(7414): 557–60.

Higgins, Pamela L., Wendy P. Heath, and Bruce D. Grannemann (2007). How type of excuse defense, mock juror age, and defendant age affect mock jurors' decisions. *Journal of Social Psychology* 147(4): 371–92.

Hirsch, Amy E. (2002). Parents with criminal records and public benefits: Welfare helps us stay in touch with society. In *Every door closed: Barriers facing parents with criminal records,* ed. Hirsch et al. (pp. 27–40). Washington, DC: Center for Law and Social Policy and Community Legal Services.

Hirschfield, Paul J., and Alex R. Piquero (2010). Normalization and legitimation: Modeling stigmatizing attitudes toward ex-offenders. *Criminology* 48(1): 27–55.

Hogue, Todd E. (1993). Attitudes towards prisoners and sexual offenders. *Issues in Criminological and Legal Psychology* 19: 27–32.

Hogue, Todd E., and Jason Peebles (1997). The influence of remorse, intent, and attitudes toward sex offenders on judgments of a rapist. *Psychology, Crime and Law* 3(4): 249–59.

Hollin, Clive R. (2002). Risk-needs assessment and allocation to offender programmes. In *Offender rehabilitation and treatment: Effective programmes and policies to reduce re-offending,* ed. James McGuire (pp. 307–32). Etobicoke, ON: John Wiley and Sons.

Holloway, Pippa (2014). *Living in infamy: Felon disenfranchisement and the history of American citizenship.* Oxford: Oxford University Press.

Holstein, James A. (1985). Jurors' interpretations and jury decision making. *Law and Human Behavior* 9(1): 83–100.

Homeboy Industries (2020). Retrieved from https://homeboyindustries.org (accessed September 1, 2020).

Horan, Rachel N. (2015). Restorative justice: The relevance of desistance and psychology. *Safer Communities* 14(3): 147–55.

Horch, Jenny D., and David C. Hodgins (2008). Public stigma of disordered gambling: Social distance, dangerousness, and familiarity. *Journal of Social and Clinical Psychology* 27(5): 505–28.

Horowitz, Irwin A., and Laird C. Kirkpatrick (1996). A concept in search of a definition: The effects of reasonable doubt instructions on certainty of guilt standards and jury verdicts. *Law and Human Behavior* 20(6): 655–70.

Horowitz, Irwin A., and David G. Seguin (1986). The effects of bifurcation and death qualification on assignment of penalty in capital crimes. *Journal of Applied Social Psychology* 16(2): 165–85.

Howe, Julie E. (2006). An ethical framework for jury selection: Enhancing voir dire conditions. In *Jury ethics: Juror conduct and jury dynamics,* eds. John Kleinig and James P. Levine (pp. 35–52). New York: Routledge.

Howe, Scott W. (1995). Juror neutrality or an impartiality array? A structural theory of the impartial jury mandate. *Notre Dame Law Review* 70(5): 1,173–245.

Hsieh, Marina (2001). "Language-qualifying juries" to exclude bilingual speakers. *Brooklyn Law Review* 66(4): 1,181–206.

Hunter, Bronwyn A., et al. (2016). A strengths-based approach to prisoner reentry: The fresh start prisoner reentry program. *International Journal of Offender Therapy and Comparative Criminology* 60(11): 1,298–314.

Hurwitz, Jon, and Mark Peffley (2005). Explaining the great racial divide: Perceptions of fairness in the US criminal justice system. *Journal of Politics* 67(3): 762–83.

Imperial County (2020). Jury service. Retrieved from www.imperial.courts.ca.gov /juror.htm (accessed September 1, 2020).

Insight Prison Project (2020). Retrieved from www.insightprisonproject.org (accessed September 1, 2020).

Irwin, John (1970). *The Felon*. Englewood Cliffs, NJ: Prentice-Hall.

Issacharoff, Samuel, Pamela S. Karlan, and Richard H. Pildes (2002). *The law of democracy: Legal structure of the political process*. New York: Foundation Press.

Itzkowitz, Howard, and Lauren Oldak (1973). Restoring the ex-offender's right to vote: Background and developments. *American Criminal Law Review* 11(3): 721–70.

Jackson, Susan E., Aparna Joshi, and Nicolas L. Erhardt (2003). Recent research on team and organizational diversity: SWOT analysis and implications. *Journal of Management* 29(6): 801–30.

Jehn, Karen A. (1995). A multimethod examination of the benefits and detriments of intragroup conflict. *Administrative Science Quarterly* 40(2): 256–82.

Jensen, Carsten (2011). Focusing events, policy dictators, and the dynamics of reform. *Policy Studies* 32(2): 143–58.

Johnson, Brian D. (2018) Trials and tribulations: The trial tax and the process of punishment. *Crime and Justice* 48(1): 313–63.

Johnson, Helen, J. Gary Hughes, and Jane L. Ireland (2007). Attitudes towards sex offenders and the role of empathy, locus of control and training: A comparison between a probationer police and general public sample. *Police Journal* 80(1): 28–54.

Jones, Melinda (2002). *Social psychology of prejudice*. Upper Saddle River, NJ: Prentice-Hall.

Judicial Council of Georgia, Administrative Office of the Courts (2005). Georgia Jury Commissioner's Handbook 10.

Kalt, Brian C. (2003). The exclusion of felons from jury service. *American University Law Review* 53(1): 65–189.

Kalven, Harry, and Hans Zeisel (1966). *The American jury*. Boston: Little, Brown.

Kam, Dara (2018). Amendment to restore felons' voting rights on Florida November ballot. *Palm Beach Post*, January 24, 2018.

Kamtekar, Rachana (2004). Situationism and virtue ethics on the content of our character. *Ethics* 114(3): 458–91.

Kang, Jerry, et al. (2011). Implicit bias in the courtroom. *UCLA Law Review* 59: 1,124–86.

Kaplan, Martin F., and Lynn E. Miller (1978). Reducing the effects of juror bias. *Journal of Personality and Social Psychology* 36(12): 1,443–55.

Kappeler, Victor E., Mark Blumberg, and Gary W. Potter (1996). *The mythology of crime and criminal justice*. Long Grove, IL: Waveland Press.

Kassin, Saul M., and David A. Garfield (1991). Blood and guts: General and trial-specific effects of videotaped crime: Scenes on mock jurors. *Journal of Applied Social Psychology* 21(18): 1,459–72.

Kassin, Saul M., and Lawrence S. Wrightsman (1983). The construction and validation of a juror bias scale. *Journal of Research in Personality* 17(4): 423–42.

———— (1988). *The American jury on trial: Psychological perspectives.* New York: Hemisphere Publishing.

Kaye, Anders (2008). Does situationist psychology have radical implications for criminal responsibility? *Alabama Law Review* 59(3): 611–78.

Kellough, Gail, and Scot Wortley (2002). Remand for plea: Bail decisions and plea bargaining as commensurate decisions. *British Journal of Criminology* 42(1): 186–210.

Keyssar, Alexander (2009). *The right to vote: The contested history of democracy in the United States.* New York: Basic Books.

Kiecolt, K. Jill (1994). Stress and the decision to change oneself: A theoretical model. *Social Psychology Quarterly* 57(1): 49–63.

Kinch, John W. (1963). A formalized theory of the self-concept. *American Journal of Sociology* 68(4): 481–86.

King, Gary (2013). *A solution to the ecological inference problem: Reconstructing individual behavior from aggregate data.* Princeton, NJ: Princeton University Press.

King, Nancy J. (1993a). Racial jurymandering: Cancer or cure? A contemporary review of affirmative action in jury selection. *New York University Law Review* 68(4): 707–76.

———— (1993b). Postconviction review of jury discrimination: Measuring the effects of juror race on jury decisions. *Michigan Law Review* 92(1): 63–130.

King, Sam (2013a). Early desistance narratives: A qualitative analysis of probationers' transitions towards desistance. *Punishment and Society* 15(2): 147–65.

———— (2013b). Transformative agency and desistance from crime. *Criminology and Criminal Justice* 13(3): 317–35.

Kjelsberg, Ellen, and Liv Heian Loos (2008). Conciliation or condemnation? Prison employees' and young peoples' attitudes towards sexual offenders. *International Journal of Forensic Mental Health* 7(1): 95–103.

Klarman, Michael J. (1998). The Plessy era. *Supreme Court Review* 1998: 303–414.

———— (2004). *From Jim Crow to civil rights: The Supreme Court and the struggle for racial inequality.* New York: Oxford University Press.

Kleinberg, Howard (1989). The issues of racism and crime are joined in Central Park attack. *Atlanta Journal-Constitution,* May 6.

Kleinberg, Jon, Sendhil Mullainathan, and Manish Raghavan (2016). Inherent trade-offs in the fair determination of risk scores. Retrieved from https://arxiv.org/abs/1609.05807 (accessed September 1, 2020).

Koch, Chantal Mees, and Dennis J. Devine (1999). Effects of reasonable doubt definition and inclusion of a lesser charge on jury verdicts. *Law and Human Behavior* 23(6): 653–74.

Kochan, Thomas, et al. (2003). The effects of diversity on business performance: Report of the diversity research network. *Human Resource Management* 42(1): 3–21.

Korte, Gregory, and Alan Gomez (2018). Trump ramps up rhetoric on undocumented immigrants: "These aren't people, these are animals." *USA Today,* May 16. Retrieved from www.usatoday.com/story/news/politics/2018/05/16

/trump-immigrants-animals-mexico-democrats-sanctuary-cities/617252002
/ (accessed September 1, 2020).

Kramer, Ronald C. (1994). Frying them isn't the answer. *Time*, May 14. Retrieved from http://content.time.com/time/magazine/article/0,9171,980318,00.html (accessed September 1, 2020).

Kramer, Ronald C., and Raymond J. Michalowski (1995). The iron fist and the velvet tongue: Crime control policies in the Clinton administration. *Social Justice* 22(2): 87–100.

Kravitz, David A., Brian L. Cutler, and Petra Brock (1993). Reliability and validity of the original and revised legal attitudes questionnaire. *Law and Human Behavior* 17(6): 661–77.

Kravitz, Mark R. (2005). The vanishing trial: A problem in need of solution? *Connecticut Bar Journal* 79(1): 9–22.

Kroll, Joshua A., et al. (2016). Accountable algorithms. *University of Pennsylvania Law Review* 165: 633–705.

Kurtz, Don, and Travis Linnemann (2006). Improving probation through client strengths: Evaluating strength based treatments for at risk youth. *Western Criminology Review* 7(1): 9–19.

Landau, Rue (2002). Criminal records and subsidized housing: Families losing the opportunity for decent shelter. In *Every door closed: Barriers facing parents with criminal records*, ed. Hirsch et al. (pp. 41–52). Washington, DC: Center for Law and Social Policy and Community Legal Services.

Langbein, John H. (2012). The disappearance of civil trial in the United States. *Yale Law Journal* 122(3): 522–72.

Lapsley, Daniel (2017). Situationism and the pyrrhic defense of character education: Commentary on Sreenivasan. In *Moral psychology: Virtue and character*, eds. Walter Sinnott-Arstrong and Christian B. Miller (pp. 171–83). Cambridge, MA: MIT Press.

Laub, John H., Daniel S. Nagin, and Robert J. Sampson (1998). Trajectories of change in criminal offending: Good marriages and the desistance process. *American Sociological Review* 63(2): 225–38.

Laub, John H., and Robert J. Sampson (1993). Turning points in the life course: Why change matters to the study of crime. *Criminology* 31(3): 301–25.

——— (2001). Understanding desistance from crime. *Crime and Justice* 28: 1–69.

——— (2003). *Shared beginnings, divergent lives: Delinquent boys to age 70*. Cambridge, MA: Harvard University Press.

Lawson, Tamara F. (2012). A fresh cut in an old wound—A critical analysis of the Trayvon Martin killing: The public outcry, the prosecutor's discretion, and the stand your ground law. *University of Florida Journal of Law and Public Policy* 23(3): 271–310.

Lawyers' Committee for Civil Rights Under Law (2013). *Democracy imprisoned: A review of the prevalence and impact of felony disenfranchisement laws in the United States*. Washington, DC: Sentencing Project.

LeBel, Thomas P. (2007). An examination of the impact of formerly incarcerated persons helping others. *Journal of Offender Rehabilitation* 46(1–2): 1–24.

——— (2012). Invisible stripes? Formerly incarcerated persons' perceptions of stigma. *Deviant Behavior* 33(2), 89–107.

LeBel, Thomas P., Matt Richie, and Shadd Maruna (2015). Helping others as a response to reconcile a criminal past: The role of the wounded healer in prisoner reentry programs. *Criminal Justice and Behavior* 42(1): 108–20.

LeBel, Thomas P., et al. (2008). The "chicken and egg" of subjective and social factors in desistance from crime. *European Journal of Criminology* 5(2): 131–59.

Lecci, Len, and Bryan Myers (2002). Examining the construct validity of the original and revised JBC: A cross-validation of sample and method. *Law and Human Behavior* 26(4): 455–63.

Lecci, Len, et al. (2000). Assessment of juror bias in a community sample. Paper presented at the 108th Annual Convention of the American Psychological Association, August 4–8, Washington, DC.

Lederman, Daniel, Norman Loayza, and Ana Maria Menendez (2002). Violent crime: Does social capital matter? *Economic Development and Cultural Change* 50(3): 509–39.

Lee, Cynthia (2013). Making race salient: Trayvon Martin and implicit bias in a not yet post-racial society. *North Carolina Law Review* 91(5): 1,555–612.

Lee, Rebecca K. (2013). Judging judges: Empathy as the litmus test for impartiality. *University of Cincinnati Law Review* 82(1): 145–206.

Lemert, Edwin M. (1951). *Social pathology: Systematic approaches to the study of sociopathic behavior.* New York: McGraw-Hill.

Lerner, Kira (2018). No longer "voiceless," Louisiana felons regain the right to vote. *Think Progress,* June 1. Retrieved from https://thinkprogress.org/no-longer-voiceless-louisiana-felons-regain-the-right-to-vote-a112f7d12ec9/ (accessed September 1, 2020).

Lerner, Melvin J. (1970). The desire for justice and reactions to victims. In *Altruism and Helping Behavior,* eds. J. MacCauley and L. Berkowitz(pp. 205–29). New York: Academic Press.

Leverentz, Andrea (2011). Neighborhood context of attitudes toward crime and reentry. *Punishment and Society* 13(1): 64–92.

Levine, Sam, and Ariel Edwards-Levy (2018). Most Americans favor restoring felons' voting rights, but disagree on how: States have taken widely varying approaches. *Huffpost,* March 21. Retrieved from www.huffingtonpost.com/entry/felonsvoting-%20rights-poll_us_5ab2c153e4b008c9e5f3c88a (accessed September 1, 2020).

Lilly, Graham C. (2001). The decline of the American jury. *University of Colorado Law Review* 72(1): 53–91.

Link, Bruce G., and Francis T. Cullen (1986). Contact with the mentally ill and perceptions of how dangerous they are. *Journal of Health and Social Behavior* 27(4): 289–302.

Link, Bruce G., and Jo C. Phelan (2001). Conceptualizing stigma. *Annual Review of Sociology* 27(1): 363–85.

Lippmann, Walter (1922). *Public Opinion*. New York: Harcourt, Brace.

Locke, Christopher Ryan (2010). Public attitudes toward mental illness: An experimental design examining the media's impact of crime on stigma. PhD. diss., Ohio State University. Retrieved from https://etd.ohiolink.edu/!etd.send_file?accession=osu1268086954&disposition=inline (accessed September 1, 2020).

Lofland, John (1969). *Deviance and identity.* Englewood Cliffs, NJ: Prentice Hall.

Lofquist, William S. (1997). Constructing "crime": Media coverage of individual and organizational wrongdoing. *Justice Quarterly* 14(2): 243–63.

Loftus, Elizabeth F. (1975). Leading questions and the eyewitness report. *Cognitive Psychology* 7(4): 560–72.

Logan, Wayne A. (2006). Constitutional collectivism and ex-offender residence exclusion laws. *Iowa Law Review* 92(1): 1–40.

Los Angeles Times Editorial Board (2017). Along with voting rights, restore jury duty to ex-inmates. *Los Angeles Times*, November 20. Retrieved from www.latimes.com/opinion/editorials/la-ed-jury-duty-felons-20171120-story.html (accessed September 1, 2020).

Losh, Susan Carol, Adina W. Wasserman, and Michael A. Wasserman (2000). Reluctant jurors: What summons responses reveal about jury duty attitudes. *Judicature* 83(6): 304–11.

Lother, William (1989). Chilling the big apple. *Toronto Star*, April 29.

Love, Margaret C. (2007). Reinventing the President's pardon power. *Federal Sentencing Reporter* 20(1): 5–15.

Love, Margaret C., and Susan Kuzma (1997). U.S. civil disabilities of convicted felons: A state-by-state survey. *National Institute of Justice.* Retrieved from www.ncjrs.gov/pdffiles1/pr/195110.pdf (accessed September 1, 2020).

Love, Margaret C., Jenny M. Roberts, and Cecilia M. Klingele (2013). *Collateral consequences of criminal conviction: Law, policy and practice.* Eagen, MN: Thompson Rueters Westlaw / NACDL Press.

Lowenkamp, Christopher T., Edward J. Latessa, and Alexander M. Holsinger (2006). The risk principle in action: What have we learned from 13,676 offenders and 97 correctional programs? *Crime and Delinquency* 52(1): 77–93.

Lynch, Mona (1998). Waste managers? The new penology, crime fighting, and parole agent identity. *Law and Society Review* 32(4): 839–70.

Lynch, Mona, and Craig Haney (2000). Discrimination and instructional comprehension: Guided discretion, racial bias, and the death penalty. *Law and Human Behavior* 24(3): 337–58.

——— (2009). Capital jury deliberation: Effects on death sentencing, comprehension, and discrimination. *Law and Human Behavior* 33(6): 481–96.

MacCoun, Robert J., and Norbert L. Kerr (1988). Asymmetric influence in mock jury deliberation: Jurors' bias for leniency. *Journal of Personality and Social Psychology* 54(1): 21–33.

MacCoun, Robert J., and Tom R. Tyler (1988). The basis of citizens' perceptions of the criminal jury. *Law and Human Behavior* 12(3): 333–52.

Machiavielli, Niccolò (1984). *The prince.* Trans. Peter E. Bondanella and Mark Musa. Oxford: Oxford University Press.

Mahoney, Bill (2019). Senate passes bill to let felons serve on juries. *Politico*, May 7. Retrieved from www.politico.com/states/new-york/albany/story/2019/05/07/senate-passes-bill-to-let-felons-serve-on-juries-1009680 (accessed September 1, 2020).

Major, Brenda, and Laurie T. O'Brien (2005). The social psychology of stigma. *Annual Review of Psychology* 56: 393–421.

Manarin, Brian P. (2019). Discriminatory and unfair practices against the indigenous peoples of Canada in the selection of criminal juries. PhD diss., University of Leicester.

Mancini, Christina, et al. (2010). Sex offender residence restriction laws: Parental perceptions and public policy. *Journal of Criminal Justice* 38(5): 1,022–30.

——— (2015). Whites' perceptions about Black criminality: A closer look at the contact hypothesis. *Crime and Delinquency* 61(7): 996–1,022.

Mann, Thomas E. (2001). Reflections on the 2000 U.S. presidential elections. *Brookings*, January 1. Retrieved from www.brookings.edu/articles/reflections-on-the-2000-u-s-presidential-election (accessed September 1, 2020).

Manza, Jeff, Clem Brooks, and Christopher Uggen (2004). Public attitudes toward felon disenfranchisement in the United States. *Public Opinion Quarterly* 68(2): 275–86.

Manza, Jeff, and Christopher Uggen (2006). *Locked out: Felon disenfranchisement and American democracy.* Oxford: Oxford University Press.

Manza, Jeff, Christopher Uggen, and Angela Behrens (2006) Disenfranchisment and civic reintegration: Felons speak out. In *Locked out: Felon disenfranchisement and American democracy,* eds. Jeff Manza and Christopher Uggen (pp. 137–64). New York: Oxford University Press.

Marder, Nancy S. (2002). Juries, justice, and multiculturalism. *Southern California Law Review* 75(3): 659–726.

Marion, Nancy E., and Willard M. Oliver (2012). Crime control in the 2008 presidential election: Symbolic politics or tangible policies? *American Journal of Criminal Justice* 37(1): 111–25.

Maruna, Shadd (2001). *Making good: How ex-convicts reform and rebuild their lives.* Washington, DC: American Psychological Association.

——— (2011). Reentry as a rite of passage. *Punishment and Society* 13(1): 3–28.

Maruna, Shadd, and Heith Copes (2005). What have we learned from five decades of neutralization research? *Crime and Justice* 32: 221–320.

Maruna, Shadd, Russ Immarigeon, and Thomas P. LeBel (2004). Ex-offender reintegration: Theory and practice. In *After crime and punishment: Pathways to offender reintegration,* ed. Shadd Maruna and Russ Immarigeon (pp. 3–26). New York: Routledge.

Maruna, Shadd, and Thomas P. LeBel (2003). Welcome home? Examining the "reentry court" concept from a strengths-based perspective. *Western Criminology Review* 4(2): 91–107.

Maruna, Shadd, and Kevin Roy (2007). Amputation or reconstruction? Notes on the concept of "knifing off" and desistance from crime. *Journal of Contemporary Criminal Justice* 23(1): 104–24.

Maruna, Shadd, et al. (2004). Pygmalion in the reintegration process: Desistance from crime through the looking glass. *Psychology, Crime and Law* 10(3): 271–81.

Maryland Farmer (1981). Letters from a Maryland farmer, IV. In *What the anti-federalists were for: The political thoughts of the opponents of the constitution,* ed. Hebert Storing (pp. 19–20). Chicago: University of Chicago Press.

Massoglia, Michael, and Christopher Uggen (2007). Subjective desistance and the transition to adulthood. *Journal of Contemporary Criminal Justice* 23(1): 90–103.

Mathews, David, and Forrest David Matthews (1999). *Politics for people: Finding a responsible public voice.* Chicago: University of Illinois Press.

Matsueda, Ross L. (1992). Reflected appraisals, parental labeling, and delinquency: Specifying a symbolic interactionist theory. *American Journal of Sociology* 97(6): 1,577–611.

Matsueda, Ross L., and Karen Heimer (1997). A symbolic interactionist theory of role-transitions, role-commitments, and delinquency. In *Developmental theories of crime and delinquency,* ed. Terrance P. Thornberry (pp. 163–213). New Brunswick, NJ: Transaction.

Mauer, Marc (1999). Why are tough on crime policies so popular? *Stanford Law and Policy Review* 11(1): 9–22.

Mauer, Marc, and Meda Chesney-Lind (2002). *Invisible punishment: The collateral consequences of mass imprisonment.* New York: New Press.

May, Bruce E. (1995). The character component of occupational licensing laws: A continuing barrier to the ex-felon's employment opportunities. *North Dakota Law Review* 71(1): 187–210.

Mayson, Sandra G. (2017). Dangerous defendants. *Yale Law Journal* 127(3): 490–568.

Mazzella, Ronald, and Alan Feingold (1994). The effects of physical attractiveness, race, socioeconomic status, and gender of defendants and victims on judgments of mock jurors: A meta-analysis. *Journal of Applied Social Psychology* 24(15): 1,315–38.

McCall, George J., and Jerry L. Simmons (1978). *Identities and interaction: An examination of human associations in everyday life.* New York: Free Press.

McCombs, Maxwell (2004). *Setting the agenda: Mass media and public opinion.* Cambridge: Polity Press.

——— (2005). A look at agenda-setting: Past, present and future. *Journalism Studies* 6(4): 543–57.

McCombs, Maxwell E., and Donald L. Shaw (1972). The agenda-setting function of mass media. *Public Opinion Quarterly* 36(2): 176–87.

McCombs, Maxwell E., Donald L. Shaw, and David H. Weaver (1997). *Communication and democracy: Exploring the intellectual frontiers in agenda-setting theory.* Mahwah: Lawrence Erlbaum Associates.

Manza, Jeff, Clem Brooks, and Christopher Uggen (2004). Public attitudes toward felon disenfranchisement in the United States. *Public Opinion Quarterly* 68(2): 275–86.

————— (2014). New directions in agenda-setting theory and research. *Mass Communication and Society* 17(6): 781–802.

McGowen, Ramsey, and Glen D. King (1982). Effects of authoritarian, anti-authoritarian, and egalitarian legal attitudes on mock juror and jury decisions. *Psychological Reports* 51(3): 1,067–74.

McIvor, Gill (2009). Therapeutic jurisprudence and procedural justice in Scottish drug courts. *Criminology and Criminal Justice* 9(1): 29–49.

McLeod, Poppy L., Sharon A. Lobel, and Taylor H. Cox Jr. (1996). Ethnic diversity and creativity in small groups. *Small Group Research* 27(2): 248–64.

McNeill, Fergus (2014). Three aspects of desistance. Blog post. *Discovering desistance.* Retrieved from https://discoveringdesistance.home.blog/2014/05/23/three-aspects-of-desistance (accessed September 1, 2020).

Mead, George H. (1934). *Mind, self and society: From the standpoint of a social behaviorist.* Chicago: University of Chicago Press.

Meili, Trisha (2003). *I am the central park jogger: A story of hope and possibility.* Waterville: Thorndike Press.

Meisenhelder, Thomas (1977). An exploratory study of exiting from criminal careers. *Criminology* 15(3): 319–34.

————— (1982). Becoming normal: Certification as a stage in exiting from crime. *Deviant Behavior: An Interdisciplinary Journal* 3(2): 137–53.

Mele, Christopher, and Teresa A. Miller (2005). *Civil penalties, social consequences.* New York: Routledge.

Meredith, Marc, and Michael Morse (2014). Do voting rights notification laws increase ex-felon turnout? *Annals of the American Academy of Political and Social Science* 651(1): 220–49.

————— (2015). The politics of the restoration of ex-felon voting rights: The case of Iowa. *Quarterly Journal of Political Science* 10(1): 41–100.

Mexal, Stephen J. (2013). The roots of "wilding": Black literary naturalism, the language of wilderness, and hip hop in the Central Park jogger rape. *African American Review* 46(1): 101–15.

Milgram, Stanley (1963). Behavioral study of obedience. *Journal of Abnormal and Social Psychology* 67(4): 371–78.

————— (1973). The perils of obedience. *Harper's Magazine* 247 (1,483): 62–77.

————— (1974). *Obedience to authority.* New York: Harper and Row.

Miller, Bryan L., and Joseph F. Spillane (2012). Civil death: An examination of ex-felon disenfranchisement and reintegration. *Punishment and Society* 14(4): 402–28.

Miller, Holly A. (2006). A dynamic assessment of offender risk, needs, and strengths in a sample of pre-release general offenders. *Behavioral Science and the Law* 24(6): 767–82.

Miller, Monica K., et al. (2011). The effects of deliberations and religious identity on mock jurors' verdicts. *Group Processes and Intergroup Relations* 14(4): 517–32.

Miller, Monica K., and Jared Chamberlain (2015) "There ought to be a law!": Understanding community sentiment. In *Handbook of Community Sentiment*, eds.

Monica K. Miller, Jeremy A. Blumenthal, and Jared Chamberlain (pp. 3–28). New York: Springer.

Miller, Teresa A. (2003). Citizenship and severity: Recent immigration reforms and the new penology. *Georgetown Immigration Law Journal* 17(4): 611–66.

Milliken, Frances J., and Luis L. Martins (1996). Searching for common threads: Understanding the multiple effects of diversity in organizational groups. *Academy of Management Review* 21(2): 402–33.

Mills, Carol J., and Wayne E. Bohannon (1980). Juror characteristics: To what extent are they related to jury verdicts. *Judicature* 64(1): 22–31.

Mitchell, Herman E., and Donn Byrne (1973). The defendant's dilemma: Effects of jurors' attitudes and authoritarianism on judicial decisions. *Journal of Personality and Social Psychology* 25(1): 123–29.

Mitchell, Tara L., et al. (2005). Racial bias in juror decision-making: A meta-analytic review of defendant treatment. *Law and Human Behavior* 29(6): 621–37.

Monahan, John, and Jennifer L. Skeem (2016). Risk assessment in criminal sentencing. *Annual Review of Clinical Psychology* 12: 489–513.

Mooallem, Jon. (2015). You just got out of prison. Now what? *New York Times*, July 16. Retrieved from https://mobile.nytimes.com/2015/07/19/magazine/you-just-got-out-of-prison-now-what.html?referrer=and_r=0 (accessed September 1, 2020).

Moore, Kelly E., Jeffrey B. Stuewig, and June P. Tangney (2016). The effect of stigma on criminal offenders' functioning: A longitudinal mediational model. *Deviant Behavior* 37(2): 196–218.

Moore, Peter (2014). Most people think felons should be allowed to vote. *Politics and Current Affairs*. Retrieved from https://today.yougov.com/topics/politics/articles-reports/2014/02/18/most-people-think-felons.

——— (2016). Most Americans think released felons should have the vote. *Politics and Current Affairs*. Retrieved from https://today.yougov.com/topics/politics/articles-reports/2016/04/26/most-americans-think-released-felons-should-have-v.

Moran, Gary, and John C. Comfort (1982). Scientific juror selection: Sex as a moderator of demographic and personality predictors of impaneled felony juror behavior. *Journal of Personality and Social Psychology* 43(5): 1052–63.

Muller, Christopher, and Daniel Schrage (2014). Mass imprisonment and trust in the law. *Annals of the American Academy of Political and Social Science* 651(1): 139–58.

Myers, Bryan, and Len Lecci (1998). Revising the factor structure of the juror bias scale: A method for the empirical validation of theoretical constructs. *Law and Human Behavior* 22(2): 239–56.

——— (2008). Individual differences in attitudes relevant to juror decision making: Development and validation of the pretrial juror attitude questionnaire (PJAQ). *Journal of Applied Social Psychology* 38(8): 2,010–38.

Narby, Douglas J., Brian L. Cutler, and Gary Moran (1993). A meta-analysis of the association between authoritarianism and jurors' perceptions of defendant culpability. *Journal of Applied Psychology* 78(1): 34–42.

National Conference of Bar Examiners and American Bar Association Section of Legal Education and Admissions to the Bar (2020). Comprehensive guide to bar admission requirements, eds. Judith A. Gundersen and Claire J. Guback. Retrieved from www.ncbex.org/assets/BarAdmissionGuide/CompGuide2020_021820_ Online_Final.pdf (accessed September 1, 2020).

Nemeth, Charlan J. (1986). The differential contributions of majority and minority influence. *Psychological Review* 93(1): 23–32.

Nodes, Kyle P. (2019). Equal dignity and unequal protection: A framework for analyzing disparate impact claims. *Duke Law Journal* 68: 149–85.

O'Brien, Patricia (2001). "Just like baking a cake": Women describe the necessary ingredients for successful reentry after incarceration. *Families in Society: The Journal of Contemporary Social Services* 82(3): 287–95.

Offenders Anonymous(2020). Retrieved from www.offenders-anonymous.org.uk /index.htm. (accessed September 1, 2020).

Office of the Pardon Attorney, U.S. Department of Justice (1996). U.S. Department of Justice, *Civil disabilities of convicted felons: A state-by-state survey.*

Ogloff, James R. P. (1991). A comparison of insanity defense standards on juror decision making. *Law and Human Behavior* 15(5): 509–31.

Ogloff, James R. P., and V. Gordon Rose (2005). The comprehension of judicial instructions. In *Psychology and law: An empirical perspective,* eds. Neil Brewer and Kipling Williams (pp. 407–44). New York: Guilford Press.

Olivares, Kathleen M., Velmer S. Burton Jr., and Francis T. Cullen (1996). The collateral consequences of a felony conviction: A national study of state legal codes ten years later. *Federal Probation* 60(3): 10–17.

Oliver, Willard M. (1998). *Community-oriented policing: A systemic approach to policing.* Upper Saddle River, NJ: Prentice Hall.

——— (2001). Executive orders: Symbolic politics, criminal justice policy, and the American presidency. *American Journal of Criminal Justice* 26(1): 1–21.

——— (2003). *The law and order presidency.* Upper Saddle River, NJ: Prentice Hall.

Orlando Sentinel Editorial Board (2018). Second chances? Not in Rick Scott's Florida. *Orlando Sentinel,* April 27. Retrieved from www.orlandosentinel.com /opinion/os-ed-rick-scott-denies-felons-voting-rights-20180427-story.html (accessed September 1, 2020).

Ostrom, Brian J., Shauna M. Strickland, and Paula L. Hannaford-Agor (2004). Examining trial trends in state courts: 1976–2002. *Journal of Empirical Legal Studies* 1(3): 755–82.

Owens, Michael Leo (2014). Ex-felons' organization-based political work for carceral reforms. *Annals of the American Academy of Political and Social Science* 651(1): 256–65.

Owens, Michael Leo, and Adrienne R. Smith (2012). "Deviants" and democracy: Punitive policy designs and the social rights of felons as citizens. *American Politics Research* 40(3): 531–67.

Pabst Jr., William R., G. Thomas Munsterman, and Chester H. Mount (1976). The myth of the unwilling juror. *Judicature* 60(4): 164–71.

———— (1977). The value of jury duty: Serving is believing. *Judicature* 61(1): 38–42.

Pager, Devah (2003). Blacks and ex-cons need not apply. *Contexts* 2(4): 58–59.

———— (2007). *Marked: Race, crime, and finding work in an era of mass incarceration.* Chicago: University of Chicago Press.

Pager, Devah, and Lincoln Quillian (2005). Walking the talk? What employers say versus what they do. *American Sociological Review* 70(3): 355–80.

Palazzolo, Daniel J., and Vincent G. Moscardelli (2006). Policy crisis and political leadership: Election law reform in the states after the 2000 presidential election. *State Politics and Policy Quarterly* 6(3): 300–21.

Panagopoulos, Costas (2010). Affect, social pressure, and prosocial motivation: Field experimental evidence of the mobilizing effects of pride, shame, and publicizing voting behavior. *Political Behavior* 32(3): 369–86.

Park, Sunyoung (2009). College students' attitudes toward prisoners and prisoner reentry. PhD. diss., Indiana University of Pennsylvania. Retrieved from http://citeseerx.ist.psu.edu/viewdoc/download?doi=10.1.1.969.6190&rep=rep1&type=pdf (accessed September 1, 2020).

Pateman, Carole (1970). *Participation and democratic theory.* Cambridge: Cambridge University Press.

Paternoster, Raymond, and Shawn Bushway (2009). Desistance and the "feared self": Toward an identity theory of criminal desistance. *Journal of Criminal Law and Criminology* 99(4): 1103–56.

Paternoster, Raymond, and Leeann Iovanni (1989). The labeling perspective and delinquency: An elaboration of the theory and an assessment of the evidence. *Justice Quarterly* 6(3): 359–94.

Paternoster, Raymond, et al. (1997). Do fair procedures matter? The effect of procedural justice on spouse assault. *Law and Society Review* 31(1): 163–204.

Patterson, Kerry, et al. (2008). *Influencer: The power to change anything.* New York: McGraw Hill.

Pelled, Lisa Hope (1996). Demographic diversity, conflict, and work group outcomes: An intervening process theory. *Organization Science* 7(6): 615–31.

Pelled, Lisa Hope, Kathleen M. Eisenhardt, and Katherine R. Xin (1999). Exploring the black box: An analysis of work group diversity, conflict, and performance. *Administrative Science Quarterly* 44(1): 1–28.

Penn, David L., et al. (1994). Dispelling the stigma of schizophrenia: What sort of information is best? *Schizophrenia Bulletin* 20(3): 567–78.

Pennington, Nancy, and Reid Hastie (1981). Juror decision-making models: The generalization gap. *Psychological Bulletin* 89(2): 246–87.

———— (1990). Practical implications of psychological research on juror and jury decision making. *Personality and Social Psychology Bulletin* 16(1): 90–105.

———— (1991–92). A cognitive theory of juror decision making: The story model. *Cardozo Law Review* 13(2–3): 519–57.

———— (1992). Explaining the evidence: Tests of the story model for juror decision making. *Journal of Personality and Social Psychology* 62(2): 189–206.

————— (1993). The story model for juror decision making. In *Inside the juror: The psychology of juror decision making,* ed. Hastie Reid (pp. 192–221). Cambridge: Cambridge University Press.

Pennington, Nancy, Reid Hastie, and Steven D. Penrod (1983). *Inside the jury.* Cambridge, MA: Harvard University Press.

Perrin, Christian, et al. (2017). "It's sort of reaffirmed to me that I am not a monster, I'm not a terrible person": Sex offenders' movements toward desistance via peer-support roles in prison. *Sexual Abuse: A Journal of Research and Treatment* 30(7): 759–80.

Petersen, Nick (2020). Do detainees plead guilty faster? A survival analysis of pretrial detention and the timing of guilty pleas. *Criminal Justice Policy Review* 31(7): 1015–35.

Petersilia, Joan (2003). *When prisoners come home: Parole and prisoner reentry.* New York: Oxford University Press.

Pettigrew, Thomas F., and Linda R. Tropp (2000). Does intergroup contact reduce racial and ethnic prejudice throughout the world? *Reducing prejudice and discrimination.* Mahwah, NJ: Lawrence Erlbaum.

————— (2006). A meta-analytic test of intergroup contact theory. *Journal of Personality and Social Psychology* 90(5): 751–83.

Pettus, Katherine Irene (2013). *Felony disenfranchisement in America: Historical origins, institutional racism, and modern consequences.* 2nd ed. New York: SUNY Press.

Petty, Richard E., Monique A. Fleming, and Paul H. White (1999). Stigmatized sources and persuasion: Prejudice as a determinate of argument scrutiny. *Journal of Personality and Social Psychology* 76(1): 19–34.

Phelps, Michelle S. (2011). Rehabilitation in the punitive era: The gap between rhetoric and reality in U.S. prison programs. *Law and Society Review* 45(1): 33–68.

Phillips, John (2019). California moves to let felons serve on juries. *Orange County Register,* June 13. Retrieved from www.ocregister.com/2019/06/13/california-moves-to-let-felons-serve-on-juries/ (accessed September 1, 2020).

Phillips, Kathrine W., et al. (2004). Diverse groups and information sharing: The effects of congruent ties. *Journal of Experimental Social Psychology* 40(4): 497–510.

Pinaire, Brian, Milton Heumann, and Laura Bilotta (2002). Barred from the vote: Public attitudes toward the disenfranchisement of felons. *Fordham Urban Law Journal* 30(5): 1,519–50.

Pinard, Michael (2010). Collateral consequences of criminal convictions: Confronting issues of race and dignity. *New York University Law Review* 85(2): 457–534.

Pitt, David E. (1989). Teenagers' "wolfpack" violence. *San Francisco Chronicle,* May 12.

Pooley, Eric (1989) Grins, gore, and videotape: The trouble with local TV news. *New York Magazine,* October 9.

POST Commission on Peace Officers Standards and Trainings (2019). Retrieved from https://post.ca.gov/Training (accessed September 1, 2020).

Powers, Ronald (1998). Friends of suspects shocked by "wilding." *Houston Chronicle.*

Pratt, Travis C. (2009). *Addicted to incarceration: Corrections policy and the politics of misinformation in the United States.* Thousand Oaks, CA: Sage Publications.

Pratt, Travis C., Jacinta M. Gau, and Travis W. Franklin (2011). *Key ideas in criminology and criminal justice.* Thousand Oaks, CA: Sage Publications.

Prendergast, Michael, et al. (2011). A multi-site, randomized study of strengths-based case management with substance-abusing parolees. *Journal of Experimental Criminology* 7(3): 225–53.

Pritchard, Mary E., and Janice M. Keenan (2002). Does jury deliberation really improve jurors' memories? *Applied Cognitive Psychology* 16(5): 589–601.

Project H.O.P.E. Reentry Initiative (2020). Retrieved from www.justice.gov/usao-sdal/programs/ex-offender-re-entry-initiative.(accessed September 1, 2020).

Protess, David L., and Maxwell McCombs (1991). *Agenda setting: Readings on media, public opinion, and policymaking.* Hillsdale, NJ: Lawrence Erlbaum Associates.

Putnam, Robert D. (2000). *Bowling alone: The collapse and revival of American community.* New York: Simon and Schuster.

Quas, Jodi A., et al. (2002). Effects of victim, defendant, and juror gender on decisions in child sexual assault cases. *Journal of Applied Social Psychology* 32(10): 1,993–2,021.

Rabe-Hesketh, Sophia, and Anders Skrondal (2008). *Multilevel and longitudinal modeling using Stata.* College Station, TX: Stata Press.

Rackley, Erika (2005). When Hercules met the happy prince: Re-imagining the judge. *Texas Wesleyan Law Review* 12(1): 213–32.

Rade, Candalyn B., Sara L. Desmarais, and Roger E. Mitchell (2016). A meta-analysis of public attitudes toward ex-offenders. *Criminal Justice and Behavior* 43(9): 1,260–80.

Randolph, Eleanor (1989). Bodybag journalism. *New York Post.*

Raphael, Steven (2014). *The new scarlet letter? Negotiating the US labor market with a criminal record.* Kalamazoo, MI: WE Upjohn Institute.

Raphael, Steven, and Michael A. Stoll (2013). *Why are so many Americans in prison?* New York: Russell Sage Foundation.

Rapp, Charles A. (1992). *The strengths model: Case management with people suffering from severe and persistent mental illness.* New York: Oxford University Press.

Rapp, Charles A., and Richard Wintersteen (1989). The strengths model of case management: Results from twelve demonstrations. *Psychosocial Rehabilitation Journal* 13(1): 23–32.

Rasberry, William (1989). Our missing anger. *Washington Post*, May 1.

Rasmussen, David M. (1996). Rethinking subjectivity: Narrative identity and the self. *Philosophy and Social Criticism* 21(5–6): 159–72.

Ratcliff, Marcus (2000). The good character requirement: A proposal for a uniform national standard. *Tulsa Law Journal* 36(2): 487–514.

Raudenbush, Stephen W., and Anthony S. Bryk (2002). *Hierarchical linear models: Applications and data analysis methods.* Thousand Oaks, CA: Sage Publications.

Rebein, Paul W., Victor E. Schwartz, and Cary Silverman (2003). Jury (dis)service: Why people avoid jury duty and what Florida can do about it. *Nova Law Review* 28(1): 144–56.

Reed, John P. (1965). Jury deliberations, voting, and verdict trends. *Southwestern Social Science Quarterly* 45(4): 361–70.

Reifman, Alan, Spencer M. Gusick, and Phoebe C. Ellsworth (1992). Real jurors' understanding of the law in real cases. *Law and Human Behavior* 16(5): 539–54.

Rhode, Deborah L. (1985). Moral character as a professional credential. *Yale Law Journal* 94(3): 491–603.

——— (2018). Virtue and the law: The good moral character requirement in occupational licensing, bar regulation, and immigration proceedings. *Law and Social Inquiry* 43(3): 1,027–58.

——— (2019). *Character: What it means and why it matters.* New York: Oxford University Press.

Rhode, Deborah L., et al. (2016). *Legal Ethics.* 7th ed. Saint Paul: Foundation Press.

Richards, H. Erle (1902). Is outlawry obsolete? *Law Quarterly Review* 18(3): 297–304.

Richards, Peter J. (2002). The discreet charm of the mixed jury: The epistemology of jury selection and the perils of post-modernism. *Seattle University Law Review* 26(3): 445–74.

Richert, John P. (1977). Jurors' attitudes towards jury service. *Justice System Journal* 2(3): 233–45.

Richeson, Jennifer A., and J. Nicole Shelton (2003). When prejudice does not pay: Effects of interracial contact on executive function. *Psychological Science* 14(3): 287–90.

Rigakos, George S. (1999). Risk society and actuarial criminology: Prospects for a critical discourse. *Canadian Journal of Criminology* 41(2): 137–50.

Ritter, Matthew A. (2002). The ethics of moral character determination: An indeterminate ethical reflection upon bar admissions. *California Western Law Review* 39(1): 1–52.

Roberts, Anna (2013). Casual ostracism: Jury exclusion on the basis of criminal convictions. *Minnesota Law Review* 98(2): 592–647.

Rogers, Paul, Lindsay Hirst, and Michelle Davies (2011). An investigation into the effect of respondent gender, victim age, and perpetrator treatment on public attitudes towards sex offenders, sex offender treatment, and sex offender rehabilitation. *Journal of Offender Rehabilitation* 50(8): 511–30.

Ronel, Natti, and Ety Elisha (2011). A different perspective: Introducing positive criminology. *International Journal of Offender Therapy and Comparative Criminology* 55(2): 305–25.

Rose, Reginald (2010). *Twelve angry men.* Elsterwick, VIC, Australia: Insight Publications.

Rosen, Jeffrey (1992). Jurymandering. *New Republic,* November 30.

Rosenberg, D. (1975). Extended review. *Sociological Review* 23(4): 967–71.

Rosenberg, Jacob (2019). Jury duty is the next big step for felons' rights. *Mother Jones,* May 21. Retrieved from www.motherjones.com/politics/2019/05/jury-duty-is-the-next-big-step-for-felons-rights/ (accessed September 1, 2020).

Rosenberg, Morris (1973). Which significant others? *American Behavioral Scientist* 16(6): 829–60.

Rosenthal, Robert (1984). *Meta-analytic procedures for social research.* Beverly Hills, CA: Sage Publications.

Rosenthal, Robert, and Donald B. Rubin (1986). Meta-analytic procedures for combining studies with multiple effect sizes. *Psychological Bulletin* 99(3): 400–6.

Ross, Barbara, and Robert Ingrassia (2002). Joy and rage over jogger 5, Morgy's decision clears them of all charges. *New York Daily News*, December 6.

Rumgay, Judith (2004). Scripts for safer survival: Pathways out of female crime. *Howard Journal of Criminal Justice* 43(4): 405–19.

Russell, Katheryn K. (1998). *The color of crime: Racial hoaxes, white fear, black protectionism, police harassment, and other macroaggressions.* New York: New York University Press.

Saks, Michael J. (1997). What do jury experiments tell us about how juries (should) make decisions? *Southern California Interdisciplinary Law Journal* 6(1): 1–53.

Salerno, Jessica M., and Shari S. Diamond (2010). The promise of a cognitive perspective on jury deliberation. *Psychonomic Bulletin and Review* 17(2): 174–79.

Salmore, Barbara G., and Stephen A. Salmore (1985). *Candidates, parties, and campaigns: Electoral politics in America.* Washington, DC: Congressional Quarterly Press.

Sampson, Robert J., and John H. Laub (1990). Crime and deviance over the life course: The salience of adult social bonds. *American Sociological Review* 55(5): 609–27.

——— (1993). *Crime in the making: Pathways and turning points through life.* Cambridge, MA: Harvard University Press.

——— (1997). A life-course theory of cumulative disadvantage and the stability of delinquency. *Developmental theories of crime and delinquency* 7: 133–161.

——— (2005). A life-course view of the development of crime. *Annals of the American Academy of Political and Social Science* 602(1): 12–45.

Sanburn, Josh (2018). How thousands of voting ex-felons could impact Florida's elections. *Medium,* November 8. Retrieved from https://medium.com/s/story/how-thousands-of-voting-ex-felons-could-impact-floridas-elections-ebc80388ff3d (accessed September 1, 2020).

Sandys, Marla, and C. Dillehay (1995). First-ballot votes, predeliberation dispositions, and final verdicts in jury trials. *Law and Human Behavior* 19(2): 175–95.

Sanghara, Kiranjeet K., and J. Clare Wilson (2006). Stereotypes and attitudes about child sexual abusers: A comparison of experienced and inexperienced professionals in sex offender treatment. *Legal and Criminological Psychology* 11(2): 229–44.

Satterthwaite, Franklin E. (1946). An approximate distribution of estimates of variance components. *Biometrics Bulletin* 2(6): 110–14.

Saxonhouse, Elena (2004). Unequal protection: Comparing former felons' challenges to disenfranchisement and employment discrimination. *Stanford Law Review* 56(6): 1597–639.

Scheufele, Dietram A. (2000). Agenda-setting, priming, and framing revisited: Another look at cognitive effects of political communication. *Mass Communication and Society* 3(2–3): 297–316.

Schneider, Meghan L. (2010). From criminal confinement to social confinement: Helping ex-offenders obtain public housing with a certificate of rehabilitation. *New England Journal on Criminal and Civic Confinement* 36(2): 335–58.

Schneider, Peter D. (2002). Criminal convictions, incarceration, and child welfare: Ex-offenders lose their children. In *Every door closed: Barriers facing parents with criminal records*, ed. Hirsch et al. (pp. 53–84). Washington, DC: Center for Law and Social Policy and Community Legal Services.

Schreier, Margrit (2012). *Qualitative content analysis in practice*. Thousand Oaks, CA: Sage Publications.

Schulz-Hardt, Stefan, Marc Jochims, and Dieter Frey (2002). Productive conflict in group decision making: Genuine and contrived dissent as strategies to counteract biased information seeking. *Organizational Behavior and Human Decision Processes* 88(2): 563–86.

Scott, Sharion (2018). Justice in the jury: The benefits of allowing felons to serve on juries in criminal proceedings. *Washington University Journal of Law and Policy* 57: 225–49.

Sealy, A. Philip (1981). Another look at social psychological aspects of juror bias. *Law and Human Behavior* 5(2–3): 187–200.

Seeds, Christopher (2017). Bifurcation nation: American penal policy in late mass incarceration. *Punishment and Society* 19(5): 590–610.

Segal, Paula Z. (2010). A more inclusive democracy: Challenging felon jury exclusion in New York. *New York City Law Review* 13(2): 313–85.

Seltzer, Richard (2006). Scientific jury selection: Does it work? *Journal of Applied Social Psychology* 36(10): 2417–35.

Selvin, Molly (2017). Homeboy Industries: A history of violence; A hope for the future. *UCLA Blue Print*. Retrieved from https://blueprint.ucla.edu (accessed September 1, 2020).

Shannon, Sarah K.S., et al. (2017). The growth, scope, and spatial distribution of people with felony records in the United States. *Anticipatory injustice: The consequences of expecting injustice in the workplace, Demography* 5(4): 1795–818.

Shapiro, Debra L., and Bradley L. Kirkman (2001). In *Advances in organizational justice*, eds. Jerald Greenberg and Russell S. Cropanzano (pp. 152–178). Stanford, CA: Stanford University Press.

Shapiro, Samuel S., and R.S. Francia (1972). An approximate analysis of variance test for normality. *Journal of the American Statistical Association* 67 (337): 215–16.

Shapiro, Samuel S., and Martin B. Wilk (1965). An analysis of variance test for normality (complete samples). *Biometrika* 52 (3–4): 591–611.

Shaw, Marvin E. (1983). *Group dynamics: The psychology of small group behavior.* New York: McGraw-Hill.

Shea, Daniel M. (1996). *Campaign craft: The strategies, tactics, and art of political campaign management.* Westport, CT: Praeger.

Shinkfield, Alison J., and Joseph Graffam (2009). Community reintegration of ex-prisoners: Type and degree of change in variables influencing successful reintegration. *International Journal of Offender Therapy and Comparative Criminology* 53(1): 29–42.

Shover, Neal (1996). *Great pretenders: Pursuits and careers of persistent thieves.* Boulder, CO: Westview Press.

Shuman, Daniel W., and Jean A. Hamilton (1992). Jury service—It may change your mind: Perceptions of fairness of jurors and nonjurors. *Southern Methodist University Law Review* 46(2): 449–79.

Sigillo, Alexandra E., and Lori L. Sicafuse (2015). The influence of media and community sentiment on policy decision-making. In *Handbook of Community Sentiment*, eds. Monica K. Miller, Jeremy A. Blumenthal, and Jared Chamberlain (pp. 29–42) New York: Springer.

Silva, Lahny R. (2015). Criminal histories in public housing. *Wisconsin Law Review* 2015(2): 375–97.

Simon, Jonathan (1988). The ideological effects of actuarial practices. *Law and Society Review* 22(4): 771–800.

———— (1998). Managing the monstrous: Sex offenders and the new penology. *Psychology, Public Policy, and Law* 4(1–2): 452–67.

———— (2000). Megan's law: Crime and democracy in late modern America. *Law and Social Inquiry* 25(4): 1,111–50.

———— (2001). Fear and loathing in late modernity: Reflections on the cultural sources of mass imprisonment in the United States. *Punishment and Society* 3(1): 21–33.

———— (2007). *Governing through crime: How the war on crime transformed American democracy and created a culture of fear*. New York: Oxford University Press.

Simon, Rita J. (1967). *The jury and the defense of insanity*. Boston: Little, Brown.

Smith, Lisa L., and Ray Bull (2012). Identifying and measuring juror pre-trial bias for forensic evidence: Development and validation of the forensic evidence evaluation bias scale. *Psychology, Crime and Law* 18(9): 797–815.

Snyder, Steven B. (1988). Let my people run: The rights of voters and candidates under state laws barring felons from holding elective office. *Journal of Law and Politics* 4(3): 543–77.

Solomon, Norman (1994). *False hope: The politics of illusion in the Clinton era*. Monroe, ME: Common Courage Press.

Sommers, Samuel R. (2006). On racial diversity and group decision-making: Identifying multiple effects of racial composition on jury deliberations. *Journal of Personality and Social Psychology* 90(4): 597–612.

Sommers, Samuel R., Lindsey S. Warp, and Corrine C. Mahoney (2008). Cognitive effects of racial diversity: White individuals' information processing in heterogeneous groups. *Journal of Experimental Social Psychology* 44(4): 1,129–36.

Sreenivasan, Gopal (2002). Errors about errors: Virtue theory and trait attribution. *Mind* 111(441): 47–68.

Stafford, Mark C., and Richard R. Scott (1986). Stigma, deviance, and social control. In *The dilemma of difference: A multidisciplinary view of stigma*, ed. Elliot Aronson (pp. 77–91). Boston: Springer.

Stangor, Charles (1998). *Research methods for the behavioral sciences*. Stamford, CT: Cengage Learning.

Staples, William G. (2005). The everyday world of house arrest: Collateral consequences for families and others. In *Civil penalties social consequences,* eds. Christopher Mele and Teresa Miller (pp. 139–59). New York: Routledge.

Starr, Sonja B. (2015). The risk assessment: An overdue debate. *Federal Sentencing Reporter* 27(4): 205–6.

Stasser, Garold (1988). Computer simulation as a research tool: The DISCUSS model of group decision making. *Journal of Experimental Social Psychology* 24(5): 393–422.

Stasser, Garold, and William Titus (1985). Pooling of unshared information in group decision making: Biased information sampling during discussion. *Journal of Personality and Social Psychology* 48(6): 1,467–78.

State of Oregon Special Election Voters' Pamphlet (1999). On file with author.

Steele, Claude M., and Joshua Aronson (1995). Stereotype threat and the intellectual test performance of African Americans. *Journal of Personality and Social Psychology* 69(5): 797–811.

Steinacker, Andrea (2003). The prisoner's campaign: Felony disenfranchisement laws and the right to hold public office. *BYU Law Review* 2003(2): 801–28.

Stern, Mark Joseph (2018). Florida just granted 1.5 million people the right to vote: That's huge. *Slate,* November 6. Retrieved from https://slate.com/news-and-politics/2018/11/amendment-4-florida-felons-voting-rights.html.

Stevenson, Megan (2018). Assessing risk assessment in action. *Minnesota Law Review* 103: 303–84.

Stole, Bryn (2019). Should Louisianans with past felony convictions serve on juries? State lawmakers consider allowing it. *The Advocate,* May 1. Retrieved from www.theadvocate.com/baton_rouge/news/politics/legislature/article_b8d7cee8-6c60-11e9-b0aa-9b59f6918e39.html (accessed September 1, 2020).

Stoll, Michael A., and Shawn D. Bushway (2008). The effect of criminal background checks on hiring ex-offenders. *Criminology and Public Policy* 7(3): 371–404.

Stone, Donald H. (1995). The bar admission process, gatekeeper or big brother: An empirical study. *Northern Illinois University Law Review* 15: 331–72.

Stryker, Sheldon (1968). Identity salience and role performance: The relevance of symbolic interaction theory for family research. *Journal of Marriage and the Family* 30(4): 558–64.

——— (1980). *Symbolic interactionism: A social structural version.* San Francisco: Benjamin-Cummings Publishing.

St. Vincent DePaul Reentry Initiative (2020). Retrieved from www.svdpcincinnati.org/About_Us/Our_Programs/Re-entry_Program/ (accessed September 1, 2020).

Sugie, Naomi F. (2012). Punishment and welfare: Paternal incarceration and families' receipt of public assistance. *Social Forces* 90(4): 1,403–27.

Sullivan, Harry S. (1947). *Conceptions of modern psychiatry.* New York: William Allison White Foundation.

Sunstein, Cass R. (2002). The law of group polarization. *Journal of Political Philosophy* 10(2): 175–95.

Sutter County (2020). Jury Service. Retrieved from www.suttercourts.com/general-info/jury-service (accessed September 1, 2020).

Sweeney, Laura T., and Craig Haney (1992). The influence of race on sentencing: A meta-analytic review of experimental studies. *Behavioral Sciences and the Law* 10(2): 179–95.

Swisher, Keith (2008). The troubling rise of the legal profession's good moral character. *St. John's Law Review* 82(3): 1,037–86.

Sykes, Gresham M., and David Matza (1957). Techniques of neutralization: A theory of delinquency. *American Sociological Review* 22(6): 664–70.

Tajfel, Henri, and John C. Turner (1979). An integrative theory of intergroup conflict. In *The social psychology of intergroup relations,* eds. William G. Austin and Stephen Worchel (pp. 33–37). Monterey, CA: Brooks/Cole.

——— (1986). The social identity theory of intergroup relations. In *Psychology of Intergroup Relations,* eds. Stephen Worchel and William G. Austin (pp. 7–24). Chicago: Nelson.

Tang, Connie M., and Narina Nunez (2003). Effects of defendant age and juror bias on judgement of culpability: What happens when a juvenile is tried as an adult. *American Journal of Criminal Justice* 28(1): 37–52.

Taxman, Faye S., David Soule, and Adam Gelb (1999). Graduated sanctions: Stepping into accountable systems and offenders. *Prison Journal* 79(2): 182–204.

Tekleab, Amanuel G., Narda R. Quigley, and Paul E. Tesluk (2009). A longitudinal study of team conflict, conflict management, cohesion, and team effectiveness. *Group and Organization Management* 34(2): 170–205.

Thatcher, David (2008). The rise of criminal background screening in rental housing. *Law and Social Inquiry* 33(1): 5–30.

Thorley, Craig, and Stephen A. Dewhurst (2009). False and veridical collaborative recognition. *Memory* 17(1): 17–25.

Tocqueville, Alexis de (1835). *Democracy in America.* New York: Vintage Books.

——— (1969). *Democracy in America.* Ed. Jacob P. Mayer. Trans. George Lawrence. Rev. ed. New York: Harper Collins.

Tonry, Michael (2004). Thinking about crime: Sense and sensibility in American penal culture. New York: Oxford University Press.

Totenberg, Nina (2020). Supreme court deals major blow to felons' right to vote in Florida. *NPR*, July 17. Retrieved from www.npr.org/2020/07/17/892105780/supreme-court-deals-major-blow-to-ex-felons-right-to-vote-in-florida (accessed September 1, 2020).

Travis, Jeremy (2005). *But they all come back: Facing the challenges of prisoner reentry.* Washington, DC: Rowman and Littlefield.

Travis, Jeremy, and Christy Ann Visher (2005). Prisoner reentry and crime in America. New York: Cambridge University Press.

Trawalter, Sophie, Jennifer A. Richeson, and J. Nicole Shelton (2009). Predicting behavior during interracial interactions: A stress and coping approach. *Personality and Social Psychology Review* 13(4): 243–68.

Trice, Harrison M., and Paul M. Roman (1970). Delabeling, relabeling, and alcoholics anonymous. *Social Problems* 17(4): 538–46.

Tyler, Tom R. (1984). The role of perceived injustice in defendants' evaluation of their courtroom experiences. *Law and Society Review* 18(1): 51–74.

———— (1990). *Why people obey the law: Procedural justice legitimacy and compliance.* New Haven, CT: Yale University Press.

———— (2003). Procedural justice, legitimacy, and the effective rule of law. *Crime and Justice* 30(2003): 283–357.

———— (2009). Legitimacy and criminal justice: The benefits of self-regulation. *Ohio State Journal of Criminal Law* 7(1): 307–59.

Tyler, Tom, Jonathan D. Casper, and Bonnie Fisher (1989). Maintaining allegiance toward political authorities: The role of prior attitudes and the use of fair procedures. *American Journal of Political Science* 33(3): 629–52.

Uggen, Christopher, and Jeff Manza (2002). Democratic contraction? Political consequences of felon disenfranchisement in the United States. *American Sociological Review* 67(6): 777–803.

Uggen, Christopher, Jeff Manza, and Angela Behrens (2004). "Less than the average citizen": Stigma, role transition, and the civic reintegration of convicted felons. In *After crime and punishment: Pathways to offender reintegration,* eds. Shadd Maruna and Russ Immarigeon (pp. 261–93). Portland, OR: Willan.

Underwood, Barbara D. (1992). Ending race discrimination in jury selection: Whose right is it, anyway? *Columbia Law Review* 92(4): 725–74.

Upton, Candace L. (2009). Virtue ethics and moral psychology: The situationism debate. *Journal of Ethics* 13(2–3): 103–15.

U.S. Department of Housing and Urban Development (2016). *It starts with housing: Public housing agencies are making second chances real.* Retrieved from www.hud .gov/sites/documents/HUD_IT_STARTS_WITH_HOUSING.PDF. (accessed September 1, 2020).

Valls, Victor, Vicente Gonzalez-Roma, and Ines Tomas (2016). Linking educational diversity and team performance: Team communication quality and innovation team climate matter. *Journal of Occupational and Organizational Psychology* 89(4): 751–71.

van Dijk, Hans, Marloes L. van Engen, and Daan van Knippenberg (2012). Defying conventional wisdom: A meta-analytical examination of the differences between demographic and job-related diversity relationships with performance. *Organizational Behavior and Human Decision Processes* 119(1): 38–53.

van Knippenberg, Daan, Carsten K.W. de Dreu, and Astrid C. Homan (2004). Work group diversity and group performance: An integrative model and research agenda. *Journal of Applied Psychology* 89(6): 1,008–22.

Vaughan, Barry (2001). Handle with care: On the use of structuration theory within criminology. *British Journal of Criminology* 41(1): 185–200.

———— (2007). The internal narrative of desistance. *British Journal of Criminology* 47(3): 390–404.

Vidmar, Neil, and Valerie P. Hans (2007). *American juries: The verdict.* Amherst, NY: Prometheus Books.

Vidmar, Neil, et al. (2003). Juror discussions during civil trials: Studying an Arizona innovation. *Arizona Law Review* 45(1): 1–82.

Viki, G. Tendayi, et al. (2012). The role of dehumanization in attitudes toward the social exclusion and rehabilitation of sex offenders. *Journal of Applied Social Psychology* 42(10): 2,349–67.

Villiers, Meiring (2010). The impartiality doctrine: Constitutional meaning and judicial impact. *American Journal of Trial Advocacy* 34(1): 71–104.

Vollrath, David A., et al. (1989). Memory performance by decision-making groups and individuals. *Organizational Behavior and Human Decision Processes* 43(3): 289–300.

von Bar, Carl L., et al. (1916). *A history of continental criminal law.* Boston: Little, Brown.

Vozzella, Laura (2017). Virginia Governor McAuliffe says he has broken U.S. record for restoring voting rights. *Washington Post,* April 27.

Vuolo, Mike, Sara Lageson, and Christopher Uggen (2017). Criminal record questions in the era of "ban the box." *Criminology and Public Policy* 16(1): 139–65.

Wagner, Peter, and Bernadette Rabuy (2017). Mass incarceration: The whole pie 2017. *Prison Policy Initiative.* Retrieved from www.prisonpolicy.org/reports /pie2017.html (accessed September 1, 2020).

Wagner, Peter, and Alison Walsh (2016). States of incarceration: The global context 2016. *Prison Policy Initiative.* Retrieved from www.prisonpolicy.org/global/2016 .html (accessed September 1, 2020).

Ward, Tony, and Mark Brown (2004). The good lives model and conceptual issues in offender rehabilitation. *Psychology, Crime and Law* 10(3): 243–57.

Ward, Tony, and Claire Stewart (2003). Criminogenic needs and human needs: A theoretical model. *Psychology, Crime and Law* 9(2): 125–43.

Warling, Diane, and Michele Peterson-Badali (2003). The verdict on jury trials for juveniles: The effects of defendant's age on trial outcomes. *Behavioral Sciences and the Law* 21(1): 63–82.

Washington Post Editorial Board (2013). Mr. McDonnell moves to restore voting rights. *Washington Post,* January 10.

Watson, Warren E., Kamalesh Kumar, and Larry K. Michaelsen (1993). Cultural diversity's impact on interaction process and performance: Comparing homogeneous and diverse task groups. *Academy of Management Journal* 36(3): 590–602.

Weaver, Beth (2012). The relational context of desistance: Some implications and opportunities for social policy. *Social Policy and Administration* 46(4): 395–412.

Weaver, Vesla M. (2007). Frontlash: Race and the development of punitive crime policy. *Studies in American Political Development* 21(2): 230–65.

Weaver, Vesla M., and Amy E. Lerman (2010). Political consequences of the carceral state. *American Political Science Review* 104(4): 817–33.

Webber, Sheila S., and Lisa M. Donahue (2001). Impact of highly and less job-related diversity on work group cohesion and performance: A meta-analysis. *Journal of Management* 27(2): 141–62.

Weir, Julie A., and Lawrence S. Wrightsman (1990). The determinants of mock jurors' verdicts in a rape case. *Journal of Applied Social Psychology* 20(11): 901–19.

Welch, Bernard L. (1947). The generalization of "student's" problem when several different population variances are involved. *Biometrika* 34(1–2): 28–35.

Welch, Michael, Eric A. Price, and Nana Yankey (2002). Moral panic over youth violence: Wilding and the manufacture of menace in the media. *Youth and Society* 34(1): 3–30.

Werner, Carol M., Dorothy K. Kagehiro, and Michael J. Strube (1982). Conviction proneness and the authoritarian juror: Inability to disregard information or attitudinal bias? *Journal of Applied Psychology* 67(5): 629–36.

West, Robin (1997). *Caring for justice.* New York: New York University Press.

——— (2012). The anti-empathic turn. In *Passions and Emotions*, ed. James E. Fleming (pp. 243–88). New York: New York University Press.

Wexler, David B. (2001). Robes and rehabilitation: How judges can help offenders "make good." *Court Review: The Journal of American Judges* 38(1): 18–23.

Wheelock, Darren (2005). Collateral consequences and racial inequality: Felon status restrictions as a system of disadvantage. *Journal of Contemporary Criminal Justice* 21(1): 82–90.

——— (2012). A jury of one's "peers": Felon jury exclusion and racial inequality in Georgia courts. *Justice System Journal* 32(3): 335–59.

White, William L. (2000). Toward a new recovery movement: Historical reflections on recovery, treatment and advocacy. Paper presented at the Center for Substance Abuse Treatment, Recovery Community Support Program Conference, Arlington, VA, April 3–5.

Whittenbaum, Gwen M., Andrea B. Hollingshead, and Isabel C. Botero (2004). From cooperative to motivated information sharing in groups: Moving beyond the hidden profile paradigm. *Communication Monographs* 71(3): 286–310.

Wilkenfeld, Joshua (2004). Newly compelling: Reexamining judicial construction of juries in the aftermath of *Grutter v. Bollinger. Columbia Law Review* 104(8): 2,291–327.

Williams, Bernard (1985). *Ethics and the limits of philosophy.* New York: Routledge.

Willis, Gwenda M., Jill S. Levenson, and Tony Ward (2010). Desistance and attitudes towards sex offenders: Facilitation or hindrance? *Journal of Family Violence* 25(6): 545–56.

Willis, Gwenda M., Sanna Malinen, and Lucy Johnston (2013). Demographic differences in public attitudes towards sex offenders. *Psychiatry, Psychology and Law* 20(2): 230–47.

Wilson, David (1996). Metaphors, growth coalition discourses, and black poverty neighborhoods in a US city. *Antipode* 28(1): 72–96.

Wilson, Drew (2018). Voters overwhelmingly support felon voting rights amendment. *Floridapolitics.com*, May 2. Retrieved from https://floridapolitics.com/archives/262686-voters-overwhelmingly-support-felon-voting-rights-amendment (accessed September 1, 2020).

Wolfe, Michelle, Brian D. Jones, and Frank R. Baumgartner (2013). A failure to communicate: Agenda setting in media and policy studies. *Political Communication* 30(2): 175–92.

Woods, LaKeesha N., et al. (2013). The role of prevention in promoting continuity of health care in prisoner reentry initiatives. *American Journal of Public Health* 103(5): 830–38.

Woolard, Jennifer L., Samantha Harvell, and Sandra Graham (2008). Anticipatory injustice among adolescents: Age and racial/ethnic differences in perceived unfairness of the justice system. *Behavioral Sciences and the Law* 26(2): 207–26.

Yankah, Ekow N. (2004). Good guys and bad guys: Punishing character, equality and the irrelevance of moral character to criminal punishment. *Cardozo Law Review* 25(3): 1,019–67.

Young, Jock (2009). Moral panic: Its origins in resistance, ressentiment, and the translation of fantasy into reality. *British Journal of Criminology* 49(1): 4–16.

Young, William G. (2006). Vanishing trials, vanishing juries, and vanishing constitution. *Suffolk University Law Review* 40: 67–94.

Zahariadis, Nikolaos (2016). Delphic oracles: Ambiguity, institutions, and multiple streams. *Policy Sciences* 49(1): 3–12.

Zeisel, Hans (1972). The waning of the American jury. *American Bar Association Journal* 58(4): 367–70.

Zimbardo, Philip G., et al. (1971). *The Stanford prison experiment: A simulation study of the psychology of imprisonment conducted August 1971 at Stanford University.* Stanford, CA: Philip G. Zimbardo.

Zimring, Franklin E., and David T. Johnson (2006). Public opinion and the governance of punishment in democratic political systems. *Annals of the American Academy of Political and Social Science* 605(1): 265–80.

Zuklie, Mitchell S. (1996). Rethinking the fair cross-section requirement. *California Law Review* 84(1): 101–50.

CASES CITED

Apodaca et al. v. Oregon 406 U.S. 404 (1972)

Avery v. Georgia 345 U.S. 559 (1953)

Ballard v. United States 329 U.S. 187 (1946)

Ballew v. Georgia 435 U.S. 223 (1978)

Carle v. United States (1998)

Carter v. Jury Commission of Greene County 396 U.S. 320 (1970)

Commonwealth v. Aljoe 420 Pa. 198 (1966)

Commonwealth v. Soares (1979)

Companioni Jr. v. City of Tampa (2007)

Duren v. Missouri 439 U.S. 357 (1979)

Edmonson v. Leesville Concrete Company Inc., 500 U.S. 614 (1991)

Glasser v. United States 315 U.S. 60 (1942)

Green v. Board of Elections City of New York 380 F.2d 445 (1967)

Hale v. Kentucky 303 U.S. 613 (1938)

Hilliard v. Ferguson 30 F.3d 649 (1994)

Holland v. Illinois 493 U.S. 474 (1990)

In re Cason 294 S.E. 2.d 520 (1982)

In re King 136 P.3d 878 (2006)

In re Matthews 462 A.2d 165, 176 (1983)

Irvin v. Dowd 366 U.S 717 (1961)

Johnson v. Louisiana 406 U.S. 356 (1972)

Lockhart v. McCree 476 U.S. 162 (1986)

Logan v. United States 144 U.S. 263 (1892)

Morgan v. Illinois 504 U.S. 719 (1992)

Norris v. Alabama 294 U.S. 587 (1935)

Patton v. Mississippi 332 U.S. 463 (1947)

People ex. rel. Hannon v. Ryan 34 A.D.2d 393 (1970)

People v. Miller (2008)

People v. Wheeler 22 Cal.3d 258 (1978)

Peters v. Kiff 407 U.S. 493 (1972)

Pierre v. Louisiana 306 U.S. 354 (1939)

Powers v. Ohio 499 U.S. 400 (1991)

Raysor v. DeSantis 591 U.S. (2020)

Rector v. State 280 Ark. 385 (1983)

Reynolds v. United States 98 U.S. 145 (1878)

R.R.E. v. Glenn 884 S.W.2d 189 (1994)

Rubio v. The Superior Court of San Joaquin County 24 Cal.3d 93 (1979)

Schware v. Board of Bar Examiners of New Mexico 353 U.S. 232 (1957)

Shows v. State 267 So. 2d 811 (1972)

Smith v. Texas 311 U.S. 128 (1940)

State v. Baxter 357 So.2d 271 (1978)

State v. Brown 334 A.2d 392 (1975)

State v. Compton 333 Or. 274 (2002)

State v. Neal 550 So.2d 740 (1989)

Strauder v. West Virginia 100 U.S 303 (1880)

Taylor v. Louisiana 419 U.S. 522 (1975)

Texas Supporters of Workers World Party Presidential Candidates v. Strake 511 F. Supp. 149 (1981)

Thiel v. Southern Pacific Company 328 U.S. 217 (1946)

United States v. Arce 997 F.2d 1123 (1993)

United States v. Barry 71 F.3d 1269 (1995)

United States v. Best 214 F. Supp. 2d 897 (2002)

United States v. Boney 977 F.2d 624 (1992)

United States v. Carolene Products Co. 304 U.S. 144 (1938)

United States v. Conant 116 F. Supp. 2d 1015 (2000)

United States v. Foxworth 599 F.2d 1 (1979)

United States v. Greene 86 Ohio App.3d 620 (1993)
United States v. Horodner 91 F.3d 1317 (1996)
United States v. Humphreys 982 F.2d 254 (1992)
United States v. Parker 19 F.Supp. 450 (1937)
United States v. Wood 299 U.S. 123 (1936)
Wainwright v. Witt 469 U.S. 412 (1985)
Washington v. State 75 Ala. 582 (1884)
Williams v. Mississippi 170 U.S. 213 (1898)

STATUTES CITED

Acts and Resolves of Massachusetts, ch. 92 (February 8, 1803)
Ariz. Rev. Stat. § 13–912(A) (2018)
Cal. Assembly Bill 535 (2018)
Cal. Civ. Proc. Code § 203
Cal. Civ. Proc. Code § 203(a)(1)-(8) (2010)
Cal. Civ. Proc. Code § 203 (a)(5) (2019)
Cal. Civ. Proc. Code § 203 (a)(10) (2020)
Cal. Civ. Proc. Code § 203 (a)(11) (2020)
Cal. Const. art. VII, § 8(b)
Cal. Penal Code §§4852.01, 4852.03, 4852.06, 4852.16, 4852.17
California Senate Bill 310 (2020)
Civil Rights Act of 1875, 18 U.S.C.A. § 243
Colo. Rev. Stat. § 13–71–105(3) (2018)
D.C. Code § 11–1906(b)(2)(B)
D.C. Code § 11–1906(b)(2)(B) (2018)
18 U.S.C. § 2113
Fed. R. Evidence § 404(a)
Fed. R. Evidence § 404(a)-(b)
Fed. R. Evidence § 404(b)
Fed. R. Evidence § 609
14 M.R.S.A. § 1211 (2012)
Ga. Code Ann. § 15–12–120.1
Ga. Code Ann. § 15–12–163(b)(5)
Ga. Code Ann. § 15–12–40
Ga. Op. Att'y Gen. No. 83–33 (1983)
Jury Plan for Superior Court of the District of Columbia, 2013 § 7(f)
Jury System Improvements Act of 2000, 28 U.S.C. § 1861
Maine Public Laws 1821, ch. 84, §3
Maine Public Laws 1971, ch. 391, §1
Maine Public Laws 1981, ch. 705, §G13
Maine Public Laws 1981, ch. 705, §G4
Maine Revised Statutes 1841, ch.135, §6

Maine Revised Statutes Annotated, tit. 21-a, §112 (2017)
Michigan Senate Fiscal Agency Bill Analysis (2003)
Nev. Rev. Stat. § 213.157(2)(a)-(e) (2018)
Ninth Circuit Jury Instructions, 2010, § 8.162
Or. Rev. Stat. § 10.030(3)(a)(E)-(F) (2017)

CONSTITUTIONAL AMENDMENTS CITED

U.S. Const. Amend. VI
U.S. Const. Amend. XIV

INDEX

ABA (American Bar Association), 39, 40
Abramson, Jeffrey, 47
African Americans, 14–15, 28, 171n1; Black juror exclusion, 179nn177,181; incarceration of, 43; jury representation, 43–44, 76; perceptions of criminality of, 115, 212n53; racially diverse juries, 65
agenda setting process, 123
Alabama: access to legal profession, 161; duration by state, 161; felon-juror exclusion policies, 150; law enforcement juror eligibility criteria, 165; misdemeanor convictions, 181n46; as permanent exclusion jurisdiction, 165, 173n66
Alaska: access to legal profession, 161; duration by state, 161; felon-juror exclusion policies, 150; felon-voter eligibility, 173–74n77; law enforcement juror eligibility criteria, 165; during sentence exclusion, 165
Allport, Gordon, 115, 212nn47,56
ambivalence. See public opinion
American Bar Association (ABA), 39, 40
American jury system, case for, 4–5
anticipatory injustice, 58
Arizona: access to legal profession, 161; duration by state, 161; felon-juror exclusion policies, 19, 150; hybrid jurisdiction, 165; law enforcement juror eligibility criteria, 165
Arkansas: access to legal profession, 161; Clinton, 126; duration by state, 161; felon-juror exclusion policies, 150;

felon-voter eligibility, 173–74n77; law enforcement juror eligibility criteria, 165; as permanent exclusion jurisdiction, 165, 173n66; Supreme Court of, 21
attainder process, 17
attentiveness, 141
authoritarianism, 50, 189n58

Ballard v. United States, 15–16
Ballew v. Georgia, 48
bar examinations, 39–41, 182n64, 182nn57–61
Barreras, Ricardo, 145
Bartlett, Elaine, 6, 192n78
Bauman, Zygmunt, 114
Baumgartner, Frank R., 125
Beckett, Katherine, 124
bias rationale, 140; explicit biases, 187n14; general biases and, 49–50; general/specific biases, 188nn33–35, 189n37; implicit biases, 187n14; in juror selection, 186n2, 187n7; predicting biases across groups, 57–58; predicting biases among convicted felons, 58–59. *See also* inherent bias rationale
blank slate ideal (tabula rasa), 47, 187n15
Boyle, Greg, 203n36
Breyer, Stephen, 205n4
Brooks, Clem, 130
Bush, George H. W., 125
Bush, George W., 25
Bushway, Shawn, 206n23

California: access to legal profession, 161; Assembly Bill 535, 27; CALSPEAKS (California Speaks Opinion Research) survey, 130–35; CDCR, 190n71; civil rights restoration, 217n3; District Attorneys Association, 137–40; duration by state, 161; felon-juror exclusion policies, 150, 190n69; felon-voter eligibility, 173–74n77; juror eligibility requirements, 173n66; law enforcement juror eligibility criteria, 165; misdemeanor convictions, 181n46; PACT meetings, 67, 190n71, 197n52; as permanent exclusion jurisdiction, 165, 192n82; POST trainings, 53, 192nn80–81; racially diverse juries, 44; Senate Bill 310, 131, 137–40, 143, 145–47, 217nn1,5; Supreme Court of, 21–22

California Department of Corrections and Rehabilitation (CDCR), 190n71

California District Attorneys Association, 137–40

CALSPEAKS (California Speaks Opinion Research) survey, 130–35

Carbone, Christina S., 122

Carle v. United States, 176n116

CDCR (California Department of Corrections and Rehabilitation), 190n71

Central Park Five, 126–27

certification process, 190n69, 210nn17,19, 218n11

character: comparing requirements of, 39–41; conventionalist formulation of, 31–32; empirical formulation of, 32–34; law's conception of, 34–36; moral character and fitness, 36–37; overview, 30–31; per se disqualifications, 37, 38 map2; presumptive disqualifications, 38 map2, 38–39

character conceptualization, 140, 141; consistency and, 180n20; context importance, 9, 30–34, 42, 45, 140; evaluative integration, 180n22; globalism and, 180n18; Harman-Doris thesis, 179nn9–10; internal traits, 180n23; situational variation, 180nn27,29; traditional concepts, 180n24; trait-relevant behavior, 180n20

Christ, Charlie, 26

Circles of Support and Accountability (CoSA) Model, 209n4

civic issues: civil banishment, 171n16; civil death concept, 17–18, 22, 175n98; engagement in, 5, 134; reintegration, 132, 134, 142

civil jury trials: decline in, 4; felon-juror exclusion policies, 20, 151

civil rights: civil liberties, 189n58; civic restrictions, 171n13; civil rights restoration, 2, 190n69, 217n3; in English law, 17

Civil Rights Act of 1875, 18, 172n56

Clinton, Bill, 126

Clinton, Hillary, 130

coding schemes, 203nn38,40

Cohen, Stanley, 214n43

collateral sanction, 7, 13, 28, 34, 77, 108, 126, 171n3

Colorado: access to legal profession, 161; duration by state, 161; felon-juror exclusion policies, 19, 20, 150; felon-voter eligibility, 173–74n77; hybrid jurisdiction, 165; law enforcement juror eligibility criteria, 165; as permanent exclusion jurisdiction, 192n82

common law model of impartiality, 47–48

community engagement: overview, 107–8, 121–22; accountability and, 209n8; closeness, familiarity, and tolerance, 113–16; community integration, 209n3; CoSA and, 209n4; desistance and delabeling, 108–13; of first-time trial jurors, 170n10; inclusion and, 142; loss of social capital and, 6

COMPAS tool, 201n19

Connecticut: access to legal profession, 161; duration by state, 161; felon-juror exclusion policies, 150; felon-voter eligibility, 173–74n77; hybrid jurisdiction, 165; law enforcement juror eligibility criteria, 165; misdemeanor convictions, 181n46; voting rights, 145

Consolini, Paula M., 170n10

constitutional protections, 176nn123–24

contact: contact hypothesis, 115; contact programs, 211n45; prejudice reduction and, 212n53; rehabilitation and, 212n52;

eligible juror participants, 192n78; comparisons to, 193n84; mock jury study???
PACT meeting people, 191n71; pretrial biases, 53–54; RJBS scores, 51, 51 table1, 53 fig.2, 53–54, 54 table2
Ellsworth, Phoebe C., 64–65
empathy, 208–9n88
English law, 17, 97
equal protection: claims, 24–25; doctrine, 23; Equal Protection Clause, 14, 24
ethical assumptions, 210n12
Ewald, Alec C., 146–47, 175n98

fear-mongering tactics, 215nn44,45,54
federal jurisdiction, 19, 197n52; access to legal profession, 161; duration by state, 161; federal criminal justice system, 4; felon-juror exclusion policies, 150; felon-voter eligibility, 173–74n77; law enforcement juror eligibility criteria, 165; as permanent exclusion jurisdiction, 165, 173n66, 192n82
Federal Rules of Evidence, 35, 181n45
Federal Sentencing Guidelines, 4
felon-juror contributions: cooperating with others, 83–87; deciphering jury instructions, 87–91; evenhanded application of law, 87–91; impartial interpretation of evidence, 83–87; overview, 77–78; reanalysis of, 80–81, 91–92; revelation of criminal past, 81–82; thoughtful deliberation, 82–83
felon-juror exclusion: benefits of, 3; consequences of, 3–4; costs of, 3; duration by state, 161–63; Federal jurisdiction, 161; felon-voter disenfranchisement and, 129–30, 178n160; history of, 17–19; invisibility of, 25–28; justifications for, 3; overview, 13–14; overview of, 8–11; policies by jurisdiction, 149–59; professed purposes for, 3; ramifications of, 3; research on, 3; studies on, 28–29. See also inherent bias rationale
felon-juror exclusion policies: California Senate Bill 310 and, 131, 137–40, 143; CALSPEAKS (California Speaks Opinion Research) survey, 130–35; flaws of, 142; implications of, 143; interna-

tionally, 174n81; by jurisdiction, 19–20, 20 map1.; legislative biasing and, 193n84; purposes for, 175n83, 179n3; reentry and, 142; scrutiny of, 176n115
felon-juror exclusion statutes, 20 map1; cross-section claims, 22–24; current, 19–20; equal protection claims, 24–25; rationales for, 20–22. See also during sentence exclusion; hybrid jurisdiction; lifetime exclusion; lifetime for cause exclusion; no exclusion
felon-juror inclusion: community engagement and, 142; CoSA Model and, 209n4; critics of, 137–40, 143; descriptive statistics, 131–32, 132 table4; impact of, 141; inclusion and, 141–42; :, inclusive impartiality, 48; perception softening and, 5; public opinion on, 134–35; public sentiment on, 142; social benefits facilitated by, 142; tactics of, 143
felon-jurors: comparisons to, 3, 193n48; interactions, 77–78; interviews of, 3, 142; as participants, 192n78
felon-voter disenfranchisement, 129–30, 131, 132, 135, 171n13, 178n160; contributions to, 217n4; felon-juror exclusion statutes and, 20; treatment of, 25–28
felon-voter rights: eligibility, 173–74n77; public support for, 131–32 reinstatement, 178n152
felony criminal record normalization, 171n1
first offense, 19, 150
Flanagan, John, 27
Florida: access to legal profession, 161; Amendment 4 ballot initiative of 2018, 130; bar admission screenings, 182n64; duration by state, 161; felon-juror exclusion policies, 150; felon-voter eligibility, 173–74n77; law enforcement juror eligibility criteria, 165; misdemeanor convictions, 181n46; as permanent exclusion jurisdiction, 165, 173n66, 192n82; voting rights restoration in, 26–27
Florida Amendment 4 ballot initiative of 2018, 130
focusing events, 25–28, 123–25
Fourteenth Amendment, 14
Franke, Todd, 203n36

exclusion policies, 151; felon-voter eligibility, 173–74n77; law enforcement juror eligibility criteria, 166; as permanent exclusion jurisdiction, 166, 173n66

New Jersey: access to legal profession, 162; bar admission screenings, 182n64; duration by state, 162; felon-juror exclusion policies, 151; felon-voter eligibility, 173–74n77; law enforcement juror eligibility criteria, 166; misdemeanor convictions, 181n46; as permanent exclusion jurisdiction, 166, 173n66

New Mexico: access to legal profession, 162; duration by state, 162; felon-juror exclusion policies, 151; felon-voter eligibility, 173–74n77; law enforcement juror eligibility criteria, 166; during sentence exclusion, 166

New York: access to legal profession, 162; duration by state, 162; felon-juror exclusion policies, 151; felon-voter eligibility, 173–74n77; law enforcement juror eligibility criteria, 166; as permanent exclusion jurisdiction, 166, 173n66; on probity rationale, 21; reentry service organizations in, 79–80; voting rights, 145, 147

noncriminal identity, certification of, 210nn19,23

non-felon-jurors, comparisons to, 3

nonviolent offense, 150; felon-juror exclusion policies, 19

normality, Shapiro-Wilk test of, 192n78

normative space sharing, 209nn6,9

North Carolina: access to legal profession, 162; duration by state, 162; felon-juror exclusion policies, 151; felon-voter eligibility, 173–74n77; law enforcement juror eligibility criteria, 166; during sentence exclusion, 166

North Dakota: access to legal profession, 162; duration by state, 162; felon-juror exclusion policies, 151; felon-voter eligibility, 173–74n77; law enforcement juror eligibility criteria, 166; during sentence exclusion, 166

North Star Opinion Research, 130

objective juror eligibility criteria, 18

occupational restrictions, statutory and regulatory, 6

Ohio: access to legal profession, 162; bar admission screenings, 182n64; duration by state, 162; felon-juror exclusion policies, 151; felon-voter eligibility, 173–74n77; law enforcement juror eligibility criteria, 166; during sentence exclusion, 166; voting rights, 145

Oklahoma: access to legal profession, 162; duration by state, 162; felon-juror exclusion policies, 151; felon-voter eligibility, 173–74n77; law enforcement juror eligibility criteria, 166; as permanent exclusion jurisdiction, 166, 173n66, 192n82, 193n83

Oregon: access to legal profession, 162; bar admission screenings, 182n64; duration by state, 162; felon-juror exclusion policies, 20, 151; felon-voter eligibility, 173–74n77; hybrid jurisdiction, 166; law enforcement juror eligibility criteria, 166; misdemeanor convictions, 181n46

ostracism, 4, 22–25

othering, 114, 116, 125, 211nn34,38

outlawry process, 17

PACT (Parole and Community Team) meetings, 67, 190n71, 197n52

pairwise kappas, 69, 203n38

pardons, 151n2, 152nn4,5,9, 153nn11–13, 154nn19, 20, 22, 155nn24,27,28,29, 156nn29,35, 157nn37, 38, 40, 158nn42, 44, 159n47, 48, 50, 52, 163, 183n68, 186n122, 190n69

Parole and Community Team (PACT) meetings, 67, 190n71, 197n52

parolees, 96, 130, 138, 139, 190n71, 197n52

participatory democracy principles, 4

Paternoster, Raymond, 206n23

Peace Officers Standards and Trainings (POST), 53, 192nn80–81

Pennsylvania: access to legal profession, 162; duration by state, 162; felon-juror exclusion policies, 151; felon-voter eligibility, 173–74n77; law enforcement

Pennsylvania *(continued)*
    juror eligibility criteria, 166; as permanent exclusion jurisdiction, 166, 173n66
permanent exclusion jurisdictions 149, 173n66, 192n82, 193n83
permanent excuse, 2
perpetual ostracism, 4
petit juries, 16, 19, 20, 150, 152nn5,7,10, 155n29, 157n39, 158n45, 172n56
Piquero, Alex, 115
PJAQ (Pretrial Juror Attitude Questionnaire), 192n73
Plaut, Victoria C., 122
plea bargaining, 4; increase in, 26; prison conditions and, 169n6; reliance on, 4
policymaking: influence on public opinion, 124–28, 134; media and, 214nn20,37
policy reform, 135
political engagement, 170n10
political ideology: civic reintegration and, 142; correctional policies and, 211n33; crime control as political tools, 213nn5–6; felon-juror inclusion and, 142; felon-voter disenfranchisement and, 129; role of, 132–35, 133 fig.4, 134 fig.5
polling of felon-voter disenfranchisement, 129–30
positive criminology, 200n8
POST (Peace Officers Standards and Trainings), 53, 192nn80–81
Powers v. Ohio, 177n128, 205n4
prejudice disqualification, 194n122
prejudice reduction: contact types and, 212n53; intergroup contact and, 212nn46–47
presumptive disqualification, 161–63
pretrial biases, 48–50; attitudes of jurors, 3; comparison of, 53; of convicted felons, 140, 190n71; presumption of, 46; protections against, 60–61; RJBS and, 191n73
pretrial confinement, 4
Pretrial Juror Attitude Questionnaire (PJAQ), 192n73
primary criminal desistance, 94, 205–6n10
prison conditions, 169n6
Probability of Commission (PC) subscale measures, 191n73

probationers, 138
probity rationale, 21, 22, 25, 30; taint argument, 30, 41–45
procedural justice theory, 59
prosecutors, 142
prosocial desistance narrative, 141; prosocial labeling, 210n15; prosocial roles, 5, 141
protectionist justifications for exclusions, 174n82
public opinion: overview, 123–24; antipathy toward offenders, 212–13n1; of convicted felons, 128–29; descriptive statistics, 131–32, 132 table4; drivers of, 128–29; on felon-juror service, 3; felon-voter disenfranchisement and, 129–30; formation of, 128, 134; influence of policymakers and the media on, 124–28; lawmakers and, 123–28; levels of punishment and, 213n2; media and, 123–28; shaping of, 142
punishment: collateral consequences of, 211n43; as criminal justice system goal, 129; culture of, 199n1; high tolerance for punitiveness, 211n33; levels of, 213n2
Putnam, Robert D., 5

racial prejudices: Black juror exclusion, 18; black juror exclusion, 179nn177,181; as drivers of public opinion, 129; effects on employment and housing, 6; jury representation and, 43; media and, 215n54; of media coverage, 127; race-based juror eligibility, 29; racial composition of juries, 43–44; radical inclusion, 209n4; watchdog effect and, 196n30
rational basis review standard, 176n122
Raysor v. Desantis, 178n152
Reasonable Doubt (RD) subscale measures, 191n73
recidivism: COMPAS tool, 201n19; rates of, 203n36; reduction of, 42, 200nn7,11, 201n23
record-based laws and statutes, 29, 176n122
Rector, Rickey Ray, 126
redemption: discounting of, 4; redemption script, 207n35; reforming policy and, 140, 143

reentry: felon-juror exclusion policies and, 142; inclusion and, 141; negative impact on, 3; primary concerns, 6–7; reflexive reformation and, 202n27; social distance and, 211n43

reflexive reformation, 202n27

reform validation, 210nn19,23

rehabilitation: certificates of, 190n69, 218n11; contact and support for, 212n52; decline of ideal, 211n33; discounting of, 4; reflexive reformation and, 202n27; reforming policy and, 140, 143

reintegration: facilitation of, 135; public support for, 134, 142; strengths-based approach to, 200n8

repeat offense, 19, 150

research methodology, 144; empirical analysis, 135, 140–42; Maine felon-juror field study, 98; mock jury experiment, 67–69, 197n52

Responsivity Principle, 200n15

restoration rights, 217n4

retributive rationale, 22

Revised Juror Bias Scale (RJBS), 51 table1, 51–56, 52 fig.1, 53 fig.2, 54 table2, 56 fig.3, 191n73, 192nn75,76,78

Reyes, Matias, 126

Rhode Island: access to legal profession, 162; duration by state, 162; felon-voter eligibility, 173–74n77; law enforcement juror eligibility criteria, 166; as permanent exclusion jurisdiction, 192n82; during sentence exclusion, 166

Richardson, Kevin, 126–27

Richie, Matt, 79

risk assessment, 200n11, 201nn16,18,19

Risk Principle, 200n15

Riverside Sheriff's Association, 139

RJBS (Revised Juror Bias Scale), 51 table1, 51–56, 52 fig.1, 53 fig.2, 54 table2, 56 fig.3, 191n73, 192nn75,76,78

RNR (Risk/Need/Responsivity) framework, 202n24

Roman law, 17

Rose, Reginald, 143–44

Salaam, Yusef, 126–27

Sampson, Robert J., 206n23

San Luis Obispo County, Certificates of Rehabilitation, 218n11

Santana, Raymond, 126–27

Scandinavia, 175n98

schema use, 204n58

Scott, Rick, 26

Scottish Drug Courts, 41–42

secondary criminal desistance, 94, 170n33, 209n3. *See also* desistance

settlements: increase in, 26; reliance on, 4

sex offenders: contact with, 212n52; public opinion and, 129; registration of, 139, 150, 173n66; reinstatement for, 216n78; wilding, 215nn45,54

Shapiro-Wilk test of normality, 192n78

Sherman, Ryan, 139–40

Silbert, Mimi, 203n36

Simon, Jonathan, 125

situational variation, 32–34

Sixth Amendment: contemporary interpretations of, 60; cross-section requirement, 16–17, 23; on impartiality, 14, 186n7

Smith v. Texas, 14–15, 16, 19

social capital: definition of, 209n5; inclusions and, 142; loss of, 6; social construction of issues, 213n11; social identity as noncriminal, 210nn19,23; social network loss, 6; tertiary criminal desistance and, 170n33

social compact theory, 22

Sommers, Samuel R., 65, 74, 196n30

South Carolina: access to legal profession, 162; duration by state, 162; felon-juror exclusion policies, 151; felon-voter eligibility, 173–74n77; law enforcement juror eligibility criteria, 166; as permanent exclusion jurisdiction, 166, 173n66, 192n82

South Dakota: access to legal profession, 162; duration by state, 162; felon-juror exclusion policies, 151; felon-voter eligibility, 173–74n77; law enforcement juror eligibility criteria, 166; during sentence exclusion, 166

sovereign authority, 4, 176n125, 177n126

Stanford Prison Project, 33–34

statutes cited, 260–61

stereotype threat model, 204n44

stigma of criminal conviction: community engagement and, 107; destigmatization process, 210n17; diverse jury deliberations and, 80; felon-voter disenfranchisement and, 96; formation of, 113–14; influence on hiring decisions, 6; intergroup contact and, 11, 115, 121–22, 142; mitigation of, 92; racial prejudice comparison, 111; self-image and, 98–100

Strauder v. West Virginia, 14, 29, 179n177

strengths-based approach, 200n9, 202nn24–26

subjective impartiality approach, 187n15

subjective juror eligibility criteria, 18

summary judgment, 4

Supreme Court: cases cited, 258–60; on cross-section claims, 23; cross-section requirement, 18, 63; on diversity and inclusion, 63–64; impartiality doctrine, 14–17; on jury system, 205n4; on legal profession, 39; race-based juror eligibility, 29. See also *specific cases; specific justices*

surveys: CALSPEAKS (California Speaks Opinion Research) survey, 132–35; PACT meeting people, 190–91n71, 192n76, 192n78; YouGov, 216n78

tabula rasa (blank slate ideal) 47, 187n15

taint argument, 30, 41–45

Taylor v. Louisiana, 16–17

temporal bans, 19

Tennessee: access to legal profession, 163; duration by state, 163; felon-juror exclusion policies, 151; law enforcement juror eligibility criteria, 166; misdemeanor convictions, 181n46; as permanent exclusion jurisdiction, 166, 173n66

terminology, controversial, 12

tertiary criminal desistance, 94, 170n33, 206n17, 209n3. *See also* desistance

Texas: access to legal profession, 163; bar admission screenings, 182n64; duration by state, 163; felon-juror exclusion policies, 151; felon-voter eligibility, 173–74n77; law enforcement juror eligibility criteria, 166; misdemeanor

convictions, 181n46; as permanent exclusion jurisdiction, 166, 173n66

therapeutic interventions, 200n7

Thiel v. Southern Pacific Railroad Company, 15, 16

Thompson, William C., 64–65

Tocqueville, Alexis de, 5, 93, 205n2

tough on crime approach, 127

traditional authoritarianism, 50, 189n58

Travis, Jeremy, 193n91

trial tax, 4, 169n6

triggering devices, 25

Trump, Donald J., 127, 130

12 Angry Men (1957 film), 143–44

Tyler, Tom, 41–42, 58

Uggen, Christopher, 130

underinclusiveness, 53

unique threat assumption, 46

United States v. Barry, 176n116

United States v. Greene, 176n116

U.S. Constitution, 23. *See also* Sixth Amendment

Utah: access to legal profession, 163; bar admission screenings, 182n64; duration by state, 163; felon-juror exclusion policies, 151; felon-voter eligibility, 173–74n77; law enforcement juror eligibility criteria, 166; as permanent exclusion jurisdiction, 166, 173n66

value-neutral science, 199n1

venue, 188n16

verdicts: delegitimizing, 43–45; general biases and, 49–50; predictors of, 49–50, 191n73, 192n75, 194n116

Vermont: access to legal profession, 163; duration by state, 163; felon-juror exclusion policies, 151; law enforcement juror eligibility criteria, 166; as permanent exclusion jurisdiction, 166, 173n66

Vidmar, Neil, 44

violent offenses, 213n8; felon-juror exclusion policies, 19; public opinion and, 130, 133–34

Virginia: access to legal profession, 163; duration by state, 163; felon-juror exclusion policies, 151; felon-voter eligibility,